LANDLORDS AND TENANTS

UNDER NIGERIAN LAWS

Containing text of
Lagos State Tenancy Law of 2011
Rent Control and Recovery of Residential Premises Law
Recovery of Premises Act/Law

Miakpo Emiaso

All Correspondence To
The Author
Miakpo Emiaso
P.O.Box 425 Ughelli
Delta State
miakpo@yahoo.com

Published by
SOS Publications
sospublications@yahoo.com

APPENDICES

PREFACE

The law of landlords and tenants is not an area of law where it could be said that there is a dearth of literature. It is indeed an over-patronised subject matter about which there is a plethora of authors.

In 2010, I authored and published *Law, Practice and Procedure: Area Customary Courts in Nigeria*. In 2011, I published *Co-operative Societies Law and Practice in Nigeria*. Both works were novel. I could say of each of them, and I did say, that each was the first and only full length work in their respective subject area.

When I mentioned it to a professor of law in the Nigerian Law School that my next work was on landlord and tenant, he admonished me not to soil a unique reputation I had already built for myself by writing on landlords and tenants which the learned professor considered too common place.

This view of the learned professor is shared by many. In my student days, I related to the subject area with contempt and made up my mind I would not accept possession briefs and, indeed, I lived up to this decision for about three years after my call to bar.

It is therefore ironic that I should write this book and in the course of which exercise I came to realize how wrong we may be in regarding the law of landlords and tenants to be too common place to deserve any serious consideration.

Landlords and tenants and their relationship may be common place but the law which regulates the relationship between landlords and tenants is not. Indeed it is so complex that Emeka Chianu, another learned law professor and an erudite author in this area of law, has had cause to lament that this area of the law is fraught with too many technicalities which ought to be eliminated but that even if they cannot be eliminated because they are too entrenched to be reversed, all avenues for introducing more should be plugged.

I have gone ahead to write this book nonetheless. Not because I disagreed with the views of the learned professor with the Nigerian Law School but because I thought there is something unique and refreshing about the style I have adopted which I believe will add some value to the study of the law of landlords and tenants.

As one who has seen and experienced the terrain both as a legal practitioner in the practice of it and one who has sat on the bench

of a court with exclusive jurisdiction for landlords and tenants matters for nearly a decade, the delivery of the discourse in this work cannot but be round and profound. It is therefore my hope and expectation that my humble effort herein will lead to an enhanced quality in the practice of the law relating to landlords and tenants, contribute in some way to legal learning and knowledge, excite healthy legal debates, robust controversies, all of which might lead to legislative action in some respect regarding the law of landlord and tenants.

The law of landlords and tenants is based both on statute and case law. I have in this work discussed and referred to over 210 decided cases twenty-four of which are foreign all of which are relevant nationwide. With regards to statutes, I have made efforts to also cover the whole country – a not-very-easy undertaking since every state has its own enactment on the subject. The saving grace in this respect is that all the enactments are substantially *impari materia* in content and principles as they have each copied from one another or from a common source. To cover the spread therefore, representative random references have been made to enactments from every part of Nigeria where necessary. However, in order not to completely lose the elegance of the discourse, the phrase 'Recovery Statutes' has been used to collectively refer to all the enactments but with the Lagos and Delta states statutes adopted as standard reference.

The Lagos State novel Tenancy Law No. 14 of 2011 was signed into law after the work had been completed. But because of the very far-reaching innovations in it, I had to stand down the work to enable me incorporate these. The Tenancy Law has therefore received ample and special attention throughout the work.

This has to be so because of the numerous alterations which this piece of legislation has brought to bear on the law of landlords and tenants. Some of the innovations in this Lagos State law are a cause for worry which only time will tell but it cannot go without saying that at a time when the call for uniform laws nationwide is gaining momentum, this law has been published with obvious and concerted efforts to be different and thereby making the study and practice of the law in this area more confusing and complex.

But the Lagos Law has to be commended for introducing provisions which now statutorily put to rest some recondite points such as the length of notice necessary for terminating a six monthly tenancy, the need or otherwise for a notice to quit in determining a tenancy for a

fixed term certain, and the requirement that notices to quit must take effect on the anniversary and at the end of a current term of the tenancy.

I have made every effort to state the law as correctly as practicable as at March 2012 but, as with every human effort, it is not impossible that some slips may have occurred inadvertently. I take responsibility for such slips, if any, which is regretted and I will appreciate it if my attention is drawn to it.

MIAKPO EMIASO
March 2012

Chapter One
Creating Landlord and Tenant Relationships

The law of landlord and tenant is a species of real property law which is sui generis regulated by special principles – Prof. Emeka Chianu.

Landlord - A landlord is any person who holds land or premises that are let to another person. He is a person who has granted a lease or tenancy to another. He may be a natural person or an artificial person such as a company or corporation or government or an agency of government.

As defined under the Recovery Statutes, a landlord is any person who, in relation to any premises, is entitled to the immediate reversion[1] of such premises.[2] The courts have also given their approval to this definition in a number of decisions[3] and, by the statutory definition, a landlord includes

(a) any person entitled to the immediate reversion under a joint tenancy or a tenancy in common;

(b) the attorney or agent of the landlord as defined above;

(c) any person who receives rent in respect of the premises under a right to receive same from any person who is in occupation thereof.

Tenant - A tenant is any person, whether natural or

1. A reversion is an interest in premises or land which a person (known as the reversioner) who has let part of his whole interest in his land or premises to another retains in the land or premises.
2. See the interpretation sections of Recovery Statutes.
3. See, for instance, the Court of Appeal in *Erhunmwunse v Ehanire* (1998) 10 NWLR (Pt. 568) 55 and *Coker v Adetayo* (1992) 6 NWLR (Pt. 249) 613.

artificial, who is in lawful occupation of premises belonging to another person known as the landlord. He is the person defined under the Recovery Statutes as any person, including a subtenant, who is

> occupying any premises whether on payment of rent or otherwise.

By this statutory definition, if the occupation is under a *bona fide* claim of right as the owner of the premises, then such a person is not a tenant.

Accordingly, a tenant is any person, not being the owner, who is in lawful occupation of premises belonging to a landlord whether the tenant is paying rent in respect of the occupation or not. The lawful occupation includes one permitted under a contract between the landlord and the tenant and one which continues after the expiration of the contractual tenancy in which case the tenant becomes what the law calls a statutory tenant.[4]

Landlord and Tenant - The relationship which exists between a landlord and a tenant is one which is a legally binding contract.[5] The contract, in the context of this book, is one which involves a person called the landlord who lets premises to another called a tenant who takes the letting as such a tenant. As between the parties, there must be a premises either in the form of land, building, flat, room or some other form of real property.

Under the general law of contracts, a valid contract comes into being when certain elements are in place which include offer, acceptance, consideration, intention to create legal relations, capacity to contract, compliance with

4. See *infra* at 23.
5. *UBA v Tejumola & Sons Ltd.* (1988) 2 NWLR (Pt. 79) 662.

formal requirements, legal objects etc. It is not intended in this book to discuss these elements of contracts law as would be requisite in a discussion on contracts law except to make some cursory references.

Offer - An offer may be described as that manifestation or indication by a person to do or refrain from doing a thing and which manifestation of indication is capable of being reacted to by another person by way of acceptance which ultimately leads to the formation of a binding contract.

For instance, where Chief Linus hangs a signpost reading *Flat To Let* in front of his house or places it as an advertisement in a newspaper to which Mr. Titus reacts by applying to Chief Linus to let the flat which application is accepted by Chief Linus, the application by Mr. Linus to let the flat will be an offer.[6] It is an indication by Linus to do a thing which, if accepted by Titus, will bring a tenancy contract into being.

The signpost or advert placed by Linus is therefore an invitation to treat which legally means a mere invitation to make offers.[7] In *Pharmaceutical Society of Great Britain v Boots Cash Chemists Ltd,*[8] it was held that the display of drugs in a chemist store was not an offer but a mere invitation by the store owner to prospective customers to make offers to buy drugs. The difference between an offer

---

6. See *Carlill v Carbolic Smoke Ball Co.* (1893) 1 Q.B. 256 where the court held that an advertisement containing an indication to do something and which was capable of an acceptance constituted an offer.
7. See Folorunsho Omojola (2004) *Omojola's General Principles of Business and Co-operative Law in Nigeria* (Darkol Press and Publishers, Lagos) at p.84.
8. (1953) 1 QB 401.

and an invitation to treat therefore lies in as to whether the indication of a party is one capable of being accepted in such a way that the acceptance results, without more, into a binding contract.

Accordingly, since the application by Titus to let the flat owned by Linus cannot result in a contract unless it is accepted by Linus, it remains an offer. But the offer by Titus would not have taken place without the invitation to the whole world by Linus for offers through his signpost or advert.

Acceptance - Where Titus offers to take Linus' flat, and the offer is one which Titus likes after taking into consideration all the surrounding circumstances relating to Titus and his offer, Linus may either agree to let his flat to Titus or decline. Where he agrees, it is said that he accepts. Once he accepts, the contract comes into being and becomes binding on both parties.

Consideration - A contract creates benefits and burdens as between the parties thereto. What burden one party suffers under the contract for the benefits which he enjoys thereunder is known in law as the consideration which he furnishes for those rights and benefits accruable to him under the contract. In *Curie v Misa*,[9] consideration was defined by the court as

> some right, benefit, profit or benefit accruing to the one party or some forebearance, detriment, loss or responsibility given, suffered or undertaken by the other.

In the contractual relationship between Linus and Titus, the loss of possession of the flat or the forebearance thereof is the consideration which Linus furnishes for the rent which

9. (1875) L.R. 10 Ex. 153.

Titus pays for the flat and vice versa. Therefore, where Linus lets his premises to Titus, Linus loses or forebears on the use of the premises and which loss or forebearance, on the other hand, operates as some right, interest, profit or benefit to Titus. What Titus loses or forebears to Linus to induce Linus to let the premises to him is to Linus the right, interest, profit or benefit he derives from the contract while to Titus it is the consideration he furnishes therefor being a loss to him or forebearance by him.

Intention to Create Legal Relations - As stated earlier, upon the acceptance of an offer, a contract comes into effect and becomes legally binding on the parties. This is because while the relationship developed right from the making of the offer to the acceptance thereof, the parties are taken or must be taken to have all through intended to create a legal relationship as between each other which is different from a mere social or domestic relationship.

In *Ebenezer v Bell*[10], the plaintiff entered the suit premises as guest of a friend who later left. The plaintiff sent rent to the defendant who instructed her lawyer to write to the plaintiff stating that the 'rent' she sent was only being accepted as money due for use and occupation of the premises and which use and occupation was without his authority. This was followed by a notice to quit.

On appeal to the Federal Supreme Court, the plaintiff contended that since the defendant accepted money from her, she had become a tenant and that although she entered the suit premises as a lodger, she became a subtenant when she began paying rent. But the apex court per Taylor FJ (Brett and Bairamian F.JJ concurring) held

10. (1963) ANLR 17.

and declared that

> there was, in my view, no intention to create a tenancy and this contention must fail.[11]

Also in *Balogun v UAC,*[12] the court refused to hold that the plaintiff was a tenant notwithstanding that he was in occupation of the premises because the court per Reed J. said

> now, there can, in my view, be no doubt that the intention of the parties ... was that there should be no occupation of the premises.

Similarly, in *Mobil Oil (Nig.) Ltd. v Johnson,*[13] the Federal Supreme Court relying on the English decision of *Isaac v Hotel de Paris Ltd.*[14] held that

> the intention of the parties and the conduct of the parties must be the deciding factor whether a tenancy has been created or the relationship was merely that of a licensor and licensee even though there was exclusive possession by the appellant and the acceptance of the amount of the rent by the respondent company.[15]

The apex court then wondered at page 111 if, by looking at the substance of this case, it could be concluded that the intention of the parties was to create a tenancy. Answering this in the negative, the court per Ademola CJF (Brett and Unsworth F.JJ concurring) declared that

> it is clear ... from the agreement ... as well as from the circumstances of the whole matter and the conduct of the parties that it was never intended that a tenancy should be created....

11. *ibid* at 21.
12. (1958) NRNLR 77.
13. (1961) ANLR 102.
14. (1960) 1 AER 348.
15. *ibid* at 110.

Capacity to Contract - Flowing from the intention to create legal relations is the requirement that the parties must have requisite legal capacities to enter into such a legally binding contract and that the contract must also, among other requirements, comply with necessary formal legal requirements for bringing the kind of contract into being.

When established, a contract between a landlord and a tenant involving the letting of premises known as a tenancy is put in place and brought into being. This is an arrangement in which an owner of premises called the landlord allows another person called the tenant to take possession of the premises usually for an agreed period of time and usually also for a consideration known as rent and which Dele Okafor describes as a

> relationship created when a person called the landlord lets premises to another called the tenant for a period of time usually but not necessarily for the payment of rent.[16]

It is a species of contract regulated by special laws made specifically for its regulation in the various states of Nigeria. In the words of Professor Emeka Chianu,

> the law of landlord and tenant is a species of real property law which is *sui generis* regulated by special principles.[17]

Formalities - A tenancy contract can either be in the form of a lease which is one for a right of exclusive possession by the tenant of premises owned by the landlord for a term

16. *Landlord and Tenant Law and Practice* (2011) De Philosophes Ventures, Agbor at 10.
17. *Law of Landlord and Tenant* (1994) Oliz Publishers, Benin City at 250.

certain or in the form of a periodic tenancy which is one for the exclusive possession by the tenant of premises owned by the landlord from time to time.

This book is more about the latter type of tenancies being a commoner type and in respect of which the greater number of suits are filed in Nigerian courts. These do not require any prescribed strict formalities in their formation to become valid as with the former some of which formalities shall now be discussed in outline only.

The Lease - The law generally requires that contracts of leases must be by way of deeds or must be in writing especially where they are for a period certain in excess of three years. This has been the position of the law from as long ago as 1676 when the Statute of Frauds[18] was enacted and section 3 thereof provides that leases must be by deed or note in writing except where the lease is for a term certain not exceeding three years.[19]

Also, in all the states of the old Western Region including Lagos, Delta and Edo where the Property and Conveyancing Law is still in force, all conveyances of land or of any interests[20] therein for the purpose of conveying same or creating a legal estate[21] are void unless made by

18. A statute of general application still in force in the northern states of Nigeria. See also Sections 77 and 79 of the Property and Conveyancing Law of the different states where the Statute of Frauds is no longer applicable namely the old Western Region.
19. *ibid* at Section 2.
20. Including periodic tenancies.
21. A right of ownership over land either in fee simple absolute in possession or for a term of years absolute being the only types of estates, interests and charges in or over land that can be created or authorized to exist as legal estates under the law.

deed and in writing.[22]

A deed, by necessary implication, must be in writing as, always, a deed is a written document signed, sealed and delivered. By this provision, it is required that all tenancies shall, at the very least, be in writing otherwise they shall be void.

Requirement of Writing not Strict - However, where a lease or tenancy is for a period not exceeding three years, the requirement as to writing shall not be strict as Section 79 of the Property and Conveyancing Law makes provisions to the effect that nothing in the provisions of the Law requiring 'all conveyances of land or of any interest therein' to be in writing

> shall affect the creation by parol of leases taking effect in possession for a term not exceeding three years ....[23]

This means that a lease i.e. a tenancy for a term certain up to but not exceeding three years made only orally and not reduced into writing shall nonetheless be valid. Even so is an interest in land

> created by parol and not put in writing and signed by the persons so creating the same, or by their agents

shall not be invalid by reason thereof and notwithstanding that it is for a period exceeding three years but shall have the force and effect of an interest at will only.[24] This means that a tenancy at will results as between the parties if they purport to enter into a contract involving an interest in land for a period of over three years without a note in writing

22. Section 77 (1) Property and Conveyancing Law (Cap. 116) Laws of Delta State 2007 which provision is *impari materia* in all the Property and Conveyancing Law states.
23. Section 79 (1) Property and Conveyancing Law.
24. *ibid.*

and signed by them.

A tenancy at will is an inferior type of tenancy contract in that it is one which can be terminated at will and at any time without notice by either of the parties. A tenancy at will most times results not from express contract or agreement but by implication as in when an owner of premises permits a person to continue in occupation of the premises by holding over but without an express agreement or contract in respect thereof. In *Odutola v Papersack Nig. Ltd,*[25] the Supreme Court of Nigeria stated[26] that

> the moment a year's rent (becomes) due and payable ... but (remains) unpaid, the yearly tenancy ... (comes) to an end by effluxion of time and the respondent becomes a tenant at will ... by continuing or remaining in possession of the property. In other words, the respondent at that stage is said to be holding over ... and in that capacity becomes a tenant at will.[27]

The Need for Writing - At the point when Linus accepts the offer of Titus in the contractual relationship between them *supra*, the terms of the contract must have been settled and agreed to. By Titus' offer, he represents or indicates to Linus that he is able, ready and willing to let the premises at terms and conditions which he specifies. That Linus accepts the offer means he accepts those terms and conditions. From the moment of the acceptance by Linus, the contract takes effect and becomes legally binding.

But what are these terms and conditions to which the parties have agreed? In the course of litigation, the

25. (2007) Vol. 148 LRN 1341.
26. Per Onu JSC at 1364.
27. See also *AP v Owodunni* (1991) 8 NWLR (Pt. 210) 391.

answer to this question could be problematic if they were not reduced into writing. The consequence for litigation especially when it is sought to terminate the relationship with a view to recovering possession and to recover pecuniary demands can sometimes be fatal. As Professor Emeka Chianu, referring to similar situations some three centuries ago, put it,

> parties to conveyances of land were perpetrating fraud as a result of the absence of written evidence of land transactions.[28]

The Statute of Frauds of 1676 was the English parliament's answer to the mischief of fraud foisted on society by the absence of writing in land and tenancy transactions. In 1959, the Western Region of Nigeria parliament enacted the Property and Conveyancing Law which is a substantial reproduction of the Statute of Frauds with modifications to suit local circumstances.

The English Statute of Frauds which is a statute of general application is still applicable in those states of the Nigerian Federation where the Property and Conveyancing Law has not been enacted and is not applicable.

The necessity of reducing into writing the terms and conditions of every contract including tenancy contracts in order to check sharp practices and fraud cannot therefore be over emphasized. A contract the terms of which have been reduced into writing is a lot easier to establish in the course of litigation and even during pre-litigation arguments than those of contracts by parol.

Therefore it is to be highly recommended always that parties to any form of contract ought to reduce the

28. *Law of Landlord and Tenant* (*supra*) at104.

terms of their agreement always into writing not only because the law requires it but as an act of prudence. In the *Odutola v Papersack*[29] case, the Supreme Court of Nigeria per Tobi JSC recommended that much when the court declared that

> it is generally accepted practice that tenancy agreement is made in writing .... I do not want to say that it is invariably made in writing; but I can say that it is mostly made in writing. Accordingly, where a party alleges the existence of an oral agreement, ... he must give credible evidence as to the ... agreement. In other words, a party alleging an oral agreement is duty bound to prove such an agreement to the hilt.[30]

Any litigation lawyer will without hesitation concede that proving 'such an agreement to the hilt' can be anything but easy.

Contents of the Writing - The writing which the various authorities talk about above is in practice generally known as 'agreement'.[31] This agreement comes in various forms usually depending on the type of premises involved and sometimes the location thereof. However, irrespective of the type of premises or the neighbourhood thereof, a standard tenancy agreement will usually contain the following:

(a) Name of the parties
(b) Description of the premises
(c) The duration of the tenancy

29. *Supra.*
30. *ibid* at 1357.
31. It is the Tenancy Agreement which is deemed to exist in Lagos State whenever premises are granted by a landlord to a person for value whether or not it is in writing. Section 3 of the Tenancy Law.

(d) Commencement date,
(e) Rent payable,
(f) Terms as to covenants, and
(g) Mode for determination.[32]

Parties - There are usually two parties to a tenancy agreement namely the Landlord[33] (or the Lessor) and the Tenant[34] (or the Lessee) These are usually human persons and in all cases must be juristic persons with requisite legal capacities to enter into contracts. The Landlord or the Lessor is the owner of the premises in whom the reversion resides arising from the tenancy contract while the Tenant or Lessee is the person to whom the Landlord lets and who takes the premises.

The agreement will be void if any of the parties lacks requisite contractual capacity. Where he is not a natural person free of disabilities,[35] he cannot contract. So also is an artificial person which is under any disability e.g. being in want of incorporation or registration. Artificial persons come in the form of companies, clubs, churches, associations, mosques, societies, and such like grouping of persons. Unless duly incorporated or registered,[36] they cannot enter into legally binding and enforceable contracts including tenancy contracts.[37]

32. *Mofia Ltd. v University of Ibadan* (1998) 5 NWLR (Pt. 549) 227.
33. Throughout this book also known as Linus.
34. Known as Titus in this book.
35. *Fawehinmi v NBA (No. 2)* (1989) 2 NWLR (Pt. 105) 494.
36. Companies and Allied Matters Act or under the Co-operative Societies Law of any of the states of the federation.
37. See *Idowu v Martins* (1974) 3 CCHCJ 344 discussed by Emeka Chianu (2004) *Law of Landlord and Tenant* (*supra*) at 114. See also *Nlewedim v Uduma* (1985) 6 NWLR (Pt. 402) 383.

The names of the parties usually form part of the beginning of the written tenancy agreement in the following manner:

AN AGREEMENT made .... day of .... 20...
BETWEEN
Mr. Ona Linus[38] of No. 1 Ona Linus Street ...
(hereinafter called the Landlord) of the one part
AND
Mr. Okupaya Titus[39] of No. 2 Tenant's Street
(hereinafter called the Tenant) of the other part.

Care must be taken in stating the names of the parties correctly including an indication of their titles, if any, as to whether they are chiefs, misters, doctors etc. The names should be written out in full avoiding abbreviations and initials.

Description of Premises - The tenancy agreement must contain an accurate description of the let premises so as to avoid any form of ambiguity which could result to unintended consequences and which may turn out to be expensive. Where, for instance, the tenancy is in respect of one room or one flat within a block consisting of rooms or flats, it is safe to identify the particular room or flat let within the block by some clear means.

A bare reference to 'one room' or one 'three bedroom flat' where there are more than one such premises within the block will be inadequate description. If the rooms or flats are numbered, it will be appropriate to identify the let premises by such numbers. If not, some detailed description such as 'the second flat on the ground floor to the left of the main gate' might be useful.

38. Name of one of the parties.
39. Name of the other party.

The predicament to which an improperly or an imprecise description of the let premises can plunge the parties is very well illustrated in the case of *Yakubu v Kaduna Furniture and Carpet Co. Ltd*[40] where the description clause in a tenancy agreement between the parties was to the effect that the letting was in respect of

> ALL THAT premises known as No. 23 Ibrahim Biu Crescent, Kaduna together with boys' quarters, garden grounds, and driveways anciliary thereto.

But No. 23 Ibrahim Biu Crescent in Kaduna comprised three bungalows each with a boys quarters. The landlord contended that one of the bungalows referred to as the 'third bungalow' did not form part of the premises let to the tenant. In construing the above description clause in the agreement, the court held that 'ALL' as used in the said clause embraced everything that formed part of 23 Ibrahim Biu Crescent and in particular the building which was styled the 'third bungalow'.

Duration of Tenancy - This is the part of the agreement that indicates for how long the tenancy shall subsist. This duration clausc is especially of great relevance and importance in leases for terms certain.

The duration clause does not only define how long the tenancy is to be for but also indicates the commencement date thereof and the expiration date. These are very important dates with regards to leases and usually run thus:

> TO HOLD UNTO the lessee a term of ... years certain from the date hereof.[41]

40. (1985) HCNLR 222 as reported by Emeka Chianu (*supra*) at 116.
41. Dating is fundamental as otherwise the tenancy may become invalid. See *Amizu v Nzeribe* (1989) 4 NWLR (Pt. 118) 755.

Accordingly, 'the date hereof' becomes the effective commencement date of the tenancy. If, for instance, the agreement is for 'five years certain', the duration of five years begins to run from 'the date hereof' which is usually which defines the period for which the parties have agreed the date the parties have agreed the contract should take effect and it is usually but not always indicated at the top of the agreement writing which introduces also the parties as illustrated *supra*.

It is therefore advisable that this date should be the same date at every other part of the written agreement especially at the attestation clause where it refers to a date and which date is usually considered the date of the execution of the agreement. This will eliminate the complications which could arise as to when the lease actually begins to run if the date of execution of the deed or agreement is consistent with the date when the deed or agreement was made.

The Commencement Date **-** The commencement date of the tenancy agreement as already explained is crucial to the validity and enforceability of the contract. In every tenancy agreement, there are usually references to a number of possible dates including

(a) the date at the beginning of the agreement,
(b) the date at the *habendum*,
(c) that indicating the date of execution,
(d) the date of sealing in the case of a deed, and
(e) the date of delivery.

In practice, the last three dates are usually reflected in the attestation in the legend 'signed, sealed and delivered' and therefore taken as one date. The date at the beginning of the agreement reflects, most times, the date the agreement was made or prepared which, again, is not necessarily so.

The date at the *habendum* is the same as the date which specifies the duration of the tenancy i.e. the date the contract becomes binding and effective (the commencement date) as between the parties through to the date when the contract comes to an end.

Where these dates (a) to (e) in any one agreement are different from one another, problems may arise whenever it is sought to enforce the terms of the agreement especially the date when the grant takes effect and when it terminates. It is therefore to highly recommended that all parts of the agreement requiring dating should, as much as practicable, carry the same date.

Rent – The Recovery Statutes[42] including the former Cap. R6 of Lagos State have always defined rent as including

> any money or money's worth whether in the form of crops, labour or otherwise paid or given as the case may be, in consideration of which a landlord has let a premises to a tenant.

Rent is a fundamental element in the contractual relationship between a landlord and a tenant. It is the

42. See the Interpretation sections. But see the more recent extensive definition under the Lagos State Tenancy Law to the effect that the term '*includes any consideration or money paid or agreed to be paid or value or a right given or agreed to be given or part of any crop rendered or any equivalent given in kind or in labour, in consideration of which a landlord has permitted any person to use and occupy any land, premises, or other corporeal hereditaments, and the use of common areas but does not include any charge for services or facilities provided in addition for the occupation of the premises*'.

consideration which the tenant furnishes under the tenancy contract. Describing the concept of rent under a landlord and tenant relationship in *Oduye v Nigeria Airways Ltd.*,[43] the Supreme Court per Oputa JSC stated that

> rent is the recompense paid by the tenant to the landlord for the exclusive possession of corporeal hereditament. … it is a payment which a tenant is bound by contract to make to his landlord for the use of the property let.

The tenancy agreement must therefore clearly specify the rent agreed as between the parties to be paid by the tenant to the landlord as consideration for the letting.

Also to be specified is how and when the stated rent is to be paid. This is to relieve the parties of any confusion as to whether the rent is, for instance, payable in advance which is the usual practice in Nigeria or in arrears which is the position under the common law.

The rent clause is the *reddendum* clause which is usually introduced with the legend, 'the tenant yielding and paying the rent reserved' but is also sometimes stated as a covenant of the tenant such as

> to pay rent annually in advance on or before the anniversary of this tenancy.

Rent Receipts – In every case, the landlord is under a duty to issue the tenant and the tenant should insist always that the landlord must issue him with a written receipt evidencing the tenant's payment of his rent. In a new tenancy, the agreement usually contains a receipt clause, where the tenant has paid rent in advance, as part of the rent clause thus 'the receipt whereof the landlord hereby acknowledges'. This acknowledgement in the agreement is

43. (1987) 2 NWLR (Pt. 55) 126, 130.

good and adequate in law in respect of the first payment of rent.

However, for subsequent payment of rent, the landlord is under duty to issue the tenant with a receipt upon the tenant's payment of his rent. Section 5 (1) of the Lagos State Tenancy Law No. 14 0f 2011, for instance, provides for this duty on the part of the landlord in the following words:

> as from the commencement of this Law, all landlords shall upon payment of rent by the tenants, be obliged to issue a rent payment receipt to their tenants in respect of such payments.

In Delta and Edo states, Section 33 of the Law prescribes that all landlords of premises in the areas to which the Law applies

> shall issue prescribed Rent Books in addition to receipts to their tenants

and any landlord who fails to issue the prescribed Rent Book to his tenant or who fails to make necessary entries as provided shall be guilty of an offence and be liable on summary conviction to a fine of fifty Naira or to imprisonment for one month or to both such fine and imprisonment.

Under the Lagos State provision, any landlord who fails to issue a rent payment receipt to his tenant in the manner prescribed under the Law shall be liable on conviction to a fine of one hundred thousand Naira only without imprisonment.

The Lagos State Law specifically provides that the receipt which the landlord issues to the tenant must state the following details:

(a) the date on which the rent was received by the landlord or his agent;
(b) the names and addresses of the landlord and the tenant;
(c) the description and location of the premises in respect of which the rent has been paid;
(d) the amount of rent paid; and
(e) the period to which the rent payment relates.

Advance Payment of Rent – In practice, it is usual for landlords to demand from their tenants payment of the rent in advance. This practice which is widespread is usually entrenched in the tenancy agreement in words such as

> to pay rent annually (or monthly, quarterly, or every six months as the case may be) in advance on or before the anniversary of this tenancy

such that it has virtually become not only the norm but the law that in Nigeria rent is paid always in advance. This is different from the common law position where the rent is always paid in arrears.

Under the common law, rent, especially in respect of periodic tenancies, is not due until the expiration of the tenancy or the expiration of the term created and is payable at midnight on the last day of the tenancy and on which day a new term is to commence. This common law position can be vacated and it is usually vacated by the parties in their agreement by providing therein how and when the rent is to be paid. But where parties fail to so provide in their tenancy agreement, the common law position will regulate the situation.

Payment of rent in advance as a norm in Nigeria has received statutory nods as, for instance, under the Lagos State Tenancy Law where, by Section 4 thereof, it is provided that a landlord may demand or receive rent in advance safe that

> it shall be unlawful for a landlord or his agent to demand or receive from a sitting tenant rent in excess of sic (6) months from a monthly tenant and one (1) year from a yearly tenant ....

And, in the case of a new or would-be tenancy, it is unlawful for a landlord or his agent to demand or receive from the tenant rent in excess of one (1) year in respect of any premises. The tenant or would-be tenant is also restricted by the provisions from offering or paying rent in excess of the prescribed periods.

By this statutory implication therefore, rent is payable in advance but only subject to a fixed or determinate period or length of time out of or beyond which the parties are not free to contract as to so do will attract the consequences stipulated in subsection (5) of Section 4 of the Law which is to the effect that

> any person who receives or pays rent in excess of what is prescribed in this section shall be guilty of an offence and shall be liable on conviction to a fine of one hundred thousand Naira or to three (3) months imprisonment.

Increase in Rent - The rent payable by a tenant must be a liquidated sum which is to say it must be certain or capable of being determined. This is only logical as the tenant cannot be made to pay a rent the exact amount of which he does not know.[44] In the nature of things, an increase of the rent fixed at the commencement of the tenancy usually becomes due for increase over time. This often creates problems between the landlord and tenant especially with

44. See *Olaniyan v Shokunbi* (1997) 6 NWLR (Pt. 509) 447.

regards to how often and by how much the rent may be increased.

This should be a matter of negotiation between the parties but in practice, the tendency is for landlords to be arbitrary and imagine that an increase could unilaterally be forced on the tenant. In *Yahaya v Chukwura*,[45] it was held that a landlord cannot unilaterally increase the previously agreed rent payable by the tenant as to do so is for the landlord to be in breach of the contract between him and tenant.

Also, the landlord cannot unilaterally change the periodicity of the tenancy nor can he unilaterally change or vary the mode of the payment of rent so that if, for instance, the tenant pays his rent annually and the landlord desires that it should be paid monthly, both landlord and tenant must negotiate this and agree.[46]

In an attempt to regulate increases in rent and possibly reduce the rancour which such exercise usually generates, the erstwhile Lagos State Rent Control and Recovery of Residential Premises Law (Cap. R6) contained provisions to the effect that standard rents were subject to review every three years or such other period as the Governor may by order prescribe and such

> increase on the standard rent at every period of review shall not exceed 20% of the standard rent prescribed....[47]

Although these provisions smirk of legislative encroachment on the freedom of persons to freely negotiate

45. (2003) 3 NWLR (Pt. 75) 20. See also *Udih v Izedonmwen* (1990) 2 NWLR (Pt. 132) 357.
46. See *Gomez v Williams* (1972) NMLR 1491.
47. Section 2 (2) and (3).

and enter into their contracts, such provisions are a welcome attempts for resolving the many difficulties usually thrown up by increases in rents.

Contractual Covenants - Every tenancy agreement contains covenants on the part of each of the parties to be performed under the tenancy contract. These are promises made by the parties to each other. For instance the landlord will usually covenant with the tenant to allow the tenant exclusive and peaceful possession of the premises let while the tenant will usually covenant to pay his rent in a particular manner e.g. monthly or yearly.

Covenants are generally binding once they form part of the tenancy contract made under seal even when they are not supported by consideration.

Modes for Determination - This is a statement in the tenancy agreement indicating how the tenancy contract may be terminated by either party. The wordings of this part of the agreement can be crucial when it is sought to bring the contract to a close especially with regards to the giving of notice to quit and the duration thereof. It has been held[48] that whenever there is a doubt as to the duration of notice which may be given for determining a tenancy, recourse shall be had to how the rent is paid. So that if the rent is paid annually, for instance, then it shall be taken that the tenancy is a yearly tenancy which requires a six months notice to determine.

Also by the provisions of Section 18 of the

48. *Adejumo v David Hughes & Co. Ltd* (1989) 5 NWLR (Pt. 120) 146; *Ebueke v Ajisafe* (1980) 4 – 6 CCHCJ 155 *Adeeyo v Roag Co. Nig. Ltd.* (1985) NBCL 92. See precedent of a tenancy agreement incorporating some of the usual covenants at Appendix C.

Recovery Statutes, the periods of time specified thereat become operational only where there is no express stipulation in the tenancy agreement as to the notice to be given by either party to determine a tenancy. In other words, once there is stipulation as to the notice to be given by either party to determine the tenancy in the tenancy agreement, the provisions of Section 18 become immaterial.

A landlord can therefore demand that his rent be paid annually in advance but inserts in the agreement that the tenancy is a monthly tenancy[49] which has the legal implication that the tenancy can be determined by a one month notice to quit. This may also be achieved directly by stating in the agreement that the tenancy, in which the rent is paid annually, may be determined by a one month notice. In *Adeeyo v Roag Co. Nig. Ltd.*,[50] the tenancy was expressly stated to be a monthly tenancy but the tenant paid his rent annually or half yearly. The tenant contended that it was entitled to a six months notice for the tenancy to be validly terminated. The court held that since the tenancy was a monthly tenancy, the notice required was one month notice and that the payment of rent by the tenant annually or half yearly was at the discretion of the tenant for its own convenience and could therefore not entitle it to six months notice.

The Periodic Tenancy - As stated *supra*, the other type of tenancy other than the lease is one for the exclusive possession of premises from time to time which is generally also known as a periodic tenancy. This means

---

49. *ibid.*
50. *Supra.*

that the tenancy is not for a specified period certain as in a lease but for a period from time to time e.g. from week to week, or from month to month, or from year to year.

From the provisions of the Statute of Frauds and the Property and Conveyancing Law discussed *supra*, the legal requirement of writing is not necessarily applicable to periodic tenancies to render them valid.[51] By their nature, even though periodic tenancies are declared to be for a period less than three years at a time such as a tenancy from month to month which is strictly speaking a tenancy for one month certain, they have the potential to, and usually do, enure for up to and exceeding three years. This is because they are usually invested with the capacity of automatically renewing themselves with the implied consent of both parties. They remain valid even when they are in place for over three years without writing. As the court put it in *Kushner v Law Society,*[52] per Lord Goddard,

> if there is a tenancy from month to month, or from quarter to quarter, or from week to week, or from year to year, it may, of course, go on for an indefinite period .... The fact that a tenancy of that kind may go on for a number of years does not make it invalid if it is not by way of deed.[53]

A deed is invariably always in writing. In effect, a periodic tenancy remains valid notwithstanding that it runs for more than three years and yet not in writing. Section 3 of the 2011 Lagos State Tenancy Law No. 14 appears to further strengthen Lord Goddard's position in this respect as the provision whittles down the requirement of the 'tenancy

51. *Kushner v Law Society* (1952) All ER 404.
52. *Supra.*
53. Or writing.

agreement' being in writing since, under this law, a tenancy agreement shall

> be deemed to exist where premises are granted by the landlord to a person for value whether or not it is …
>
> (a) express or implied;
>
> (b) oral or written or partly oral or partly written; or
>
> (c) for a fixed period.

But the arguments in support of the need for and the advantages accruable to writing generally are nonetheless applicable *mutatis mutandi* to periodic tenancies notwithstanding that the absence of writing is not fatal.

When reduced into writing, which is to be highly recommended, all the contents as discussed above in respect of a lease must also be provided for in the agreement for the periodic tenancy.

The Statutory Tenant - There is a sense in which it is sometimes said that our laws do not recognize the contractual tenant but that every tenant is a statutory tenant – a type of tenancy where the element of agreement, as in the contractual tenancy, is absent.

This, it is argued, is because the various state enactments[54] on landlords and tenants in Nigeria define the term 'tenant' to exclude the elements of a contract as between the landlord and the tenant which, it is further argued, is more of a common law position than under Nigerian statutes. According to Tom Anyafulude,

> every state has enactments on landlord and tenant…. Consequently, issues relating to landlord and tenant including the question of tenancy ought to be

54. The Recovery of Premises and the Rent Control and Recovery of Residential Premises laws.

> approached within the context of these statutes rather than from common law concepts and principles. The common law notion of tenancy is different from the concept of tenancy under the statutes.[55]

There is therefore the contractual tenancy that is consciously created by way of agreement between the landlord and the tenant as parties thereto in accordance with the common law rules of contract[56] and which is different from the statutory tenancy that is a creation of statute devoid of the intentions of the parties.

The common law is part of Nigerian law by virtue of the various reception statutes. These statutes provide, as in Section 2 of the Law (Miscellaneous Provisions) Law of Lagos State, that

> the common law of England and the doctrines of equity, together with the statutes of general application that were in force in England on the first day of January, 1900, shall be in force in the Lagos State.[57]

The rules of contracts law are in the main wholly developed by the common law courts of England except as in those

55. *Principles of Recovery of Premises in Nigeria through the Cases* (2010) Snaap Press Ltd., Enugu at 15 -16.
56. The contractual tenancy is therefore the same as the common law tenancy.
57. See the various reception statutes especially Law (Miscellaneous Provisions) Act applicable nationwide. See also A.O. Obilade (1979) *The Nigerian Legal System* (Sweet & Maxwell, Great Britain) at 70 and Section 3 of Laws of England (Application) Law (Cap. 123) Annotated Laws of Delta State (2007) which provides that '*from and after the commencement of this Law and subject to the provisions of any written law, the common law of England and the doctrine of equity observed by Her Majesty's High Court of Justice in England shall be in force throughout the state*'.

limited areas in those states[58] which have enacted statutes on the subject matter of contracts. This means that tenancies formed under the common law cannot without controversies be described as being invalid in Nigeria in such strength that the courts in Nigeria ought only to approach

> issues relating to landlord and tenant including the question of tenancy ... within the context of ... statutes rather than from common law concepts and principles.

All statutory tenancies are merely consequential in nature. They arise and come into being as consequences of developments arising from a prior subsisting common law or contractual tenancy. There cannot be a statutory tenancy without some form of a pre-existing common law tenancy.

This is even obvious from the definition of 'tenant' as contained in the Recovery Statutes of the various states which is that

> a tenant *includes* a sub-tenant or any person occupying any premises whether on payment of rent or otherwise but does not include a person occupying premises under a bona fide claim to be the owner thereof. (Emphasis supplied).[59]

That a tenant 'includes' the kind of tenants listed, presupposes that there are other kinds of tenant especially, it is humbly submitted, a pre-existing tenant who is landlord to the 'sub-tenant or any person occupying' the premises. The learned author of *Law, Practice and Procedure: Area Customary Courts in Nigeria,*[60] declares that

58. E.g. the old Western Region states.
59. Interpretation section of all Recovery Statutes.
60. Miakpo Emiaso (2010) Peakmans Ltd., Lagos at 26.

> in interpreting statutes, there is a difference between … 'means' and 'includes'. Whereas 'means' is restrictive … and will not permit of any extraneous meanings, 'includes' is not … and would admit of additional items.

The facts of all the cases[61] usually cited in a discussion of the rights and incidences of the statutory tenant bears out the point that every statutory tenant depends on an original tenancy. Stating this position succinctly, Professor Emeka Chianu[62] states that

> it is impossible to talk of a statutory tenancy where no previous relationship of landlord and tenant ever existed

and cited the case of *Sadiku v Samoua*[63] where Adedipe J., in further stress thereof, the learned jurist declared that

> it is only where a subtenant lawfully in possession holds over after the termination of the term created by the head lease, (that) he becomes a statutory tenant, notwithstanding that there was never any privity of contract between him and the headlessor.

The point being made here is that every landlord and tenant relationship commences originally as a contract. It is then known as a contractual tenancy where the tenant is also known as a contractual tenant. This is the same thing as what is known as a common law tenancy where the tenant is also known as a common law tenant. It is this tenancy that puts the tenant in occupation of premises in the first place since nobody moves into another's premises unilaterally without threatening a breakdown of law and order in some form.

---

61. See *Pan Asian Co. Ltd v Nicon* (1982) 9 S.C 1; *Sobamowo v Federal Public Trustee* (1970) 1 ANLR 257; *Okedare v Hanid* (1955) 15 WACA 17; and *Enigbokan v Akinosho* (1957) SCNLR 9.
62. *Law of Landlord and Tenant* (*supra*) at 28.
63. (1964) LLR 159.

From the common law or contractual tenancy may sometimes but not always spring the statutory tenancy or statutory tenant. This then becomes what Aniagolu JSC describes as an exception when, in *Pan Asian African Co. Ltd. v Nicon,*[64] the learned justice of the Supreme Court of Nigeria declared that

> there are ... some exceptions provided by statutes[65] ... under which a tenant is entitled to remain in possession,[66] after the expiry of the term,[67] as a statutory tenant.

The statutory tenant is a statutory tenant not only because the Recovery of Premises laws define him in a particular manner but also because, under these laws, he is conferred with certain protective rights which, under the strict common law rules of contract, he may not possess. He is, as Aniagolu JSC would say, specifically protected by special enactment of the legislature from being affected by the general law whose rigors are mitigated by special statutes.[68] Therefore, when the Recovery Statutes define 'tenant' as

> *include*(ing) *a sub-tenant or any person occupying any premises* whether on payment of rent or otherwise but does not include a person occupying premises under a bona fide claim to be the owner thereof,

the 'sub-tenant' or the 'any person' who is so 'occupying' the premises must be taken to have so occupied the said premises lawfully arising or consequential from a right

---

64. *Supra.*
65. The Recovery of Premises laws of the various states.
66. The exclusive possession lawfully obtained under the common law tenancy.
67. Under the original common law tenancy.
68. The Recovery of Premises laws of the various states.

under an original contractual or common law tenancy which confers legality on the 'occupying' in the definition and without which the 'occupying' will be unlawful. It is this original occupying which gives the tenant the personal right he exercises in protecting his 'holding' as an occupier and not as one with a demise or an estate in the premises.

As Eso JSC (as he then was) put it in *Oduye v Nigeria Airways Ltd*,[69]

> when a person occupies premises lawfully, he becomes a protected tenant *qua* a status arising from statute creating statutory tenancy.... What is necessary is lawful occupation.

The intention and purpose of the statutes is to protect the occupier's possession of premises by extending to him the rights of a tenant properly so called and abolishing the landlord's common law right of unilateral re-entry exercisable upon due determination of the tenancy either by the service of an appropriate notice to quit or upon the effluxion of time in respect of a lease. In effect, a tenant who is holding over after the expiration of his term certain or whose tenancy has been validly determined by notice is now, by the statutes, entitled to the due process of appropriate notice or notices, legal proceedings, and order of court before he can be lawfully ejected.

Indeed, the statutory tenant is so called because of the protections which the statutes confer on him as any such 'occupying' of premises in the absence of a contract before the enactment of these statutes in Nigeria following the English Rent Restriction Acts, will render the tenant one at sufferance and whose possession of the premises

69. *Supra.*

could be recovered under the common law by the landlord simply exercising his right of re-entry without it amounting to self-help or trespass.[70]

Types of Landlord and Tenant Relationship – From the above discussion, it is clear that there can be only two broad types of tenants known to our laws. These are the

(a) common law tenancy which is also known as the contractual tenancy and the

(b) statutory tenancy.

The contractual tenancy has the inherent capacity of developing into other forms of sub-tenancies and types. These include the lease and the periodic tenancy which are types of tenancies under the contractual tenancy. On its own, the periodic tenancy, which is more common than the lease, comes in six sub-types[71] namely the

(a) Weekly tenancy[72]

(b) Monthly tenancy

(c) Quarterly tenancy

(d) Half yearly tenancy[73]

---

70. *Ezenwa v Oko* (1980) IMSLR 377 as cited by Emeka Chianu in *Law of Landlord and Tenant* (*supra*) at 26.

71. Section 18 Rent Control and Recovery of Residential Premises Law (Cap. 180) Annotated Laws of Delta State 2007 which is same in content as Law No. 4 of Bendel State 1977 applicable in Edo State ; Section 17 in Plateau State ; Section 13 Tenancy Law in Lagos State.

72. No longer applicable in Lagos State. See Section 13 of that state's Tenancy Law No. 14 of 2011.

73. Unlike the other sub-types, this is not specifically provided for in any of the Recovery Statutes except the Lagos State Tenancy Law. But these statutes all provide for the tenancy at will which, strictly speaking, is but *quasi*-contractual in nature as therein lies some consent of the landlord.

(e) Yearly tenancy and the

(f) Tenancy at will.

All Recovery Statutes in Nigeria make provisions relating to the above sub-types of contractual landlord and tenant relationship except the half-yearly tenancy which is nonetheless a very common type of tenancy in practice. The classification or identification of tenancies into types have fundamental legal consequences especially with regards to how the rent is paid and the length of notices required to validly determine the relationship.

The Tenancy at Sufferance - The tenancy at sufferance has been described as the cousin or next of kin[74] of the tenancy at will. But their parents are really not directly related. Both types of tenancy usually arise from a holding over by a contractual tenant but whereas a tenancy at will arises from such holding over with the agreement of the landlord, the holding over in the case of the tenant at sufferance arises without the agreement or consent of the landlord.

In effect, the tenancy at sufferance is a perfect example of a statutory tenancy because the tenant holds over without a contract but is nonetheless protected, just like the tenant at will, by the recovery of premises statutes against ejection without due process. His parent is the Recovery of Premises laws hence he is referred to at all as a 'tenant' otherwise he would be a trespasser for being in occupation of some other person's premises without that other person's consent or agreement.

Both the tenant at will and the tenant at sufferance are therefore statutory tenants with the tenancy at will still

74. *Wheeler v Mercer* (1956) 3 AER 631, 634.

retaining some element of consensus *ad idem* as between the landlord and the tenant and thereby qualifying as a *quasi*-contractual tenancy. This is because the consensus between the parties is not with respect to all matters and issues which should make up a contract. For instance, the tenant will be without a well defined or specific estate or demise.

A tenant on whom a notice to quit has been duly served is a tenant at sufferance because the notice served on him by the landlord is an indication on the part of the landlord that he no longer consents or agrees to the tenant's continued occupation of the premises after the expiration of the notice. If during the pendency of the notice to quit, the tenant sublets the premises to another, the occupation of that other will be unlawful and will therefore disqualify that other from the protection of the statutes as he is not and cannot become the landlord's subtenant who is entitled to protection under the statutes.

The same situation applies to a supposed subtenant who is put in occupation of premises in breach of a covenant on the part of the tenant not to sublet the premises. The occupation, being in breach of covenant, will be unlawful and will not be protected by the statutes.

Chapter Two
Terminating Landlord and Tenant Relationships

Except ... with tenancies for a fixed term, a quit notice is an imperative of the law in the determination of landlord and tenant relationship
– Miakpo Emiaso *infra* at 74.

Introduction - Every human relationship comes to an end some day. Even with marriages where the intention is that the marriage should last forever, the parties themselves know that it will certainly come to an end some day as they are even made to take their marriage vows with this in mind when they declare to each other that their union shall be 'till death do us part'. So they part upon death. The relationship, especially when it is not one under customary law, comes to an end upon the death of one of the parties.

In landlord and tenant relationships, several reasons may give rise to the need to bring the relationship to an end. In some cases, death could be one of the reasons. The reasons could be the need for the tenant to relocate as a result of job demands or some other reasons, he may have risen in his station in life and so he needs a bigger, more comfortable premises, the landlord may no longer want him for sundry reasons.

This last reason is about the most usual and commonest reason for seeking the end of a landlord and tenant relationship. The law prescribes specific modes, notwithstanding the reasons, for giving effect to a party's desire to bring his landlord and tenant relationship to a close.

Effluxion of Time – This is one mode of bringing a landlord and tenant relationship to a close. Usually, all it requires is the patience of the parties. This mode is particularly applicable to tenancies for fixed terms i.e. leases. A tenancy for a fixed term has a specified life span and thus predetermined date of its coming to an end. If Linus and Titus had entered into a tenancy contract for a fixed period of three years from the 1st of January 2001, the parties will, *ab intio*, know that the tenancy will come to an end on the 31st of December 2003. Therefore, the parties do not need any notices to bring an end to the relationship or any notices to inform them that the relationship is to come to an end on the predetermined date. As Taylor CJ. put it in *Tinuola v Okon,*[1]

> … in the case of a fixed term, both the landlord and the tenant are aware of the date of the termination of the contractual agreement. The tenant is aware of the fixed date on which he is to quit and deliver up possession, and no further notice to quit is required.

Therefore a notice to quit is unnecessary where, by the agreement of the parties, the tenancy is for a fixed term.

Position Statutory in Lagos State - Indeed, Section 13 (5) of the Lagos State Tenancy Law No. 14 of 2011 has statutorily provided for this position in the following words:

> In the case of a tenancy for a fixed term, no notice to quit shall be required once the tenancy has been determined by effluxion of time ….

In such a situation the landlord is ordinarily only under a legal duty to serve the 'Seven Days' notice of his intention to proceed to court to recover possession[2] although service of a notice to quit nonetheless does not and cannot operate

1. (1966) ANLR 469, 473.
2. See the last leg of Section 13 (5) of the Lagos State Tenancy Law No. 14 of 2011.

as a waiver of the legal effect that the tenancy had come to an end by effluxion of time.[3]

A tenancy is for a fixed term where, by the agreement of the parties, the tenancy is stated to be for a certain period of time e.g. a number of months or years or some other definite period of time, or until a particular day, or contingent on an event the occurrence of which the tenancy is to come to an end. In any of these situations, the issue and service of a notice to quit will ordinarily be a surplusage.[4]

But, as it is usually said, sometimes it is better to err on the side of surplusage and thereby fulfill all righteousness. In so doing, the Supreme Court has also held in *AP v Owodunn*[5] that whenever there is a holding over, a statutory tenancy comes into being and

> once there is an incident of statutory tenancy, the tenant becomes a weekly, monthly or yearly tenant depending upon the term of the original grant

and that therefore, the tenancy can only be lawfully terminated in accordance with the manner and length of term of the original grant between the landlord and tenant.

This means that where a yearly tenant, for instance, holds over, he becomes either a tenant at sufferance or one

3. *Otegbade v Adekoya* (1962) ANLR 760. But see also the Supreme Court in *Odutola v Papersack* (2007) 48 LRCN 1341, 1370 to the effect that the statutory tenant is nonetheless entitled to a seven days notice to quit. This position is however not any longer tenable in Lagos State by virtue of Section 13 (5) of the Tenancy Law No. 14 of 2011.
4. *Tinuola v Okon* (*Supra*. But see also the Supreme Court later in *Odutola v Papersack* (*Supra*).
5. (1991) 15 NSCQR 308

at will depending as to whether he holds over with his landlord's consent or not.

Where such holding over is in respect of a yearly tenancy however, the Supreme Court of Nigeria, sixteen years after it decided *AP v Owodunni*,[6] has also emphatically held that

> from the moment a year's rent became due and payable … but remained unpaid, the yearly tenancy … came to an end by effluxion of time and the respondent thereupon became a tenant at will … by continuing or remaining in possession …. In other words, the respondent at that stage is said to be holding over … and in that capacity, became a tenant at will … (who) was entitled to no more than a week's notice.[7]

Statutory Notices – There are two statutory notices which are required to be served prior to or leading to the institution of proceedings for the recovery of possession and or *mesne* profits. They are the

(a) Notice to Quit (where necessary) and

(b) 'Seven Days' notice in all[8] cases.

They are referred to as statutory notices because they are specifically provided for in the Recovery Statutes. Section 18 of the Recovery Statute for Delta and Edo states which contains provisions exactly *impari materia* with the provisions of all other states Recovery Statutes makes express provisions for the quit notice while the preceding section provides for the 'Seven Days' notice.

The Notice to Quit - This is the notice expressly required

6. *Supra.*
7. Per Onu JSC in *Odutola v Papersack* (*Supra*).
8. But see the discussion *infra* on the questionable nature of this mandatory practice.

by the Law for bringing to an end a tenancy contract between a landlord and a tenant. It can be served by either party on the other party.

As pointed out earlier, the notice to quit is not, strictly, applicable to leases or tenancies for a fixed term. It is expressly provided for in the Recovery Statutes and is specifically in relation to

(a) tenancies at will;
(b) weekly tenancies;
(c) monthly tenancies;
(d) quarterly tenancies;
(e) half-yearly tenancies[9] and
(f) yearly tenancies.

The quit notice, where it is prescribed by law, is indispensible. It is a strict requirement of law and all Recovery Statutes nationwide provide for it as above in the following introductory words:

> where there is no express[10] stipulation as to the notice to be given by either party to determine the tenancy, the following period of time shall be given:

There are a number of technical legal requirements which the law requires the notice to quit to satisfy to be valid and effective. Some of these requirements and effects of a quit notice are as follows:

(a) A notice to quit once served automatically determines the tenancy at the expiration of the notice.[11]

9. Lagos State only vide Section 13 (1) (d) Tenancy Law No. 14 of 2011.
10. The Lagos Tenancy Law does not use this word.
11. *Total Nig. Plc v Morkah* (2002) 9 NWLR (Pt. 773) 496; *Udih v Izedonwan* (1990) 2 NWLR (Pt.132) 357.

(b) A notice to quit, in order to be effective, ought to determine the tenancy at the end of a current term.[12]

(c) A half a year's notice to quit in the case of a yearly tenancy is not valid if it is to take effect on any date other than that on which a current term of the tenancy would expire.[13]

(d) A tenancy, whether or not rent has been paid, cannot be determined by a notice to quit while the term is in operation.[14]

(e) A notice to quit determines the tenancy but the determination may be waived by agreement of both parties and in such a situation, a new tenancy is created and not a continuation of the old tenancy.[15]

(f) While a notice to quit is running, another notice may validly be given without thereby waiving the first notice so that the tenancy will determined by which ever notice first expires.[16]

A tenant who pays his rent every six months and is issued receipts accordingly is deemed to be a yearly tenant and such tenancy can only be terminated by a six months notice to quit and not by a month's notice.[17]

(g) A tenant at will is entitled to one week notice to quit before action can be instituted against him.[18]

---

12. *AP v Owodunni* (1991) 8 NWLR (Pt.210) 391.
13. *Awobiyi v Igbalaiye Brothers* (1956 – 66) 4 NSCC 123.
14. *Ekunife v Wayne WA Ltd.* (1989) 5 NWLR (Pt. 122) 422.
15. *Udih v Izedonwan* (*Supra*).
16. *Balogun v Ajufo* (1948) 1 – 3 CCHCJ 404.
17. *Ebueke v Ajisafe* (1980) 4 – 6 CCHCJ 155.
18. *Shugaba v Ta'abu* (2000) 16 NWLR (Pt. 71) 1.

(h) Wrongly stating the date the tenancy was determined in the seven days notice renders the seven days ineffectual.[19]

(i) Stating an inaccurate date on which owner is to apply for court processes against the tenant is sufficient error to oust the court's jurisdiction.[20]

(j) Errors in dates on statutory notices cannot be orally explained or corrected.[21]

(k) Statutory notices served in a claim which has failed abates with the case and a landlord wishing to bring a new action after the former one had collapsed must serve fresh notices.[22]

(l) A notice to quit must specifically describe the nature and type of the premises and not only the address.[23]

(m) A notice to quit must relate to the whole premises sought to be recovered.[24]

(n) A notice to quit must be clear and certain.[25]

(o) A notice to quit which is clear, certain, and unambiguous is valid notwithstanding that it does not comply with the forms in the Schedule to the Recovery Statutes.[26]

(p) A notice to quit which omits the words 'which

19. *Otegbade v Adekoya* (*Supra*).
20. *Akeju v Shonibare* (1968) 2 ANLR 159.
21. *Awe v Said* (1961) ANLR 477.
22. *Enifeni v Ademofe* (1980) 1 CCHCJ 1.
23. *Oshodi v Okafor* (1975) CCHCJ 1093.
24. *Onya v Jalingo* (1974) ECSLR 113.
25. *Lyster v Goldwin* (1841) 2 Q.B. 143.
26. *Otegbade v Adekoya* (*Supra*)

you hold of him as tenant thereof' is invalid.[27]

(q) A notice to quit may be given at any time prior to the date of determination of the current term of tenancy, but it shall not be effective if the time between the giving of the notice and the time when the tenancy is to be determined is less than the respective periods set out in the Recovery Statutes.[28]

(r) A statutory notice not signed by the party giving it nor the capacity in which he was giving it is void.[29]

(s) A notice to quit is not necessary to determine a tenancy for a fixed term.[30]

(t) Parties may by agreement vary length of notice prescribed by law.[31]

(u) A notice to quit given not to expire on the anniversary of the tenancy is invalid.[32]

Notice to Quit and Forms - The Recovery Statutes nationwide also provide for the format of quit notice in their schedules. These are as in Forms B, C, and D[33] to the schedules to the various Recovery Statutes nationwide. The first of these forms i.e. Form B is the form which a landlord

---

27. *Fasade v Nwabunike* (1974) 12 CCHCJ 1868.
28. *Ochie v Ajose* (1968) ANLR 437; *Awe v Saidi* (*supra*).
29. *Idowu v Adekanmi* (1975) 6 CCHCJ 923.
30. *Tinuola v Okon* (1966) ANLR 469; *Alokolaro v Mawdew Ventures Ltd.* (1975) 12 CCHCJ 2029; Section 13 (5) Tenancy Law (Lagos).
31. *AP v Owodunni* (1991) 8 NWLR (Pt. 210) 399.
32. *Owoade v Texaco Africa Ltd.* (1973) ANLR 89.
33. In Lagos State, the Tenancy Law has dropped Form D while Forms B and C have been relabeled TL2 and TL3 respectively.

issuing a quit notice personally uses. It is entitled

> *Notice to Quit Signed by the Landlord Himself*

and it has to be personally signed by the landlord. This notice opens with the words:

> I hereby give you notice to quit and deliver up possession of the ....

The second form i.e. Form C is the form which an agent to the landlord or a legal practitioner acting for him issues on behalf of the landlord. This form is entitled

> *Notice to Quit Given by an Agent or Legal Practitioner of the Landlord*

and is required to be signed by such agent or legal practitioner issuing same who must have been so authorized by the landlord to issue and sign the notice. This notice opens with the words:

> I hereby, as agent (Legal Practitioner) for ... your landlord, and on his behalf give you notice to quit and deliver up possession of the ....

Form D[34] is entitled

> *Notice by Landlord to Quit Lodgings*

and contains a short command in its entirety thus:

> I hereby give you notice to quit and deliver up on ... the ... day of ... 20... the rooms or apartments with the appurtenancies in my house ... which you hold of me.

It is to be signed personally by the landlord so issuing it.[35]

Use of Forms not Mandatory – The use of the above forms by all persons especially legal practitioners and estate agents involved in recovery of premises litigation and in all cases is to be highly recommended. The law does

34. No longer applicable in Lagos State.
35. For live precedents of these forms, see the Schedule to any of the Recovery Statutes nationwide.

not expressly prescribe their use as a mandatory requirement but their use in substantial compliance fastens proceedings in the court because it helps to avoid long and unnecessary arguments as to compliance and regularity of processes.

This is generally the acceptable attitude of the courts whenever the use of forms is prescribed in any statute. It is informed by a provision in the Interpretation Act to the effect that

> where a form is prescribed by an enactment, a form which differs from the prescribed form shall not be invalid for the purposes of the enactment by reason only of the difference if the difference is not in a material particular and is not calculated to mislead.[36]

By the above provision of the Interpretation Act, nothing is to be inferred as meaning that prescribed forms may not be used altogether. If anything, the provision is to the effect that prescribed forms, even though may be different, may nevertheless be used where the difference is not material. Where therefore material differences are injected into the prescribed forms such that substantial compliance is put to question, a court may be entitled to hold that such use of form, on such ground, is invalid.

Furthermore, Section 34 of the Recovery Statute for Delta and Edo states provides, as in all other states' statutes that

> subject to the express provisions, if any, of the rules, the forms contained in the First Schedule, may, in accordance with any instructions contained in the said forms, and with such variation as the circumstances of

36. Section 23 (Cap. 192 Laws of the Federation of Nigeria) 1990.

> the particular case may require, be used in the cases to which they apply, and when so used, shall be good and sufficient in law.[37]

Again, this provision has not suggested a complete disregard of the forms but merely permits modifications and variations thereto as particular circumstances would render necessary. As Bellamy J. put it in *Otegbade v Adekoya*,[38]

> it is true (the notice to quit) does not follow the form of notice to quit to be found in the Schedule to the Recovery of Premises Act. But this does not render invalid a notice to quit which is otherwise good. ... To say that a tenancy can only be determined by a notice to quit as in Form B ... appears to me to involve deleting from ... the Act the words 'or otherwise duly determined', and I do not see my way to doing this.

Contents of the Notice to Quit – A quit notice ought necessarily to be in writing although it has been held that, under the common law which appears to be the current recovery of residential premises law in the Federal Capital Territory of Abuja[39] in the absence of statutory provisions, oral notices to quit will suffice to terminate periodic tenancies.[40]

It has also been said that, notwithstanding the prescribed forms contained in the schedule to the Recovery Statutes, there is no provision in the statutes requiring that a

37. All other Recovery Statutes nationwide contain this provision.
38. (1962) 2 ANLR 760, 765.
39. See Salami JCA in *FCDA v Nwanna* (1998) 4 NWLR (Pt. 544) 73
40. See Professor Emeka Chianu (2004) *Law of Landlord and Tenant* (*supra*) at 242. See also *Obadina v Agro Services Corporation* (1985) HCNLR 215.

notice to quit should be in any particular form and that it could even take the form of a normal routine letter provided the contents reflect the intention to bring the tenancy to a close and other necessary essentials in relation thereto.

This is only logical because the provisions as to the use of forms are only in relation to the format of the forms which may be modified or varied to suit particular circumstances but not the contents thereof. Therefore, once a notice to quit reflects the essential elements which every valid notice to quit ought, by law, to reflect, it will suffice to 'otherwise duly determine' the tenancy irrespective of the form in which the notice to quit is presented. The essential elements of a valid notice to quit include:

Names of the Parties – The names of the parties must be contained in the notice to quit. This is almost elementary as every piece of writing from one person to another must invariably contain the names of the person writing and that of the person to whom the writing is addressed.

Here however, it is not necessarily the name of the person writing or that of the person to whom the writing is addressed but the names of the landlord and that of the tenant. The precedent as in Form C has a blank space for inserting the name of the landlord even though he is not the person writing but the person on whose behalf the writing is done by his agent or his legal practitioner. The precedent runs thus:

> I hereby, as agent (legal practitioner) for ... *Chief Ona Linus* ..., your landlord, and on his behalf give you notice to quit and deliver up possession of ....

Before this opening statement of the Form C are, first, the words 'To CD' below which is 'Sir'. The 'CD' represents Okupaya Titus, the tenant, while the 'Sir' beneath it is the traditional 'salutation' in formal letter writing.

In practice, and especially when the notice to quit is issued by a legal practitioner, it is done on the legal practitioner's letter-headed paper so that the reference to the first person pronoun 'I' in the opening leaves no one in doubt as to the person referred to. However, where this is not done on a letter-headed paper, it might be prudent that the full names of the person doing the writing is indicated in the space between the 'I' and 'hereby' thus:

> I, Barrister Loya, hereby, as legal practitioner for Chief Ona Linus, your landlord, etc.[41]

Therefore, if well utilized, Form C creates no difficulty in presenting this essential element of the notice to quit relating to the names of the landlord and the tenant.

With regards to the use of Forms B and D however, the precedent forms do not have blank spaces as in Form C for inserting the landlord's name. Therefore, where a letter-headed paper is not used, care must be exercised in clearly writing the landlord's name out in full upon which he signs. In practice, it is not uncommon to have persons affix indecipherable writings as their signatures at the bottom of the notice. This will not do, as the 'name' so signed cannot be read with any useful meaning.

A safe approach to avoid falling into the above error is for the landlord to adopt the modification as above whereby he inserts his name between the opening first person pronoun 'I' and 'hereby'.

Description of Premises – Following immediately after stating the parties in the prescribed forms, especially Forms

41. An agent of the landlord should do same as appropriate.

B and C, is a reference to the type of premises which is the subject of the notice to quit. Using the forms as guide therefore, it is correct to state that a quit notice must contain a description of the particular premises the tenant is required to quit and deliver up possession.

Stating the bare address of the premises will not suffice in this respect.[42] It is required that if the premises is a flat, then the notice to quit shall specifically say so that it is a flat. More than that, it will be necessary to say what kind of flat e.g. a three bedroom flat. If it is a room, the notice shall specifically say so that it is one room; and if it is a room and a parlour, the notice to quit shall specifically say so that it is a room and a parlour. The precedent as in Forms B and C is to the effect that the tenant is given notice to quit and deliver up

> possession of the ... *two bed room flat* ... with the appurtenances ...

Address of the Premises – The address or exact location where the premises, the possession of which the tenant is required to quit and give up, is situate shall also be specifically stated in a valid notice to quit.

The address shall not only be the street name and the number thereat where the premises is located but it shall also name the town or local government. This is clear from the wordings of the prescribed Forms B and C which is that the tenant is required to deliver up possession of the premises with the appurtenances

> situate at ... *No. 1 Ona Linus Street*, in the town of *Kaduna*
>
> OR

42. *Oshodi v Okafor* (*Supra*); *Onyia v Jalingo* (*Supra*)

situate at ... *No. 1 Ona Linus Street*, in the local government of *Chukun*

OR

situate at ... *No. 1 Ona Linus Street*, in the town of *Kaduna* in *Chukun* local government.

Nature of Tenancy **-** Although the prescribed forms in all but Lagos State do not require that the type of tenancy as to whether it is a weekly, monthly, quarterly, or yearly tenancy be stated, it has been held[43] that stating it will enable the court determine whether the notice is adequate in validly determining the tenancy.

This stands to reason but it has to be submitted, with due respects, that the point as to whether a notice to quit is adequate or otherwise in validly determining a tenancy is usually a point that will come up during evidence in the course of trial[44] and, since this is not a requirement of the prescribed forms or a requirement of any express provisions in the Recovery Statutes, its omission ought not to have the effect of rendering a notice to quit invalid.

In stating the type of tenancy held by the tenant, the prescribed forms can be modified or varied by inserting this fact between the words 'as' and 'tenant' thus:

… which you hold of me[45] as *a monthly* tenant thereof …

OR

43. *Olaoye v Mandilas* (1949) 19 NLR 59.
44. Except in those High Courts where 'front loading' is a requirement under their Rules of Court and Magistrate Courts in Lagos State under the Tenancy Law.
45. As under Form B. Not applicable in Lagos State whose Form TL2 has it as '*which you hold as …… tenant*' dropping the 'me'

> … which you hold of him[46] as *a monthly* tenant thereof …

The Holding as Tenant – The expression 'which you hold of … as a tenant' indicates the capacity or status in which the addressee is served the notice to quit. This status is that of a tenant and the prescribed forms require that this should be part of the notice.

In *Fasade v Nwabunike*,[47] Linus issued Titus a notice to quit through his lawyer using the format as in Form C in the schedule to the Recovery Statutes. The words 'which you hold of him as tenant thereof' were omitted. Dosunmu J. of the Lagos High Court held that this was

> more than a case of omission …. It is certainly a case of a form of notice differing in a material particular from the prescribed form and to that extent it is not saved by the provisions of the Interpretation Act … (and therefore) the notice is invalid for the purpose of determining the … tenancy.

Dates – In every notice to quit, there are usually two dates. One is the date on which the notice is issued. The other is the date on which the tenant is to quit and to give up possession of the premises. The latter is contained in the body of the notice in the following manner:

> which you hold of me as tenant thereof on the … day of … 20….

This date is very material because this is the date on which the tenancy expires and therefore the date on which the

46. As under Form C. Not applicable in Lagos State whose Form TL3 has it as '*which you held as …… tenant*' dropping the 'him'.
47. *Supra.*

status of the tenant as tenant comes to an end. Care must therefore be taken in inserting this date as it should correspond with the date on which, as a matter of fact, the tenant's tenancy can be lawfully terminated.[48]

The date on which the notice is issued is usually stated at the bottom of the notice to quit just before the signature of the person issuing same. It is stated thus:

Dated this … day of … 20…

Although this date is not very material, it may play some crucial role during the evidence in trial especially in those jurisdictions where the provision of the Recovery Statutes relating as to how[49] the notice to quit is to be served is not strictly complied with. In such jurisdictions this date could be as important a determinant as the date of service. By reference to the prescribed forms, this date like the other date as to when the tenant's tenancy determines, is required to be contained in a valid notice to quit.

During the trial, a third date may become an issue. This is the date the notice to quit is served. It is not a date to be reflected on the notice to quit. This is reflected in the evidence as to service. It is usually more easily proved by reference to the affidavit of service as deposed to by the bailiff of the court who served it.

Length of Notice to Quit – Parties are free to fix in their

48. See the discussion *infra* on the length of notice to quit.

49. See Section 32 of the Recovery Statute for Delta and Edo states which, like all other Recovery Statutes, provides that '*service of any notice under (the statute) ... shall be effected in accordance with the provisions of the law for the time being in force relating to the service of civil process of magistrates' courts*'. But see Section 22 of the Lagos State Tenancy Law No. 4 of 2011 which now excludes 'notice' from this provision.

contract the length of notice required to bring the tenancy to an end. This is usually included in their written agreement. Where however there is no such express stipulation agreed by the parties, Section 18 of the Law provides, as in all other states' laws, that the length of notice shall be:

(a) one week in the case of a tenancy at will
(b) one week for a weekly tenancy
(c) one month for a monthly tenancy
(d) one quarter for a quarterly tenancy and
(e) half a year for a yearly tenancy.

Although it has been held[50] *obitre* and it is generally so accepted that a six months notice is required to determine a six-monthly tenancy, the Recovery Statutes generally do not make provisions for the length of notice required for the determination of a half-yearly or six-monthly tenancy.

But in Lagos State, Section 13 (d) of the state's 2011 Tenancy Law dispenses with the weekly tenancy and now introduces 'three (3) month's notice for a half-yearly tenant.' In effect, only Lagos State has a provision relating as to the length of notice which is required to determine a half-yearly tenancy.

When in doubt as to the length of notice to be given in the absence of express stipulation, reference shall be had

50. See Cole J. of the then Lagos High Court in *Ebueke v Ajisfe* where he declared that '*when a landlord is generous enough to demand and receive rent from a tenant payable six monthly, he must be benevolent enough to give the tenant a period of six months to quit premises*' after observing that '*there is no provision in ... the Recovery of Premises Law of determination for a six monthly tenancy*'. ...

in evidence as to how and when the rent is paid.[51] The references to the type of tenancies are references to tenancies from week to week, month to month, quarter to quarter or year to year as the case may be and it has been held that a month's notice is a calendar month's notice and not a thirty days' notice.[52]

The Tenancy at Sufferance: Length of Notice for – The Recovery Statutes nationwide do not make provisions for tenancies at sufferance notwithstanding that this type of tenancy often occurs in Nigeria. Indeed, it is almost a daily occurrence in our courts to hear a defendant state that he tendered his rent but the landlord has refused to accept same. It is obviously for this reason that the 2011 Lagos State Tenancy Law No. 14 now provides in its Section 29 that

> … where a landlord refuses to accept the current rent from a tenant, the tenant may, upon application to the court, pay such rent to the court's Registry.

Refusal of rent by a landlord usually happens because the landlord has firmly made up his mind not to allow the defendant remain in occupation of the premises. In effect, the tenant is rendered a tenant at sufferance being one who now occupies the premises of another person without the consent or agreement of that other person who is the owner of the premises.

He is therefore in the nature of a statutory tenant who has been described as the next of kin[53] of the tenant at

51. *Adejumo v David Hughes & Co. Ltd* (1989) 5 NWLR (Pt. 120) 146; *Ebueke v Ajisafe* (1980) 4 – 6 CCHCJ 155 *Adeeyo v Roag Co. Nig. Ltd.* (1985) NBCL 92.
52. See 'How Long is a Month?' *infra.*
53. *Wheeler v Mercer* (1956) 3 AER 631; (1957) AC 416.

will. But whereas the statutes have made provisions for the length of time by way of notice to determine the tenancy of the tenant at will, no such or similar provisions have been made in any of the Recovery Statutes for the tenancy at sufferance.

According to Nnaemeka-Agu in *AP v Owodunni*,[54] the Recovery Statutes have only created statutory tenants and that

> in fact, there is no room for that class of tenancy *(i.e. the tenancy at sufferance)* under the law *(the Recovery Statutes) hence* they (the legislature) did not therefore have to make any separate provisions as to the length and nature of notices necessary for the determination of a tenancy at sufferance.

The learned jurist of the Nigerian apex court apparently holds the view that a tenant at sufferance is unknown to our statutory laws but recognizes that once a contractual tenancy

> comes to an end by effluxion of time or otherwise and the tenant holds over without the will or agreement of the landlord, he becomes a tenant at sufferance (which) is strictly a common law[55] concept'.[56]

This common law concept, known as tenancy at sufferance is, according the learned jurist, a kind of tenancy

> in which the original grant by the landlord has expired, usually by effluxion of time, but the tenant holds over the premises. In such a case, the tenant's right to occupation of the premises to which he had come in

54. *Supra.*
55. The common law of England is still part of Nigerian law by virtue of and to the extent permissible under the reception statutes.
56. *op. cit.*

> upon a lawful title by grant is at an end but, although he has no more title as such, he continues in possession of the land or premises without any further grant or agreement by the landlord on whom the right to the reversion resides.[57]

The honourable Justice Nnaemeka-Agu then explained that a necessary precondition for the existence of a tenancy at sufferance is that the tenant must have in the first place come upon the premises lawfully and that although he no longer now had an estate,

> the law will deem his right to possession to have continued on the same terms and conditions as the original grant till possession has been duly and properly wrested from him. It is a form of tenancy which … depends upon the law and not the agreement of the parties and can only be determined either by the landlord's lawful act of forcible entry,[58] where it is still possible,[59] or by a proper action for ejectment after due notices as prescribed by law.[60]

In effect, the tenant at sufferance is as entitled to the protections which the Recovery Statutes provide as other statutory tenants so that it becomes a correct statement of the law that a tenant at sufferance is also a statutory tenant

57. *ibid* at 332.
58. A right at some time in the remote past known only to the common law.
59. Not any more possible anywhere in Nigeria by virtue of the various Recovery Statutes. See also *Iheanacho v Uzochukwu* (1987) 2 NWLR (Pt. 487) 257; Lord Denning MR in *Agbor v Metropolitan Police Commissioner* (1969) WLR 707; *Adekunle v Adegboye* (1992) 2 NWLR (Pt. 223) 305, 309; *NSC Nig. Ltd. v Innis Palmer* (1992) 1 NWLR (Pt. 218).
60. *AP v Owodunni* (*supra*) pp.332 - 3.

who is entitled to 'due notices as prescribed by law'. But there is no express prescription by the Recovery laws as to the length and nature of notices necessary for the determination of a tenancy at sufferance.

The Statutory Tenant - However, the tenant at sufferance is very similar to the tenant at will with which it is next of kin and about both of which the Supreme Court of Nigeria has said that they differ materially from each other

> only in the sense that whereas a tenancy at sufferance is a concept of the common law

in operation only in those parts of Nigeria, if any,[61] where there are no Recovery Statutes, the tenant at will is expressly a statutory tenant. In effect, there really is no difference between both except as to their source of origin as law.

They are both tenants holding over, and, every tenant holding over is a statutory tenant. The one holds over with the consent and agreement of the landlord. The other holds over without the consent and agreement of the landlord. Consequently, the latter otherwise fits more the bill of a naked trespasser. But it is not trespass because it arises from a prior lawful entry and occupation of premises.

In *Pan Asian African Co. Ltd. v Nicon Ltd.*,[62] Idigbe JSC (as he then was) explained the no-difference between the tenant at sufferance and the tenant at will in lights similar to the difference between twelve and one dozen so well that there is nothing to add such that the learned jurist deserves only to be quoted here in *extenso* thus:

> At common law, a tenant who entered premises on a

61. See *FCDA v Nwanna* (*supra*).
62. (1982) ANLR 229.

lawful demise or title but wrongfully continued in possession, after the expiration of the period under the demise or title without the consent (assent) or dissent of the person next entitled, is a tenant at sufferance; again, anyone who continues in possession of premises without agreement after a particular estate is ended is also a tenant at sufferance.

Accordingly, where … a tenant for a fixed term refuses at the expiration of his tenancy to vacate possession and wrongfully (i.e. without the consent of the landlord) continues in possession, he would at common law be a tenant at sufferance.

However, in recent times, the laws relating to controlled, protected or regulated tenancy intervened to give such a tenant a special tenancy; hence we find the 'statutory tenant' being defined – for example – as 'a tenant who retains possession by virtue of the Rent Acts and not as being entitled to a tenancy'.[63] Put simply, the statutory tenant is an occupier who, when his contractual tenancy expires, holds over and continues in possession by virtue of special statutory provisions.

He has also been described as 'that anomalous legal entity … who holds the land of another contrary to the will of that other person who strongly desires to turn him out. Such a person will not ordinarily be described as a tenant".[64]

… The expression 'statutory tenant' has also been defined as 'a compendious expression to describe the right of a tenant of a protected premises to remain in possession of those premises, notwithstanding the

63. His lordship then referred to Section 49 (1) of the 1954 English Housing Repairs and Rents Act (2 and 3 Elix. 2, C.53).
64. His lordship then referred to Scrutton LJ in *Shutter v Hersh* (1921) 1 K.B. 438, 448.

determination of his contractual interest until such time as either he voluntarily gives up possession, or the court, on cause shown, makes an order against him to deliver up possession'.[65]

Accordingly, it has been, quite appropriately, described as a 'status of irremovability'.[66]

Since no one is entitled to embark on self help in the effort to recover possession of premises or, as Lord Denning MR (as he then was) would say, that

> no one is entitled to take possession of premises by a strong hand or with a multitude of people,[67]

or as the Court of Appeal declared in *NSC Nig. Ltd. v Innis-Palmer*,[68] that

> a landlord has not the right to invade premises in the lawful occupation of a tenant and cast his goods and belongings away even for safe keeping without his consent,

even the tenant at sufferance, it is humbly submitted, is entitled, at the very least, to the quantum of due process to which at least its next of kin, the tenant at will, is entitled. Under the Recovery Statutes, the next of kin to the tenant at sufferance i.e. the tenant at will is entitled to a one week notice for the valid determination of his tenancy. All the Recovery Statutes nationwide provide for this using exactly the same words. It is that

---

65. His lordship then referred to Jenkins LJ in *American Economic Laundary Ltd. v Little* (1951) 1 K.B. 400, 406.
66. His lordship then referred to Lush J. in *Keaves v Dean; Nunn v Pelegrini* (1924) 1 K.B. 685,
67. *Agbor v Metropolitan Police* (*Supra*) WLR 703, 707, *Adekunle v Adegboye* (*Supra*), *NSC Nig. Ltd v Innis-Palmer* (*Supra*).
68. (1992) 1 NWLR (Pt. 218) 422.

> where there is no express stipulation as to the notice to be given by either party to determine the tenancy, the following periods of time shall be given -
>
> (a) in the case of a tenancy at will or a weekly tenancy, a week's notice; ...[69]

A Week not Seven Days - A week is a week. This must be different from seven days in the contemplation of the law. Whereas seven days may be computed from any day of the week, a week must be calculated with reference to when a calendar week begins and ends. This, in Nigeria, is that a week begins on Monday and ends on Sunday.

If the lawmaker had intended seven days in this section of the Recovery Statute, he would have stated so, just as he did in the preceding section, where his intention must be taken to have been seven days and he so stated that

> ... to recover possession on a date not less than seven days from the date of service of the notice.[70]

But a tenant at sufferance need not necessarily be equated to a tenant at will simplistically. Being a tenant holding over without the consent or agreement of the landlord, the position of the tenant at sufferance ought more to be precarious[71] than that of the tenant at will who holds over with the consent or agreement of his landlord.

Ironically however, there is a sense in which it can be said that the position of the tenant at sufferance may be

69. Section 13 (1) (a) (Lagos); S. 18 (a) (Delta/ Edo); S. 17 (Plateau). Also *Odutola v Papersack Nig. Ltd.* (*Supra*).
70. But observation must be made that in *Odutola v Papersack Nig Ltd.* (*supra*), the Supreme Court of Nigeria, in this regard, used 'one week' interchangeably with 'seven days'.
71. This is so under the common law. See *Thunder Weaver v Belcher* (1803) 3 East 449.

less precarious than that of the tenant at will who is statutorily entitled to but only one week notice for the due determination of his tenancy. The one week notice is fixed and certain with respect to the tenant at will. It is statutory. This is not the case with the tenant at sufferance who is entitled to notice of a length which is not necessarily fixed and certain but is fluid depending on his original grant.

In *AP v Owodunni*,[72] the Supreme Court of Nigeria held that whenever there is a holding over, a statutory tenancy comes into being and

> once there is an incident of statutory tenancy, the tenant becomes a weekly, monthly or yearly tenant depending upon the term of the original grant

and that therefore, the tenancy can only be lawfully terminated in accordance with the manner and length of term of the original grant between the landlord and tenant.

This means that where a yearly tenant, for instance, holds over, he becomes either a tenant at sufferance or one at will depending as to whether he holds over with his landlord's consent or not. Whether he holds over with agreement or not, he is a statutory tenant. His tenancy can only be terminated in accordance with the manner and length of notice under his original grant from which he now holds over.

This is that as a yearly tenant at sufferance, he will be entitled to a six months notice to quit except there was such express stipulation otherwise in the original grant. By this decision of the Supreme Court of Nigeria, the same situation applies to the other types of tenancy as to monthly or quarterly.

---

72. *Supra.*

The position of the law therefore is that a statutory tenant is entitled to the same length of notice for the valid determination of his tenancy while holding over just as he was entitled to during the lawful pendency of his original grant and that his holding over does not change anything in this regard.[73]

This is the position of the Supreme Court of Nigeria taken in 1991. The position appears, with due respect, to have ignored the express provisions of the Recovery Statutes to the effect that where a statutory tenant is a tenant at will, he shall be entitled to a one week notice.

Under our legal system, statute is superior to judicial precedent and accordingly, it must, with due respect, be a correct statement of the law that the decision of the apex court in this respect can hardly represent the position of the law in as far as the decision is inconsistent with the statute which is that a tenant at will, irrespective of the nature and the type of his original holding, is entitled to only a week's notice to quit.

However, in 2007, some sixteen years later, the *Odutola v Papersack Nig. Ltd.*[74] case came up for the determination of the Supreme Court of Nigeria which therein held unequivocally and emphatically per Onu JSC that

> from the moment a year's rent became due and payable ... but remained unpaid, the yearly tenancy ... came to an end by effluxion of time and the respondent thereupon became a tenant at will ... by continuing or remaining in possession .... In other words, the

73. See Nnaemeka-Agu in *AP v Owodunni* (*supra*) at 334 -5.
74. *Supra*.

> respondent at that stage is said to be holding over … and in that capacity, became a tenant at will … (who) was entitled to no more than a week's notice.[75]

Rubbing it in, Tobi JSC who delivered the lead judgement, after concluding that the tenancy in issue was one at will, proceeded thus:

> In Exhibit P6 … the 1st appellant gave the respondent seven day's notice to quit. … I do not think I should take the issue further. The notice, Exhibit P6, is valid.[76]

In arriving at this decision in the *Papersack* case, the Supreme Court of Nigeria did not overrule itself with regards to its 1991 position in *AP v Owodunni.* But the two decisions are clearly diametrically opposed to each other. Whereas the latter case sought to stick strictly to the provisions of the Recovery Statutes relating to the length of notice for the determination of a tenancy at will, the former categorises tenancies at will in terms of their original contractual grant in arriving at what length of notice is required to determine what category of tenancy at will.

In their effect, whereas *Owodunni* over indulges the yearly tenant who is holding over, *Papersack* works hardship on him. Notwithstanding that the *Owodunni* case was not expressly overruled by the apex court, the *Papersack* decision, being later in time and obviously founded on a strict application of statutory provisions, is to be taken as representing the current position of the law.

The *Owodunni* case is, with due respect, to be preferred as it accords more with the doing of substantial justice. But for the holding that a tenancy at sufferance is

75. *ibid* at 1364.
76. *ibid* at 1360.

unknown to our statutory laws on the subject, the respondent in the *Papersack* case, with due respect, was nothing short of a tenancy at sufferance as the evidence showed clearly that the respondent was not the appellants' original tenant and that it even took possession of the premises not only without the consent or agreement of the appellants but without the appellants' knowledge.

Papersack and Hardship - The hardship which the *Papersack* decision visits on the yearly tenant holding over is illustrated by the provision of the proviso to the section in all Recovery Statutes nationwide specifying the length of notice for the different types of tenancies. This proviso allows a monthly tenant holding over a three months period from the date his rent becomes due and payable but remains unpaid before his tenancy determines. The proviso runs thus:

> … in the case of a monthly tenancy, where a tenant is in arrears of rent for three months … the tenancy shall determine ….

This proviso is a reflection of the spirit and purpose of the Recovery Statutes which is to protect the tenant in his possession of premises.[77] But *Papersack* certainly is not in consonance with this spirit and purpose.

Six Months Arrears in Lagos - Under the Lagos State Tenancy Law No. 14 of 2011 the provision is now direct and no longer comes as a proviso. This Lagos law now allows a monthly tenant to be in arrears of his rent up to six months, as against three months, before his tenancy determines by operation of the law. The provision is to the effect that

77. *AP v Owodunni* (*supra*) at 344.

> in the case of a monthly tenancy, where the tenant is in arrears for six (6) months, the tenancy shall lapse and the court shall make an order for possession and arrears of rent upon proof of the arrears by the landlord.[78]

However, the protection in this proviso is conferred not across board but only on the monthly tenant other than in Lagos State. The reason for the discriminatory provision is not clear except that the monthly tenant is the commonest type of tenant in Nigeria and, as a result, although the provision is discriminatory, most Nigerian tenants beneficiaries thereof.

But what is good for the goose, it is said, is good for the gander. The requirements of justice, equity, balance, and fair play ought to be brought to bear on the provision so as to extend the protection to all types of tenancies. This is what the decision in *AP v Owodunni* has attempted to do and must have informed the new Lagos position that

> in the case of a quarterly or half-yearly tenancy, where the tenant is in arrears of one (1) year rent, the tenancy shall lapse....

But if a monthly tenant can be allowed to be in arrears of his rent for three months (and, in Lagos State, he can be in arrears of his rent for up to one year where he is either a quarterly or a half-yearly tenant) before his tenancy stands determined by operation of the law, why not a yearly tenant and even more so? Instead, *Papersack* has now decided, ironically, that the yearly tenant is not entitled to fall into arrears in his rent even for a single day before his tenancy determines but that

> from the moment a year's rent became due and payable

78. Section 13 (2) Tenancy Law No. 14 of 2011.

> … but remained unpaid …the yearly tenancy … came to an end

and the tenant becomes a tenant at will by reference and reliance on the two English decisions namely *Howard v Shaw*[79] and *Wheeler v Mercer*[80] and thereafter that, by the provisions[81] of the Recovery Statutes, the tenant, having become a tenant at will was entitled to no more than a week's notice[82]

Papersack and Validity of Notices to Quit - This decision of the Supreme Court of Nigeria appears, with due respects, to have ignored the requirement of the law that every valid quit notice must be issued and served at such dates and times so that it not only meets the length of time provided by law or the stipulations of the parties for the determination of the tenancy but also that the notice to quit must expire at the end of a current term or the anniversary of the tenancy.[83]

If therefore as by the apex court's decision in this case, a year's rent becomes due and payable, for instance, on the 1st day of January but remains unpaid by the 2nd of January and on which date a week's notice was served on the tenant or on any date thereafter but before the 24th of December, how will this one week notice operate so as to validly terminate the tenancy on the 31st of December since such notice will not be expiring on a date corresponding to

79. (1841) 8 M & M & W 118.
80. *Supra*
81. *Supra.*
82. Section 15 (1) of the Lagos State Rent Control and Recovery of Premises Law. All Recovery Statutes nationwide have the same provision.
83. *ibid* at 1364 per Onu JSC.

the anniversary of the tenancy but before it?

To be effective, going by the *Papersack* decision, the one week notice must be served not later than the 24th of December such that there is a clear one week from the date of issue and service to the 31st of December being the anniversary date of the tenancy. Yet, this cannot be entirely free of difficulties as there is also the requirement, ignored also by the *Papersack* decision, that the notice to quit which the tenant is entitled to, in order to be valid, must be such that he gets one whole term which, in this case, is one year.[84]

Clearly, a notice to quit issued and served on the 24th of December can hardly provide the tenant with a whole term notwithstanding that it satisfies the requirement of the one week length of time. Nor can a notice to quit issued and served on the 2nd of January in respect of a yearly tenancy whose expiration or anniversary is the 31st of December as the term will then be short by at least one day.

However, all of the above analyses come to naught if it is taken that what *Papersack* has decided ultimately is that the yearly tenancy held by the tenant is extinguished and transformed to a tenancy at will merely by reason of the tenant's rent falling into arrears and remaining unpaid by the moment. Therefore all that is now required is a resort to the provisions of the Recovery Statutes which is to the effect that a tenancy at will can be determined by a one week notice and which notice can be issued and served at any time.

84. AP v Owodunni (*Supra*). But see the Lagos Tenancy Law which has done away with these requirements.

Papersack Binding in Lagos State - By the enactment of the Tenancy Law No. 14 in Lagos State and upon its coming into effect on the 24th of August 2011, the *Papersack* decision with respect to yearly tenancies remains firmly binding and effective in Lagos State notwithstanding that this law extends the protection hitherto provided only to monthly tenancies (whereby they remain undetermined for three months while the tenant's rent remains unpaid) to quarterly and half-yearly tenancies. Section 13 (3) of the Law No. 14 in extending this protection to the quarterly and half-yearly tenancies provides that

> in the case of a quarterly or half-yearly tenancy, where the tenant is in arrears of one (1) year rent, the tenancy shall lapse ….

In similar wordings, subsection 2 of the same section of this law extends the protection with respect to monthly tenancies from three months to six months.

However, in all of these novel provisions which have radically altered the position of the recovery laws in these respects, no consideration whatsoever has been given to the yearly tenant in like manner.

Therefore, whereas the tenancies of monthly tenants and those of quarterly and half-yearly tenants remain protected for up to six months and one year respectively where the tenant's rent falls into arrears and remains unpaid, there is no such-like protection for the yearly tenant under the Lagos State Tenancy Law No. 14. For the yearly tenant, his tenancy remains subject to a six months notice for its termination pursuant to Section 13 (1) (e) of the law and to the decision in *Papersack* which is to the effect that from the moment a year's rent becomes due and payable but remains unpaid, the yearly tenancy comes to an end.

The Half-Yearly Tenancy - The Recovery Statutes nationwide except Lagos State do not make provisions for the length of notice for the determination of a six monthly tenancy notwithstanding that this type of tenancy is not in practice unknown. But it is generally accepted that a six months notice is required to determine a six-months tenancy.

According to Professor Emeka Chianu, it is enough to say that, with respect to the determination of half-yearly, quarterly, or weekly tenancies, the length of notice required is the period of the tenancy itself so that a weekly tenancy requires a week's notice, a quarterly tenancy a quarter's notice and a half-yearly or six-monthly tenancy, six months notice.[85] The learned law professor then cited *Adeeyo v Roag Co. Ltd*[86] in support of his assertion and quoted the dictum of Cole J. in *Ebueke v Ajisafe,*[87] a 1980 Lagos High Court decision, to drive the point home thus:

> There is no provision in (the section) of the Recovery of Premises Law of determination for a six monthly tenancy, but law is sometimes common sense, and common sense dictates that when a landlord is generous enough to demand and receive rent from a tenant payable six monthly, he must be benevolent enough to give the tenant a period of six months (notice) to quit (the) premises.[88]

---

85. *Law of Landlord and Tenant* (*supra*) at 240. See also the Supreme Court in *AP v Owodunni* (*supra*).
86. *Supra*.
87. (1980) 4 – 6 CCHCJ 155.
88. *ibid* at 158.

Although, Cole J. sounds comical in the above dictum of his, the reality in practice is that the serving of a six months notice to quit in respect of the determination of a half-yearly tenancy is generally accepted as correct.

There is no other direct pronouncement of a more superior court of record on the issue and until such a pronouncement is made, it is humbly submitted that the correct position of the law for now ought to be as posited by the professor of law and the learned justice of the Lagos High Court. This conclusion does not relate to Lagos State which has enacted a 2011 Tenancy Law expressly providing for a three months notice for the determination of a half-yearly tenancy in Section 13 (1) thereof.

How Long is Half a Year? This question may sound stupid at first contact as, obviously, half a year ought clearly and without dispute to be half of twelve months being the number of months which make up one year. Of course it is also obvious that the issue is taken for granted as it ought naturally be and most courts including even the Supreme Court usually gloss over the fine disputations that may sometimes arise in the computation of times and periods for doing such things as the serving of quit notices.

The actual numerical computation of any period in law whether the period be expressed in weeks, months or in years is ultimately done with reference to the number of days making up the period.[89] This is why, as far back in time as 1895, Lindley LJ. had held that in computing half a year or a six months period, the computation must consist of 182 days. In line with this, Smith J. of the Lagos High

89. *Akeredolu v Akinremi* (1985) 2 NWLR (Pt. 10) 787, 798.

Court had held in *Lasaki v Dabian*[90] that the

> length of a half a year's notice must be 182 days … reckoned by including the one extreme and excluding the other.

Illustrating the effect of this position, Professor Chianu computed the period between the 1st day of September to the 28th day of February which though adds up to six months falls short of 182 days by one day and therefore inadequate in satisfying the requirement that a yearly tenancy can only be determined by a six months notice. The learned professor then concluded that

> half a year means half the days of a year (*i.e. half of 365 days*) and in this regard, six months is not necessarily equivalent to half the days of the year[91]

since, again as the learned professor of law correctly illustrates, a six months notice to quit served on the 1st of March to expire August 31st, for instance, will be in excess of six months by two days.

The Monthly Tenant – This is a tenant whose tenancy runs from month to month. He is a periodic tenant but which, though his term is only for one month which means that at the end of a month the term expires by effluxion of time, he is, in the nature of things, automatically allowed to continue in possession almost as a matter of right. This operates from antiquity like an implied term of the contract between the landlord and the tenant and of which the court in *Gandy v Jubber*[92] states that

> there is no re-letting (but that), at the commencement of

90. (1957) NRNLR 12.
91. *Law of Landlord and Tenant* (*supra*) at 255.
92. (1865) 9 B & S 15.

> every (new) year, month, or week, there is a springing interest which (automatically) arises and which can only be determined by a proper notice to quit.

Citing *Gladstone v Bower*,[93] Professor Chianu says of this automatic springing interest that

> after the first term of one month or year, there is an automatic renewal of the term by operation of law[94] from the anniversary of the tenancy for successive periods of one month or one year as the case may be.[95]

Because of the operation of this automatic springing interest which works most times in the general interest of the tenant, the most common mode of determining a monthly tenancy is by way of the notice to quit. This is a notice for a period of one month[96] except there is some express stipulation to the contrary. This is provided for in all the Recovery Statutes nationwide thus:

> where there is no express stipulation as to the notice to be given by either party to determine the tenancy, the following periods of time shall be given –
> (a) in the case of a tenancy at will or a weekly tenancy, a week's notice;
> (b) in the case of a monthly tenancy, a month's notice;
> (c) in the case of a quarterly tenancy, a quarter's notice;[97] and
> (d) in the case of a yearly tenancy, half a year's notice.

93. (1960) 1 QB 170, 178.
94. This is not statutory but must be a reference to the common law.
95. *Law of Landlord and Tenant* (*supra*) at 250.
96. See Section 18 (b) of the Delta State Rent Control and Recovery of Residential Premises Law. All other states Recovery Statutes nationwide have this provision verbatim.
97. The Lagos State Tenancy Law now provides for a half-yearly tenancy determinable by a three months notice to quit.

The periods of time stipulated by this provision become applicable only when and if the parties had not stipulated some other period of time in their terms of contract for bringing the tenancy to an end. This is clear from the opening statement in the provision which is that

> where there is no express stipulation as the notice to be given....

This means that parties to a tenancy contract are free to make for themselves stipulations as to length of periods of notice for determining a tenancy. Therefore, if for instance, parties to a monthly tenancy stipulate that the tenancy as between them may be terminated by a one week notice or by a three months notice, the courts will give effect to the stipulation and will not interfere with same since courts do not make contracts for persons and, further, the Recovery Statutes permit parties in this regard to contract freely.

How long is a month? When the Recovery Statutes provide for 'a month's notice' to determine a monthly tenancy, it is clear that this also means 'one month'. But what is, and, how long is 'a month'? Is a month a period of thirty days? If so, is the period of thirty days any period of thirty days calculated from any day within a calendar month? And, is a month a reference to any of the months as is on the calendar?

According to the Interpretation Act, a 'month' means 'a calendar month reckoned according to the Gregorian calendar'. The Gregorian calendar is the calendar currently in use worldwide and was introduced in 1852 by Pope Gregory XIII and is said to be a modification of a previous Roman calendar. Therefore, a month is any of the months January to December as contained in the calendar. This is the law. It is statutory. It is binding on parties except where they have made express stipulations providing otherwise in their contract.

Also the English House of Lords, in what may be considered the common law position, has held in *Dodds v Walker*,[98] that a calendar month

> ends upon the day in the next ensuing month having the same number (of days) as that on which the computation began, but if the ensuing month has not the same number (of days) as that on which the computation began, then the month ends on the last day on the next ensuing month

but Chianu respectfully disagrees with this definition which makes a month a period from 1st of one month to the 1st of the next month or from 10th to the 10th except where the next month does not contain the day and in which case the month ends on the last day thereof. The learned law professor proffers instead, with due respects, that

> the proper computation should be the numerically corresponding date in the next month less one day[99]

and that, since a basic month is made up of 30 days, being an approximation of 29 days, 12 hours and 44 minutes by reference to the exact lunation of the moon,

> a month should be ... from any day of any month ... in the calendar to a corresponding day in the next month less one (day and), where there is no corresponding day (in the next month), then the last day of the following (next) month.[100]

98. (1981) 1 WLR 1027.
99. *Law of Landlord and Tenant* (supra) at 250.
100. *ibid* at 249.

Without meaning to join the fray, it is humbly submitted that, in practice, the learned professor's mode of computation is the popularly accepted and applied mode. This is that the period of a month is from any day of a month to the corresponding date of the next month less one day, that is, for instance from the 1st of one month to the 1st of the next month less one day or from the 10th to the 10th less one day as the case may be.

Terminating Monthly Tenancy by Operation of Law – There is a proviso to the section of the Recovery Statutes relating to the periods for the termination of tenancies which is peculiar to the one month tenancy in all but Lagos[101] State. This is that provided

> in the case of a monthly tenancy, where a tenant is in arrears of rent for three[102] months after the commencement of (the Law) the tenancy shall determine ....[103]

This means that in a monthly tenancy, the contractual relationship between a landlord and his tenant automatically comes to an end whenever the tenant's rent falls into arrears for three months. The three months must be consecutive.

The provision refers in real terms to a monthly tenant holding over and who by virtue of such holding over is a statutory tenant in the class of a tenancy at will. By this logic, the provisions of subsection (a) of the section of the

---

101. It is a direct provision in Section 13 (2) of Tenancy Law in Lagos State.
102. Six months in Lagos State.
103. Section 18 of the Law (Delta and Edo). Section 17 (Plateau State). Section 15 (Cross River State).

Recovery Statutes stipulating periods for the termination of different types of tenancies as well as such judicial authorities as *Amalgamated Press of Nig. Ltd. v Haastrup*[104] and *Odutola v Papersack Nig. Ltd.*,[105] the monthly tenant would, but for this express proviso, be entitled only to a week's notice for the due determination of his monthly tenancy.

Discriminatory Nature of Proviso - But the proviso is discriminatory in favour only of the monthly tenant in all but Lagos State. This must be due to the reality that the monthly tenant is the commonest type of tenancy in Nigeria and the law maker must have assumed that the proviso will, as it is, affect all tenants or, at the very least, most of them. Set against the position of the yearly tenant who holds over, the proviso works hardship and its unfair character in relation thereto is laid bare.

However by Section 13 (2) and (3) of the Lagos State Tenancy Law No. 14 of 2011, the discriminatory effect of the provision has been reduced as it has now been extended to cover the quarterly and half-yearly tenancies which shall stand determined only when these tenants' rent fall into arrears up to one year.

Features of a Valid Notice to Quit – As stated earlier, there are legal technicalities prescribed by the law which every quit notice must comply with to render it valid as otherwise the action which follow may fail because a valid quit notice is an important condition precedent to the institution of an action for the recovery of possession of premises. These legal technicalities include:

104. (1966) ANLR 346.
105. *Supra*

.***Effective at End of Term*** - In every case, a valid quit notice must be issued, served and expressed so as to terminate the tenancy at the end of a current term while still complying strictly with the length of time required by law to terminate the tenancy by notice. As the Supreme Court held in *Owoade v Texaco Africa Ltd*[106] after calling in aid the English decision in *Soames v Nicholson,*[107]

> the general rule is that where nothing is said (in the contract between the parties) about the time at which *(the tenancy)* is to be determined, it can only be put an end to by notice expiring at the date corresponding to that of its commencement.

Position in Lagos State Different – The above age-long rule of law has now been modified by Section 13 (4) the Tenancy Law No. 14 of Lagos State in that, from the commencement of this law on the 24th of August 2011, notices to quit in Lagos State in respect of quarterly, half-yearly, and yearly tenancies need no longer be issued, served and expressed to terminate the tenancy at the end of a current term.

The provision effectively overrules the Supreme Court's decision in *Owoade v Texaco Africa Ltd*[108] and all other judicial authorities in this respect. By it, notices for the termination of quarterly, half-yearly, and yearly tenancies

> need not terminate on the anniversary of the tenancy but may terminate on or after the date of expiration of the tenancy.

The provision is not one of those easily understood

106. *Supra.*
107. (1902) 1KB 157
108. *Supra.*

legislative draftings. It curiously now requires that some clear difference be placed between the *anniversary date* of a tenancy and the *date of expiration* of the tenancy which previous understanding meant one and the same date. This is so as a tenancy, safe for the monthly tenancy, need no longer be made to terminate by notice on the *anniversary date* of the tenancy but may be made to terminate *on* the *date of expiration* of the tenancy or *after* the *date of expiration* of the tenancy.

Before the enactment of this provision by the Lagos State legislature, the nearest provision in terms of similarity in effect is in Section 19 of the Law[109] which is to the effect that notices to quit

> may be given at any time prior to the date of termination of current terms of tenancy, but they shall not be effective if the time between the giving of the notice and the time when the tenancy is to be determined is less than the respective periods[110] set out

in the section of the Recovery Statutes providing for the periods for the determination of various types of tenancies.

Notice a Necessity – Except as is usual with tenancies for a fixed term certain, a quit notice is an imperative of the law in the determination of the relationship between a landlord and a tenant. Therefore, where there has been an express stipulation as to the notice to be given by either of the parties to determine the tenancy, such notice, whcther it is

Notice can be Given any Time - The quit notice, whether given in situations where there is an express stipulation or

109. See Section 19 of the Law; Section 15 Lagos State prior to the 2011 Tenancy Law No. 14 of 2011; *AP v Owodunni* (1991) 15 NSCQR 308; *Awe v Saidi* (1969) ANLR 477.

110. See *infra*. But see also Emeka Chianu op. cit. at 255 – 259.

not can be given at any time but so that
(i) it meets the length of time provided by law or by the stipulation of the parties,
(ii) the tenant must have at least one whole term[111] of the tenancy from the date of the service on him of the notice to quit and when the notice takes effect,
(iii) it expires at the end or expiration of the current term as a tenancy can only be terminated at its expiry date.[112]

What this means in effect is that a monthly tenant, for instance, may be served a quit notice at any time of any day in one month to have effect at end of the following month. By way of illustration, if Linus serves Titus a quit notice on the 2nd of a month, say March, to determine a monthly tenancy, Linus would validly be entitled to do so since the law is that a quit notice may be served 'at any time' – a term which the Supreme Court has said in *Awe v Saidi*[113] and *Awobiyi v Igbalaye Brothers*[114] mean that the notice must be given at any date earlier than the date of termination of a current term and which will fit in for a week, in case of weekly tenancy, a month, in case of a monthly tenancy, or six months in case of yearly tenancy, but if given on a date which will make it less than the necessary period of a week, a month or six months as the

111. Except the yearly tenant who is entitled to a term less half the term.
112. *AP v Owodunni* (1991) 15 NSCQR 308;
113. *Supra.*
114. (1965) NMLR 306.

case may be, the notice is ineffective. For instance, a notice due to be given on 1st March for a yearly tenancy which expires six months after that date, may be given at any time earlier than 1st March.[115]

However since the quit notice must also be served so that its effective date or its expiration must correspond with the end of a current term which is the end of a month and still meet the stipulated length of time, in this case, one month, the quit notice served by Linus cannot be effective on the 31st of March because then the one month period will be short by one day. It cannot also be effective on the 1st of April because that date will not correspond with the end of a term which should be at the end of a month.[116]

The notice will however not be invalid but will only become effective at the end of the next month i.e. the 30th of April. If however Linus proceeds to taking any step following the service of the quit notice e.g. serving on Titus a seven days notice of his intention to recover possession from Titus before the 30th of April, then the quit notice will become invalid for purposes of the subsequent suit if filed. Therefore, a month's notice to quit served on the first day of the same month will necessarily be short of one month by one day and thereby invalid.[117]

The computation of the length of notice in recovery of possession processes is strict. Care must therefore be

115. Per Ademola CJN in *Awe v Saidi* (*Supra*).
116. But see *Odutola v Papersack Nig. Ltd.* (*supra*) where the Supreme Court has held that a yearly tenant becomes a tenant at will the 'moment' his rent falls due and payable but remains unpaid and is therefore then entitled only to a one week notice to quit.
117. *Oyekoya v G.B Ollivant* (1969) ANLR 80.

taken in writing out the quit notice particularly with respect to the dates thereon as the insertion of a wrong date will invalidate the notice.

Generally, a quit notice must be free of ambiguity and its contents certain and definite in every respect.

Effect of the Notice to Quit – For the purpose of the recovery of premises laws, there are two kinds of tenants recognized by law. These are

(a) the *contract tenant* and

(b) the *statutory tenant*.[118]

The contract tenant is that tenant who has an estate or demise arising from his agreement with the owner of premises who, under the agreement, agrees to let premises to the tenant. Such a tenant enjoys rights under the contract of tenancy just as he is subject to duties under it. Both parties freely agree to contract with respect to the premises and the law does not make for them their contract.

On the other hand, the statutory tenant is a tenant who, though not having an estate or demise in relation to premises, nevertheless occupies same sometimes without the consent or agreement of the owner of the premises. Notwithstanding that he does not have an estate, he remains in possession of the premises and enjoys the protection of the law in respect of his possession thereof.[119] Such a person will not ordinarily be described as a tenant but he is nonetheless regarded as an

> anomalous legal entity … who holds the land of another

118. *AP v Owodunmi* (*Supra*) at 342. See The Statutory Tenant at Chapter One.
119. See Idigbe JSC in *Pan Asian African Co. Ltd v Nicon Ltd* (*supra*) at 259.

> contrary to the will of that other person who strongly desires to turn him out.[120]

A usual mode of creating a statutory tenancy is when a notice to quit is served on the contractual tenant. This has the effect of converting a contractual tenancy into a statutory tenancy when the tenant remains in possession beyond the effective date of the notice to quit served on him.

Except the tenancy for a fixed term certain, the usual mode by which a tenancy is brought to an end is by way of the notice to quit.[121] In other words, the notice to quit has the effect of relieving the parties of all contractual obligations and rights because the contract which binds them as landlord and tenant is brought to an end by virtue of the notice to quit.

Therefore once the notice to quit takes effect, the tenant ceases to be under a duty to pay rent since rent is the consideration paid only by a tenant. A tenant turned 'trespasser' does not pay rent but 'damages'.[122]

The 'damages' which such a 'trespasser' pays is known in law as *mesne* profits instead because there had existed as between the parties what may be called a quasi-tenancy arising from a prior tenancy but which has been determined lawfully. Explaining this kind of 'damages' which only someone who is in occupation of premises is liable to pay, the Supreme Court in *AP v Owodunni* states

120. See *ibid.*
121. There are other ways including expiration of the term otherwise also known as effluxion of time, forfeiture, surrender, merger, satisfied term, enlargement, disclaimer and frustration.
122. *AP v Owodunmi* (*Supra*).

that

> *mesne* profits are the rents and profits which a trespasser has, or might have received or made during the occupation of the premises (i.e. after the due determination of a prior tenancy), and which therefore he must pay over to the true owner as compensation for the tort which (the tenant) has committed[123]

and that because a claim for *mesne* profits is based on trespass committed by a person unlawfully occupying another's premises, it is inappropriate to use the term in respect of a person in lawful occupation as a tenant and that a claim founded on *mesne* profits can only be maintained when the tenancy has been duly determined and the tenant becomes a trespasser.

Rent and *Mesne* Profits Distinguished – Rent is different from *mesne* profits in that while rent is usually a liquidated amount arising from contract as usually agreed by the parties in the form of the consideration which flows from the tenant to the landlord for the letting, possession, and use of premises, *mesne* profits is never a liquidated sum but dependent on computation from the date when the contractual relationship between the landlord and the tenant is terminated and the date when the tenant gives up possession.

Rent is paid by the tenant to his landlord while there subsists between them a tenancy contract but *mesne* profits is paid by the tenant to his landlord where the tenant retains possession of the premises after the tenancy contract had ended arising from the service on him of a notice to quit. Accordingly, *mesne* profits is recoverable as from

123. *ibid* at 344.

the expiration of the tenancy for so long as the tenant remains in possession of the demised premises without a contract.

Only a tenant pays rent. Sometimes, a tenant's rent falls into arrears giving rise to a cause of action for arrears of rent only. But where the status of 'tenant' is taken off a tenant, he ceases to be under a duty to pay rent. However, if he remains in possession after so ceasing to be a tenant, he is regarded technically by the law as a trespasser but of a kind arising specially from the particular pre-existing relationship of landlord and tenant and with entirely different consequences from those of a general trespasser.

In a claim for only arrears of rent while a tenant is still in possession of the premises *qua* tenant, the tenant is considered as, and is usually, still in lawful and valid possession as the relationship of landlord and tenant subsists. Here, the landlord does not contest the tenant's right to possession but contends only that the tenant is owes him rent.

A trespasser does not pay rent but damages. Therefore, a tenant whose tenancy has been validly determined but is holding over becomes a trespasser of a special kind arising from a relationship he had with the landlord as a tenant. The damages to which such an ex-tenant trespasser is liable is a special kind of damages known in law as *mesne* profits which is

> only another term for damages for trespass, … which arises from the particular relationship of landlord and tenant.[124]

Damages for Use and Occupation: There is a kind of

124. *Osawaru v Ezeiruka* (1978) 6/7 SC 135.

damages very like *mesne* profits but different. It arises where a person lawfully enters upon and occupies another's land or premises but without an actual agreement with that other person being the true owner of the land or premises.

According to the Supreme Court in *AP v Owodunni*,[125] where a tenant enters upon a premises lawfully but occupies the land or premises of another without an agreement or consent of the true owner, he pays no rent because there is no demise and he has not an estate. He will rather be liable for damages for his use and occupation of the land or premises.

An action for damages for use and occupation arises out of an implied agreement between the parties that the user or occupier will pay for the use and occupation out of what the Supreme Court referred to as a 'quasi-tenancy' and not from a relationship between landlord and tenant. According to the Supreme Court,

> *mesne* profits starts to run from the date of service of the process for determining the tenancy (i.e. the quit notice) while damages for use and occupation starts to run from the date of the holding over.[126]

But the apex court has also explained in *Debs v Cenico Ltd*[127] that where the tenancy is for a fixed term, *mesne* profits may be claimed from the date of its effluxion.

A claim for rent is always liquidated while the claim for *mesne* profits is unliquidated and calculated based

125. *Supra* at 341.
126. *AP v Owodunni* (*Supra*) at 341. It is humbly submitted that this date from which *mesne* profits starts to run is the date the served quit notice takes effect.
127. (1986) 3 NWLR (Pt. 32) 846.

on the real and current rental value of the premises but usually using the previous rent as a guide.

Monthly Tenant and *Mesne* Profits – As can be seen from the above discussion, a tenant pays rent while *mesne* profits is paid only by a trespasser ex-tenant. A tenant is not liable to pay *mesne* profits until his tenancy has been lawfully determined and he is holding over. In other words, a demand for 'rent' can no longer be made on the tenant who now is liable only for *mesne* profits.

The proviso to section 18 of the Law is to the effect that a monthly tenant whose rent falls into arrears for three months ceases to be a tenant from the beginning of the fourth month as the tenancy thereby determines after three months.[128] By this provision, it is incorrect to sue a monthly tenant for arrears of rent in excess of three months since by the fourth month he is no longer liable to pay rent but *mesne* profits.

In like manner, it is now incorrect in Lagos State to sue a monthly tenant for arrears of rent in excess of six months or to sue a quarterly or half-yearly tenant for arrears of rent in excess of one year since by the seventh month, in respect of a monthly tenant, and by the 13th month, in the case of a quarterly and half-yearly tenants, these tenants would have ceased to be tenants by operation of the law and would then only be liable to pay damages in the nature of *mesne* profits.[129]

128. All other Recovery Statutes nationwide have this provision except Lagos State where the provision allows the monthly tenant this protection for six months and the quarterly tenant and half-yearly tenant for one year.
129. See Section 13 (2) and (3) of the Lagos State Tenancy Law.

Generally therefore, where a monthly tenant is owing his monthly rent for more than three months (six months in Lagos State) and the landlord desires to sue for same, he shall sue for arrears of rent only for three months and the remaining 'arrears' must be claimed as *mesne* profits.

But in Lagos State, where the tenant is either a quarterly tenant or a half-yearly tenant and he is owing his rent for more than one year, the landlord is to sue him in respect of the arrears only for twelve months i.e. one year and the remainder must be claimed as *mesne* profits.

Who may Issue the Notice to Quit – As has been shown, the relationship between a landlord and a tenant is a contractual one. By the doctrine of privity of contract, no other person can exercise any powers or rights or incur duties thereunder except by the parties thereto. Accordingly only the landlord may sign and issue the tenant with a quit notice and vice versa.

Notice to Quit by Agent - The parties may however act through agents or attorneys lawfully engaged and invested with specific and sufficient powers to act in relation to the contract. Such donated powers are usually in writing for ease of proving same during proceedings.

The Recovery Statutes all define 'agent' specially and in such a manner that only the landlord may engage an agent in the contractual relationship between a landlord and tenant. The Interpretation Sections of all the Recovery Statutes define 'agent' to mean

> any person usually employed by the landlord in the letting of a premises or in the collection of the rents thereof or specially authorized to act in a particular manner by writing under the hand of the landlord in relation to a premises.

From the definition, it is clear that only a landlord can, under the Recovery Statutes, employ an agent in relation to the contract between him and his tenant. The definition must therefore be considered as special in relation to landlord and tenant law as it is one-sided and different in this respect from the general definition of the concept of agency which includes that an agency is a

> relationship that exists between two persons when one, called the agent, is considered in law to represent the other called the principal, in such a way as to be able to affect the principal's legal position in respect of strangers to the relationship by the making of contracts or the disposition of property.[130]

By this generally accepted definition of agency, either of the 'two persons' in the 'relationship' can be 'principal' or 'agent' unlike the definition in the Recovery Statutes which allows only the landlord to employ an agent who must be

(a) any person usually employed by him
 (i) in the letting of premises, or
 (ii) in the collection of rents thereof, or
(b) a person specially authorized under his hand by writing to act in a particular manner in relation to premises.

Appointment of Agent Need not be Written – Where the person appointed as agent by the landlord is a person the landlord has usually and regularly employed in the letting of premises or the collection of rents in respect of the premises, by the provision, it will not be necessary or mandatory that the appointment should be in writing. This will be due to the fact that arising from the 'usual' dealings

130. Fridman (1971) *The Law of Agency* (Butterworths, London) at p.8.

over time, the agent would have been well known to the tenant in this respect.

In *Olusi v Solana*[131] for instance, the court held that the notice served by the landlord's agent was valid notwithstanding that the agent was not employed by authorization in writing. Delivering the judgement of the court, Hubbard J. declared that

> it is not correct that persons authorized in writing are the only persons ... who can give a notice as in Form E. ...(and that) it is clear on the evidence that (the person) who gave the notice ... was the appellant's agent by virtue of the fact that he is usually employed by the landlord in the collection of their rents of the premises.

However, in *Nianda v Alake*,[132] there was no evidence that the landlord had given his daughter any authorization in writing neither was there any evidence that the daughter was a person usually employed by the landlord in the letting of the premises or the collection of the rents thereof. A notice issued by the daughter was held invalid.

Therefore, it is advisable, that except there is manifest evidence that the person held out as agent of the landlord and who has issued notices as such agent on behalf of a landlord is well known especially by the tenant as one who is usually employed by the landlord as agent, the agent should be engaged in writing.

Notice to Quit by Solicitors - In this regard, it has been held that a solicitor who, in the ordinary course of his profession usually represents his client, especially in possession matters, has an inherent authority in law to

131. (1956) LLR 18.
132. (1972) NNLR 23

represent and act for his client in such matters without being specially so authorized in writing. In *Nianda v Alake*,[133] the court, with great respects, found itself unable to agree with the earlier decision in *Ayiwoh v Akorede*[134] that, under our laws, a solicitor unless specially authorized in writing cannot give or sign a notice to quit since the relevant provision did not specify who should give or sign a statutory notice to quit

> unlike the specific requirements contained in the same section for a notice of intention to apply to the court for possession

and that in the circumstance of the case

> … the statutory notice to quit was not bad even though it was given by the landlady's solicitors who were not proved to have been authorized in writing to do so.

This may well be so but the court may require that such a solicitor establishes to its satisfaction that the landlord has in fact always been his client in the ordinary course of his professional business as a legal practitioner.

Notice to Quit by Estate Agent – A common feature of recovery processes in Nigeria is the Estate Agent. These are persons engaged professionally in the business of letting premises, collecting rents, and recovering possession from tenants, on behalf of landlords. In other words, these are professional persons who, being in the business of letting of premises and collecting rents are

> … employed by … landlord(s) and tenants in the letting of … premises or in the collection of the rents thereof, or specially authorized to act in a particular manner by

133. *Supra.*
134. (1951) 20 NLR 4.

writing under the hand of the landlord or tenant in relation to a premises

and they are a very common sight in Recovery Courts.

Although it cannot be said of most of them that they have undergone any training[135] with respect to their line of business nor are they required under any law to possess any qualifications to be such agents as is applicable in some other lines of business e.g. insurance agents,[136] and in some other jurisdictions,[137] but some of them are quite useful in providing estate-related services to both landlords and tenants.[138]

Estate Agents Subject to Agency Laws - Though not trained and not subject to any statutory supervision or

135. There may be a few who have studied courses like Estate Management at polytechnics and universities but are not part of the kind of 'agents' usually found in our Recovery Courts.
136. See Section 34 of the Insurance Act 2003, for instance, which provides that '*no person shall transact business as insurance agent unless he (a) possesses a certificate of proficiency issued by the Institute, and (b) is licensed in that behalf under this Act*'.
137. Take Singapore, for instance, where they have an Estate Agents Act 2010 requiring that *'subject to (the) Act, no person shall —*
    (a) exercise or carry on or advertise, notify or state that he exercises or carries on, or is willing to exercise or carry on, the business of doing estate agency work as an estate agent;
    (b) act as an estate agent; or
    (c) in any way hold himself out to the public as being ready to undertake, whether or not for payment or other remuneration (whether monetary or otherwise), estate agency work as an estate agent,

    unless he is a licensed estate agent. (Section 28 (1) thereof).
138. They assist tenants in searching for and getting accommodation at a fee. This part of their business is not covered by the definition of 'agent' in the Recovery Statutes as pointed out *supra*.

control, these estate agents, it is humbly submitted, are however subject to the general common law rules of agency which imposes fiduciary duties on agents.

These duties include, whether he is acting for a landlord or a tenant as his principal, the duty

(a) not to make secret profits;
(b) to render true and accurate financial accounts;
(c) obey his principal's instructions strictly;
(d) perform his agency in good faith;
(e) perform his agency with skill and care; and
(f) personally perform his duties.[139]

It must be pointed out that the agent as defined in the Recovery Statutes is different from the estate agent in that while the agent need not be a paid professional in business, the estate agent is and is usually paid by his principal for his services. Notwithstanding this difference, both types of agent are subject to the above common law duties.

Appointment of Agent – Unlike the solicitor, the appointment of an estate agent by a landlord must comply with the provisions of the Recovery Statutes relating to authorization by writing under the hand of the landlord as discussed above except the estate agent falls into the first two kinds whereby he is a person usually employed by the landlord either to let the premises or to collect rents thereof.

Notice to Quit by Agent of an Agent - A quit notice signed by an agent of the landlord's agent is invalid as the general rule is *delegatus non portes delegare* which is that a person to whom authority or power has been delegated

139. For further readings on the duties and rights of an agent, see Miakpo Emiaso (2011) *Co-operative Societies Law and Practice in Nigeria* (Peakmans Ltd., Lagos) at 185 *et seq*.

cannot himself further delegate the same authority or power to another. It is what is meant by the duty of an agent to perform his functions under his agency personally.

However, where the particular function of the agent is one which requires special skill which the agent does not possess, he may delegate that part of his function to another. For instance, an estate agent, not being trained in law and without the requisite legal knowledge to handle the technicalities of court litigation, may delegate such functions to a lawyer and will not be in breach of his duty not to delegate.

This will accord with what has been described as the implied authority of an agent to delegate those of his functions which are by trade and usage delegable. Statutory notices are legal documents required by the law to come with certain specific features and which a non-lawyer may not be conversant with. Therefore, where a non-lawyer agent appoints a lawyer to issue and serve statutory notices, such delegation of functions will not be in breach of his agency duties not to delegate.

In *Allam & Co. Ltd v Europa Poster Services Ltd.*,[140] the agent appointed by a landlord instructed a solicitor to issue and serve statutory notices. The court held that the agent's instruction did not amount to an 'unauthorised delegation of the agent's authority'.

The court was of the view that the position of the solicitor was like that of someone employed by another to write from that other's dictation; and that it would be different if the agent appointed by the landlord was the

140. (1968) 1 WLR 638.

solicitor, in which case, it will be taken that the solicitor's special skill with regards to the particular duties was what the landlord relied on in appointing him as his agent to serve the statutory notices.

Set against the decision of the Nigerian court in *Onyia v Jalingo*[141] which is binding, this English decision must, with the greatest respects, be seen as being more persuasively appropriate than binding and is to preferred. In the Nigerian case, an agent appointed by a landlord as 'caretaker' by power of attorney to recover premises. The caretaker then appointed a solicitor in writing to issue the statutory notices.

Declaring the notices invalid, the High Court of the then East Central State per Araka J. relying heavily on the common law agency maxim of *delegatus non potest delegare* and on the 1876 English decision of *Tarry v Ashton*[142] declared that

> a solicitor, unless specially authorized by the landlord in writing, is not competent to give the relevant notices under the Recovery of Premises Law.

Araka J. then explained further that the caretaker in this case was not competent to give the solicitor authority to serve the statutory notices and that it is only the landlord who can give such authority to the solicitor unless the power to so authorize a solicitor had been incorporated in the power of attorney creating the agency relationship.

Although this circumloquitous approach of the East Central State High Court has been described[143] as an

141. (1974) 4 ECSLR 118.
142. (1876) 1 QBD 314.
143. See Emeka Chianu op.cit. at 328.

absolutely unnecessary burden on the landlord and his agent, it has been recommended in consequence that powers of attorney and letters of authority in this regard should be expressed so as to empower the agent or attorney to employ the services of skilled experts such as legal practitioners to facilitate the effective discharge of the agent's or attorney's powers and functions.

Where however a notice to quit is unauthorized, it cannot be subsequently ratified after it has been served. In *Nianda v Alake,*[144] there was no evidence that the landlord had given his daughter any authorization in writing neither was there any evidence that the daughter was a person usually employed by the landlord in the letting of the premises or the collection of the rents thereof. A notice issued by the daughter was held invalid.

Effect of Notice to Quit on Sub-Tenant - A notice to quit served on the main tenant by the landlord is sufficient to terminate a subtenant's tenancy. This is because, as the court explained in *Ewuoso v Afolabi,*[145] the only legal relationship is between the landlord and the tenant and that

> there can be no question of the landlord serving a notice to quit on the subtenant as there is no legal relationship between them. The subtenant derives his title from the tenant and once the interest of the tenant is determined that of the subtenant disappears *ipso facto.*

This is clearly the common law position where contract is the basis of the relationship between a landlord and his tenant; and it is also clearly different from the provisions of Section 13 of the Law which is to the effect that

144. (1972) NNLR 23.
145. *Ewuoso v Afolabi* (*Supra*).

> where a landlord at any time lets any premises and his tenant, not being expressly prohibited in writing from subletting, sublets such premises or any part thereof, the subtenant of such premises or any part thereof shall be deemed for the purpose of (the Law) to be tenant of the landlord.[146]

Accordingly, a subtenant, where he is deemed a tenant of the landlord (as under the Recovery Statutes), is entitled to a notice to quit from the landlord. But where he is not a tenant to the landlord but is only a tenant at sufferance to the landlord, then he shall not be entitled to a notice to quit from the landlord.

A person can only be a subtenant if his occupation of the premises is lawful. This means that the subtenant's status as such subtenant is known to law only where his possession of the premises is lawful and not in breach of a covenant in the head-tenancy forbidding the head tenant to sublet. In *Sadiku v Saimoua*[147] the tenant was expressly prohibited from subletting the premises without the landlord's consent. This covenant was breached by the tenant who put a third party in possession of the premises. In an action by the landlord to recover possession, the third party argued that he was a statutory tenant and that he was therefore entitled to a notice to quit.

Dismissing the third party's contention, the Lagos High Court per Adedipe J. held that

> it is only where a subtenant (who is) lawfully in

146. The provision is contained in all Recovery Statutes nationwide including section 11 of Cap. R6 (Lagos State) but the provision is missing from the 2011 Tenancy Law No. 14; Section 14 (Cross River State); and section 23 (Plateau State).

147. (1964) LLR 159.

possession holds over after the termination of the term created by the head lease, that he becomes a statutory tenant, notwithstanding that there was never any privity of contract between him and the head lessor.

Notice to Quit must be Exact - In every case, the exact length of the notice to quit must be stated thereon and proved at the trial. A notice to quit stated to take effect upon the occurrence of a contingency is bad in law but mere inaccuracies such as in the spelling of the tenant's name or the description of the premises, if the tenant is not misled thereby, may not be fatal. But the correct address of the premises must be stated.

Notice to Quit Determines Tenancy - A notice to quit, once served on the tenant, terminates the tenancy upon the expiration of the period stated thereon and it cannot be recalled, withdrawn or cancelled. But a new tenancy may be created by the parties thereafter. This may sometimes be created by the conduct of the landlord as in when he accepts rent for a new term from the tenant subsequent to his serving the quit notice.

Notice of Owner's Intention: Section 17 of the Recovery Statutes nationwide requires that so soon as the term of a tenancy or the interest of the tenant shall have ended or shall have been duly determined by a notice to quit in writing or otherwise and the tenant neglects or refuses to quit and deliver up possession of the premises, then the landlord or his agent may cause the tenant or person neglecting or refusing to vacate to be served a written notice of his intention to proceed to court for an order to recover possession of the premises on a date calculated from the date of the service of the notice on him not being less than seven days.

Generally, service of this notice which is also known as the 'Seven Days Notice', is considered a condition precedent to the institution of proceedings in the court for recovery of possession.[148] Failure to serve the seven days notice has been held to render proceedings in court invalid.[149]

Attention must however be drawn to the language of the Recovery Statutes nationwide and as in Section 17 of the Law which is to the effect that the landlord 'may' cause the seven days notice to be served on the tenant. This will, in law and under the strict rules of interpretation of statues, mean that the service of the seven days notice is only permissive and not mandatory.

But learned authors[150] and the courts have always taken the position, from a long time back, that the requirement is mandatory. One of the earliest decisions in this respect is *Lasaki v Dabian*[151] where the High Court of the then Northern Region held per Smith J. that

> the plaintiff has not served on the defendant a notice as in Form E of his intention as landlord to take proceedings to recover possession. This is a statutory requirement which is *an essential prerequisite to the commencement of proceedings in court* and the failure to serve such a notice on the defendant precludes the court

148. *AP v Owodunni (Supra).*
149. *Lasaki v Dabian* (1957) NRNLR 13; *Otegbade v Adekoya* (1962) 2 NLR (Pt. 1) 52, 57.
150. See, for instance, Tom Anyafulude (2010) *Principles of Recovery of Premises* (Snaap Press Ltd, Enugu) at 150 and 155.
151. *Supra*. See also *Eleja v Bagudu* (1994) 3 NWLR (Pt. 334) 536 a more recent decision which decided that *'service of the notice of intention to recover premises ... is a condition precedent to the exercise of jurisdiction'*.

> from making an order for possession even when a valid notice to quit has been served.

This position has been repeatedly replicated by all courts including the Supreme Court of Nigeria notwithstanding that the language of the Recovery Statutes has always been and still is that

> …when and as soon as the term or interest of the tenant of any premises determines or has been duly determined by a notice to quit …such tenant … neglects or refuses to quit and deliver up possession … the landlord … or his agent ***may*** cause the person so neglecting or refusing to quit … to be served with a written notice … signed by the landlord or his agent of the landlord's intention to proceed to recover possession on a date not less than seven days from the date of service[152] of the notice.

With the greatest respects, there is nothing in this statutory provision which makes the serving of the seven days notice

> an essential prerequisite to the commencement of proceedings in court

since the requirement of the law is only that the landlord or his agent ***may*** cause the notice to be served. Even the more recent Lagos State Tenancy Law No. 14 of 2011 retains the permissive '***may***'[153] in its Section 16 which reproduces the provision verbatim except for the change of the last word thereat from 'service' to 'notice' which in itself is certain to create its own problems.

---

152. Section 16 of the Lagos State Tenancy Law No. 14 of 2011 puts this rather awkwardly as '*on a date not less than seven (7) days from the date of the notice*'.
153. But see Section 13 (5) where the mandatory 'shall' is used that '*where the landlord intends to proceed to court to recover possession, he shall serve a seven (7) days written notice of his intention tto apply to recover possession …*'.

There are, of course, judicial pronouncements of superior courts that, sometimes, the legislator is taken to mean a compulsion when he uses the word 'may' instead of 'shall' and vice versa in certain statutes.[154] But, it has to be submitted with the greatest respects, the courts have all proceeded with respect to the meaning of 'may' in this particular section of the Recovery Statutes as though it is taken that it means a compulsion rather than a permissive provision without a direct pronouncement thereon.

Seven Days Notice Merely Advisory – Service of the seven days notice has nonetheless become an important aspect of the recovery of premises proceedings more as a matter of practice than of law. Its object is not to determine the tenancy but merely to give notice, or 'warning', or advice to the tenant that the landlord intends to institute legal proceedings against the tenant and which legal proceedings shall be instituted any time after the expiration of seven clear days from the date of the service on the tenant of the seven days notice.

The notice then operates as an advice to the tenant to prepare his mind for the suit to follow and work out his strategies for confronting and defending same since its purpose

> is to unequivocally apprise the tenant that the landlord is determined to recover possession from him and the tenant should be prepared to defend the landlord's claim.[155]

This is the same purpose which the service on a defendant

154. See, for instance, *Ifezue v Mbadugha* (1984) ANLR 256.
155. See Emeka Chianu op.cit. at p.318.

of a court process serves.[156] In other words, in recovery actions, the tenant is notified of the impending action in court twice before the actual trial of the action in the court. One is a pre-action notice known as the 'seven days' notice while the other is a notice of the action itself which takes place when the writ of summons is served on him whereupon the court becomes properly seised of the suit. These two notifications are besides the notice to quit.

Features of the Seven Days Notice – As with the notice to quit, there are technical legal requirements which the seven days notice of owner's intention to apply to recover possession must comply with to render same valid and effective as otherwise the suit would be rendered incompetent and the court would be without jurisdiction. These include:

Speaks from Death of Tenancy - It is premature and therefore to no point or issue to serve the seven days notice while the tenancy still subsists. The Recovery Statutes all provide that the seven days may be served only

> when and as soon as the term or interest of the tenant … determines or has been duly determined by a written notice to quit ….

Therefore, the tenancy must have first been effectively determined and brought to an end before the notice of owner's intention is issued and served.

156. See Miakpo Emiaso (2010) *Law, Practice and Procedure: Area Customary Courts in Nigeria* (Peakmans Ltd., Lagos) at p. 223. See also and *United Nigeria Press Ltd. v Adebanjo* (1969) ANLR 422 where the Supreme Court declared that the object of all types of service of court process is to give notice to the other party so that he might be aware of the suit against him and, if he so desires, be able to resist the claim.

Positive Demand for Peaceable Possession – Service of the seven days notice becomes only necessary only when the tenant neglects or refuses to quit and deliver up possession of the premises or any part thereof hence, by reference to the wordings of Form E, the landlord is now required to demand from the tenant that 'unless peaceable possession' of the premises be given to him on or before the expiration of seven clear days from the service of the notice on the tenant, he shall apply to the court for a summons to eject any person from the premises.

Capacity of Giver – The precedent form of the seven days notice as in Form E in the schedule to the Recovery Statutes opens with a statement indicating the capacity in which the giver of the seven days notice does so as to whether he is the owner of the premises or an agent of the owner. In effect, where the giver does not employ the use of the prescribed Form E, he will be required to remember to indicate the capacity in which he gives the notice.

In *Idowu v Adekanmi*,[157] the court held that the failure by the giver of a statutory notice to sign the notice or to indicate the capacity in which he gives the notice renders the notice void.

Describe the Premises – A description of the premises as to whether it is a one room or a three bedroom flat is a requirement of the seven days notice.

Location of Premises – The address of the physical location where the premises is situate is also a requirement of the seven days notice.

Nature of Tenancy – The nature of the tenant's tenancy must be accurately stated as, for instance, where a yearly

157. (1975) 6 CCHCJ 923. See also *Awoniyi v Eletu* (1963) ANLR 539

tenancy was described as a monthly tenancy in the notice of the owner's intention to apply to recover possession, the notice was held to be invalid.[158]

In Lagos State, under the newly promulgated Tenancy Law No. 14 of 2011, the lawmaker has, in the Schedule to the law, provided two forms namely

(i) Form TL4 entitled *Notice to Tenant of Owner's Intention to Apply to Recover Possession* and

(ii) Form TL5 which is entitled *Notice to Tenant of Owner's Intention to Apply to Recover Possession for Effluxion of Time*

in place of Form E in use by all other Recovery Statutes.

Section 16 of the Lagos Tenancy Law which contains the substantive provision for the service of the seven days notice does not, however, contain a reference to Form TL5 but provides only that the

> landlord or his agent may cause the tenant to be served with a written notice as in Form TL4, signed by the landlord or his agent ....

The difference between the two Lagos State new forms is as to the nature of tenancy. Whereas the first form i.e. Form TL4 is for periodic tenancies e.g. a tenancy from year to year or from month to month, the second form i.e. Form TL5 deals with leases of tenancies for fixed terms certain.

Mode by which Tenancy Determined – It is a feature of every notice of owner's intention to apply to recover possession to state whether the tenancy came to an end by

158. *Oyebanji v Registered Trustees of the Nigerian Branch of the Sadrajuman Ahmadiyya Qadian* (1974) 5 CCHCJ 789; See also *Fanimokun v Soetan* (1974) 8 CCHCJ 1225; *Hassan v Okesuji* (1977) 11 CCHCJ 2573.

effluxion of time or by notice to quit or by some other form. This is the purport of the part of Form E which provides in respect of the

> tenancy ... which expired (or was determined by notice to quit from the said ....)(or otherwise as the case may be).

This part of Form E accommodates all modes possible by which a tenancy may come to an end. It provides for situations where the tenancy is terminated by effluxion of time as well when it is determined by notice to quit. More than these two usual modes, the form provides for situations where a tenancy comes to an end by some other mode other than by effluxion of time and the notice to quit.

As already pointed out *supra*, there are now two forms in Lagos State replacing the general Form E. The new Lagos State Form TL4 still retains the general

> tenancy ... which expired or was determined by notice to quit ... *et al*,

while Form TL5 which is meant for tenancies for fixed terms certain now simply provides for a

> tenancy ... which was determined by effluxion of time ....[159]

Date Tenancy Determined – The seven days notice of the owner's intention to apply to court to recover possession must state the exact date the tenancy was determined either by effluxion or by notice to quit.[160] A misstatement of this date may be fatal to the action for possession. This is because the notice of owner's intention is unnecessary and

159. By Section 13 (5) of the Tenancy Law, a notice to quit is no longer necessary to determine a tenancy for a fixed term determined by effluxion of time in Lagos State.
160. *Akeju v Shonibare* (1968) ANLR 555; *Awoniyi v Eletu* (1963) ANLR 539, 541.

goes to no issue without a prior determination of the tenancy. It must be proved during the action. In *Awoniyi v Eletu*,[161] the then Lagos High Court per De Lestang, relying on the English decision of *Bowden v Rollinson*[162] in interpreting Section 7[163] of the Recovery of Premises Act in this respect, held that a notice which wrongly described the time when the tenancy was determined was invalid.

Also, in *Otegbade v Adekoya*,[164] Bellamy J. (also of the then Lagos High Court) held that where the notice of owner's intention inaccurately stated that the tenancy was determined by notice to quit on the 30th of November instead of the 31st of December, the

> inaccuracy renders the notice of intended application ineffectual (and that therefore) it follows that the landlord was not entitled to come to the court for an order for possession (as then) the learned magistrate (court) had no jurisdiction to make the order applied for.

But see the Supreme Court in *Nigerian Joint Agency Ltd. v Arrow Engineering and General Transport Co. Ltd.*[165] and *Sunmonu v Yesufu*[166] where the courts came to conclusions to the effect that where an inaccuracy as to the date when the landlord intends to apply to the court to recover possession as stated in the seven days notice is in excess of the period prescribed by the Recovery Statutes, then the defendant cannot be heard to complain that he has in any way been prejudiced by the plaintiff by so doing.

161. *Supra.*
162. (1948) 1 A.E.R. 841.
163. Same provision as in Section 17 of the Law.
164. (1962) 2 ANLR (Pt.2) 760.
165. (1970) ANLR 324.
166. (1972) NMLR 169.

In the *Nigerian Joint Agency*[167] case, the date for the determination of the tenancy was the 31st of May. This was erroneously stated to be the 1st of June in the notice of owner's intention. This is one day later. Madarikan JSC delivering the judgement of the Supreme Court of Nigeria, referred to and relied on the English Court of Appeal decision in *Sidebotham v Holland*[168] and held that

> on the facts of (this) case, we are satisfied that whilst the plaintiffs should have put the date of determination of the tenancy as the 31st May, 1967, the defendants have not in any way been prejudiced by the act of the plaintiff in putting the date one day later i.e. 1st of June ....

What these latter decisions mean is that the requirement of accurately stating the date of the determination of the tenancy in the notice of owner's intention to apply to court is not strict. It is not necessarily absolute especially where the interest of the person on whom the notice is required to be served is not thereby prejudiced.

In the other cases[169] where the courts have been strict in applying the provision of the statutes, the notices in issue were short of the statutorily prescribed period thereby exposing the interests of the defendants to prejudice. In other words, *Nigerian Joint Agency Ltd. v Arrow Engineering and General Transport Co. Ltd* and *Sunmonu v Yesufu* are authority for the view that where the period of notice given in the notice of owner's intention is in excess of the statutorily prescribed period of seven days and the defendant is thereby not prejudiced, the notice will still be

167. *Supra.*
168. (1895) 1 Q.B. 378.
169. *Akeju v Shonibare* (1968) ANLR 555; *Awoniyi v Eletu* (1963) ANLR 539; *Otegbade v Adekoya* (1962) 2 ANLR 760.

valid notwithstanding that the date stated thereon is or has been inaccurately stated.

Date of Application to Court – Another important date which the seven days notice of owner's intention to apply to recover possession must contain and be stated accurately is the date on which the landlord intends to make his application to court.

In *Awoniyi v Eletu,*[170] the court in interpreting what was then the equivalent provision of the current Section 17 of the Recovery Statute which provides for the service of the seven days notice declared that the section required that

> the notice shall state the landlord's intention to proceed to recover possession '*on a date not less than seven days from the date of service of the notice*'. The notice in the present case didn't comply with this requirement because a wrong date was inserted in it. ... (Section 10) provides that a landlord cannot apply to the court until the time stated in the notice has expired.[171]

In this case, the seven days notice was served on the 17th of May. In it, the giver stated he shall apply to court on the 29th of April of the same year. The court was of the view that this defect could not be considered a mere technicality which the court could disregard in view of the provisions of Section 10[172] of the same Act which provided that a landlord could not apply to court until the time stated in the seven days notice of owner's intention has expired. The relevant part of Form E in this regard expressly states that the giver of the notice

170. *Supra.*

171. *ibid* at 541.

172. The equivalent provision of Section 20 (1) of the Law, Section 24 of Tenancy Law (Lagos State).

> shall on the ... day of … apply to the …court for a summons…

following the expiration of seven clear days calculated from the date of service[173] of the notice on the defendant. Proving[174] the date of service of statutory notices is crucial as the different periods prescribed by the Recovery Statutes for doing different acts or taking different steps are calculated from the date of service and not the date on the dated on the notice.

In *Nnadozie v Oluoma*,[175] the notice to quit was dated 29th March. It required the tenant to quit and deliver up possession on the 30th of April but was served on the tenant on the 1st of April. The court held that the relevant date for the purpose of computing the 30 days notice to quit was not the date on the notice being the date it was prepared, but the date it was served. The notice was therefore held to be insufficient and consequently invalid.

Fact of Tenant Holding Over – In construing Form E, it is required that before inserting the date on which application shall be made to court, the fact of the premises being held over by the tenant shall be indicated. This is in the words

> which premises are now held over and detained from the said ….

173. Although Forms TL4 and TL5 of the new Lagos State Tenancy Law No. 14 of 2011 retains the 'date of service' as the material date, its Section 16 puts it as '*seven days from the date of the notice*'.
174. See *Eke v Ula* (1977) 1 IMSLR 517 where Amadi-Obi J. of the Imo State High Court held that '*evidence of the date of serving the notice must be given at the hearing to enable the court know whether or not (the Law) had been complied with'*.
175. (1963) ENLR 77.

The holding over by the tenant is, of course, the basis for the issuance of the seven days notice and the proceedings which are to follow since, otherwise, these will be unnecessary.

The Court – The court at which the application for possession is to be made must also be stated in the seven days notice of owner's intention. This is usually a court which is seised with jurisdiction for possession matters within the particular local government where the premises sought to be recovered or any part thereof is situated.

Summons to Eject 'Any Person' – The application to court is for a summons to eject 'any person' from the premises sought to be recovered. At the stage of issuing the seven days notice, the tenancy would have been terminated but the tenant refuses or neglects to quit or deliver up possession. Although Section 20 which provides for the issuance of the seven days notice still uses the word 'tenant', the person from whom possession is to be recovered has ceased to be a tenant from the date of effluxion of time or of the coming into effect of the notice to quit.

This then explains why Form E talks of a summons to eject 'any person' and not necessarily the tenant therefrom the premises. This also is why the deputy sheriff of the court, upon arrival at the suit premises to levy execution of the court's judgement for possession, will carry out his authorization in that respect even when he does not meet the tenant but meets other persons in the premises who allow him access thereto. The judgement for possession is one *impersonam*. It attaches to the premises and not the tenant as a person. Recovering it involves the deputy sheriff gaining access thereto and not in literally taking, collecting or receiving it from the tenant.

Date of Notice – The date the notice is actually issued is then inserted at the bottom thereof. This is different from the date of service[176] which is the more material date from which the length or period of the notice is computed for purpose of determining its effective date.

Signature of Giver - As shown in *Idowu v Adekanmi,*[177] a statutory notice not signed by the giver is void. The giver's signature is closely tied to the identity and capacity of the person who issues and gives the notice. Therefore the seven days notice of owner's intention to apply to court for recovery of possession of premises must be signed by the person who issues the notice.

Licensee Entitled to Seven Days Notice – Where a person in Lagos State occupies premises as a licensee but upon the expiration or valid withdrawal of his licence he refuses or neglects to quit and deliver up possession, Section 14 of the Tenancy Law provides that he shall be entitled to service of a seven days notice of the owner's intention to apply to recover possession of the premises.

A licensee is a person with permission to enter or occupy another person's land or premises for an agreed purpose but without conferring a right to exclusive possession, or any legal right or estate. A licence confers a personal right on the licensee to occupy the premises which can be withdrawn or revoked by the licensor at any time where it is a bare licence i.e. a gratuitous permission.

176. But see Section 16 of the Lagos State Tenancy Law which puts the effective date as '*seven days from the date of the notice*'.
177. *Supra.*

A contractual licence may however not be withdrawable or revocable except in the manner specified in the contract between the parties. Also, a licence coupled with an interest is irrevocable or withdrawable.

The reference in the above provision to an expiration of licence is a reference to either a licence under contract or one coupled with an interest where the interest is for a fixed term. The provision in this respect is clear as the same rules applicable to the termination of tenancies for fixed terms apply. But the provision is silent as to the mode of terminating or withdrawing a bare license or the length of notice required therefor.

However it is the law generally that a licensee in occupation of land is without any legal interest or estate in the land and that he is therefore entitled only to reasonable notice for the license to be determined and the personal right to which the licensee is entitled is withdrawn.[178]

Abandoned Premises in Lagos State – Also, by Section 15 (2) (a) of the Lagos Tenancy Law, another situation which calls for the service of a seven days notice of owner's intention to apply for recovery of possession is where the premises is abandoned. Premises will be deemed abandoned the Tenancy Law where

(a) the tenancy of the tenant has expired,

(b) the tenant is not in occupation of the premises

(c) despite his non-occupation of the premises, the tenant has not given up lawful possession of the premises.

Usually, where the above situation arises, the rent in

178. See *Akpiri v West African Airways Corporation* 14 WACA 195; *Sobamowo v Federal Public Trustee* (1970) 1 ANLR 257.

respect of the premises will also remain unpaid and the tenant's whereabouts will be unknown. Before the enactment of this provision, landlords faced with this kind of situation were usually at a loss as to what to do to recover possession since they cannot find the tenant to demand rent from or to serve statutory on.

The provision has ostensibly come to rescue this situation by providing for a mode for the recovery of such premises which is abandoned. However the provision of the last limb of paragraph (a) of the subsection 2 is open to abuse in that the seven days notice is merely required to be pasted on the abandoned premises unilaterally without leave of court. This has the capacity of rendering almost every premises in Lagos abandoned.

It is humbly recommended that it will be more in the interest of justice that the court's prior leave be sought and obtained by the landlord before such pasting. The application for such leave should be supported by affidavit detailing strong and convincing grounds for the grant of such leave.[179]

179. See the discussion on 'Force Open' *infra* at page 357.

Chapter Three
The Action for Recovery of Possession

It is not the law ... that a landlord has unbridled right to invade premises in lawful occupation of a tenant ... when the intention of the landlord is to recover possession.
– Obaseki JSC in *Eliochin Nig. Ltd.v Mbadiwe* (1986) 11 NWLR (Pt.14) 47, 49

Possession Matters – A recovery action is a suit commenced in an appropriate court for the purpose of recovering possession of premises and other purposes connected therewith subsequent to the termination of a landlord and tenant relationship. Such connected purposes include matters relating to such issues as rent and ancillary rights of the parties to landlord and tenant relationships.

Recovery actions are also generally referred to as possession matters which is a reference to all such causes and matters in relation to the jurisdiction and powers specifically conferred on those specialized courts referred sometimes referred to as Rent Tribunals in most states of the federation. Recovery of possession matters relate to proceedings in court in connection with

(a) the recovery of possession of premises,
(b) rent or arrears of rent,
(c) *mesne* profits, and
(d) the enforcement of ancillary rights and duties arising from the contractual relationship between a landlord and tenant

but do not include claims which raise issues as to title to land or any interest in land.

In *Erhumwunse v Ehanire*,[1] the plaintiff claimed

1. (2003) FWLR (Pt. 170) 1511; *Odutola v Samuel* (1956) 1 FSC 76.

before the Area Customary Court in Benin City possession of the suit premises from the defendant who, at all material times, was in possession thereof. The plaintiff claimed defendant had sold the premises to him. This the defendant denied. The Supreme Court per Uwais CJN (as he then was) held that

> the dispute between the parties involves land.... Although the claim ... was *inter alia* to recover possession of the house which (the plaintiff) claimed to have purchased from the (defendant), the ... defence is a denial of the sale of the property .... This puts title to the house in issue

and therefore the Customary Court lacked jurisdiction to entertain the suit.

Generally, the scope of recovery actions is traditionally restricted to the first three types of proceedings (a), (b) and (c) listed above.[2] This restriction is inferred from construing the provisions of the Recovery Statutes which do not provide for any other kind of claims. For instance, a consideration of the Form F which is the writ or plaint for commencing the recovery action shows that only the claims for possession, arrears of rent, and *mesne* profits are provided for therein.

The court in *Oku v Awanah* was of this view when it held that the Recovery Statutes under their special procedure for the recovery of possession of premises also provide only for

> claims for arrears of rent and *mesne* profits but (they do) not contemplate the joinder of any claim for damages which are outside the scheme[3]

2. *Oku v Awanah* (1961) ANLR 116.
3. *ibid* at 118.

of the Recovery Statutes. The High Court in the latter case of *Adejumo v David Hughes & Co. Ltd.*[4] relying on this decision, held that in an action for recovery of possession the plaintiff is not allowed to join other claims in the writ.

But on appeal, the Court of Appeal, disagreed with and upturned this decision on the strength of the provisions of Order 16 Rule 2 of the Lagos State High Court (Civil Procedure) Rules which is to the effect that

> no cause of action save an action for declaration of title shall, unless by leave of the court or a judge in chambers, be joined with an action for the recovery of land except claims in respect of *mesne* profits and arrears of rent in respect of the premises claimed ....[5]

By this Rule of the Lagos State High Court, it is clear that certain other claims can be joined in an action for recovery of possession. Such other claims include one for

(a) declaration of title which can be joined without leave of the court, or

(b) *mesne* profits, or

(c) arrears of rent, or

(d) damages for breach of contract under which the premises are held, or

(e) any wrong or injury to the premises claimed, or

(f) payment of principal money or interest secured by or for any other relief in respect of a mortgage or charge of the land.[6]

---

4. (1989) 5 NWLR (Pt. 120) 146.
5. See also Order 14 Rule 4 of the High Court of Delta State (Civil Procedure) Rules 2009.
6. Order 16 Rule 2 of the 1994 High Court (Civil Procedure) Rules, Lagos State.

The learned appellate jurist Akpata JCA in overruling the *Oku v Awanah*[7] decision in the *Adejumo v David Hughes & Co. Ltd*[8] case declared that it seemed to him that

> the learned trial judge was not quite right that other claims cannot be joined in an action for recovery of possession.

His lordship then went on to hold that the only claims which appeared improper to him in the action were the claims for the

> (1) order that the defendant sign the draft tenancy agreement and
>
> (2) order that the defendant pay all electricity and telephone bills and other rates and taxes due.

The grounds upon which the above two claims would be improper are obvious. Courts do not make contracts for parties.[9] The court made this clear in the *AP v Owodunni*[10] case when it declared that

> it is fundamental that the courts will neither make a contract for the parties nor inquire into the adequacy of a consideration.

Therefore to have granted the order in claim (1) for an order of the court compelling the defendant to sign the draft tenancy agreement would have amounted to the court interfering with the rights of the parties to freely contract.

Claim for Electricity Bills - With regards to the claim on electricity and other bills, it has been stated[11] that thc

7. *Supra.*
8. *Supra.*
9. See *AP v Owodunni* (*supra*) at 335.
10. *Supra.*
11. See G.N. Dele Okafor (2011) *Landlord and Tenant Law and Practice* (*supra*) at 66.

reason why plaintiffs cannot claim these is because they represent revenue to the government or agencies of government and therefore, since the monies do not belong to the landlords as plaintiffs, they cannot claim same by action.

However, where a landlord has settled these bills to the appropriate government agency prior to filing his writ and he can prove this by tendering valid receipts thereof, then, it is humbly submitted, he would be entitled to the amount actually paid by him by way of reimbursement from the tenant who accumulated the bills which the landlord can claim by action.

Such a claim will be ancillary to a claim for recovery of possession and can be joined in an action for recovery of possession. The provision in Order 16 Rule 2 of the Lagos High Court Civil Procedure Rules forbidding joinder of other claims to a recovery of possession claim is not absolute as it provides that to join other claims to a possession claim only requires that the plaintiff obtains leave of the court.

Courts with Recovery Jurisdiction - The jurisdiction for recovery of possession is exercised by magistrate courts in most states. These are then sometimes redesignated as Rent Tribunals. In Delta, Edo and Osun states, the jurisdiction is vested in the Customary Courts.[12]

In *Erhumwunse v Ehanire*,[13] the plaintiff claimed possession of the suit premises from the defendant who, at

12. See Section 7 of the 1977 Bendel State Rent Control and Recovery of Residential Premises Law No. 4 as applicable to Delta and Edo states.
13. *Supra*.

all material times, was in possession thereof. He filed the action in the Area Customary Court Benin City claiming the defendant had sold the premises to him. This the defendant denied. The Supreme Court per Uwais CJN (as he then was) held that

> the dispute between the parties involves land.... Although the claim ... was *inter alia* to recover possession of the house which (the plaintiff) claimed to have purchased from the (defendant), the ... defence is a denial of the sale of the property .... This puts title to the house in issue

and that since the house was situate in an urban area and by virtue of the provisions of Section 39 (1) of the Land Use Act, the Area Customary Court lacked jurisdiction to hear the case.

It follows that if the suit premises had been in a non urban area, the said customary court in Edo State would have had jurisdiction therefor by virtue of that court's establishing statute which expressly confers jurisdiction over land in rural areas on it.[14] The Area Customary Courts in Delta and Edo states and the District Customary Courts in Osun State are the only customary courts with jurisdiction for recovery actions in Nigeria. These are unique kinds of customary courts with very wide civil jurisdiction.[15]

Nigeria is a federation[16] with a federal constitution[17]

14. See Section 20 (1) and the First Schedule pursuant thereto (Item 1). See also Miakpo Emiaso (2010) *Law, Practice and Procedure: Area Customary Courts in Nigeria* (Peakmans Ltd., Lagos) at 66.
15. Miakpo Emiaso (*supra*) at 1.
16. Section 2 (2) Constitution of the Federal Republic of Nigeria 1999.
17. Constitution of the Federal Republic of Nigeria 1999.

having two express legislative lists – an Exclusive Legislative List and a Concurrent Legislative List. The Exclusive List contains legislative items which only the Federal Government 'shall have powers to make laws …'[18] while the Concurrent List contains those legislative items which

> both the federal and state governments shall have powers to make laws … to the extent prescribed in the second column opposite thereto

in Part II of the Second Schedule to the constitution[19] while by Section 4 (7) (a) thereof, a Residual Legislative List is created which by necessary implication confers legislative powers on the states in that, in addition to powers to legislate on items on the Concurrent List,

> the Houses of Assembly of (states) shall have powers to make laws for … any matter not included in the Exclusive Legislative List set out in Part I of the Second Schedule to (the) constitution.

In effect, whatever matter is not contained in either of the two express legislative lists shall fall into residue and shall be a matter exclusively for the states to legislate upon.

Neither of the express Exclusive and Concurrent Legislative lists contains a reference to possession matters or landlords and tenants. This makes landlords and tenants a matter clearly 'not included in the Exclusive Legislative List' and therefore a matter over which states Houses of Assembly 'shall have powers' to exclusively 'make laws' on.

By the constitutional arrangement, the Federal

---

18. See Section 4 (7) (b) *ibid.*
19. Section 4 (2) *ibid.*

Capital Territory is regarded as a state with legislative powers therefor vested in the National Assembly.[20]

In consequence, every state in Nigeria has enacted for itself a Rent Control and Recovery of Residential Premises Law and a Recovery of Premises Law. These Recovery Statutes contain provisions stipulating which courts shall exercise the jurisdiction in respect of which the statute is enacted. For instance, Section 6 of the Lagos State's erstwhile Cap. R6 stipulated that

> there shall be established in each local government area (a) tribunal for the purposes of (the Law) to be called Rent Tribunal

which tribunal shall have jurisdiction to determine in respect of any residential accommodation the standard rent payable[21] and to which tribunal a landlord may apply

> for the issue of a writ or enter a plaint ... against (a) tenant ... neglecting or refusing (to quit and deliver up possession) ... for the recovery of same.[22]

The Recovery Statutes of most other states contain similar provisions. Sections 4 and 20 of the Bendel State (now Delta and Edo states) Recovery Statute, for instance, contain the same provisions verbatim.

States in the North - Section 7 (1) of the Plateau State Rent Control and Recovery of Residential Premises Law

20. See Section 299 of the 1999 Constitution.
21. Section 7 (1) Rent Control and Recovery of Residential Premises Law (Cap. R6) Laws of Lagos State 2003. The current law is the Tenancy Law No. 14 of 2011 the provisions of which respecting jurisdiction is different vesting same on Magistrate's Courts and the High Courts.
22. Section 16 (1) *ibid.*

(Law No. 1 of 1998) provides, for instance, that as from the commencement of the Law

> District Courts shall hear and determine all cases and matters arising from the provisions of the Law.

Similar provisions are made for most of the states in the North of the country. The District Courts (not District *Customary* Courts) are courts found in the north of Nigeria and are similar in their character and jurisdiction to magistrate courts of the south of Nigeria. They exercise the jurisdiction for possession matters in all the states where they exist except in states where, by special enactments such as the Rent Control and Recovery of Premises laws, rent tribunals have been established.

Abuja – The Federal Capital Territory, Abuja is constitutionally regarded as a state. Section 299 of the 1999 Constitution provides that the Constitution 'shall apply' to the territory

> as if it were one of the states of the Federation; and accordingly, all the legislative powers … vested in the House of Assembly … shall … vest in the National Assembly.[23]

Currently, no Rent Control and Recovery of Premises statute has been enacted by the National Assembly[24] for the territory for the control of rent and the recovery of residential premises besides the Recovery of Premises Act (Cap. 544) of 1990. Therefore all courts in the territory, safe the customary courts, are seised of the jurisdiction for recovery of residential premises.

---

23. Section 299 (a) Constitution of the Federal Republic of Nigeria 1999.
24. See *FCDA v Nwanna* (1998) 4 NWLR (Pt. 544) 73, 86.

Section 3 of the said Recovery of Premises Act (Cap. 544) 1990 of Abuja provides that

> proceedings under (the) Act may be brought in any court of competent jurisdiction

while Section 2 thereof defines 'court' as including

> the High Court and Magistrates' courts but does not include a customary court.

Lagos State – The Lagos State House of Assembly in 2011 enacted a Tenancy Law the preamble to which proclaims that is a

> law to regulate rights and obligations under tenancy agreements and the relationship between the landlord and the tenant including the procedure for the recovery of premises and for connected purposes.

Section 48 of this new Lagos Recovery Statute repeals the Rent Tribunals (Abolition and Transfer of Functions) Law 2007 but is silent as to the Rent Control and Recovery of Residential Premises Law (Cap. R6) but provides further that proceedings under the law shall be brought

> at the High Court where the rental value of the premises exceeds the jurisdiction of the Magistrates' Court as provided by the Magistrates' Courts Law.

In effect, jurisdiction for possession matters in Lagos State is no longer vested in Rent Tribunals but in Magistrates' Courts and the state High Court where the rental value of the premises sought to be recovered exceeds the monetary jurisdiction of a Magistrates' Court.

Delta and Edo States - In Delta and Edo states, the jurisdiction which used to be exercised by the erstwhile Rent Tribunals[25] is now exclusively conferred on the Area

25. Established vide Section 4 of the Rent Control and Recovery of Residential Premises Law (Law No. 4) Laws of Bendel State 1977.

Customary Courts in these states by virtue of Section 20A of the Customary Courts Law 1984[26] (Laws of Bendel State as applicable to Delta and Edo states) in the following words

> the jurisdiction and powers formerly conferred on the Rent Tribunals … are hereby transferred to and shall be exercised by the Area Customary Courts….

Although these courts are known as customary courts they wield very wide civil and criminal jurisdictions and are invested with the exclusive jurisdiction for recovery of residential premises under the Rent Control and Recovery of Residential Premises Law[27] (Law No. 4) Laws of Bendel State 1977 as applicable to Delta and Edo states.

States in the East - Under the Recovery of Premises Law (Cap. 113) Laws of Eastern Nigeria, a customary court, unlike the position in Delta, Edo and Osun states, does not have jurisdiction for recovery actions as Section 3 of this Law expressly defines 'court' to exclude a customary court.[28]

Osun State - A court similar to the Area Customary Courts with exclusive jurisdiction for recovery of residential premises actions is the District Customary Court in Osun State established pursuant to Section 3 of that state's 2006 District and Customary Courts Law. This court is seised of jurisdiction for possession matters subject to a rental value limit of N250,000.00 while its subordinate Customary Court also has the jurisdiction subject to a rental value limit

26. Reenacted verbatim for Delta State in 1997.
27. Published as Cap. 180 in the Annotated Laws of Delta State 2007.
28. See Tom Anyafulude (2010) *Principles of Recovery of Premises in Nigeria Through the Cases* (Snaap Press Ltd., Enugu) at 635.

of N50,000.00.

In the exercise of this jurisdiction, these Customary Courts in Delta, Edo and Osun states observe the provisions of the Rent Control and Recovery of Residential Premises Law[29] section 7 (3)[30] of which expressly provides that the court shall be bound by the practice and procedure in civil matters in the magistrate's courts.

This means that whenever the Area Customary Courts in Delta and Edo states or the Customary Courts in Osun State are exercising their jurisdiction over possession matters, they do so as hybrid courts in that they assume the position of a regular magistrate court while still retaining their character and composition as customary courts.

Scope of Jurisdiction and High Courts

The scope of the jurisdiction for recovery of possession suits conferred on the above courts does not exclude the original jurisdiction of the various states High Courts in appropriate cases to hear and determine cases relating to landlords and tenants.

In Lagos and Osun states,[31] the jurisdiction for possession matters conferred on the Magistrates' Courts and the Customary Courts respectively is restricted monetarily. This is that if the annual rental value of the premises sought to be recovered is in excess of the Magistrates' Court's or the Customary Court's jurisdiction in terms of monetary limit, the suit becomes *ultra vires* the

29. Section 20A (2) of the Delta and Edo states Law.
30. Although this section and Section 4 of the Law has been deleted by Edict No. 6 of 1985, their effect on the Area Customary Courts remain valid.
31. As in most other states.

jurisdiction of the court and must then be instituted in the High Courts of the respective state.[32]

This monetary restriction is however not applicable to the Area Customary Courts in Delta and Edo States since nothing in the Recovery Statute for these two states suggests any monetary limitation in jurisdiction for recovery actions.

There is however the provision of Item 6 to the First Schedule of the Customary Courts Law in these two states which is to the effect that the Area Customary Court's jurisdiction for causes or matters under any law not being under customary law shall not exceed N500,000.00 in Delta State and N600,000.00 in Edo State. Does this provision affect the jurisdiction for recovery actions since these actions are 'causes or matters other than customary law' causes?

If this question is answered in the affirmative, then the recovery of possession jurisdiction of the Area Customary Courts is restricted to a maximum rental value of N500,000.00 and N600,000.00 for Delta and Edo states respectively.

But when these courts sit over recovery of premises actions, they do not sit as Customary Courts and they are regulated not by the Customary Courts Law but by the Rent Control and Recovery of Premises Law which does not contain a limitation provision in relation to the monetary value of the jurisdiction for recovery actions.

32. Section 2 (4) Lagos Tenancy Law 2011; Item 7 Second Schedule pursuant to section 13 (Osun) and Item 7 Third Schedule (Osun) Customary Court put at N50,000.00 in causes or matters relating to landlord and tenant.

The High Courts are reputed to possess 'unlimited' jurisdiction under the Nigerian constitution. Section 236 (1) of the 1979 constitution was express in this respect.

Although the 1999 constitution advisedly does not expressly provide for an 'unlimited' jurisdiction for High Courts (since there can really be no such thing as a court with unlimited jurisdiction), it has however provided for a jurisdiction enabling High Courts

> to hear and determine *any* civil proceedings in which the existence or extent of a legal right, power, duty, liability, privilege, interest, obligation or claim is in issue....

The provision is nonetheless wide enough to include possession matters in appropriate cases[33] and more especially as it is the position of the law that the powers and jurisdiction of a High Court cannot be removed except by express provisions of a statute.[34]

A recovery action must be instituted in the appropriate court as otherwise the action would be invalid. Where the Rent Control and Recovery of Residential Premises Law expressly provided that the Law 'shall apply to all residential accommodation throughout'[35] the state and that

> the governor may from time to time by order exempt the application of the Law to any particular accommodation or area,[36]

the Supreme Court held that the action which was

33. See *Casagrande v Omololu* (1983) 1 FNR 414.
34. See *Abu v Odugbo* (2001) FWLR (Pt. 69) 1260, 1316.
35. Section 1 of the 1976 Lagos State Rent Control and Recovery of Residential Premises Law.
36. Section 3 *ibid.* See also Section 3 Plateau State Rent Control and Recovery of Premises Law No. 1 of 1988.

commenced in the Lagos High Court

> was instituted in the wrong forum, in the High Court instead of the Rent Tribunal established under Section 2 of the Rent Control and Recovery of Residential Premises Law 1976

and held further that the High Court ceased to have jurisdiction for recovery actions on the establishment of the Rent Tribunals relying on Section 34 (1) of the aforesaid 1976 Law[37] which provided that

> in so far as jurisdiction is conferred on the tribunals in respect of the causes or matters mentioned in the foregoing provisions of this Law, the High Court, Magistrate Courts, or any other court of the state, shall, to the extent that jurisdiction is so conferred on the tribunals, cease to have jurisdiction in relation to such causes or matters.

By this provision of the 1976 Lagos State Recovery Statute, the jurisdiction of the High Court was expressly ousted by the statute and thereby rendering the *Pan Asian* case an inappropriate action to be filed at the High Court despite the constitutional provision in Section 272 thereof.

Types of Premises – The Recovery Statutes of the various states, except Lagos State, relate only to residential premises and usually do not extend to cover jurisdiction for non-residential premises. Accordingly all "landlord and tenant" matters where they relate to residential premises are the exclusive preserve of all those courts and tribunals including the Customary Courts in Delta, Edo and Osun states specifically conferred with the jurisdiction.

---

37. *Pan Asian African Co. Ltd. v Nicon Nig. Ltd.* (1982) ANLR 229, 254 per Obaseki JSC. See the Supreme Court also in *Sule v Nigerian Cotton Board* (1985) ANLR 291.

Commercial Premises - The jurisdiction under the Rent Control and Recovery of Residential Premises provisions do not usually cover premises which are non-residential such as stores, shops and other premises used for commercial purposes. In most states, these fall within the jurisdiction of the regular magistrate courts and the High Courts and are governed, not by the Rent Control and Recovery of Residential Premises laws, but by the Recovery of Premises laws of the respective states and of the Federal Capital Territory of Abuja.

There is no clear legal reason for the split in jurisdiction as between residential and non-residential premises and the Lagos State House of Assembly, ostensibly in reaction to this want of reason, has provided that the Lagos State Tenancy Law No. 14 of 2011

> shall apply to all premises within Lagos State including business and residential premises unless otherwise specified.[38]

This provision has commendably and effectively removed the distinction between residential premises and business or commercial premises in terms of which court has jurisdiction for what type of premises in Lagos State.

In Delta and Edo states, the jurisdiction for commercial premises is concurrent and co-ordinate between regular Magistrate Courts and the Area Customary Courts.

As pointed out *supra*, the 1963 Eastern Nigeria Recovery of Premises Law defines 'court' in its Section 2 to exclude customary courts. Also, under the Plateau State Recovery of Premises Law (Cap. 115) and Cap. 544 of the

38. Section 1 (1).

Federal Capital Territory's Recovery of Premises Act, 'court' is defined in Section 2 thereof respectively as including

> the High Court and District Courts but does not include a native court.

The equivalent Section 2 of the 1976 Recovery of Premises Law (Cap. 142) Laws of Bendel State as applicable to Delta and Edo states does not define 'court' to exclude customary courts as is the case in the Eastern, Northern and Federal Capital Territory statutes but declares simply that 'court' includes the High Court and Magistrate Courts.

By this definition of 'court' in these statutes, it is beyond dispute that the Delta and Edo states statute confers recovery of commercial premises jurisdiction on all courts including the High Court and magistrate courts. Therefore, the argument in some quarters especially in these two states that the Area Customary Court does not have jurisdiction for commercial premises cannot be a correct statement of the law on the point.

Besides, the Area Customary Courts in Delta and Edo states can also exercise the jurisdiction for commercial premises via the provisions of Item Six of the First Schedule to the Customary Courts Law (Law No. 2) 1984 of Bendel State pursuant to Section 20 thereof which is applicable to both states.[39] This Item, provides that the Area Customary Court can hear and determine

> causes or matters under *any* law (other than customary law) including bye-laws, where the amount of debt, demand, or damages does not exceed N500,000.00

39. This Law has been reenacted for Delta State as Customary Courts Law 1997 and published as Cap. 47 in the Annotated Laws of Delta State 2007.

in Delta State and N600,000.00 in Edo State. This means that although this court is referred to as a customary court, its jurisdiction is not limited to customary law suits alone but extends to 'causes or matters under any law' not being customary law. Such non-customary law causes or matters necessarily include recovery actions in respect of commercial premises provided that their annual rental value does not exceed N500,000.00 if the action is taken out in Delta State and N600,000.00 if taken out in Edo State.

Conditions Precedent to Instituting Recovery Actions – The filing of the writ or plaint as provided by the various Recovery Statutes will be incompetent if the conditions precedent to its filing are not met. An incompetent suit is incurably bad in law and is liable to be struck out.[40] By its incompetence, the court itself is divested of jurisdiction.[41] The conditions precedent and which must be met before a competent recovery action can be instituted are:

Termination of Landlord and Tenant Relationship – A recovery action only becomes necessary after the contractual relationship between the landlord and the tenant has formally been effectively terminated. There are three modes by which such termination can be validly brought about. These are:[42]

Effluxion of Time – The first is where the fixed time fixed by the parties for the coming to an end of the relationship becomes due. This is usually with respect to leases or tenancies for a fixed period in which case the tenancy

40. *Pan Asian African Co. Ltd. v Nicon Nig. Ltd.* (*supra*).
41. *Madukolu v Nkemdilim* (1962) ANLR 581.
42. See Chapter Two for a more detailed discussion.

determines naturally and as agreed by the parties from the commencement of the relation. None of the parties is ordinarily required to be reminded of this determination date as the date is known by them *ab initio.*

Notice to Quit – The second and the more common mode for bringing the contractual relationship between a landlord and a tenant to an end is the quit notice. This is the requirement of the section of the Recovery Statutes to the effect that where the parties by their contract have not expressly stipulated the notice to be given by either party to determine the tenancy the periods stipulated in the section shall operate to determine the respective types of tenancies. Such a notice to quit has and performs the fundamental function of effectively terminating the contractual relationship between a landlord and his tenant provided that the notice itself is valid.

Operation of Law – The section of the Recovery Statutes providing for the periods for determining contractual tenancies where parties have not made stipulations thereto as discussed above contain a proviso which operates to terminate a monthly tenancy without the need of a quit notice. This happens where the tenant is in arrears of his rent for three consecutive months and it is then said that the tenancy terminated by the operation of the provisions of the Law.

Another instance where a contractual tenancy determines without a quit notice but by operation of law is the unique situation created by the Supreme Court in the *Odutola v Papersack*[43] case whereby a yearly tenancy

43. (2007) Vol. 148 LRCN 1342.

determines

> the moment a year's rent (becomes) due and payable … but (remains) unpaid, the yearly tenancy comes to an end by effluxion of time.[44]

Holding Over – A recovery action only becomes necessary where, despite the valid termination of the contractual tenancy relationship, the tenant neglects or refuses to quit and deliver up possession. Such a tenant is said to be holding over as a result of which the law sees him as a trespasser of sort and refers him as, not any longer a contractual tenant, but a tenant at sufferance if he so holds over at the displeasure of the landlord.

However, where he so holds over with the consent of the landlord, he is referred to as a tenant at will whose possessory interest is protected by the Recovery Statutes so that he is also known as a statutory tenant.[45]

Expiration of Seven Days Notice – No competent recovery action can be commenced unless the notice of owner's intention to recover possession has not only been served but the time stated in the notice has done its full course of seven days.

The issue and service of this notice which is also known as the 'Seven Days Notice' itself can only be valid after the due determination of the relationship of landlord and tenant between the parties. Its service on the defendant has been held as a condition precedent to the institution of recovery proceedings in the court[46] and failure to serve it

44. Per Onnoghen JSC at 1368.
45. See the discussion on this type of tenant *supra* at 53.
46. *AP v Owodunni* (*Supra*).

has been held to render proceedings in court invalid.[47]

Attention must however be drawn to the language of the section of the Recovery Statutes providing for the service of this 'Seven Days Notice' which is to the effect that the landlord 'may' cause the seven days notice to be served on the tenant neglecting or refusing to quit and deliver up possession. The usage of the permissive 'may' in the section will, with due respects, in law mean that the service is only permissive and not mandatory. According to the Supreme court in *Ifezue v Mbadugha*,[48]

> whenever a statute declares that a thing 'shall' be done, the natural and proper meaning is that a peremptory mandate is enjoined.

This is elementary interpretation of statutes but it is also true that the courts have also held that in some statutes and depending on the mischief which the statute was intended to remedy, the lawmaker may be taken to mean a compulsion when he uses the word 'may' instead of 'shall' and vice versa as, in the words of Bello JSC in *Ifezue v Mbadugha*,[49]

> the ordinary meaning of the word 'shall' is mandatory and consequently the section may be construed *prima facie* mandatory. Under the circumstances,[50] the word 'shall' may also be construed as directory .... The subsection is capable of mandatory and directory meaning.

47. *Lasaki v Dabian* (1957) NRNLR 13.
48. (1984) ANLR 256.
49. *Supra*.
50. The Supreme Court was in this case considering the circumstances of Section 258 (1) of the 1979 Nigerian Constitution that '*every court ... shall deliver its decision ... not later than three months ....*

However, until there has been an interpretative pronouncement of a superior court of records with respect to specific legislative provisions no one may be allowed to deviate from the ordinary rules for interpreting such legislation. With respect to the provisions of the Recovery Statutes nationwide employing 'may' in the service of the 'Seven Days Notice', the Supreme Court may have impliedly intervened rightly or wrongly that the service is an imperative.

In *Pan Asian African Co. Ltd. v Nicon Nig. Ltd.*,[51] for instance, the Supreme Court, immediately after quoting Section 15 of the 1976 Lagos State Rent Control and Recovery of Residential Premises Law, which provided that the

> ... landlord ... or his agent may cause the person so neglecting or refusing to quit and deliver up possession to be served ... a written notice ... signed by the landlord or his agent of the landlord's intention to proceed to recover possession on a date not less than seven days from the date of service of the notice,

and is *impari materia* with other Recovery Statutes nationwide, proceeded to hold and declare that it was clear from the provision of the quoted section that

> the notice of intention to proceed to recover possession as in Form E signed by the landlord or his agent *must* be served.[52]

In other words and in effect, the Supreme Court has declared by this holding that the 'may' in the section of the various Recovery Statutes requiring the service of the 'Seven Days Notice' has the same meaning as 'shall' and

51. *Supra.*
52. *ibid* at 248.

is therefore an imperative and a mandatory condition precedent to the institution of recovery actions. This the Supreme Court has only consequentially done without a direct invitation or application to it from the bar or by a litigant to so do and the court may think otherwise someday should there be a direct invitation to it to strictly construe the true meaning and purport of 'may' in this particular provision.

Seven Days Notice need not be Served on Tenant - It is premature and therefore to no point to serve the 'Seven Days Notice' while the tenancy still subsists. Its object is not to determine the tenancy but merely to give notice or 'warning' not necessarily to the tenant but to any person who is in occupation of the premises who is 'neglecting or refusing to quit and deliver up possession that the landlord, having already determined the tenancy, intends to institute legal proceedings against such 'person so neglecting or refusing to quit or deliver up possession' for the recovery of the premises the subject matter of the contract which had come to an end and that the legal proceedings shall be instituted any time after the expiration of seven clear days from the date of the service[53] on the person of the 'Seven Days Notice'.

Grounds for Recovery of Possession – The Recovery Statutes nationwide contain provisions specifying grounds upon which a court shall order the recovery of possession of any premises by a landlord from a tenant. This provision is generally to the effect that

> no order or judgment for recovery of possession of any

53. Section 16 of the Lagos Tenancy Law No. 14 of 2011 puts this date as 'the date of the notice' and not the date of service.

premises to which the Law applies or for the ejectment of a tenant therefrom shall be made or given UNLESS THE (COURT) CONSIDERS IT REASONABLE to make such order or give such a judgment AND UNLESS either

(a) the court has power so to do under the provisions set out in the Second Schedule OR

(b) the court is satisfied that suitable alternative accommodation is available for the tenant (Emphasis supplied).[54]

The provision is that the court is to make an order or judgment for possession only upon the existence of two grounds to wit that

(i) it considers it reasonable so to do AND

(ii) unless any of the situations or conditions prescribed in paragraph (a) or (b) of the subsection is present.

Reasonableness – Therefore, the first factor which a court must take into consideration before making an order for possession in favour of a landlord is whether it is reasonable to do so. This requirement of reasonability is paramount in every case. The court decides whether it is reasonable or not to make the order taking into account all the circumstances of the case as at the date of hearing and will decide the point as an ordinary man of the world employing common sense.

The point is not whether it is reasonable for the landlord to seek possession but whether it is reasonable for the court to grant it taking prevailing and all surrounding circumstances into account. In other words, it is the court

54. See Section 27 of the Law which, except in Lagos State, is *impari materia* with all other Recovery Statutes.

which decides the reasonability or otherwise of the application in exercise of its discretion done judicially and judiciously.

The ground of reasonability is paramount and is an imperative but must be accompanied by any other ground or grounds as stipulated in the paragraphs (a) or (b) of Section 27 (1) of the Recovery Statute. These other grounds are that first, there is a suitable alternative accommodation for the tenant or secondly, any of the nine situations listed in paragraphs (a) to (i) of Schedule II to the Recovery Statute is present in the event that there is no proof of alternative accommodation.

What this means is that the Recovery Statutes do not contemplate that possession can be ordered in favour of the owner (landlord) as a matter of course or only because he 'wants' it. It requires that the landlord, as plaintiff, must satisfy the court as to the ground or grounds on which he relies for justifying an order for possession. These grounds are provided for in substantially the same wordings in all the Recovery Statutes nationwide[55] and, as has been shown above, are basically two. These are

(a) that it is reasonable to make the order in every case (discussed *supra*) and

(b) availability of alternative accommodation for the

55. For reasons of elegance and ease of reference, the Delta State Rent Control and Recovery of Residential Premises Law 1977 published as Cap. 180 in the Annotated Laws of Delta State 2007 the provisions of which are substantially *impari materia* with all other Recovery Statutes nationwide except Lagos State has been adopted as the standard reference, source and guide throughout this book in which any reference to 'the Law' or 'Recovery Statute' is a reference to that Law except the context otherwise indicates.

tenant.

Alternative Accommodation - Before making an order for the recovery of possession in favour of the owner, Section 27 (1) (b) of the Law requires that the court must be satisfied that there is a suitable[56] alternative accommodation for the tenant and the onus is on the landlord to prove the availability of such alternative accommodation.[57]

The provision does not place a burden on the landlord to provide the alternative accommodation but that the court shall be satisfied that there is suitable alternative accommodation for the tenant. The decision in *Dawodu v Solanke*[58] does not place the burden of providing an alternative accommodation on the landlord either but only requires that the burden of 'satisfying' the court that there is an alternative accommodation which is suitable to the tenant shall be discharged by the landlord.

It is also the requirement under the provision and by the decision in *Dawodu v Solanke* that the alternative accommodation shall be available, not in the future, but at the time the order is made or at the time the order is to take effect.

By the provisions of Section 23 of the erstwhile Lagos State Rent Control and Recovery of Residential Premises Law (Cap. R6), it will appear that the burden for proving alternative accommodation was expressly shifted

56. Section 22 of the erstwhile Lagos Statute (Cap. R6) does not use this word but in the Schedule. The Tenancy Law does not have this provision.
57. *Dawodu v Solanke* (1956) LLR. 15.
58. *Supra.*

from the landlord or, at the least, the section clarifies the position that there is no duty on a landlord so to do by providing that

> … where, in the opinion of the (court), it is expedient so to do, it may allow a tenant up to a maximum of six months to look for alternative accommodation.

This means that the court may make the order for possession notwithstanding that there is no immediate availability of an alternative accommodation for the tenant but that the tenant may be allowed time not exceeding six months from the date of the order to look for an alternative accommodation for himself. If, at the expiration of the six months, the tenant shall be unable to secure an alternative accommodation for himself, then the court's order for possession in favour of the landlord shall take effect and he shall be at liberty to levy execution against the tenant therefor.

Standard of Alternative Accommodation - For the alternative accommodation to be suitable, the court must be of the opinion that the accommodation is reasonably suitable to the:

(i) needs of the tenant and his family as regards proximity to place of work

(ii) means of the tenant and

(iii) needs of the tenant and his family as to nature, extent and character.[59]

Generally, the alternative accommodation shall

(a) be of a kind similar to the one being recovered from the tenant,

59. Section 27 (2).

(b) not expose the tenant to less security in tenure

(c) not be of a higher rent and

(c) be one suitable for the tenant comparable to accommodation for persons in the tenant's station in life.

Possession without Alternative Accommodation –The provision as to availability of alternative accommodation for the tenant is not absolute. There are exceptions. This is because although Section 27 (1) (b) of the Recovery Statute precludes the court from making an order or giving a judgment for possession in favour of the owner except he has discharged the burden of proving availability of alternative accommodation for the tenant, the restriction is subject to the provisions of paragraph (a) of the same subsection under which the court is not to make the order unless it has power to do so by virtue of the provisions set out in the Second Schedule to the Law.

The said schedule provides for situations where the court can make the order for recovery of possession without proof of alternative accommodation subject however to the court considering it reasonable to do so. In its introductory provision, the schedule declares that

> a (court) shall, for the purpose of Section 27 of (the Law), have power to make or give an order of ejectment for the recovery of possession of any premises to which (the Law) applies or for ejectment of a tenant therefrom without proof of suitable alternative accommodation (where the {court} considers it reasonable so to do if ...)

any of the situations listed in the schedule from paragraphs (a) to (i) is present. These situations which operate as exceptions to the requirement as to proof of alternative accommodation are as follows: [60]

Arrears of Rent - Where the tenant's rent lawfully due by virtue of the Recovery Statute is in arrear for one month after it has become due, then the landlord would be relieved of the burden of proving alternative accommodation before being entitled to an order of the court for possession. In this situation, where the tenant pays his rent monthly in advance, such rent will only be in arrear for the required one month at the end of the month for which it ought to have been paid but was not paid.

The arrears of rent for one month which dispenses with the need to prove alternative accommodation is different from the arrears of rent as provided for in the proviso to Section 18 of the Recovery Statute which dispenses with the requirement of a notice to quit in determining a tenancy in the case of a monthly tenancy.[61]

Breach of Covenant - Tenancy agreements usually carry with them sundry duties and covenants to be performed by the parties during the pendency of the contract. Such covenants, on the part of the tenant to perform, usually include, for instance, covenants not to sublet[62] the premises and to pay rent[63] promptly.

Where therefore the tenant falls in breach of an express covenant of the tenancy agreement, it shall no longer be necessary for the landlord to prove the availability of alternative accommodation for the tenant

60. See generally Schedule II to the various states' Recovery Statutes.
61. See also Section 13 (2) and (3) of the Lagos Tenancy Law 2011 for provisions relating to rent arrears dispensing with the notice to quit.
62. *Kuyoro v Mawdew Ventures Ltd.* (1975) 7 CCHCJ 1087.
63. *Osawaru v Ezeiruka* (1978) 6-7 SC 135.

before an order for possession may be made by the court against the tenant. In *Osawaru v Ezeiruka*[64] the Supreme Court held that the failure of the tenant to pay rent promptly as provided in the tenancy agreement amounted to a breach of covenant which availed the landlord to recover possession without proof of alternative accommodation.

If the landlord has by express statements or conduct waived his right to rely on or enforce the breach, he will be denied by the court from subsequently relying on same as entitling him to the relief of not proving alternative accommodation before obtaining an order of court for possession. Acceptance of rent from the tenant by the landlord with knowledge of the breach is however not a waiver.

Notice to Quit by Tenant – There will be no need for the landlord to prove availability of an alternative accommodation for the tenant if the tenant had served the landlord with a notice of his intention to quit and deliver up possession of the premises and the landlord has, in reliance thereof, contracted with a third party to acquire interest in the premises either by selling or letting same or taking some other steps in relation thereto such that he would be seriously prejudiced if he could not obtain possession.

The notice which is required to activate this exception is an actual notice preferably in compliance with the provisions of the Law relating as to notices. An implied notice or a suggestion thereto or a mere agreement to give up possession will be insufficient.

64. *Supra.*

Public Interest **-** Where the premises are reasonably required for any purpose which is in the public interest or public good and the landlord proves this fact before the court, then he shall not be required to prove alternative accommodation before being entitled to the court's order for possession.

It will be a purpose in the public interest if it is sought to use the premises for a public school or hospital by a government or some other public spirited or charitable institution such as a non-governmental organization reputed to be engaged in non-profit making charitable purposes; or where it is sought to construct a public highway or railway which runs through the land on which the premises is built.

In every case, what amounts to public interest is determined by the court taking into account the peculiar circumstance of each case especially with regards to the true meaning of public interest. A wealthy individual seeking recovery of premises for the purpose of building a fee-paying university may not be a purpose of public interest even though by the special circumstances of the community where the university is sought to be built the public will benefit thereby.

In *Olaoye v Mandilas*[65] the plaintiff sought to recover possession with a view to knocking down the existing structure and constructing a bigger and better structure 'in the interest of the public'. The court disagreed with him that his bigger and better structure was necessarily in the best interest of the public within the contemplation of the law.

65. (1949) 19 NLR 59.

Nuisance – Paragraph (e) to the Schedule 2 of the Law contains a number of situations which will activate the exception to proving alternative accommodation in favour of a landlord. The paragraph provides that a landlord shall be relieved of the burden to prove alternative accommodation where the tenant or any person residing or lodging with him or being his sub-tenant has:

(a) been guilty of conduct which is a nuisance or annoyance to adjoining occupiers, or

(b) has been guilty of using the premises as a brothel, or

(c) the tenant or that other person has been convicted of using the premises or allowing the premises to be used for an illegal purpose, or

(d) that the condition of the premises has deteriorated owing to acts of waste by, or neglect or default of, the tenant or any such person, and

(e) where such person is a sub-tenant or lodger, that the tenant has not taken such steps as he ought reasonably to have taken for the removal of such sub-tenant or lodger.

The language of the exceptions created under this heading of nuisance is such that the tenant or that other person residing or lodging with the tenant or being the tenant's subtenant must first have been 'found guilty' as in (a) and (b) herein above or 'convicted' as in (c) of the stated crime.

In the *Osawaru v Ezeiruka*,[66] case, the evidence showed that the tenant used the premises as a brothel. The Supreme Court held in the circumstance that the provision gives a landlord the right to remove a tenant who is using

66. *Supra.*

his premises, among other things stated in the Act, as a brothel but that

> the tenant does not have to be convicted in a court of law for using the premises as a brothel before being ejected (as in the case of using the premises for an illegal purpose where a prior conviction is necessary). It is enough that the court is satisfied that he has been using the premises as a brothel.[67]

The conduct which amounts to a nuisance or annoyance to adjoining occupiers in any particular case will depend on factors peculiar to the nature of the neighbourhood or locality, the stations in life of the persons living within the particular neighbourhood and their life style, the consideration as to whether the tenant's conduct is a temporary or permanent nature etc.

In *Omole v Taylor*,[68] the tenant's wife was a quarrelsome woman who incessantly quarreled with the wife of the landlord's father and shouted and clapped her hands noisily in the middle of the night to the annoyance of the 67 year old father of the landlord. The High Court of Lagos State per Kazeem J. held that

> the evidence of loud noise in the middle of the night to the annoyance of the respondent's father would alone be sufficient to constitute nuisance.

Also in *Idowu v Adekanmi*,[69] the then Lagos High Court per Adefarasin J. held that

> a tenant who habitually and repeatedly brings undesirable friends to his flat dancing and drinking and making a noise and stamping on the floor above his

67. Per Aniagolu JSC.

68. (1976) 4 CCHCJ 1169.

69. (1975) 6 CCHCJ 923.

landlord or other tenants to their annoyance creates a nuisance.

The above decisions of the Lagos High Court should serve as sufficient authority for the legal view that noise especially in the middle of the night such as is usually generated during 'dancing and drinking and making a noise and stamping on the floor' and such like noise during what is now known as 'night vigil' by some religious groups within residential areas and which causes annoyance to persons in adjoining premises is nuisance.

Dangerous Overcrowding **-** Where the premises are so overcrowded as to be dangerous or injurious to the health of the inmates, and the court is satisfied that the overcrowding could have been abated by the removal of any lodger or subtenant (not being a parent or child of the tenant) whom it would, having regard to all the circumstances of the case, including the question as to whether other accommodation is available for him, have been reasonable to remove, and that the tenant has not taken such steps as he ought reasonably to have taken for his removal, then upon the landlord eventually taking out a suit for the recovery of possession from the tenant, the landlord shall not be required to prove alternative accommodation to be entitled to an order for possession.

Not every overcrowding is material under this heading. The overcrowding must be such that

(a) will be injurious to the inmates of the premises,

(b) it is as a result of the presence in the premises of persons other than the tenant and his relations including his parents and or children,

(c) such other persons include the tenant's friends, subtenants, or lodgers,

(d) the tenant could have taken steps to prevent the overcrowding which steps he has not taken

(e) the steps open to the tenant in all the circumstances include that there is an availability of alternative accommodation.

Notice of Abatement - Where the premises are the subject of an abatement notice or similar notice issued by a public authority and it is shown by the landlord that compliance with the terms of such notice is only possible through the ejectment of the tenant,[70] it shall not be necessary for the landlord, in an action for recovery of possession from tenants in occupation of the premises, to prove alternative accommodation. This exemption is however dependent on the proviso that the court may impose a condition for the return of the tenant to the premises when compliance has been made with the terms of the notice.

An abatement notice is one which is usually issued and served on premises on grounds that the premises have become a threat to health or life and which calls on either the landlord or the occupier of such premises to remove or arrest the threat. It can be issued and served by a public health authority, the town planning authority or fire service.

For the court to be satisfied that the premises does in fact pose a threat to health or to life, it may sometimes be necessary to make a visit to the *locus in quo*[71] for the purpose of the court inspecting the premises the state of which is clearly material to the proper determination of the question as to whether it poses a threat to health and or

70. *Aboaba v Kalaiwo* (1961) ANLR 753.

71. See Chapter Seven on Incidental Proceedings at the Recovery Trial *infra* at 280.

life.[72] As the Supreme Court explained in *Umar v Bayero University Kano,*[73]

> there are certain matters of fact that cannot be resolved by the trial court by mere judgement of demeanour of the witness. The *locus in quo* must be seen.

This is more so as it is known that some landlords who are desperate in their desire to eject tenants they consider recalcitrant connive with some public officers, especially local government officials, to issue and serve on them spurious abatement notices.

Where the threat to be abated is of such a nature and magnitude that it cannot be removed or abated while the occupants are in possession of the premises, it is usual for the landlord to then require that the occupants give up possession to enable the removal take place.

But such an order for the recovery of possession is not necessarily always of a permanent nature hence the proviso which allows the court to impose the condition that the occupiers shall be allowed to return to the premises when compliance has been made with the terms of the abatement notice.

An abatement notice on its own does not operate as an ejectment order or authority for the landlord to forcefully eject the tenants or occupants of the premises without an appropriate court order. A subsequent application for and an order of court to this effect is an imperative. This is what De Lestang J. meant in *Aboaba v Kalaiwo*[74] when he held that

72. See Chapter Seven on Incidental Proceedings at the Recovery Trial *infra* at 280.
73. (1998) 4 NWLR (Pt. 86) 85.
74. *Supra.*

before an order for possession can be made on such ground, it must be shown that compliance with the terms of the abatement notice is only possible through the ejectment of the tenant.

In *Ogunsanya v Arab Brothers Ltd.*,[75] the landlord, upon receipt of an abatement notice which was also served on the occupants immediately proceeded to demolish the house. He was successfully sued by the tenants for trespass. Explaining the purport of the exemption, the court, per Coussey J. held that the Recovery Statutes enjoined a landlord to apply for and obtain an order of the court for ejection of the tenant upon the notice of abatement for his own protection against the rights of the tenants.

Substantial Repairs - Where the premises require substantial repairs on account of which it is necessary for the tenant to vacate possession to enable the repairs to take place, there will be no need to prove the availability of alternative accommodation before the court makes an order in favour of the landlord for possession.

Under this heading, the meaning of the word 'repair' is very material. This is because to repair a thing is different from a replacement thereof. Therefore a whole house is to be demolished with a view to replacing it with a completely new and better one upon a more modern plan, this will not be a 'repairs'.

In *Oyename v Sulu*,[76] the suit premises was a hall. The evidence showed that it was to be demolished and new premises of an entirely different kind showing a house comprising three self-contained flats erected in its place. As

75. (1952) 14 WACA 107.
76. (1962) ANLR 1053.

to whether this amounted to repairs, Onyeama Ag. CJ unhesitatingly held that 'such a conversion would not ... amount to repairs in law' and that it was not open to doubt that in certain cases repairs might involve renewal but, quoting Buckley LJ in *Lurcott v Wakely*,[77] the learned Acting Chief Justice held that

> repair always involves renewal; renewal of a part; of a subordinate part .... Repair is restoration by renewal or replacement of subsidiary of a whole

so that if the premises were in such a state that they had to be demolished and rebuilt, the case would not be one of repairs at all whether substantial repairs or otherwise. To repair is therefore the restoration by renewal or replacement of subsidiary parts of a whole and not the replacement or renewal of the whole.

The evidence which the court will require to act upon in granting the exemption which this head presents must be strong and cogent. This is because the court may refuse to order possession if it is not satisfied that it is reasonable to do so upon evidence which supports making the order. This is what the court did in *Animashaun v Oduntan*[78] where the trial magistrate refused to make an order for possession in favour of the landlord on the ground of substantial repairs because, in his view, the repairs were such that could be effected while the tenant retained possession. His decision was upheld, on appeal, by the Lagos State High Court.

To enable the court determine in justice whether in fact the premises are in need of substantial repairs, it might

77. (1911) 1 KB 905, 923.
78. (1975) 1 CCHCJ 81.

be necessary for the court to, like under the heading for notice of abatement, make a visit to the *locus in quo.*[79] Also under this head, there is the proviso that the court may impose a condition for the return of the tenant when the repairs are completed.

Personal Use **-** Where the premises are reasonably required by the landlord for

(a) his personal occupation or

(b) for the occupation of his child who is over eighteen years old or

(c) the occupation of either or both of his parents,

then the need to prove alternative accommodation on the part of the landlord before being entitled to an order for possession shall be dispensed with.

The order for possession on the ground of personal occupation is made subject to the avoidance of greater hardship which may be caused by the grant or refusal thereof and it will not be made unless the person for whose benefit it is sought to recover possession is either

(a) the landlord's child (whether son or daughter) of who must be over 18 years of age or

(b) the direct parent (either father or mother) of the landlord.

The occupation for which the suit premises is required by the landlord must be an immediate one. Where the occupation is one required for some time in the future, the order sought will be refused.[80]

79. See Chapter Seven on Incidental Proceedings at the Recovery Trial *infra* at 280.

80. See *Oyename v Sulu*. (*Supra*).

Also the occupation must be for the benefit of the landlord so that where it is sought to use the premises for the expansion of the landlord's business, it was held that the exemption availed the landlord.[81] This is because, it has been argued,[82] the requirement is for the landlord's 'occupation' which need not be occupation for residence especially since the provision does not use the word 'residence'.

But it may be apt to draw attention to the legal fact that the Law which regulates these proceedings is, with due respects, the Rent Control and Recovery of *Residential* Premises Law. Accordingly, it would seem more appropriate that the view be taken that the occupation under the contemplation of the Law should be one for personal residential purposes. So that if the landlord seeks the possession for the purpose of expanding the business of 'his' company duly incorporated, then the provision would not avail him in view of the separate legal personality of the company.

The burden of proving that the premises are reasonably required for the personal use of the landlord lies on the landlord while the burden for proving greater hardship resides in the tenant.Where the suit premises is family property or is subject of joint landlords, the court will grant the order for possession if it is the wishes of the joint landlords that their premises is sought to be recovered for the use or occupation of any one or more of them.[83]

81. *Adebajo v Odunlami* (1949) 19 NLR 55.
82. See Emeka Chianu (2004) *Law of Landlord and Tenant* (*supra*) at 368.
83. See *Coker v Adetayo* (1992) 2 NWLR (Pt. 249) 612.

This is because the definition of 'landlord' under the Recovery Statutes is such that it could mean just one of many landlords just as it could also mean two or more of them.

Making the order for possession under the head of the requirement for personal use, the court takes into account the proviso thereto that the order must be refused if it is satisfied that having regard to all the circumstances of the particular case including as to whether there is an alternative accommodation for the landlord or the tenant, greater hardship would be caused to either of the parties by granting the order than by refusing to grant it.

The circumstances of the case which the provision requires the court to take into account are as varied as can be imagined. Professor Chianu describes them as open-ended.[84] What is required therefore is that the court considers the varied circumstances as they present themselves the way the reasonable man on the street will do and always having the justice of the case in mind.

Hence, in *Ibrahim v Oguunlesi*,[85] the defendant tenant was a banker. She was for this reason considered to have the requisite financial means to procure an alternative accommodation for herself and her failure to do so was held against her.

Also in *Martins v Ogunsanya*,[86] the evidence showed that the landlord occupied one of the two rooms in the premises while she let out the second room. She then collected money from another person and renovated a third

84. Emeka Chianu (2004) *Law of Landlord and Tenant* at 373.
85. (1975) 7 CCHCJ 1255.
86. (1976) 10 CCHCJ 2981.

room which she let to this other person. She then sought to recover possession from the first tenant on the ground that she wanted the room for her personal use as a single room was no longer convenient for her.

The court held that she could not render the tenant homeless and thereby cause him greater hardship while she stayed in two rooms more so as she had the opportunity of using the room she had let to the new tenant.

***Employee Tenant* -** Another ground for which the landlord may recover possession without proof of alternative accommodation is where the tenant was an employee of the landlord and whose occupation of the premises is in consequence of or dependent on the contract of employment which has ceased and the premises is now required for the use and occupation of a new employee.

This ground is not provided for in the Schedule but see Obi-Okoye[87] who is of the view that a landlord may recover possession from his former employee without proof of alternative accommodation. The learned author did not give reasons for his views. Professor Chianu however holds a different view and states[88] that

> even with the proof of a valid notice to quit and the expiration of the notice of the landlord's intention to proceed to recover possession, the employer is further expected to provide a suitable alternative accommodation for the employee/tenant before he can recover possession.

Relying on Section 25(1) of the 1976 Lagos State 'Rent

87. *Essays on Civil Proceedings* (1983) Elmina Books Ltd, Enugu, at 38.
88. *Law of Landlord and Tenant* (2004) at 97.

Control Law' for his views, the position taken by the learned professor is to be preferred except to humbly defer with due respects, with part of the view that 'the employer is further expected to provide' the suitable alternative accommodation.

With due respects, no such burden is placed on any landlord by any of the Recovery Statutes. Section 25 (1) (b) of the Lagos Recovery Statute which the learned professor quoted in full and relied upon is to the effect that

> no order or judgement for the recovery of possession of any premises to which (the) Law applies or for the ejectment of a tenant therefrom shall be made or given ...
>
> (b) unless the (court) is satisfied that suitable alternative accommodation *is available* for the tenant.(Emphasis supplied).

The provision is silent on who provides the alternative accommodation and certainly does not say the duty is that of the landlord. Indeed, Section 23 of the 2003 Lagos State Rent Control and Recovery of Residential Premises Law Cap. R6 which contains this provision[89] is to the effect that

> notwithstanding the provision of Section 22 of this Law, where, in the opinion of the (court), it is expedient so to do, it may *allow a tenant* up to a maximum of six months *to look for an alternative accommodation*.(Emphasis supplied).

89. The Lagos Tenancy Law of 2011 does not contain this provision except the reference in Section 27 (5) that '*the court shall, in making an order for possession ... have regard to all the circumstances of the case including where appropriate, the question as to whether other premises are available for the landlord or tenant.*

Clearly, this latter day enactment leans more to the view that the duty to provide a suitable alternative accommodation is that of the tenant himself and not that of the landlord. Somehow, Professor Chianu realizes this much when at page 98 of the same book, he writes that

> one mitigating principle is that Section 25 (1) (b) does not require the landlord to provide the alternative accommodation.

As seen in the *Ibrahim v Oguunlesi*[90] case, the court held against the defendant because evidence showed that as a banker she was in a comfortable financial position to be able to provide an alternative accommodation for herself but failed to do so. The court was considering the issue of greater hardship but the decision pointed in the direction that the duty of providing alternative accommodation is not that of the landlord.

Legal Status of Employee-Tenant - Two types of employee tenant are recognizable under this head. These are the service occupant and the service tenant.

Service Occupier - A service occupant is an employee who occupies the premises of his employer because such occupation is necessary for the performance of the employee's duties. In the words of Bairamian JSC in *The Appraiser v Nigerian Railway Corporation*,[91]

> in a service occupancy, the servant is not the rateable occupier. The test is whether the occupation is subservient and necessary to the service.[92]

A service occupant, being a person occupying premises belonging to his employer for the purpose of being able to

90. (1975) 7 CCHCJ 1255.
91. (1964) ANLR 57.
92. *ibid* at 63.

perform his duties under his contract of employment, is not a tenant but a mere licensee. As such licensee, he is not entitled to the protections which the Recovery Statutes afford a tenant and as such cannot maintain an action in trespass against his licensor.[93] This is because, as explained in Woodfall's *Law of Landlord and Tenant*,[94]

> an agent or servant who is allowed to occupy premises belonging to his principal for the more convenient performance of his duties, acquires no estate therein ….

That a service occupant is not a tenant was beyond dispute. That he is a licensee is a latter day categorization. Denning LJ identified this category of an employee's holding in *Torbett v Faulkner*[95] when he declared that

> previously, the holding of a servant was classified either as a service occupancy or a service tenancy. There was no third category. But nowadays, it is recognized that there is an intermediate position. He may be a licensee. A service occupancy is, in truth, only one form of licence. It is a particular kind of licence whereby a servant is required to live in the house in order the better to do his work.

Service Tenant – A service tenant is a tenant. He is entitled to all the rights, benefits and protection which the Recovery Statutes confer. He is an employee who occupies premises belonging to his employer but whose occupation is not necessarily one which is required by the employee for the better performance of his duties. He occupies the premises only as part of his terms or conditions of service as a fringe benefit to him of the contract of employment.

93. See *Chukwumah v SPDC Nig. Ltd.* (1993) 4 NWLR (Pt. 289) 512.
94. 21st Ed. at p.294.
95. (1952) 2 TLR 659.

The test in distinguishing between a service tenant and a service occupant is as Bairamian J. put it in the *Appraiser v NRC*[96] case that

> in a service occupancy, ... the occupation (of the premises by the employee) is subservient and necessary (but that) if (this) test is not passed in the case of a particular ... servant, (then such an employee) ... is a tenant (albeit one) at will even though he does not pay rent for his occupation.

Accordingly, whenever an issue as to the status of an employee has arisen in an action for the recovery of premises as to whether he is a tenant or a licensee, the court must proceed in its effort to determine this status by enquiring whether the employee's occupation was one which was necessary for the performance of his duties under his employment and therefore subservient thereto. If the court finds an affirmative result to this test, then the employee is a licensee but otherwise he is a tenant. A tenant at will.

Legal Significance of Distinction – A licensee is not a tenant. Accordingly, the provisions of the Recover Statutes which are strictly in relation to tenants do not relate to licensees. The effect is that the licensee is not entitled to the protections which the Recovery Statutes afford a tenant. One such effect is that the licensee is not entitled to the notices prescribed in the Recovery Statutes before he can be ejected from the premises which he occupies as such licensee.

By the nature of a licence, a licensee does not 'occupy' premises in the context of the section of the

96. *Supra.*

Recovery Statutes[97] which defines ‘tenant’. A licensee, unlike a tenant, cannot be in exclusive occupation of premises and his ‘occupation’ is usually of a temporary nature. A tenant has a legal interest or estate in the premises he occupies but a licensee’s interest in premises is no more than a mere personal right to possession. The Recovery Statutes nationwide define ‘tenant’ as including

> a subtenant or any person occupying any premises whether on payment of rent or otherwise but does not include a person occupying a premises under a bona fide claim of right as the owner of the premises.[98]

This means that to be a tenant under the Law, a person must be occupying premises in such a manner that the provisions of the Recovery Statutes will relate to him. But it is not every kind of occupation that will serve the purpose.

According to Lewis JSC in *Sobamowo v The Federal Public Trustee*,[99] ‘occupying the premises here means lawful occupation’, but that according to Lush J. in *The Queen v St. Pancras Assessment Committee*,[100]

> it is not easy to give an accurate and exhaustive definition of the word ‘occupier’. Occupation includes possession as its primary element. But it also includes something more. Legal possession does not of itself constitute occupation.... A person who without having

97. Section 36 of Cap. R6 (Lagos) for instance.
98. Section 2 of the Law as in all other Recovery Statutes but this same provision in some states e.g. Section 143 of the Enugu State Landlord and Tenant Law (Cap. 101) of 2004, do not include ‘subtenant’.
99. (1970) ANLR 261.
100. (1877) 2 Q.B.D. 581, 588.

> any title takes actual possession of a (premises) whether by leave of the owner or against his will, is the occupier. Another element however ... necessary to constitute the kind of occupation which the Act contemplates ... is permanence

and that therefore, in the learned view of the Nigerian Supreme Court, for there to be an

> 'occupying' the premises within the meaning of 'tenant' in Section 2 of the (Recovery Statutes), one must establish actual use, which is lawful, of the premises so as to have actual possession of the premises coupled with such degree of permanence as would amount to occupation.

A licensee, being a service occupant of premises, does not in law occupy premises. The real occupant is his employer and his occupation is like that of one who has merely a right to possession of the premises with a view to, as in *Balogun v UAC*,[101] carrying out certain acts thereat at the behest of his employer.

In other words, the licensee possesses but does not occupy premises since his possession is not actual and is without the requisite degree of permanence. Hence, under the Recovery Statutes, he is not a tenant. But the licensee does or may have an occupation of some sort and since

> no one is entitled to take possession by a strong hand or with a multitude of people (but) must regain it by due process of law[102] (and) it is not the law ... that a landlord has unbridled right to invade premises in lawful occupation of a tenant ... when the intention of the

101. (1958) NNLR 77.
102. Lord Denning in *Agbor v Metropolitan Police* (1969) WLR 703, 707.

landlord is to recover possession,[103]
even the licensee is entitled to some sort of due process before his possession can be recovered from him and in this regard, Professor Chianu is of the view that

> where the employee is considered a service occupant, he is a licensee and as such may be entitled to a reasonable notice to vacate the premises.[104]

Reasonable notice in this context will depend on the circumstance[105] of each case and it is to be determined ultimately by the court but it is humbly submitted that where the employee paid rent on the premises, reasonable notice should be determined according as to how he paid the rent where practicable.

The service tenant is a tenant. Unlike the service occupant, his possession of premises belonging to his employer is protected by the Recovery Statutes. Upon the cessation of his contract of employment, a service tenant becomes a tenant at will[106] and, in accordance with the provisions of the Recovery Statutes, is entitled, not to a reasonable notice, but to a one week notice.[107]

What the above analyses represent is that whether the employee occupying his employer's premises does so either as a service tenant or a service occupant, his possession of the premises does not necessarily come to an

---

103. Obaseki JSC in *Eliochin Nig. Ltd.v Mbadiwe* (1986) 11 NWLR (Pt.14) 47, 49
104. (2004) *Law of Landlord and Tenant* (*supra*) at 92.
105. *Smith v West African Pictures Co. Ltd.* (1975) 6 CCHCJ 933.
106. *Appraiser v NRC (supra).*
107. Section 14 of Cap. R6 (Lagos); Section 18 of the Law (Delta and Edo); Section 17 of Law No. 4 of 1998 (Plateau State).

end upon the cessation of his employment.[107]

The courts have shown that the contract of employment is different from that of landlord and tenant which is independent of the former and that therefore the necessary legal steps for recovery of possession must be taken and followed to recover possession from the employee tenant. This is that appropriate notices must be served on the tenant by the employer landlord and if the tenant still detains the premises from the landlord, the landlord shall commence appropriate legal action in the proper court and obtain an order on the merit thereof to eject the tenant.

Recovery of Possession from Inherited Tenant – It sometimes happens that Linus as landlord of premises which he has recently purchased or has become entitled to by inheritance seeks to recover possession thereof from Titus as a sitting tenant who was put into possession by the predecessor in title of Linus and to whom the sitting tenant paid rent in furtherance of his tenancy contract evidenced by a tenancy agreement in writing.

Under the general principles of the law of contract and especially with regards to the principle of privity of contract, Linus will be a stranger to the tenancy contract between Titus and Linus' predecessor in title and will therefore be unable claim a benefit or be under a burden thereunder. In other words, Titus cannot determine the tenancy by a notice to quit or by any other form.

107. See *Sule v Nigerian Cotton Board (Supra), African Petroleum Ltd. v Owodunni* (1991) 8 NWLR (Pt. 210) 391.

In *Ehizogie v Utunye*,[108] the plaintiff claimed to have inherited the suit premises under a sharing of her late father's estate and had also obtained the court's declaration in her favour in respect thereof whereupon she served a notice to quit on the defendant and thereafter a notice of owner's intention to recover possession. At the trial, the defendant contended that the plaintiff was not his landlord since she was not the person who put him into possession and he has never paid rent to her. Delivering judgement disagreeing with the defendant, the court, in parts, said:

> The other ground upon which the defendant has contested the plaintiff's entitlement to judgement is that the plaintiff is not his landlord since she did not put him into possession but one other person called Osasere, who is his landlord who, through his mother, Mary Ogbebo, put him into possession.
>
> We shall concentrate on whether the plaintiff can maintain this action as landlord of the plaintiff. Defence counsel has answered this question firmly in the negative on the ground that the plaintiff did not put the defendant into possession and therefore no landlord and tenant contractual relationship exists between the parties.
>
> Who is a landlord under our laws? And who is a tenant? Section 2 of the Rent Control and Recovery of Residential Premises Law 1977 of Bendel State (hereinafter to be referred to as the Law) defines a landlord as the person, in relation to any premises,
>
> > 'who is entitled to the immediate reversion of the promises or, if the property is held in joint tenancy or tenancy in common, any of the

108. Unreported suit No. UACC/1/09 delivered on the 17th of June 2010 by the Uvwie Area Customary Court III CORAM Miakpo Emiaso – President; S.O. Ukuko and B.O. Edumijeke - Members.

> persons entitled to the immediate reversion and includes
> (a) the attorney or agent of any such landlord; or
> (b) any person receiving (whether in his own right or as an attorney or agent) any rent from any person for the occupation of any accommodation in respect of which he claims a right to receive the same.'

In his final address to court, learned counsel to the defendant cited to us *Olorunkoje v Rokosun* 20 NLR III, 119 and submitted on the point that a tenant cannot deny the title of the person who let him into possession. We agree with him as this represent substantially the provision of Section 7 (2) of the Rent Control and Recovery of Residential Promises Law (supra).

Counsel also submitted, citing *Akinlosho v Enigbokan* 21 NLR 76, 77, that where there is no relationship of landlord and tenant between the parties, the plaintiff's action must fail.

The definition of 'landlord' reproduced from the statute as above clearly does not bear out learned counsel's contention. Plaintiff testified in this suit that the suit premises was hers having inherited it from her father. She told the court that after her father's death, his estate was shared and the suit premises was shared to her. That she also took steps to validate the sharing by seeking a court declaration to that effect and tendered Exhibit P1.

Exhibit P1is a judgement of this court entered on the 20th of March, 2008, the last paragraph of which reads as follows:

> *This court has carefully considered the uncontroverted evidence of the plaintiff and we are satisfied that she has made out a case for the*

> *declaration sought. Accordingly, it is hereby declared that by virtue of the sharing of the estate of the plaintiff's father to wit Ogbemudia Okhuorobo Ogbebo as evidence in Exhibit ACCA 1 and which sharing is valid and subsisting, the plaintiff is the beneficial owner of all that house at No.1, Ogbebo Close, behind Urhobo College, Effurun; and the one acre of land lying behind and situate at Ogbebo Estate, Jakpa Road, Effurun effective from the date of the sharing to wit 31st day of July, 2005.*

Upon the strength of this judgement which is not shown to have been appealed against by anybody and therefore subsisting and valid, the suit properly became the property of the plaintiff who also became the person, in relation to the property, entitled to the immediate reversion.

We disagree with the submission of the learned defence counsel that the plaintiff's action must fail because of an absence of an express landlord and tenant relationship between the parties since a landlord, as has been seen from the definition of the term in the law, is not necessarily a person who receives rent from a particular defendant but the person entitled to the immediate reversion of the promises.

Plaintiff then led evidence in proof of her claim for possession, arrears of rent and *mesne* profits. This was on the 26th of May, 2009. She was thereafter cross examined on behalf of the defendant by M.G. Omokete.

In her evidence, plaintiff testified inheriting the defendant as a monthly tenant of her father and that she served a 7-day notice on the defendant, who has refused to pay her rent. She then urged court to give her judgement as per her claim as failed.

> It must be observed that the plaintiff's evidence above in respect of her entitlement to possession, arrears of rent and *mesne* profits remain *uncontroverted* by the defendant, who has contested this action by denying the plaintiff's status to be entitled to the immediate reversion of the suit promises. In the circumstance, we believe the evidence of the plaintiff and hold that she shall be entitled to judgement and we order as follows:
>
> (a) That the plaintiff do recover possession forthwith from the defendant of the premises known as No. 1, Ogbebo Close behind Urhobo College, Effurun.

The situation, from the arguments canvassed in the above suit, can be resolved by either of two ways. The first is for Linus as the new landlord to take steps to properly inherit Titus as his tenant by formally entering into a fresh tenancy contract with Titus subject however to Titus accepting him as Landlord. Where Titus accepts Linus as his landlord, and Titus, still desiring to recover possession may then accept rent from Titus as a monthly tenant. This way, he would only be under a legal requirement to subsequently issue a one month's notice to quit on Titus to determine the fresh tenancy of which he is now a party and under which he can exercise rights as appropriate.

The other way in resolving the situation which is to be preferred as being faster and free of difficulties is to adopt the position as was in *Pan Asian African Co. Ltd v Nicon*[109] where the respondents had purchased the suit property while the appellants as sitting tenants were in the process of negotiating a fresh tenancy with the respondents' predecessors in title. The respondents refused to accept the

109. *Supra. Ehizogie* was actually decided along this reasoning.

appellants as tenants and insisted appellants give up possession and filed the action therefor.

Deciding in favour of the respondents, the Supreme Court held that upon the respondents' purchase of the property, the appellants as sitting tenants, became statutory tenants of the respondents since the respondents now became entitled to the immediate reversion of the property. Obaseki JSC, delivering the lead judgement of the apex court, declared that

> there is evidence that the tenants made all efforts, though unsuccessful including payment of rent to the respondents, to attorn contractual tenants to them. Since Section 40 (3) of the (Lagos State Rent Control and Recovery of Residential Premises Law) No. 9 of 1976 stipulates that the provisions of the Law shall apply to all leases and the respondents were unwilling to renew the tenancy agreement, it became mandatory for the respondents to comply with Section 15 of the Law to set in motion the processes leading to ejectment of the appellants and recovery of possession under Section 25. Section 15 clearly requires the service of a written notice as in Form E on the appellants as
>
> (1) the term of years or interest in the premises granted to them had ended; and
>
> (2) they have neglected or refused to quit and deliver up possession of the premises.
>
> Since the respondents bought the interest of the appellants' landlord in the property as from 1st June 1977, the respondents became (the landlords) entitled to the immediate reversion of the premises.
>
> Learned counsel for the respondents contended that as there was no contractual relationship between them in respect of the premises the appellants cannot

> become their statutory tenants. A statutory tenancy is a creation of statute for the benefit of the tenant and does not depend on the will or acceptance of the landlord or on the existence of a contractual tenancy.[110]

In effect, the Supreme Court has provided a straight forward approach to resolving the situation where the plaintiff became the landlord of the defendant subsequent to the tenant's subsisting tenancy agreement with a previous landlord in respect of the premises. This is that by the change of ownership of the premises, the sitting tenant ceased to be a contractual tenant and became a statutory tenant who is then entitled to the benefits of that status as provided in the Recovery Statutes.

The plaintiff in this situation will then at the trial of the action for recovery of possession be required to satisfy the provisions of Section 25 (1) (e) of the Recovery Statutes[111] requiring him to prove his title since such title had 'accrued since the letting of the premises'.

110. *ibid* at 252.

111. Section 27 (4) (e) Tenancy Law (Lagos State). Section 19 (1) (e) Recovery of Premises Act/Law (Abuja and Plateau State).

Chapter Four

Form and Commencement of the Recovery Action

The law of landlord and tenant is fraught with ... technicalities. If the courts are reluctant to eliminate them because they are too entrenched to be reversed, all avenues for more should be plugged.

- Emeka Chianu[1]

Generally, there are two principal modes for commencing actions in Nigerian courts. These are the summons and the originating motion. The reference to summons is a reference to all kinds of summonses known to our laws including the writ of summons and the originating summons.

Motions – A motion generally is an application, usually in writing, but which can also be made orally in appropriate cases where the Rules of court so permit, made to a court usually for an interlocutory relief.

The Interlocutory Motion - Such a motion is made within the pendency of the substantive suit in which the applicant seeks the court's pronouncement in respect of an issue incidental or collateral to the main object of the substantive suit. This kind of motion is known as an interlocutory motion and is usually made on notice to the other party but may also in certain circumstances permitted by the Rules be made *ex parte*.

The Originating Motion – There is also the originating motion which is different from the interlocutory motion in that it is used to commence an action. It is used to seek a substantive relief and, as the name suggests, commence the action.

But an originating motion can be used to commence

1. *Law of Landlord and Tenant* (2004) Oliz Publishers, Benin at 282

an action only if the Rules of the particular court permit. For instance, Order 2 Rule 2 of the Lagos State Magistrates' Courts Civil Procedure Rules provides that

> subject to any Law or Rule, an originating application may be commenced in the Magistrates' Court ...

while Order XI (a) of the Delta State Customary Courts Rules expressly provides that

> an action for customary letters of administration shall be commenced by a motion supported by an affidavit ....

Summons - A summons is a court order to a person directing the person to appear in court at a specified place and time. In usage, it is very similar in meaning to the writ which is also a court order but which directs that some act be done by the person to whom it is addressed or that he should forbear from doing something. There are different kinds of summons and the originating summons and writ of summons are two examples of the summons.

The difference between a 'summons' and a 'writ' usually becomes blurred when the two words are used together as in the 'writ of summons'. In modern usage, the two words are now usually used separately and interchangeably to mean one and the same thing.

The Originating Summons - This is a kind of summons used in initiating proceedings where the facts of the action are not in issue so that a trial involving the oral examination of witnesses is unlikely. Actions commenced by originating summons are proceedings involving only questions of law as against disputed issues of facts.

The originating summons is used to initiate an action where the principal or main issue for determination is the interpretation or construction of some written law, deed, document, an instrument made pursuant to a written law, a Will, a contract or some other question of law, where it is unlikely that there will be any substantial dispute of facts. In other words, whenever the facts giving rise to the cause of action are not disputed by the parties, then an originating summons will suffice in commencing such an action.

The difference between the originating motion and the originating summons lies therefore in the legal fiction that while in an action commenced by the originating summons there is no disputation as to the facts constituting the action, this may not be so with the originating motion.

The Writ of Summons - The writ of summons which is also generally referred to simply as the summons is the most commonly used mode for commencing all forms of actions including the recovery action. Order 1 of the Customary Courts Rules 2007 of Delta State which is the same *verbatim* for Edo State, for instance, defines the summons as a

> document issued by a court calling upon the person to whom it is directed to attend before the court or to produce any document or thing to the court at a certain time or place.

But it is to be observed that the Civil Form A (i) in the Schedule to the said Rules which is headed 'civil summons' is wider in the scope of what a summons does than the definition of summons as contained in the Order I thereof. Whereas the definition only calls

> upon the person to whom it is directed to attend … or to produce…,

the form further to requires the person to whom it is directed to attend the court for the purpose of 'answer*(ing)* the plaintiff's claim …'.

Therefore, a fuller and more appropriate definition of the 'summons' could be that it is a document or a process issued from a court at the instance of a plaintiff indicating the plaintiff's claim against a defendant and calling upon the defendant to attend the court to answer to the claim of the plaintiff or to produce any document or thing at a certain date, time, and place specified thereon.

The writ of summons has also been defined as a formal document issued by a court and which contains the claim of a plaintiff against a defendant to 'cause an appearance to be entered' for him in an action at the suit of the plaintiff within a specific period of time, usually eight days, after the service of the writ on him, or to attend court on a named date to 'answer to a suit' by the plaintiff and with a warning, as the case may be, that in default of his causing an appearance to be entered for him or to appear in court, as commanded, the plaintiff may proceed therein and judgement may be given in the defendant's absence.[2]

This definition which is more directly related to High Court proceedings where the formal entering of appearance is applicable is sufficiently wide to encompass the essence and nature of a summons.

It is important to include in the definition that the document is issued by the court and at the instance of the plaintiff because, in any event, no summons can be issued without an application first being made for it to thc court by someone (usually the person commencing or originating the action i.e. the plaintiff) who desires that the defendant

2. See the adoption of this definition by Fidelis Nwadialo in *Civil Procedure in Nigeria* (1990) MIJ Professional Publishers Ltd., Lagos at 172.

be summoned by force of law to attend the court.

Form A (i) as contained in the First Schedule of Forms to the Delta State Customary Courts Rules 2007 entitled 'Civil Summons', for instance, provides (after the usual heading naming the court and the parties) thus:

> You are hereby summoned to appear at a court holden at … on the …day of … 20…at… O'clock to answer the plaintiff's claim as follows:

This is a command by which the defendant is summoned to 'attend before the court' to answer the plaintiff's claim as endorsed thereon.

All summonses, irrespective of the issuing court nationwide, use these 'command words' and immediately following the command words is usually a blank space which is designed to contain the endorsement of the plaintiff's claim against the defendant. Here, the plaintiff is expected to indicate a summary of his claim e.g.

> The plaintiff's claim is for possession of the three bedroom flat at No. 1 Linus Street, Benin; the sum of N300,000.00 being arrears of rent for the months of January, February and March [3] 2011; and *mesne* profits at the rate of N100,000.00 per month from April 2011 till possession is given up.

This is the plaintiff's claim. Not the particulars or statement of his claim. Following after this on the standard writ form is the phrase 'Particulars of Claim' in courts of summary jurisdiction such as the Magistrates' Courts, the Rent Tribunals, and the Customary Courts.

The standard writ form for the High Court bears the phrase 'Statement of Claim'. Below these phrases is a

3. In Lagos State, the arrears of rent can be for up to six months. See Section 13 (2) Lagos State Tenancy Law.

blank space where it is expected that the plaintiff will indicate some details of the facts which have informed his claim.

It is to be noted however that generally and in the special case of recovery actions, the Recovery Statutes contain special forms and modes for commencing such actions which shall be discussed herein *infra.*

Format of the Summons - The format of the general writ of summons is substantially the same in all courts. It is generally headed with the name and location of the court followed by the suit number and the parties. Next follows the 'command words' and the indorsement of the claim and relief sought. The Particulars or Statement of Claim (as the case may be) then comes next. The heading format of a standard writ of summons looks like this:

IN THE …….. COURT OF … STATE
HOLDEN AT………………..

Suit No ………………

Between:

CHIEF LINUS ONA ……………………………………Plaintiff
And
MR. TITUS OKUPAYA ……………………………Defendant

It has the general name of the state court or of the Federal Capital Territory on the topmost line. This is usually followed by a line indicating the particular court and the location where the summons is filed. Then follows the name of the town or the particular location where the court sits. This heading format is also used in the filing of motion papers either as originating or as interlocutory motions.

The writ of summons form is usually printed in standard form and made available at the various court registries upon the litigant's request usually at a fee. They can also be obtained from book sellers usually around the court premises. In these standard form writs of summons are blank spaces for the insertion of appropriate information as required.

The writ of summons can also be generated by the litigant or his counsel in substantial similarity to the standard form with latitude to vary same as the circumstances of his case may require.

The suit number (when known after official filing) is inserted in the blank space provided immediately beneath the name and description of the court. This is followed by the names of the parties which should be written out always in full. Initials should be avoided. Where a party has a title other than the usual 'Mr.' or 'Mrs.' or 'Miss', such a title should be indicated. This helps to better describe and identify the party and reduce chances of name coincidences and name mix-ups.

Each party should be properly described either as plaintiff or defendant. No one person can be both a plaintiff and defendant in the same suit even if he attempts to do so in different capacities. The names used must be the names of real and living persons not of dead persons.[4]

The 'command words' - Immediately after the names of the parties, the 'command words' of the summons which summons or orders the defendant to attend the court so as to answer the plaintiff's claims follows. They command, or summon or call upon the defendant to appear before the named court. The words used in the standard form are:

4. *Management Enterprise Ltd v Otusanya* (1987) 2 NWLR (Pt.55) 179.

> You are hereby summoned to appear at a court holden at ... on the ... day of ... 2 ... at ... O'clock to answer the plaintiff's claim as follows:

The Claim - A blank space then follows wherein the litigant is expected to indorse his claim. This indorsement is a concise statement of the nature of the claim he makes and the remedy or relief he seeks and it is similar in courts of summary jurisdiction to the usual 'general indorsement' of the High Court writ of summons which is essentially to bring to the notice of the defendant and the court the nature of the action and the relief or remedy sought by the plaintiff in general terms e.g.

> ... possession of the three bedroom flat at No. 1 Linus Street, Benin; the sum of N300,000.00 being arrears of rent for the months of January, February and March [3] 2011; and *mesne* profits at the rate of N100,000.00 per month from April 2011 till possession is given up.

It is inserted after the 'O'clock a.m.' in the 'command words' as a separate sentence.

Issuing the Summons - In the courts with summary jurisdiction for recovery suits, upon the receipt of the application of the litigant for a writ of summons following the presentation of the plaint as in Form F,[5] the Registrar or the appropriate officer of the court as is authorized in that behalf takes out the writ of summons form usually as in Form G[6] which he completes and presents to the Administrative Judge or Chief Magistrate or, in the case of Customary Courts, to the Administrative President or any such other member or officer of the court as is authorized

5. Now Form TL6B in Lagos State.
6. Form TL6A in Lagos State.

in that behalf in accordance with the provisions of the court's Rules for signature.

Where the process has been filed in a Registry serving more than one court, the Administrative Judge or Chief Magistrate or President or such other officer who signs the summons also assigns the suit to one of the courts within the particular jurisdiction of that Registry.

When the duly completed writ of summons has been signed aforesaid, the summons is said to have been issued. There is usually no provision for sealing in the courts with summary jurisdiction but it is the usual practice under the Rules of some High Courts to have the seal of the court embossed on the writ of summons before its issue is said to be complete.

The Registrar is then expected to produce or cause to be produced FOUR copies of the issued summons where there is only one defendant. Where there are more than one defendant, the Registrar shall cause to be produced as many additional copies as there are additional defendants.

One copy of the summons should then be placed in the court's file while a copy should be given to the plaintiff or plaintiffs. Of the remaining two copies, one shall be for service on the defendant while the other should be for the endorsement by the defendant upon his being served and as evidence of the service.

The copy endorsed by the defendant upon the service of the summons on him is then attached or exhibited to the affidavit of service by the court bailiff as proof and thereby putting the service almost entirely beyond doubt.

The endorsement required to be made by the

defendant should be on the face of the summons and not at the back thereof. It should also not be on a 'Dispatch Book'. The person served shall acknowledge the service by writing such words as

original (or copy of) writ of summons received by me

on the front of the writ of summons or other originating process as is served on him and affixing his signature or mark and date thereunder. The time of the service could also be indicated thereon.

Where the defendant is illiterate, some other form of endorsement could be adopted as the circumstance permits. Otherwise, it would be sufficient for the bailiff to make an appropriate note indicating the circumstance of the service on the endorsement copy of summons. Also where the defendant refuses to acknowledge the service by endorsing the endorsement copy, the bailiff may note thereon as appropriate that the defendant 'refused to sign'.

The bailiff then deposes to an affidavit of service to which he annexes or exhibits the duly endorsed copy of the summons. This then shall be sufficient proof of the service of the process unless the contrary can be and is proved.

The sworn affidavit of service which is also generally known as 'proof of service' is then placed in the court's file. This should generally be folio two or three in the court's file following the writ of summons and claim[7] depending as to whether these are on separate pages.

---

7. In current practice in some courts, especially in Delta State, only the 'claim' may be found in the court's file as the writ of summons is not placed in the court's file. It is humbly suggested that this ought not to be so as the court should be in a position to see the originating process itself and not only the claim of the plaintiff which operates as the application for the court's writ of summons.

Special Nature of Recovery Actions – The above discussion is in general terms and in the main relates to commencement of actions generally. Recovery actions are specially regulated. The court in *Oku v Awanah*[8] recognized this much when it declared that Recovery Statutes under their special procedure for the recovery of possession of premises also provide only for claims for arrears of rent and *mesne* profits. These special procedures for recovery actions are entrenched and as numerous as they are technical such that a learned writer[9] has had cause to observe that

> the law of landlord and tenant is fraught with enough technicalities (and that) if the courts are reluctant to eliminate them because they are too entrenched to be reversed, all avenues for more should be plugged (and further that) the public and the profession can do with some broad legal principles.[10]

In the special procedure of recovery actions, the plaintiff's claim and particulars of claim are usually to be found in the 'writ or plaint against tenant or person refusing to deliver up possession' as in Form F[11] the use of which form is not discriminatory as to court so that it can be used even in recovery actions filed in non-summary jurisdiction courts such as the state High Courts.

The Plaint or Writ - The Recovery Statutes all make provisions to the effect that if upon the expiration of the

---

8. (1961) ANLR 116.
9. Professor Emeka Chianu.
10. *Law of Landlord and Tenant* (2004) Oliz Publishers, Benin at 282.
11. See Appendix A. This form is now referred to as Form TL6B in Lagos State and entitled '*Annexed Claim Against Tenant or Person Refusing to Deliver up Possession*'.

time stated in the Seven Days Notice already served on a tenant of the landlord's intention to recover possession from the tenant and, if such tenant neglects or refuses to quit and deliver up possession of the premises accordingly, the landlord may apply to the appropriate court for the issue of a writ or to enter a plaint as in Form F (TL6B in Lagos State) in the Schedule to the Recovery Statute, and at the landlord's option, either against such tenant or against such person so neglecting or refusing, in the court in the local government area where the premises is situate for the recovery of same and thereupon a summons as in Form G (TL6A in Lagos State) shall be issued from the court to such tenant or person so neglecting.[12]

This provision under the Lagos Tenancy Law now confusingly runs thus:

> … the landlord may file a claim by way of summons as in Form TL6 and B for recovery of possession ….

The Lagos Form TL6B which is the same as Form F in other jurisdictions is no longer a plaint which serves as an application to court for the issue of a summons but now operates as the summons directly just as Form TL6A which is the same as Form G in other jurisdictions and which is the summons for recovery of possession.

The Form TL6B is entitled 'Annexed Claim against Tenant or Person Refusing to Deliver up Possession' which suggests that this form is to be annexed as a 'claim' to some other process which is likely the Form TL6A in the usual manner as the writ of summons. The provision of Section 24 of the law is, with due respects, inelegantly to

12. Section 24 Tenancy Law (Lagos); Section 20 (1) of the Law (Delta and Edo); Section 10 of Cap. 554 of 1990 (Abuja).

the effect that

> … the landlord may file a claim by way of summons as in Form TL6 and B.

The conjunctive 'and' employed by the lawmaker would mean that both Forms A and B must be filed together with Form B which opens with the words 'the claimant is entitled …' operating as the plaintiff's 'claim' and is to be 'annexed' to Form A which opens with the words 'you are summoned to attend…' operating as the summons.

What the provisions in Section 20 of the regular Recovery Statutes and Section 24 of the Lagos Tenancy Law mean is that a landlord (now better referred to as 'the owner' since the landlord and tenant contract has been determined) who is desirous of recovering possession of premises from his tenant, having first determined the tenancy contract between him and the tenant, and having served on the tenant a written notice of his intention to proceed to recover possession[13] on a date not less than seven days from the date of the service thereof, shall, upon the expiration of the seven days notice, and the tenant neglecting or refusing to quit and deliver up possession, may, at his option, apply to the appropriate court in the local government area where the premises is situated or located for a writ or plaint against the tenant or any person being in possession of the premises but refusing or

13. See Section 17 of the Law (Delta and Edo) No. 4 of 1977. For reasons of elegance and convenience, except otherwise expressed, all references to sections of Recovery Statutes throughout this book are to this Delta and Edo states Law the provisions of which are substantially *impari materia* with all other Recovery Statutes nationwide except the Lagos State Tenancy Law No. 14 of 2011 which contains fundamentally different provisions in some respects.

neglecting to quit or give up possession for the recovery of the premises.

Use of Forms and Variation - This writ or plaint is as in Form F[14] contained in Schedule 1 to the Recovery Statutes. It is to be advisedly used in all cases as the use of the forms in the Schedule, though merely permissive, is good and sufficient in law. The forms are permitted to be used with such variations as circumstances of particular cases require.

One such variation which is required in every case, it is submitted, is the inclusion in the writ or plaint of the grounds for seeking possession. This is necessary so as to enable the court keep in focus such grounds for possession since Section 27 of the Law precludes the court from making any order or giving any judgement for recovery of possession unless, among other considerations, it has powers so to do pursuant to the provisions contained and set out in the Second Schedule to the Recovery Statute.

Endorsing Grounds on Plaint - As stated above, Section 20 of the Law allows for the institution of proceedings for the recovery of possession by applying to the court for the issue of a writ or to enter a plaint as in Form F (TL6B in Lagos State) contained in Schedule I to the Recovery Statutes which by the provision of Section 34 of the Law may be used 'with such variations as the circumstances of the particular case may require'.

Relying on these provisions and the fact that the summons for recovery of possession of tenements as in Form G or Form TL6A in Lagos State requires that the defendant appears before the court to answer the plaintiff's claim for possession 'on the ground stated on the

14. See Appendix A. Form TL6B in Lagos State.

particulars of claim hereto annexed, it is to be highly recommended that the owner (formerly the landlord), in filing his plaint, should endorse thereon the grounds[15] upon which he relies for seeking the order of possession. In Lagos State, this endorsement, by the provisions of Section 16 of the Tenancy Law is required to be on the Seven Days Notice of the owner's intention to recover possession. This is because concluding part of this section provides that

> ...the landlord or his agent may cause the tenant to be served with a written notice as in Form TL4, signed by the landlord or his agent, of the landlord's intention to proceed to recover possession, stating *the grounds* and particulars of the claim, on a date not less than seven (7) days from the date of the notice.

As already pointed out *supra*, statutory notices in Lagos State are not processes of court. In this regard, it is to be submitted that the grounds be better endorsed on the plaint by which the plaintiff commences his action for the recovery of possession and which is a process of court.

The Form TL4 referred to in the provision is *impari materia* with the Form F of the regular Recovery Statutes and provides no additional space for 'stating the grounds and particulars of the claim' as required. Therefore, the plaintiff can achieve the objective by modifying the plaint as in Form G or TL6A being a process of court to be served by an official of the court stating the grounds immediately below the endorsed claim for possession and before his signature thus:

> The plaintiff claims possession and N...... for arrears of rent and *mesne* profits at the rate of N...from the ... day

15. See 'Grounds for Recovery of Possession' *infra* at 131.

of …… 20…. until possession is given up.

GROUNDS

The grounds for seeking possession are

(i) Reasonablenes (ii) Arrears of rent
(iii) Personal Use (iv) Substantial Repairs
(v) Nuisance (vi) Etc. etc.

Signed …………………..
Landlord[16]

Filing the Recovery Action - Having satisfied all conditions precedent to the institution of the action for recovery of possession of premises including the service of the seven days notice but the tenant still neglects or refuses to deliver up possession of the premises, then, upon the expiration of the time stated in the seven days notice, the owner (formerly the landlord) may validly commence legal proceedings in the appropriate court[17] with competent jurisdiction for the recovery of possession of the premises from the tenant.

The landlord may join a claim for arrears of rent and for *mesne* profits in the claim for possession. The claim for arrears of rent and for *mesne* profits are treated as one claim.[18]

The suit is commenced by the landlord when he obtains and files a writ or plaint[19] as in Form F (TL6B in

16. See precedent of a plaint at Appendix A.
17. The Area Customary Courts in Delta and Edo states, Customary and District Courts in Osun State.
18. Section 23.
19. As in Appendix A.

Lagos) together with a summons[20] for recovery of possession of tenements as in Form G (TL6A in Lagos) in Schedule 1[21] of the Recovery Statutes issued from the court.

The Recovery Plaint - The plaint bears the claim of the plaintiff together with the particulars of his claim while the summons contains the proverbial command words summoning the defendant to appear before the court to answer the plaintiff's claim for recovery of possession of the premises. The plaint opens with the plaintiff's allegation claiming possession of the premises thus:

> The plaintiff is entitled to the possession of ... premises situate at …

and goes to state other allegations of the plaintiff's claim such as arrears of rent and *mesne* profits. The plaint also contains statements alleging

> (a) the letting of premises by the landlord to the tenant,
> (b) the rent payable under the letting,
> (c) the expiration of the letting or determination thereof by notice to quit,
> (d) the service of the seven days notice (a copy of which is annexed),
> (e) a description of the mode by which the said seven days was served on the defendant,
> (f) and the refusal of the defendant to deliver up possession.

The Recovery Summons - The summons for the recovery of possession as in Form G (TL6A in Lagos) of Schedule 1

20. As in Appendix B.
21. The Lagos Tenancy Law has only one unnumbered Schedule.

to the Recovery Statutes is different from the regular Civil Summons as in Form 6 of Appendix 1 of the Lagos Magistrates' Courts (Civil Procedure) Rules and in Form A (i)) in the First Schedule to the Customary Courts Rules for Delta and Edo states.

The summons for recovery of possession, like every summons of court, contains the legendary command words for the defendant to appear before the court as its opening line. This is followed by the reason for the command which is for the defendant to answer the plaintiff's claim to recover possession of premises which is concisely described thereon clearly indicating the location of the premises which must be an address of a place within the territorial jurisdiction of the court.

The summons further contains a declaration of the plaintiff's allegation of the grounds on which he claims to be entitled to the possession. This is that the claim for possession is on 'ground(s) stated in the particulars of claim hereto annexed' to the summons. This means that the ground or grounds upon which the plaintiff claims possession must always be endorsed on the plaint to be annexed to the summons.[22]

Seven Days Notice to be Annexed to Plaint - The plaint itself requires that a duplicate copy of the seven days notice served on the tenant prior to the institution of the suit should be annexed thereto together with a description of how the seven days notice was served. This is clearly the purport of the part of the plaint Form F (TL6B in Lagos) which runs thus:

22. See *supra*.

> the plaintiff did serve on the defendant …….. a notice in writing of his intention to apply to recover possession of the said premises (a duplicate of which notice is hereto annexed) by ……(describe the mode in which the service was affected[23]) ….

After filing the suit, a copy each of the summons, the plaint, and the seven days notice annexed thereto are served[24] on the defendant by the bailiff of the court. The original copies are placed in the court's file and paged seriatim.

Defendant's Reaction – The service of any writ of summons or other court process on a party gives notice of the existence of the suit against him. This is so that having become aware of the suit against him, he might if he so desires, resist the claim. In a recovery action, the defendant has a number of options open to him upon his receipt of the process. These include:

Dispute Claim or Counterclaim - The defendant may dispute the claim or may bring a counterclaim against the plaintiff. Whether he disputes the claim or files a counterclaim, the instructions on the summons require him to, within a number of days after service on him of the summons (usually eight days[25]), file a defence to the claim or a counterclaim thereto using the part of the Form G contained in the summons for this purpose. The relevant part of the Summons Form G (TL6A in Lagos) which is addressed to the defendant reads that

23. It is humbly submitted that this ought to read: 'the mode by which the service was effected'.
24. See Chapter Five on Service of Recovery Processes *infra* at 186.
25. The exact number of days is not specified in the Form or in the Recovery Statutes.

> if you dispute the claim or have a counterclaim, you should within … days after service of this summons on you, inclusive of the day of service, send to the Registrar a defence or counterclaim for which the form below may be used.

Dispute Part of Pecuniary Claim - The defendant may dispute part only of the amount claimed by the plaintiff as arrears of rent and or *mesne* profits and admit the difference. In such a case, he is required to pay the amount admitted by him into court while only the part he disputes goes to trial.

Admit Claim and Ask for Time - Where the defendant admits the whole or part of the claim but desires that he be given time to pay up or to give up possession, he is at liberty to within the number of days specified in the summons file an admission in court using the form or space provided for this purpose at the bottom of the summons Form G.[26] This form or space at the bottom of the summons form states thus:

> I dispute the claimant's claim because … (the defendant is then expected to state here the facts he relies on in support of his defence);
>
> or
>
> I admit the claimant's title and his right to immediate possession and offer to give up possession on ….[27]

The above steps are designed in the Recovery Statutes to assist the defendant know what to do in the circumstance of his having been served a court process. If the defendant who, usually, is not a lawyer makes good use of these provisions, he would avoid spending money paying for the

26. See Appendix B.

27. The form contains other alternatives including as to counterclaim.

services of a lawyer and facilitate the speedy disposal of proceedings by either narrowing the issues for trial or outrightly rendering a trial unnecessary.

Unfortunately, these laudable provisions in the Recovery Statutes are, in practice, outrightly ignored not only by litigants but especially by defence counsel, sometimes deliberately, as a way of 'buying' time and thereby delaying the proceedings which can hardly be the intendment of the lawmaker or in the interest of justice.

Counterclaim – A counterclaim is an action or claim filed by a defendant in an action in which he claims, within the same suit, against the plaintiff a remedy or relief in respect of any matter irrespective of how, where, or when the cause of action or claim has arisen instead of filing a separate action.

In substance, a counterclaim is a cross-action[28] by which the plaintiff thereof, instead of filing a separate suit against the defendant in his cross-action who is the plaintiff in the already subsisting suit, inserts his cause of action or claim into the already subsisting suit of the plaintiff and describing his cross action as such counterclaim. The counterclaimant's claim must be one to which he is entitled under relevant laws and rules of court to raise by way of a counterclaim.[29]

Sometimes, a tenant who has been served with a summons in a recovery action may also have a claim against the landlord which he wants the court to also determine. Such a tenant does not need to file a separate suit as he can bring his claim by way of a counterclaim. By

28. *Oragbaide v Onitiju* (1962) 1 ANLR 32, 37.
29. *Oyegbola v Esso West Africa Incorporated* (1966) ANLR 162.

process of a counterclaim, a person who has been sued as a defendant in an action and who also has a claim against the plaintiff may, instead of filing a separate suit, file his claim in the same suit in which he has been sued as defendant. He then becomes a defendant/counterclaimant while the plaintiff becomes a plaintiff/defendant.

The defendant/counterclaimant does not file his counterclaim as a defence to the plaintiff's subsisting claim but as a distinct action albeit within the same suit with the same suit number.

The Set-off – A tenant who has been sued in a recovery action may also react by way of a set-off which is a claim very similar to a counterclaim yet it is not in that a tenant who sets up a defence by way of a set-off is actually saying that the plaintiff says I am owing him XYZ Naira in rent arrears, but he is also owing me ABC Naira in debts from unpaid balance in cost of goods I supplied him.

The following are some other differences between a counterclaim and a set-off:

(a) a set-off is available only for making money claims while the counterclaim can be used for both monetary claims and other kinds of claims.

(b) A set-off is only in the nature of a cross-claim which can be raised only as a defence to a plaintiff's claim but a counterclaim is a cross-action in its own right as a separate suit to which a defence can be and is usually raised.

(c) A set-off swims or sinks with the action so that a discontinuance, dismissal or stay of the action *ipso facto* also brings the set-off to an end. This is not so with a counterclaim which swims or sinks on its own being a distinct and separate action from the plaintiff's suit. If the plaintiff discontinues his suit or it is dismissed or stayed, the discontinuance, dismissal or stay does not affect the counterclaim in any way and may be proceeded with.

(d) Where a set-off may be pleaded as a counterclaim, a counterclaim can only be pleaded by way of a set-off only where it is a monetary claim.

Any cause of action can be set up by a defendant as a counterclaim whether it is of the same nature or type with the plaintiff's claim and it is immaterial that the cause of action has arisen out of the same transaction or not. But it must be one which can be tried by the same court and within the same proceedings of the plaintiff. In this respect, the cause of action of the counterclaimant must be one for which the court has jurisdiction. If the court lacks the jurisdiction for the cause of action had it been independently filed, then the fact of its being filed as a counterclaim cannot invest the court with the jurisdiction which it does not have.

A claim by a co-defendant against a fellow defendant in the same suit is not a counterclaim. A counterclaim must be a suit by a defendant against a plaintiff who has sued the defendant. The plaintiff is therefore a necessary party to a counterclaim and he needs not be counterclaimed against in the same capacity or status in which he has sued the defendant/counterclaimant.

Procedure – Neither the Law establishing most of the courts with summary jurisdictions which exercise recovery jurisdiction nor their Rules contain provisions as to counterclaim. However, where ever a litigant can validly bring an action before a court there also lay a right of action to bring a counterclaim.

Procedurally, in courts where pleadings are filed and whose Rules of court have made provisions for counterclaims, the defendant/counterclaimant is usually required to insert his counterclaim as part of the statement of defence but specifically pleading same separately usually following after the paragraphs making up the statement of defence and under the heading 'Counterclaim' and then introduced by such words as

> … and by way of counterclaim, the defendant repeats the allegations of facts contained in the ... and claims as follows:
>
> The defendant counterclaims against the plaintiff the sum of N500,000.00 being monies expended by the defendant in renovating the premises … etc.

Summary Procedure - However, under the summary jurisdiction of the Recovery Courts, it is sufficient for the defendant/counterclaimant to file his counterclaim as a separate process but within the same suit and with the same suit number. It is important that the defendant formally files his counterclaim notwithstanding that the court is a court of summary jurisdiction. Such process is headed in the usual manner as follows:

IN THE .... COURT OF ... STATE
HOLDEN AT..................

Suit No ....

Between:

CHIEF ONA LINUS……..............................Plaintiff

And

MR. OKUPAYA TITUS...........................Defendant

And Between the said

MR OKUPAYA TITUS ......Defendant/Counterclaimant
And the said
CHIEF ONA LINUS ....Plaintiff/Defendant

The heading, COUNTERCLAIM, is then inserted followed by an endorsement of the claim by way of counterclaim e.g. as follows:

> The defendant counterclaims against the plaintiff the sum of N500,000.00 being monies expended by the defendant in renovating the premises .... etc.

The Particulars of the Counterclaim is then settled thereunder and signed in the usual manner.

Recovery Actions in Customary Courts – As already discussed in Chapter Three, customary courts in most parts of Nigeria are expressly divested of the jurisdiction for possession matters except in Delta, Edo and Osun states. In these three states, when these customary courts sit in respect of possession matters, they acquire a hybrid character as both such customary courts and as regular magistrate courts. This is because in such proceedings these courts are required to

> observe the provisions of the Rent Control and Recovery of Residential Premises Law

and Section 7 (3) of the said Rent Control and Recovery of Residential Premises Law in turn provides that

> subject to the provisions of (the) Law, a (court) shall be bound by the practice and procedure in civil matters in the Magistrates' Courts[29]

despite that they are customary courts retaining their characteristics as such customary courts including, for instance, sitting with a President and two other members[30] in Delta and Edo states as against Magistrates who constitute the court sitting alone. The effect of this is that the Civil Procedure Rules made for the Magistrates' Courts are binding on these customary courts with respect to recovery action just as they are binding on Rent Tribunals in those states where the courts with summary jurisdiction for recovery suits are so designated.

But it is generally said that there are no particular forms or modes prescribed for commencing proceedings in the customary courts or that the mode or form of their commencements is not material. What is important, it is stressed, is that substantial justice is done. But, as can be seen from the above analysis, this does not mean that causes or matters, especially recovery causes or matters, can be brought to the customary courts in an indefinable and indiscriminate manner.

What the notion simply represents is that a court of appeal shall not set aside any proceedings or declare them a nullity and thereby defeat the objects of justice only by reason of how the proceedings were brought to or commenced in the customary courts. Indeed the Rules of these customary courts make provisions for how causes and matters shall be commenced.

These should be complied with all the time. Although there are provisions also in the Rules in support of substantial compliance with the Rules, it must be stressed that substantial compliance does not mean a wholesale disregard of the Rules but that they may be

29. See also Section 2 (5) of the Lagos State Tenancy Law No. 14 of 2011 which refers also to '*the practice and procedure in civil matters in ... or the high court...*'.

30. In Osun State, the District Customary Court is presided over by a legal practitioner of no less than seven years post call sitting alone to constitute the court.

modified to suit particular circumstances. They are not to be observed in the breach in the name of substantial compliance such that what is obtained becomes substantial non-compliance.

Chapter Five
Service of Recovery Processes

The regularity or validity of court processes and their proper service ... is a condition precedent to an order for possession ...
- *Akeju v Shonibare* (1968) 2 ANLR 159

Service - The process leading to the recovery of premises is commenced by the issuance and service of statutory notices followed by the issuance and service of the summons applied for by the landlord or his agent following the expiration of the period stated in the seven days notice of owner's intention to apply to recover possession.

Upon the due issue of the summons from the registry of the court to eject any person from the premises sought to be recovered, it becomes a process of the court and the next thing to be done in order to effectively activate the jurisdiction of the court is to serve it on the defendant/defendants.

Service of the summons or any other process of court is the bringing to the notice of the other party that such a process against that other person has been filed or instituted. Such service is usually accomplished by delivering the process to that other party in a manner prescribed by the Rules of court. The court will be without jurisdiction without service of the process.

Object of Service - The Supreme Court in *United Nigeria Press Ltd v Adebanjo,*[1] has explained that the object of all types of service of a writ of summons or other court process is to give notice to the other party on whom

1. 1969 ANLR 422. See also *Eimskip Ltd v Exquisite Industries Ltd* (2003) 4 NWLR (Pt. 809) 88, 117.

service is required to be effected so that he might be aware of the suit against him so that, if he so desires, will be able to resist the claim.

Service of court process is therefore a fundamental requirement for the effective activation of the competence of the court with regard to the cause or matter and the failure to serve gives rise to an incurable fundamental vice. The Rules of court usually prohibit the court from assuming jurisdiction over any cause or matter which depends upon any process being served unless service is proved or deemed to have been effected or admitted by the person on whom the summons is required to be served.

Therefore, where service of a court process is required, as the summons is, failure to serve it operates as a fundamental vice which makes every step taken in the proceedings including the proceedings themselves and the judgement thereon, if any, a nullity and liable to be set aside.[2]

Applicable Law for Service of Process - The applicable law relating to service of recovery processes is to be found in the various states Recovery Statutes, the Magistrates' Court Laws, the Magistrates Civil Procedure Rules; as well as the High Court Rules and Customary Courts Rules in the relevant states. These statutory provisions and Rules of court are substantially the same in all the states except in the numbering of sections and orders. A reference to one of them is therefore as good a reference to any of them and, for purposes of this chapter, references shall be made interchangeably to the Lagos State and Delta State provisions.

2. *Obimonure v Erinosho* (1966) ANLR 245.

Statutory Notices are Court Processes – The statutory notices, namely the notice to quit and the notice of owner's intention to apply to recover possession, by virtue of the requirement that they have to be filed[3] at the court registry before they are served, are court processes. Therefore, some of the rules relating to service of court processes to be discussed in this chapter will relate to them.

How and by whom Statutory Notices Served – The Recovery Statutes provide that service of any of the statutory notices (i.e. the quit notice or the seven days notice) shall be effected in accordance with the law for the time being in force in relation to the service of civil processes in the magistrate's court.

Section 28 of the erstwhile Lagos State Rent Control and Recovery of Residential Premises Law (Cap. R6) which is *impari materia* with Section 32 of the Law and all other Recovery Statutes provision in this respect runs thus:

> service of any notice[4] under the provisions of this Law or any summons, warrant or other process shall be effected in accordance with the provisions of the Law for the time being in force relating to the service of the civil process of magistrate's courts and if the defendant cannot be found and his place of dwelling shall either

3. See Section 32 of the Rent Control and Recovery of Residential Premises Law (Delta and Edo) hereinafter referred to simply as 'the Recovery Statute' or 'the Law' which is *impari materia* with all other Recovery Statutes including Section 28 of the Lagos State Law prior to the enactment of its Tenancy Law No. 14 of 2011 Section 22 of which now omits 'notice' from this provision. See also Adefarasin CJ. in *Idowu v Adekanmi* (1975) 6 CCHCJ 923.
4. Section 22 of the Lagos Tenancy Law omits the word 'notice'.

not be known, or admission thereto cannot be obtained for serving any such process, a copy of the process shall be pasted on some conspicuous part of the premises sought to be recovered and such pasting shall deemed good service on the defendant.

The Magistrate's Court (Civil Procedure) Rules make rules for normal modes and substituted modes of serving its civil processes. These are that the process shall be served by delivering same on the person to be served (the personal service) or where this cannot be conveniently effected, the court may, upon being satisfied by affidavit evidence that it is necessary to do so, order that the service be effected by some other substituted means.[5]

What the above means is that statutory notices must be served the way a normal court process is served i.e. they must be served by such officers of the court as are authorized by law. Such officers are usually the bailiffs and other messengers appointed by the Judicial Service Commission, and police officers. Their statutory duties include service and execution of all writs and other processes issued from the court.[6]

But, in practice, statutory notices are in, some parts of the country,[7] ordinarily not regarded or considered as court processes for purposes of service. They are treated as private documents raised or produced by either counsel in chambers or the landlord or his agent. Being private

5. See Order 4 Rules 3 and 4 (a) to (e) of Magistrate's Court (Civil Procedure) Rules (Delta and Edo), Order 6 Rule 1 and 2 (a) to (e) Lagos State.
6. See Section 40 Magistrates' Court Law (Lagos State); Section 17 Customary Courts Law (Delta and Edo states).
7. In Lagos State, for instance.

documents, they do not therefore come within the 'writs and other processes' of court which court bailiffs and messengers or the police are under a statutory duty to serve. To bring them within the ambit of civil processes of a magistrate's court, statutory notices must first be filed at the registry of the court and appropriate filing and mileage fees paid.

This is the requirement of the Recovery Statutes as shown above. It is only upon their filing that statutory notices can be properly referred to as 'processes of court' for which the court bailiff or messenger or a police officer shall be under a duty to serve and which service becomes the only valid service recognized by law.

In *Ayinla v Fagbemi,*[8] Onyeama J. of the then Lagos High Court correctly held that

> service by a person not authorized to serve a process would be an invalid service for the law requires particular formalities to be observed in connection with the service of notices under the Recovery of Premises *laws.*

In effect, only a bailiff of the court or any other officer of the court appointed in that behalf can serve a statutory notice as to do otherwise will render not only the service but also the notice invalid.[9]

This is in agreement with the provisions of Section

8. (1964) LLR 119.
9. *ibid* where statutory notice served by a solicitor's clerk was held invalid but this is no longer the law in Lagos State in view of the proviso to Order 6 Rule 6 of the Magistrates' Court Rules which is to the effect that '*service of any notice of determination of tenancy or of intention to recover possession under the Recovery of Residential Premises Law may be served by the landlord or his agent as if he were a bailiff.* Consider also Section 22 Tenancy Law. See *infra.*

32 of the Recovery Statute requiring that service of statutory notices be

> effected in accordance with the provisions of the Law for the time being in force relating to the service of the civil process of magistrate's courts.

Also Section 17 of the Customary Courts Law for Delta and Edo States provide that the state Judicial Service Commission shall appoint fit and proper persons as bailiffs and messengers of the court whose duties shall be to

> (a) effect the service and execution of all writs and other processes ....

By subsection 4 of this section, no person other than a duly appointed bailiff or messenger shall carry out or purport to or attempt to effect the service and execution of writs or other processes of the court.

Apart from the position in Lagos State where the proviso to Order 6 Rule 6 of the Magistrates' Court Rules is to the effect that

> service of any notice of determination of tenancy or of intention to recover possession under the Recovery of Residential Premises Law may be served by the landlord or his agent as if he were a bailiff,[10]

there is nothing in the other Recovery Statutes nationwide to suggest that service of statutory notices may otherwise be effected. Besides, the provision of the Recovery Statutes, safe for Lagos State, helps to check sharp practices since the registry dates stamped on the notices upon their filing can be of great assistance to the court in doing justice. Even though the learned Nsofor J. in *Emekwuru v Inyama*[11] had expressed the view that

---

10. Statutory notices are not processes of court in Lagos State.
11. (1980) IMSLR 74, 76.

> the law has not designated any particular person or officer to serve the notice on the tenant,

and that the

> resort to the services of the court bailiffs to effect the service of notices to quit is nothing more than a matter of convenience

his lordship did not lose sight of the importance of serving the statutory notices through bailiffs and other court officers when his lordship declared also in the same passage of his judgement that

> it facilitates the proof of such service and so avoids the possible denial of the defendant that he was so served.

Statutory Notices not Court Processes in Lagos State – As already pointed out above, Section 22 of the Lagos State Tenancy Law No. 14 of 2011 now provides for the service of court processes omitting the word 'notice' and thereby excluding notices as processes of court which are required to be served in accordance with the provisions of the law for the time being in force relating to the service of civil process of Magistrates' Courts or the High Court.

There is now a Section 17 (1) of this law instead which provides that service of statutory notices 'shall be by proper service as prescribed under Sections 18 and 19' of the Tenancy Law. Proper service is then defined in subsection (2) as

> service in such a manner that it can be established to the satisfaction of the court that the person to be served will have knowledge of any of the notices.

Proper Service on Residential Tenant Personal – Section 18 of the this Lagos innovative Tenancy Law proclaims that

> proper service on a tenant of residential premises shall

> be personal service

and that the court will be satisfied that a tenant of a residential premises will have knowledge of any statutory notice served on him if the plaintiff establishes that the tenant was personally[12] served which in this respect will include[13] but not limited to

> (a) service on the tenant in person;[14]
> (b) delivery to any adult[15] residing at the premises to be recovered;
> (c) by courier where the tenant cannot be found, by delivering same at the premises sought to be recovered and the courier shall provide proof of delivery; or
> (d) affixing[15] the notice on a prominent[16] part of the premises to be recovered and providing corroborative[15] proof of service.

The bare provision requiring that notices be affixed on a prominent part of the premises is too open-ended and open to abuse. Affixing the notice on the 'front door or entrance of the premises to be recovered' would be more specific and less vague. This is the provision of Order 6 Rule 2 (d) of the Lagos Magistrates' Court Rules in relation to substituted service of court processes generally which is to the effect that

> where it appears to the court that … for any reason … service in respect of any process whatsoever … cannot

12. Section 18 Tenancy Law.
13. See Section 18 (1) to (4).
14. This is the usual mode nationwide. See *infra*.
15. Delivering to '*any adult residing at the premises*', or '*affixing … on a … part of the premises*' without leave of court first sought and had leaves itself open to abuse by landlords and agents.
16. This is vague as to what part of premises is prominent and as to what amounts to corroborative proof.

conveniently be effected, the court, after being satisfied by affidavit that it is necessary so to do, may order that service be effected

(d) by affixing the process together with a copy of the order in a *conspicuous* position in the *entrance or on a door* of the usual or last known place of abode or business of the person to be served. (Emphasis supplied)

and which is to be preferred to the bare provisions of the Tenancy Law especially when it is realized that the 'affixing' in the Tenancy Law is without a prior court order and it is not by way of substituted service but it is 'proper service' which, with due respects, is certainly not personal even the law defines it so.

Proper Service on Business Tenant – Where the tenant to be served with statutory notices is a tenant of a business premises, Section 19 of the Tenancy Law in Lagos State provides that the court shall be satisfied that the tenant will have knowledge thereof if the notice is

(a) delivered to a person at the business premises sought to be recovered; or

(b) affixed to on a prominent part of the premises sought to be recovered and providing corroborative proof of service.

The introduction of the concept of *proper service* in relation to the service of statutory notices by the Tenancy Law of Lagos State amounts to legalizing a procedure which has long been in practice, albeit in breach of the statutory provision in this respect, in that state. It is a procedure which neglects the provisions of Section 28 of Cap. R6 that

service of any notice under the provisions of this Law …

> shall be effected in accordance with the provisions of the Law for the time being in force relating to the service of the civil process of Magistrate's Courts ....

Under which the notices would first be filed in the court's Registry and thereby render them as court processes and which must be served by officers of the court in whom the court would repose greater confidence and trust.

With the greatest respects, there is nothing attractive in the concept of proper service as presently defined especially in the face of the provisions of Section 22 of this Law which has omitted the service of 'notices'

> in accordance with the provisions of the law for the time being in force relating to the service of civil

processes of the courts and the provisions of Order 6 Rule 6 of the Magistrates' Courts Civil Procedure Rules which permits landlords and their agents to serve statutory notices 'as if they were bailiffs'.

This is bound to encourage massive abuse of the court process relating to service of these notices and will ultimately lead to monumental injustice especially in a state like Lagos State where '*jankara*'[17] practice in relation to actions for recovery of premises is well known and very common.

Not withstanding this legalization, the attraction in the old practice as provided for in Section 28 of Cap. R6 which had always been obeyed in its breach in any event, is still to be preferred in the interest of justice. It is to be reintroduced and conscious steps taken by the courts to

17. A practice whereby judgements and orders of court are obtained by fraud in the absence of or without serving the defendant or the person against whom the judgement or order is obtained.

ensure compliance.

There is no provision in the new Lagos Law forbidding a landlord or his agent from following the old but neglected practice with a view to minimizing the time which is usually wasted in unnecessary arguments in court as to whether statutory notices were validly served. As Mbanefo CJ. put it in *Nnadozie v Oluoma,*[18]

> there is nothing to prevent a landlord serving his tenant notice by himself or through his solicitor[19] but I suppose this invariably leads to argument as to whether it has in fact been served or not, and landlords in Port Harcourt prefer to use the services of court bailiffs in this respect.

These words of the learned Chief Justice of the then Eastern Region (as he then was) some nearly five decades ago still holds water today in Lagos in the face of the provisions of Sections 17, 18, and 19 of the Tenancy Law No. 14 of Lagos State.

How and by whom Summons Served – All the Rules of courts make specific provisions relating to the service of their processes. These provisions are substantially the same in relation to all Recovery Courts. The applicable Rules are usually those of the magistrates' courts all of which provide for both normal and substituted modes for service of court processes as well as for service out of jurisdiction.[20]

Order III Rule 2 of the Customary Court's Rules for Delta and Edo states, for instance, provides that any

18. (1963) ENLR 77. See also Nsofor J. in *Emekwuru v Inyama* (1980) IMSLR 74, 76.
19. This, except in Lagos, can hardly be a correct statement of the law in view of the provisions of Section 32 of the Recovery Statute.
20. See, for instance, Order 4 Magistrates' Court (Civil Procedure) Rules for Delta and Edo states; Order 6 (Lagos).

process, including the summons, issued by the court and requiring service shall be served upon the person to whom reference is made therein by such officers of the court as are authorized by law in that behalf.

These officers usually include the Sheriff of the court who also is usually the court's Chief Registrar at the very apex, the Deputy Sheriff, bailiffs and messengers the last two being the ones who actually carry out the service of processes in the name of the court sheriff. In some cases, the court may direct a police officer and, in some courts, an officer of a local government, attached to the court to effect service of the court process including the summons.

Section 40 of the Magistrates' Courts Law (Cap. 127) Laws of Lagos State 1994 in this regard provides that

> all summonses, warrants, orders, judgements, writs of execution or other process or proceedings, whether civil or criminal … respecting any cause or matter *may* be served or executed … by a bailiff of the court or by a member of the police force to whom the same may be directed or any other member of the police.

Similarly, Section 17 of the Customary Courts Law (Delta and Edo) provides that the Judicial Service Commission of the state shall appoint fit and proper persons as bailiffs and messengers of the court whose duties *shall* include to effect the service and execution of all writs and other processes issued from the court.

No person other than a duly appointed bailiff or messenger shall carry out or purport to or attempt to carry out the duties of a bailiff or messenger.[21] Accordingly, even

21. Subsection 4 of Section 17 of the Customary Courts Law (Delta and Edo).

though Section 40 of the Lagos State Magistrates' Courts Law employs the permissive *may*,[22] only a bailiff or messenger of court can effect service of the summons (especially) or other process of the court requiring service. This position is further strengthened by the provision of Order 6 Rule 6 (Lagos) in which the imperative '*shall*' is employed to the effect that

> service of process *shall* be effected by a bailiff of the court or a member of the police force (as provided by Section 40 of the Law) but a magistrate may order service to be effected by any person designated by him.

Modes of Service – There are mainly three modes of serving the summons. These are

(a) the personal service,
(b) the substituted service, and
(c) the service other than personal.

By the various court Rules, provision is made for these three modes of service in what the law describes as

(a) normal service which is same as personal service,
(b) substituted service which is resorted to where personal service cannot be conveniently effected, and
(c) service other than personal service being a mode of service in situations where no mode of service has been prescribed by any Law or Rule of court.

Order 4 Rule 3 (1) of the Delta and Edo states Magistrates' Courts (Civil Procedure) Rules,[23] for instance, provides that

22. Section 17 of the Customary Courts Law (Delta and Edo) uses the mandatory '*shall*'.
23. See also Order 6 (Lagos State).

normal service is that kind of service of a summons which, subject to the Magistrates' Courts Law and of any other written law, is effected by delivering same together with the plaint annexed thereto on the party to be served.

But where it appears to the court, either with or without an attempt at service in accordance with the provisions of the above Rule of the said Order 4, that for any reason such service in respect of any process whatsoever cannot conveniently be effected, the court, after being satisfied by affidavit that it is so to do, may order that service be effected in some other form not being normal service. Such other form of service is described as substituted service.[24]

Normal Service – Normal service consists mainly in the delivering of the court process to the person to be served personally in the following circumstances:

Personal Service – By personal service, Rules require that the summons shall be served personally on the person to whom it is addressed. This is accomplished by delivering the process personally on or to the person who is required to be served.

Because of the fundamental nature of service in litigation, the rule regarding personal service of the summons must be complied with except in those situations permitted by the Rules or where the court considers that it is just and expedient to direct otherwise.

Accordingly, except by leave of court, service on the spouse or agent of the person to be served is not good service. Even where a husband and his wife are sued together, each of them shall be separately served personally

24. Order 4 Rule 4 (Delta and Edo); Order 6 Rule 2 (Lagos).

unless the court otherwise directs. Similarly, a defendant cannot be served through a co-defendant.[25] Each defendant must be separately served personally.

In effecting personal service, the court bailiff or such other officer of court as is authorized by law in that behalf must hand the summons to the defendant or leave it with him personally after ensuring that the person is in fact the defendant or the person to be served.

Personal Service on Person Resisting Service - Where the defendant refuses to accept the service or threatens the bailiff with violence, the bailiff or process server shall inform the person to be served in clear and concise language the nature and content of the process and thereafter leave the process by dropping same with the person to be served.[26]

Order 6 Rule 10 of the Lagos State Magistrates' Court Rules provides for how personal service of a court process is to be effected on a person resisting service in the following words:

> where service is to be effected by delivering a document to the person to be served (i.e. personal service) and such person refuses to take the document, it is sufficient to inform such person of the nature of the document and to throw it down near him.

In *Martins v Komolafe*,[27] the tenant refused service of the process. The server then informed him of the contents and pasted same on the door of the tenant in the tenant's presence. The Lagos High Court per De Lestang CJ held

25. *Management Enterprises Ltd v Otusanya* (1987) 2 NWLR 179.
26. *Martins v Komolafe* (1961) LLR 14.
27. *Supra.*

this constituted good service explaining that the object of the rule is to ensure that the process is left with the person to be served and that it did not matter whether the process was thrown at the feet of the person to be served or placed on a table nearby or posted on the door in the presence of the person to be served and that

> so long as (the person to be served) is made aware of the contents of the (process) and so long as it is left behind, the service … is good.

Also, in *Green v Olorunkoya*,[28] the process was served on the tenant contained in an envelope. The court held the service to be good service since the essential thing is that the person serving knows what he is serving and the person being served knows what is being served on him.

Accordingly, if, as in the *Olorunkoya* case, the person to be served the process contained in the envelope is not informed of the content of the envelope so that he is aware thereof, the service will be invalid.[29]

Copy to be served - It is usual to serve a duplicate copy of the summons or process. The original copy is normally placed in the court's file as the first page. But it is to be observed that the Customary Courts Rules for Delta and Edo states in all its provisions[30] relating to service refer to 'the process' and not a copy thereof.

Service other than Personal Service - Apart from personal service, the Rules provide for other forms of service not being personal. Rule 11 of Order 6 of the Lagos State magistrates' Court Rules provides that

28. (1974) 7 CCHCJ 1031.
29. See the English decision in *Banque Russ v Clarke* (1894) W.N. 203.
30. Except Order III Rule 4 (a) Customary Courts Rules 2007 (Delta).

where in any proceedings in the court any process is required to be served on any person and no other mode of service is prescribed by any Law or Rule

then the provisions which follow thereunder shall apply. These provisions are:

Address for Service by Person to Served – Where an address has been given by the person to be served, service shall be sufficiently effected by sending the process by registered post to such address or by delivering the process at the address for service to an adult person employed or residing at such address.

Proprietor of Business – If the person to be served is the proprietor of a business, service shall be sufficiently effected by delivering the process at his place of business or sending it by registered post to his last known place of business.

Person to be Served Represented by Counsel – Where the person to be served is acting by a legal practitioner, service shall be sufficiently effected by delivering the process at or sending it by registered post the legal practitioner's address for service.

This is similar but quite different from the position in Rule 8 of this same Order where a legal practitioner represents that he is authorized to accept service of an ordinary summons on behalf of a defendant. Under Rule 8, there is no requirement as to service by registered post but only that it shall be sufficient to deliver the summons to such legal practitioner if the legal practitioner shall endorse upon the process server's copy of the summons a memorandum stating that he accepts service thereof on behalf of the defendant and gives an address for service within the state.

In all of the above situations where process has been served by way of registered post, it shall, unless the contrary is proved, be deemed to have been served at the time when the registration slip would have reached the person to be served in the ordinary course of post, and in proving service of the process, it shall be sufficient to prove that the process was properly addressed, franked or prepaid, and sent by registered post.

Service on Public Servant – Also by Order III Rule 3 (2) of the Customary Courts Rules for Delta and Edo states, where it is intended to serve a person who is employed in the public service of the state government or a local government in the state, the service may be effected by posting the summons or other process to the head of department wherein the person to be served works or, in the case of a local government to the secretary of the local government council where the person to be served works.

The head of department or the secretary, as the case may be, shall, upon his receipt of the summons or other process, arrange for service upon the person to be served.[31] For proof of this kind of service, it shall be sufficient for the head of service or secretary, as the case may be, to write to the court stating that the person has been served.[32]

Substituted Service - There often arise situations where personal service is impossible or cannot be conveniently effected so that service by some other mode becomes imperative. The Rules have accordingly made provisions for such situations.

31. Order III Rule 3 (2). This procedure is applicable in all the states of the federation by different statutory provisions.
32. Order III Rule 3 (3).

By Order III Rule 4of the Customary Courts Rules for Delta and Edo states and Order 6 Rule 2 of the Lagos State Magistrates' Courts (Civil Procedure) Rules, whenever it appears to the court that, for any reason, personal service of the summons or any other process of court cannot be conveniently effected, the court may, upon being satisfied by affidavit or sworn evidence that it is necessary to serve the summons or other process by substituted means, order that the service may so be effected.

The court may make the order for substituted service either before or after some previous attempt at personal service had been made. In practice, a court will almost always insist that some attempt at personal service be first made before an application for substituted service may be brought to court for consideration. Where no previous attempt had been made to personally serve the process, the reason or grounds upon which the court will grant the leave for substituted service must be strong, cogent and very convincing.

One of such strong and very convincing reason would be when the tenant is dead and there is exhibited a certificate of death duly issued by the National Population Commission evidencing the death and nobody can be found claiming to be the relation of the tenant whose rent has fallen into arrears. In situations such as this, the application for substituted service may be granted without evidence of a previous attempt at personal service.[33]

Substituted Service Without Leave of Court? Service of the summons or other process by substituted means can be resorted to only with leave of court as otherwise such

33. See the discussion on Force Open *infra*.

service will be invalid. However, the provisions of Section 32 of the Law seem to suggest that service of all kinds of process can be effected by substituted means without leave of court where the person to be served cannot be found and his dwelling place unknown. The section provides that

> service of any notice under the provisions of this *(Law)* or any summons, warrant or other process shall be effected in accordance with the provisions of the law for the time being in force relating to the service of the civil process of magistrate's court and if the defendant cannot be found, and his place of dwelling shall either not be known, or admission thereto cannot be obtained for serving any such process, a copy of the process shall be pasted on some conspicuous part of the premises sought to be recovered, and such pasting shall be deemed good service on the defendant.

The provision does not restrict itself to 'service of any notice' under the Law but extends to 'any summons' which must be taken to include the writ of summons for commencing the suit. It refers also to 'warrant or other process' which must be taken to include warrants for possession. These can all be served, under the provision, by pasting same on some conspicuous part of the premises sought to be recovered apparently without the need of the plaintiff satisfying the court by affidavit that it is necessary so to do and without first obtaining leave of the court so to do.

Indeed, Nsofor J. of the then Imo State High Court in *Emekwuru v Inyama*[34] was unhesitant in holding that the Recovery Statute in Imo State

> has done away with the necessity to obtain leave of court

34. *Supra.*

> for substituted service of the notices or summons or warrants etc provided the conditions therein set out exist.

Influenced apparently by this decision of Nsofor J. and that of Hubbard J. in *Chiwete v Amissah*[35] where the court also held that

> it is doubtful ... that an application ... should be necessary for substituted service either of a notice to quit or of a notice of intention to proceed to recover possession. I have certainly not heard of one being made and I suggest that substituted service of such notice[36] should be deemed to be governed by the second limb of section 28,

Professor Emeka Chianu also without any hesitation declares that

> there is no need to obtain an order of court for substituted service to effect it.

It is with the greatest respects to their lordships and the erudite learned law professor that it is humbly submitted that the provisions of Section 32 of the Law (Section 28 of Cap. R6 in Lagos) is clear and without any ambiguity and it is doubtful if their lordships' position represents a correct statement, spirit and intendment of the law.

There is no legal justification for the dismembering of section 28 as Hubbard J. did in *Chiwete v Amissah* nor is there any legal reason advanced by his lordship why, after dismembering the section, the second limb only should be made applicable to substituted service. The Recovery Statutes provide that for service of process, the Magistrate Courts' civil procedure Rules shall apply. This also means

35. (1957) LLR 1.
36. His lordship refers here only to notices but in *Emekwuru v Inyama* Nsofor J. extends it to the '*summons, warrants etc*'.

that where there is need to serve the defendant by substituted means because

> the defendant cannot be found, and his place of dwelling shall either not be known, or admission thereto cannot be obtained for serving any such process, a copy of the process shall be pasted on some conspicuous part of the premises sought to be recovered

applying the provisions of the Magistrates' Court Law and the Magistrates' (Civil Procedure) Rules and this is that for substituted service, the court shall make orders therefor

> after being satisfied by affidavit that it is necessary so to do.

The court cannot be 'satisfied by affidavit', it is humbly submitted, unless an application has been made to it with respect to the subject matter of substituted service supported by the 'affidavit'.

The correct statement of the law therefore is that whenever it appears to the court, upon an application made to it, that service of any court process required to be served personally cannot for any reason whatsoever be so served conveniently, the court may order that such process be served by some other mode. This court ordered 'other mode' is what is known as substituted service.

This service by some other mode which is mostly by pasting is done only upon leave of the court. The order therefor is made only after the court is made satisfied by affidavit or sworn evidence that it is necessary to do so.[37]

Forms of Substituted Service - The term 'substituted service' is applicable to different modes of non-personal

37. *United Nigeria Press Ltd v Adebanjo* (1969) ANLR 431; Order 4 Rule 4 Magistrate Courts (Civil Procedure) Rules; Order III Rule 4 Customary Courts Rules (Delta and Edo), Order 6 Rule 2 (Lagos).

service by which notice of the process is brought to the defendant or the person to be served. The mode adopted in each particular case will depend on the peculiar circumstance of each case provided that the mode adopted will meet the object of service i.e. to bring the process to the notice of the person to whom the process is addressed.

In all the courts with jurisdiction for possession matters, the appropriate Rules and practice accommodate and make provisions for the following modes of serving processes by substituted means:

Service on Agent - The court may order that service be effected by delivering the process to some person who is an agent[38] of the person to be served or to some other person connected or related to the person to be served.

For the court to make this kind of order for substituted service, the court must be satisfied that there is a 'reasonable probability' that the copy of the process would, in the ordinary course of things, come to the knowledge of the person to be served through that agent or through that other person.

Service by Advertisement - Substituted service may also be effected with leave of court by advertising the process in some newspaper circulating within the jurisdiction of the court.

As in all types of service, the object of this mode is to bring to the notice of the person to be served the existence of the process against him. The court will have to be satisfied that this object will be met in the circumstance of each case before making the order for advertisement in a

38. Order III Rule 4 (a) Customary Courts Rules (Delta/Edo); Order 6 Rule 2 (a) Magistrates' Court (Civil Procedure) Rules (Lagos).

newspaper. Therefore, where the court serves a rural community where newspapers are a rarity and the parties are mostly from a non-literate populace, the court will be more circumspect in making orders for service by advertisement in newspapers.

This is particularly so with quite a number of Area Customary Courts in Delta and Edo states which are usually located deliberately in rural areas to serve communities where newspapers are not a common feature of the people's lives. Besides, even where newspapers are available, the cost element of advertising may be a problem to the litigant.

Service by Pasting - By this mode of substituted service which is perhaps the most common, the process is ordered to be affixed to a conspicuous place at the usual or last known place of abode or of business of the person to be served. The pasting need not be at the premises sought to be recovered. It is to be pasted at

> the usual or last known place of abode or business of the person to be served[39]

where there is a probability that the person sought to be served will come to a knowledge or an awareness of the process served.

Order 6 Rule 2 (d) of the Lagos Magistrates' Court Rules provides for this as

> affixing … in a conspicuous position in the entrance or on a door of the usual or last known place of abode or business of the person to be served

which is to be preferred as it specifies that the pasting be in a 'conspicuous position in the entrance or on a door'.

39. Order III Rule 4 (c) Customary Courts Rules.

Unavoidably, the person to be served, if in fact the place is his usual place of abode, will make us of the entrance or door and will inevitably come upon the process which has been conspicuously pasted thereat.

But see Section 18 (d) of the Lagos Tenancy Law No. 14 of 2011 which now requires that statutory notices may be served by substituted means without leave of court merely by

> affixing the notice on a prominent part of the premises to be recovered and providing corroborative proof of service.

There is no prescription in the Tenancy Law as to what may suffice as 'prominent' and this is bound to create interpretative problems in the courts. Also the affixing is to be done at the 'premises to be recovered' and not at a usual place where the person to be served frequents. Again, this may raise doubts as to whether the pasting will command the requisite 'reasonable probability' that the process will in the ordinary course of things come to the knowledge of the person to be served.

In order to obviate these type of doubts, some courts, in practice, while making orders for pasting, sometimes advisedly include a directive that photographic evidence of the pasting be provided as part of the proof of the service. This is to check or reduce the abuse to which this mode of substituted service can be subjected and perhaps meet the 'corroborative proof' requirement of the new Section 18 (d) of the Lagos Tenancy Law.

The practice of photographic evidence as corroborative proof in all situations of substituted service by pasting is, in all humility to be recommended. When ordered, the photographs are to be annexed to the affidavit of service and appropriately numbered as exhibits in the usual manner.

Pasting on Abandoned Premises in Lagos – By Section 15 of the Lagos Tenancy Law, where the tenancy in respect of any premises has expired and the tenant has not occupied the premises since the expiration of the tenancy and has not given up lawful possession thereof, the premises will be deemed to be abandoned.

To recover possession of such an abandoned premises, subsection 2 (a) of Section 15 of the Tenancy Law requires that the

> landlord shall issue a seven days notice of the landlord's intention to recover possession … which shall be served by pasting the notice on the abandoned premises.

The provision does not require that the pasting shall be effected by a prior leave of court sought and obtained.

Pasting on the Court House – The Lagos Magistrates' Court Civil Procedure Rules provides another mode of substituted service which requires that the court processes may be served

> by notice affixed in a conspicuous position at the court house or some other place of public resort in that part of (the state) wherein the proceedings in respect of which the service is made have been instituted.[40]

It would appear in this situation that it is not merely the pasting of the process that is required but a pasting of a notice as to the process which is to be pasted. Obviously, this mode of service is fraught with problems and the averments in support will need to be strong, cogent and very compelling for a court to be satisfied that it is

40. Order 6 Rule 2 (c).

necessary so to do and order service to be effected on the person to be served by such notice.

The person to be so served must be someone who frequents the particular court premises or such other place of public resort or possibly works there such that the pasting of the notice of the court process thereat will in the ordinary course of things bring to his knowledge the existence of the court process.

Service by other Manner **-** The Rules provide that the court may make orders for substituted service in such other manner as the court may direct.[41] This means that the list of the modes for substituted service is not closed as the court may, in its discretion, make orders as to any other mode not listed but which in its view will meet the requirements of the objects of service and the interests of justice.

Substituted Service: Procedure for - The application for substituted service in all cases is brought by way of motion *ex parte* supported by affidavit. The prayer seeks leave of the court to serve the specific process of court by substituted means.

The Prayer - The process sought to be served must be properly described and the mode of substituted service to be adopted specified on the motion paper. Also the address or the place where the pasting is to be done must be clearly and specifically described so as to enable the court come to a proper determination whether the object of service will be met thereby. A fair illustration of the prayer in the motion paper should read like:

> Take notice etc… for an order granting leave to the applicant to serve the writ of summons on the

41. Order III Rule 4(d) Customary Courts Rules; Order 6 Rule 2 (e) (Lagos).

defendant by

either

(a) pasting same on the front door of the defendant's last known place of abode (or place of business) at No. 1 Linus Ona Street, Enugu

or

(b) delivering same to Mrs. Titus Okupaya who is the defendant's wife (or agent) who now occupies the premises at No. 1Linus Ona Street, Kaduna

or

(c) advertising same in the *Posetion Newspaper* being a newspaper in circulation within the jurisdiction of this honourable court

or

(d) notice hereof affixed to the entrance of this honourable court.

The Affidavit in Support - The efforts made at personal service by the bailiff must be deposed to in the affidavit in support in good and sufficient details e.g. how many times and at what dates and times of the day the attempts were made. The fact that the person sought to be served cannot be found or that his place of dwelling is not known, or that although his place of dwelling is known but admission or access thereto cannot be obtained for purpose of serving the process shall also be deposed to by the process server.

After deposing to all relevant facts as above, the deponent shall then aver that he believes that by the mode of substituted service proposed, the court process will come to the notice and knowledge of the person to be served.

Bailiff to Depose to Affidavit - The affidavit in support of an application to serve the writ of summons or other originating process by substituted means shall be deposed to by the bailiff of the court or such other officer of the court as has been authorized to serve the process and whose duty it is statutorily to serve all originating processes.

An affidavit deposed to by any other person in this regard e.g. the applicant himself or counsel or counsel's staff will not do. The service of originating processes is the statutory duties of court officers[42] and the court will more likely believe its own officers in statements of facts and circumstances to which the officer deposes of his own personal knowledge in line with the provisions of Section 115 of the Evidence Act 2011 than the statements of any other person who, most likely, has an interest in the proceedings and more likely ready to depose to falsehood and mislead the court.

Since the Law mandatorily requires that service of originating processes shall be by the bailiff or such other court officers as are duly authorized in that regard, it is only they who should depose to the facts and of the circumstances why personal service is impossible or not convenient and why resort must be had to substituted service.

Although Section 115 of the Evidence Act 2011 permits a deponent to depose to such statements of facts and circumstances which, from information, he believes to be true, the provision still does not permit any other person to depose to an affidavit in support of an application for substituted service of a writ of summons or other originating process. The provision only requires that where the depositions of facts and circumstances are not within

42. See 'How and by whom Summons Served' *supra* at 196.

the personal knowledge of the bailiff or court officer, e.g. because he never attempted personal service of the summons for reasons which the plaintiff gave him why personal service was unnecessary and which he believes, he shall depose to the affidavit and state the fact of his being so informed and that he so believes.

Time for Service - The Customary Courts Rules are silent on time of day during which service can be made but provides[43] that service shall not be made on a Sunday or a public holiday unless the court so directs by order endorsed on the process to be served. Order 6 Rule 9 of the applicable Lagos Rules however expressly provides for service of court processes

> between the hours of 6 am and 6 pm on any weekday and between the hours of 6 am and 2 pm on Saturdays.

Accordingly, service of the summons or other court processes shall not be made on a Sunday or on a public holiday. But service may be made on a Saturday and weekdays.

Generally, even where the Rules are silent as to time for service of process, it is accepted that service is to be effected on weekdays during usual working hours that is from dawn till 6 p.m. on weekdays and till 2 p.m. on Saturdays. Wherever there are no specific rules for what time of day service may be effected, service done during a reasonable time of the day not being a Sunday or a public holiday between dawn to dusk will be good service.

In exceptional circumstances, the court may by order grant leave to effect service at any time of the day or day. Where the court so directs, the order shall be endorsed

43. Order III Rule 6.

on the process to be served.

A process served on any prohibited day or time without leave of court is however not a nullity but a mere irregularity which can be cured by a subsequent application to court to properly serve the process. The applicable Lagos Rules provide that service effected on a Sunday or public holiday or on a Saturday after 2 pm

> shall not be invalid but shall be deemed to have been made on the nearest following day which is not a Sunday or a public holiday.[44]

The Rule refers to a public holiday and not a work-free day. The term public holiday enjoys a constitutional flavor and only the Federal Government, by reliance on Item 51 of the Exclusive Legislative List of the 1999 Constitution of the Federal Republic of Nigeria, can declare a public holiday by legislation.

A state government cannot therefore declare a public holiday and where it declares a work-free day, it shall not operate as a public holiday for purposes of the Rules relating to service of process. Also, it is doubtful if a 'public holiday' declared by the Federal Government but not backed up by appropriate legislation will suffice for the purposes of the Rules relating to service of process for, then, the declaration is no more than a work-free day which is not what the Rules contemplate.

Other Kinds of Service not being Personal - Substituted service is non-personal service. It is an exception to the rule that service of the summons must be

44. Order 6 Rule 9 (Lagos). See *Idowu v Adekanmi* (1975) 6 CCHCJ 923 where the court held service at 7.30 pm as valid on the next following day.

personal. There are other exceptions to the personal service rule. These include service such as on an infant, on a company, partnership, an insane person, a prisoner, person living on board a ship etc.

Special rules, by way of exception, apply to these situations. For instance, service on an infant is good service if made on his father or mother or guardian or any person with whom the infant resides or under whose care the infant is kept. An infant tenant (or even landlord) is however an uncommon occurrence.

Although the Rules of some courts are silent on most of these exceptions, they are accepted as part of the general law and rules for service of court processes which may be obtained from other legal sources such as the common law and statute.

Company - Section 78 of the Companies and Allied Matters Act 1990 makes provision for how a court process may be served on a company. By it, a court process shall be served on a company in the manner provided by the Rules of the court. The Customary Court Rules and the Magistrates' Courts (Civil Procedure) Rules are silent on the mode of service of court process on a company except for the indirect provision in the latter to the effect that service shall be effected on a corporation aggregate by delivering the summons

> to the mayor or other head officer, personally, or to the town clerk, clerk, treasurer, or secretary personally.[45]

The Rule uses the phrase 'corporation aggregate' which, in law, means a registered or incorporated entity with legal personality consisting of a number of members exceeding

45. Order 6 Rule 1 (1) (c).

one. Its opposite is a corporation sole which consists of only one member. A company is a usual and common example of a corporation aggregate.

Therefore, notwithstanding the rather confusing listing of a 'mayor' and 'town clerk' as possible persons on whom service on a corporation aggregate may be effected, this provision must be taken to refer to companies and service on the 'head officer' of the company or on its 'clerk', 'treasurer', or 'secretary' will be good service on the company.

In practice however, it is usual to serve documents on companies by leaving the document at, or sending it by post to the registered office of the company. It is therefore humbly submitted that with regard to the service of court processes, the same mode of serving documents on companies which is *impari materia* with the provisions of Section 78 of the Companies and Allied Matters Act will be sufficient as good service of summons and other court processes on a company.

Partnership - Generally, every partner is an agent of the partnership. Therefore service of a summons on any one or more of the partners is good service where the partnership has been sued in the partnership name.

It will also be good service if the service is done by delivering the process at the principal place of business of the partnership to any person who, at the time of the service, appears to have the control or management of the partnership business. However, where the partners are sued personally but on behalf of the partnership, service must be effected by delivering the summons on the partner named in the summons personally.

Where the partnership has been dissolved before the filing of the suit and this fact is known to the plaintiff, the summons must be served personally upon every person in Nigeria sought to be made liable.[46]

Insane Person - Where an insane person has been sued, the lunatic can be effectively served by delivering the process on the person under whose care he is or with whom he resides and, where he is in an asylum, by delivering the process to the person appearing to be the superintendent or person appearing to be in control or head of the asylum. Where the lunatic is not known to be under any body's care but roams destitute, then it is doubtful if he can be effectively served.

Prisoner - Where the person to be served is a prisoner, delivery to the person in charge of the prison as head thereof shall be good service.

Person Living on Board Ship - To serve a person who lives or works in a ship, it will be sufficient to deliver the summons or other process to the person who, at the time of the service, appears to be in control or in charge of the ship.

Proof of Service - As has been stated earlier, a written statement from the head of department in the civil service of the federal or state government or the secretary of a local government, as the case may be, that the person to be served, being an employee in the public service, has been served, shall be sufficient proof of service on the employee unless the contrary is proved.

Appearance in Court as Proof of Service - The appearance in court of the person named in the process to

46. See generally Order 6 Rule 1 (b) Lagos State Magistrates' Courts (Civil Procedure) Rules.

be served is perhaps the best proof of service. In *Ido/Osi Local Government v Aluko,*[47] the Ilorin Division of the Court of Appeal per Muntaka-Coomassie JCA declared that the rigour of an affidavit of service can be greatly reduced where the person served appears in court and that in such a situation, there shall be no further need to insist on a proof of service.

This strong evidence of service is however subject to the court being able to establish the true identity of the person appearing in court. There are known instances of persons impersonating other persons in court as the defendants particularly in possession matters filed by, especially, estate agents where persons impersonate tenant-defendants.

Order III Rule 5 of the Customary Courts Rules provides that proof of service shall be by evidence on oath. The court can therefore rely on this provision to put the person appearing in court in the witness box and to make him admit on oath the service on him and verify his identity as the defendant.

Affidavit of Service - The same Rules require that an affidavit of service shall be sufficient proof of service in all cases where service of any process has been effected by a bailiff or such other person as is appointed by the court.

The bailiff or such other officer after effecting service deposes to this affidavit setting out the fact of the service showing the place, date and time of the service. The affidavit must describe the kind of process served and how the bailiff came to identify the person served as the person

47. (2007) All FWLR (Pt. 352) 1807, 1817.

named in the process and on whom service was intended to be made.

The affidavit of service is *prima-facie* proof of service upon which the court can act but it does not preclude the defendant from rebutting the service where there was no service in fact. Such a rebuttal would have to be founded upon very strong, cogent and unassailable credible evidence. A successful rebuttal of service renders the entire proceedings incurably null and void and will have to be set aside.

Under the Lagos Magistrates' Court Rules, proof of service can also be established other than by an affidavit. This is by an endorsement on a true copy of the summons under the hand of the process server in which he sets out the fact, place, mode and date of the service and this shall be prima facie evidence of the matters stated in the endorsement.[48]

Service out of Jurisdiction: The Recovery Statutes all require that the action for recovery of possession be commenced in a court where the premises sought to be recovered is situated. This is the purport of the last limb of the Form E in which the landlord gives notice to the tenant that he intends to

> apply to the court acting for the ...... local government (being the district, division or place in which the premises or any part thereof is situated) for a summons to eject any person therefrom.

Also Section 24 of the Lagos Tenancy Law now expressly provides for this that the landlord may, upon the expiration of the seven days notice,

48. Order 6 Rule 7.

> file a claim by way of summons ... for recovery of possession ... against the tenant ... in the magisterial district or High Court Division where the premises is situated.[49]

Such district or division where the claim by way of summons is filed also becomes the jurisdiction where the claim is to be heard. But it may happen that the person to be served, at the time of filing the claim, lives or resides outside the district, division or place of filing and where the premises sought to be recovered is situated.

This will therefore mean that the process will have to be served at a district, division or place different from the district, division or place with jurisdiction for hearing and determining the claim where it has been filed. In other words, the summons will have to be served out of jurisdiction. Such service out of jurisdiction could be either inter-local government areas or inter-state.

The various court Rules make provisions for such situations where service has to be effected out of jurisdiction. In Lagos State, every magistrate court has jurisdiction throughout the state. Section 8 of the Magistrates' Court Law provides that

> every magistrate shall have jurisdiction throughout Lagos State.

This means that in Lagos State, one can only talk of an inter-state service out of jurisdiction since irrespective of the district, division, local government or place where the claim is filed, the whole state is but only one jurisdiction. Accordingly, the provision for service out of jurisdiction in

49. The clause '*where the premises is situated*' is not contained in this section of other Recovery Statutes.

Lagos State as contained in Order 6 Rule 3 of the Magistrates' Court Rules is to the effect that

> no summons for service on a defendant in Nigeria, outside of Lagos, shall issue without leave of the court.

The application for the leave of court to serve out of jurisdiction must be made in open court supported by affidavit or 'other evidence' in which the applicant for leave must show one or more of the following i.e. that the

(a) cause of action arose wholly or in part in Lagos,
(b) subject matter of the suit is in Lagos, and
(c) plaintiff has *prima facie* a good cause of action.[50]

The leave shall be refused unless the applicant makes it sufficiently to appear that the action is a proper one for service out of the jurisdiction under the Order. Where the leave is to be granted, the court may make it a condition that security for costs shall be furnished by the plaintiff before the leave is granted.[51]

Upon its grant, the Rules require that the court shall observe the provisions of the Sheriffs and Civil Process Act[52] with respect to service of processes outside a state.[53] A copy of the court's order shall then be sent to the court which is to execute the order of service.[54]

In Delta, Edo and Osun states, the jurisdiction for possession matters is vested in the Customary Courts of

---

50. Order 6 Rule 3 (a) and (g).
51. Rule 4. The costs may have to extend to cater for transportation and lodging depending on the distance from Lagos.
52. A federal enactment. See Section 111 thereof.
53. Rule 4 (1).
54. Rule 4 (2).

these states. This jurisdiction is restricted territorially to one or two local government areas within the state.

Delimiting the area of jurisdiction of the customary court, Section 9 of the Customary Courts Law for Delta and Edo states provides that a Customary Court shall exercise such jurisdiction within the territorial limits of any one or more local government council areas or as may be directed by a warrant under the hand of the President of the Customary Court of Appeal but that no two or more local government council areas shall be served by one Customary Court unless the local government council areas belong to one ethnic group and have or are reputed to have a common historical origin or community of interest in traditional and customary matters.[55]

What this means is that ordinarily, a Customary Court shall have its territorial jurisdiction limited to one local government council area but that where it has become expedient or necessary for the court to serve more than one council area, then such two or more council areas must belong to a common ethnic group or tribe, with a common ancestry or common interest in tradition and custom. Such extension of territorial jurisdiction has to be authorized by a direction under the hand of the President of the state's Customary Court of Appeal.

Section 19 of the Customary Courts Law for Delta and Edo states provides that a customary court shall have jurisdiction over all persons. The combined effect of Sections 9 and 19 of the Law therefore is that while the court has jurisdiction over all persons, such persons must

55. See also section 13 of Osun State District and Customary Courts Law 2006 for a similar territorial delimiting provision.

be within the territorial limits of the court's jurisdiction.

This arrangement is different from what is obtainable in some other states, e.g. Lagos State, where the jurisdiction of a customary court is stated to be "over all persons within the state". Under the Lagos State provision, for instance, the jurisdiction of a customary court over persons covers the whole state irrespective of the local government where the person is found, located or domiciled. Service of a customary court process in Lagos State is therefore effected following the rules and procedures already discussed above without any legal complications.

But under the arrangement in Delta, Edo and Osun states where the customary court's jurisdiction is limited territorially within the state, special procedural rules are made for service of process outside the court's territorial jurisdiction but within the state.

The Rules[56] for Delta and Edo states which are *impari materia* with those of Osun State provide that when a Customary Court desires that any summons or any other process be served outside the limits of its territorial jurisdiction but within the state, the court shall forward such summons or other process to the Customary Court within whose territorial jurisdiction the summons or other process is to be served.

Upon receipt of the summons or other process by the Area Customary Court in whose territorial jurisdiction the summons or other process is to be served, the receiving Area Customary Court shall immediately endorse on the summons or other process an order for its due service and

56. Order IV.

shall arrange for such service without delay.

Where there is no customary court in the place where the summons or other process is to be served, the forwarding court shall forward the summons or other process to the magistrate court having jurisdiction in the area where the summons or other process is to be served which shall arrange service in the manner aforesaid.

Service out of Jurisdiction outside the State - The Rules are silent on the procedure to be adopted when summonses or other court processes are to be served out of jurisdiction beyond the state. It is however submitted that, where such a situation arises, service shall be effected using the same procedure discussed above as though the person to be served is out of jurisdiction but within the state.

The reverse procedure is adopted when summonses and other processes from outside the state are forward to and received by an Area Customary Court.[57]

Leave to Serve out of Jurisdiction - Under the Rules of most courts, service of process out of jurisdiction can be done only with leave of court. This is not so in the Area Customary Court whose Rules are silent on the need to seek and obtain leave of court to serve out of jurisdiction.

In effect, the summons or other process to be served out of jurisdiction can be served without leave of court provided the proper address for service has been endorsed thereon. However, an application to the court for leave to serve out of jurisdiction with a view to satisfying "all righteousness" will, it is respectfully submitted, not be refused by the court.

57. See Order V.

Chapter Six
Proceedings at the Recovery Trial

The first man to speak in court always seems right until his opponent begins to question him. – Proverbs 18:17

Introduction

The word 'hearing' is generally used in litigation to also mean 'trial' which, in turn, involves the public presentation of the cases of the contending parties before the court beginning, in a court of summary jurisdiction, with the defendant's plea through to the judgement of the court.

The hearing or trial of a suit consists of all the evidence called by the parties, final addresses and the judgement of the court but does not include proceedings of interlocutory nature occurring during the course of the suit and which are incidental to the principal object thereof.

The Plea - In trials before courts where pleadings are used e.g. the High Court, an oral plea from the defendant in civil proceedings is unnecessary as all denials and admissions would have been done in the statement of defence.

In trials before courts of summary jurisdiction as most Recovery Courts are however, the oral plea of the defendant is vital for the commencement of the proceedings. This involves the reading of the claim to the defendant by the court and calling upon him to plead either by admitting the claim as read to him or resisting it. The oral plea is an exercise in civil proceedings before courts of summary jurisdiction whereby the defendant is called upon to respond in concise, clear and precise words to the claim of the plaintiff.

Upon the defendant entering his plea in a recovery

action, issues become properly joined as between the parties. This is different from the position in the High Courts where issues are joined upon the exchange of pleadings and where oral pleas in civil causes are unknown except with respect to criminal trials where the oral plea of the accused person is extracted and recorded in the same manner as in all other courts including courts of summary jurisdiction.

The Recovery Statutes do not make provisions for how the plea of the defendant is to be extracted but Order IX Rule 1 of the Customary Courts Rules provide for a 'plea in civil and criminal matters' whereby the subject of a charge or claim shall be read out by the clerk of the court to the defendant or accused who shall be asked how he pleads to it and his answer shall be recorded. Rule 14 of Order 17 of the Lagos Magistrates' Court Rules also provides that

> if on the day of hearing, both parties appear, the plaint shall be read to the defendant and the Magistrate shall require him to make his answer or defence thereto ....

In extracting the oral plea of a defendant, it has been held, especially in criminal trials, that

> (a) the claim must be read over and explained to the defendant to the satisfaction of the court by the registrar or other officer of the court,
> (b) it must be read over and explained to the defendant in a language he understands, and
> (c) the defendant must be called upon to react by pleading thereto unless the court is confronted with circumstances why it may order otherwise.[1]

These requirements are with respect to a criminal trial but

1. *Tobby v The State* (2001) FWLR (Pt. 52) 2081.

are also useful to civil proceedings in summary form. The plea in all cases must be entered by the defendant personally and not through counsel or proxy.

The response of the defendant when called upon to react to the claim is 'Not liable' where he resists the claim and 'Liable' where he admits the claim. This must be clear and unequivocal and must be recorded by the court.

Joined Issues - Where the defendant appears in court and admits the plaintiff's claim by pleading liable thereto, then no issues are joined as between the parties and the court may proceed to give its judgment[2] after hearing the statements of the parties.[3] This procedure is also provided for in Order IX Rule 4 of the Customary Courts Rules.

Hearing the statements of the parties, where the defendant admits the plaintiff's claim, is a more usual practice in criminal proceedings during which the prosecutor is called upon to review the facts which gave rise to the charge. The facts as reviewed are recorded by the court before pronouncing its judgment but, in practice, a review of facts in civil proceedings is uncommon as the court in its summary jurisdiction would usually proceed to pronouncing its judgment once the defendant has pleaded liable to the claim. By Order IX Rule 4 (1) of the Customary Courts Rules,

> where the defendant admits the claim or part thereof, the court shall proceed to give judgement therefor or for the part admitted.

---

2. Order 17 Rule 5 Magistrates' Court (Civil Procedure) Rules.
3. There are views to the effect that issues are joined irrespective of how the defendant pleads since the plea one way or the other is what confers jurisdiction on the court to proceed to the next stage in the proceedings.

Generally however, where the defendant pleads not liable to the claim or part thereof, issues are said to be joined as between the parties and the cause shall thereupon proceed to trial. This the court may immediately embark upon being a court of summary jurisdiction. It may however adjourn the trial to another date depending on the convenience of the court and also to enable the parties prepare properly for the trial.

Non-Appearance of Parties – The Rules of court provide that if on the return date when the cause is called and both parties do not or the plaintiff does not appear, the court shall strike out the cause or matter unless there is some good reason for keeping it on the list. If kept on the list for good reason, the reason shall be recorded and a new hearing date fixed.[4]

Absence of Defendant - If the defendant in does not appear on the return date, the court shall, where there is evidence that he has been served with the court process, proceed to hear and determine the cause or matter in his absence on the evidence of the plaintiff and his witnesses if he has any. This is what Rule 4 of Order 17 of the Lagos Magistrates' Court Civil Procedure Rules means in providing that

> if the defendant does not appear, the court, upon proof of service and of facts entitling the plaintiff to relief, may give such judgement or make such order as may be just.

A judgement of the court in this situation is a default judgment which is liable to be set aside for good reason shown. However, if there is some good reason for

4. See, generally, Order 17 Magistrates' Court (Civil Procedure) Rules; Order VII Rules 1 and 2 of the Customary Courts Rules.

adjourning the hearing, the court shall record the reason and another hearing date fixed.

Also, where the defendant is absent in court on the hearing date but he had filed an admission in writing admitting the plaintiff's claim, the court may give judgment for the plaintiff based on the defendant's written admission and without further proof of the service of the claim.[5]

Reinstating Struck Out Cause - Generally speaking, when a plaintiff is absent in court on the return or hearing date fixed for his matter, it is usually taken that he has lost interest in prosecuting his case or that he is in want of diligence in prosecuting it. Hence the cause will be struck out in accordance with the Rules.[6]

However, a cause struck out may be revived and replaced on the list by leave of court[7] granted upon application to it. The Magistrates' Rules provide in this respect that where any proceedings have been struck out

> ... the court may reinstate them for hearing on the same or any subsequent day on such terms as the court may deem just ....

Considerations for Reinstatement - The grant reinstating such a struck-out cause is not obtained as a matter of course. It is granted only upon reasonable cause[8] shown for reinstating it. Reasonable cause will involve, among others,

(a) the reason (or reasons) for the failure to appear in court at the hearing.

5. Order VII Rule 3 of the Customary Courts Rules.
6. Order VII Rules 1 and 2 of the Customary Courts Rules.
7. Order 17 Rule 2 (2) Magistrates' Court (Civil Procedure) Rules; Order VII Rule 5 of the Customary Courts Rules.
8. *Williams v Hope Rise Voluntary Society* (1982) ANLR 1.

(b) whether the application to reinstate is brought timeously
(c) whether the applicant's case is manifestly unsupportable and
(d) the applicant's conduct throughout the proceedings.

Setting Aside Default Judgment - Similar to the reinstating of a cause struck out is the setting aside of a court's judgment or order entered in the absence of the defendant. Such a default judgment (i.e. judgment in default of appearance or and defence) may be set aside upon reasonable cause shown by the applicant and upon such terms as the court may deem fit.[9] Section 49 of the Lagos Magistrates' Courts Law provides for this in the following manner –

> a Magistrate, at the same or or any subsequent sitting of the court, may set aside any judgement or order given or made against any party in the absence of such party, and the execution thereupon, and may grant a new trial or hearing, upon such terms, if any, as he may think just, on application and on sufficient cause shown to him for that purpose.

The application to set aside is made to the same court whose default judgment is sought to be set aside because a default judgment is not a final[10] judgment over which the court would have become *functus officio* and whose only challenge would lie in an appeal.[11]

9. Order VII Rule 6 of the Customary Courts Rules.
10. But see Section 38 of the Lagos Tenancy Law which provides that '*any judgement by default under this Law shall be final and remain valid and may only be set aside …*'.
11. *Ogolo v Ogolo* (2006) 2 FWLR (Pt. 309) 2152 at 2166.

The grant of the application is not obtained as a matter of course. It is at the discretion of the court exercised judicially and judiciously. The conditions upon which the court will exercise its discretion in favour of the applicant are similar to those for reinstating a struck-out cause discussed *supra* but include also a consideration whether the party in whose favour the judgment subsists i.e. the respondent, would be prejudiced or embarrassed if the judgment is set aside so as to render such a course inequitable.

The conduct of the applicant throughout the proceedings i.e. from the service of the summons or motion on him to the date of the judgment or ruling and even during the pendency of the application to set aside would be material in rendering his application worthy of sympathetic consideration.[12]

Section 38 of the Lagos Tenancy expressly provides grounds on which a Magistrate[13] may set aside a default judgement. The section provides that

> any judgement by default under this Law shall be final and remain valid and may only be set aside upon application to the Magistrate on grounds of fraud, non-service, lack of jurisdiction, or upon such terms as the court may deem fit.

The Recovery Trial – Although a trial is all the proceedings from the taking of the plea in a summary trial to the delivery of the judgment, the actual trial i.e. the actual hearing of the cause is the taking of evidence in respect thereto and this begins when the first witness is

12. *Williams v Hope Rise Voluntary Society* (*supra*).
13. The section refers only to a Magistrate.

called by the party beginning, usually the plaintiff, into the witness box to testify.

A trial in this regard is contrasted from what appeal courts do where evidence is not usually led. Trial courts try issues by listening to and considering evidence. Appeal courts do not. According to Oputa JSC (as he then was) in *Egbe v Adefarasin*[14]

> now (the Supreme Court) as well as the Court of Appeal are appellate courts. They do not try issues. Rather they examine the way issues had been tried by trial courts in order to ensure that the case was properly tried.[15]

The trial of causes in the trial courts therefore usually begins with the plaintiff calling evidence in proof of his claim and thereafter the defendant calls evidence in challenge of the plaintiff's evidence.[16]

Defendant to Show Non-liability - Section 25 of the Recovery Statutes however provides for the hearing of the recovery suit in words which suggest that the defendant is first to prove his 'innocence' or non-liability to the plaintiff's claim failing which before the plaintiff shall prove his case for possession. This is contrary to the rules procedure and of the law of evidence which is that he who asserts or alleges must prove.

The Recovery Statutes provision opens with the following words:

> if the defendant shall not at the time named in the summons or any adjournment thereof show good cause to the contrary, then on proof....

14. (1987) ANLR 1.
15. *ibid* at 16.
16. See Order 17 Rule 16 Magistrates' Court Rules; Order IX Rule 5 Customary Courts Rules.

This suggests that the defendant has to first 'show good cause to the contrary' before the plaintiff proceeds to prove his case. In other words, the trial in a possession matter opens with the defendant showing good cause why the order for possession against him should not be made by the court. It is when the defendant 'shall not' be able to 'show good cause to the contrary' that proof is then required of the plaintiff of the sundry matters[17] listed in Section 25 (1) (a) to (f) of the Recovery Statutes upon which the court may order that possession be given up by the defendant to the plaintiff.

In practice generally however and notwithstanding the above provision, trials for possession matters, open and proceed in the same manner in which trials in other kinds of suits are conducted. The defendant, when he appears in court in response to the summons, takes his plea and the matter proceeds in the usual manner depending on how the defendant pleads.

If the defendant pleads admitting the claim, judgment is entered in favour of the plaintiff and the matter comes to an end. Where the defendant pleads not liable to the claim, the action proceeds to the trial with the plaintiff opening and calling evidence in proof of:

(a) his status in relation to the defendant,
(b) type of premises occupied by the defendant,
(c) type of tenancy,
(c) the determination of the tenancy either by notice or operation of law and the reason or reasons therefor,

---

17. See *infra*.

(c) the valid service of statutory notices, especially the seven days notice, on the defendant,
(d) the rent payable for the premises and the arrears where applicable,
(e) plaintiff's title where such title has accrued since the letting of the premises,
(f) the defendant's neglect or refusal to deliver up possession despite the due determination of the tenancy and the service on him of statutory notices,
(g) service of the summons,
(h) grounds entitling plaintiff to recover possession.

The evidence in proof of the above facts usually runs thus in court:

I know the defendant. He is my tenant in respect of a two bed room flat at No. 1 Linus Ona Street, Calabar (*or as the case may be*).

He is a monthly tenant paying N10,000.00 per month as rent.

The defendant is not a good tenant. He does not pay his rent and is owing me rent for two months. He last paid his rent in … month and I issued him a receipt for it. This is the duplicate of the receipt which I issued him when he last paid his rent. I seek to tender it.

(*The court admits and marks it as an exhibit*).

Since then he has not paid any rent despite repeated demands from me.

I then decided to recover possession of the flat from him and I issued and served on him a one month notice to quit. I filed the one month notice at the Registry of this court before serving it on the defendant.

This is a duplicate copy of the one month notice to quit which I served on him. I seek to tender it.

(*The court admits and marks it as an exhibit*).

The notice to quit (or better still, the exhibit) was served on the defendant by Mr. …, a bailiff of this court after I pointed at and identified the defendant to the bailiff.
Despite the service of the notice to quit on the defendant, he did not give up possession of the premises.
I then issued and served on him a seven days notice of my intention to apply to this court to recover possession of the premises from him. This is a copy of the seven days notice which I served on the defendant. I seek to tender it.
(*The court admits and marks it as an exhibit*).
The seven days notice was issued and served on the defendant the same manner the notice to quit was served on him.
Despite the service of the seven days notice on the defendant, he still refuses to deliver up possession of the premises to me.
Hence I filed this action to recover possession, the arrears of rent and *mesne* profits as per my plaint.
The plaint was served on the defendant by way of a writ of summons duly issued from this court. It was served on the defendant by a bailiff of this court after I pointed at and identified the defendant to the bailiff.
I urge the court to give me judgement as per my claim.
That is my case.

If the plaintiff is led in evidence by counsel, the questions from counsel are framed in such a way as to elicit the above answers. If the plaintiff is not the landlord but an agent of the landlord, appropriate evidence is led to show this relationship in which case the evidence begins with identification of the agent and his relationship with the landlord thus:

My name is …. etc. I am an estate agent.

> The plaintiff is the owner of the premises situate at … who appointed me in writing to issue statutory notices to the defendant and to file this action.
> I have a copy of the writing by which I was appointed by the plaintiff in court. The original copy has been tendered in evidence at another suit and I have been unable to retrieve it. I seek to tender the copy of the writing.
> (*The court admits and marks it as an exhibit*).

He then leads evidence in relation to the defendant and the claim as above modifying same as appropriate to suit the circumstance of his relationship to the defendant in the course of his agency.

When the plaintiff is done with his testimony, the defendant, if he so desires, cross examines the plaintiff. The cross examination will be determined by the nature of evidence presented by the plaintiff, and like every cross examination, it is designed to discredit the plaintiff's evidence. This sequence is repeated with the plaintiff's witnesses, if he calls any. The plaintiff then closes his case.

Thereafter the defendant opens his defence, if he has any, by calling evidence. He is cross examined by the plaintiff if the plaintiff so desires. When he is done with his testimony and those of his witnesses, if he had any, the defendant closes his case.

Parties then address court where necessary and judgment is entered incorporating the order of the court as provided for in either Form J, K or L (Form TL7 only in Lagos) in the schedule to the Recovery Statute.

Trial in Lagos by Written Deposition – In Lagos State, Section 27 of the Tenancy Law provides that

> in any matter under (the Tenancy Law) relating to any

> fact required to be proved at the trial of any action, evidence shall be by written deposition or oral examination of witnesses in open court or a combination of both.

By subsection 3 thereof, the oral examination of a witness during his evidence in chief at the trial shall be limited to confirming his written deposition and tendering in evidence all disputed documents or other exhibits.

Also, all agreed documents or other exhibits shall be tendered at the trial from the bar i.e. counsel shall hand same to the court from the bar, or by the party where he is not represented by a legal practitioner in which case, same shall be handed to the court by the party from the witness box.[18]

The Tenancy Law does not define 'written deposition' but this must be taken to mean a reference to an oath which could be by way of

(a) an affidavit in which case the provisions of the Evidence Act in relation thereto will have to be complied with beginning in the usual manner that

> I, … of … do solemnly and sincerely swear that this is my name and handwriting and that the facts deposed by me in this affidavit are the truth, the whole truth and nothing but the truth[19] or

(b) a statutory declaration as contained in the First Schedule to the Oaths Law[20] thus:

> I, … of … do solemnly declare that … (which is

18. Subsection 2.
19. See Form A in the First Schedule to the Oaths Law (Cap. 137) Laws of Lagos State 1994.
20. *Supra.*

then followed by the facts to which the declarant deposes to in numbered paragraphs).

In both (a) and (b), the attestation i.e. the concluding part shall be in the usual manner thus:

DECLARED (or Sworn to) at … in the … this … day of … 20…

BEFORE ME

……………………………………

Commissioner for Oaths

Tenant to First Defend in Lagos - The Tenancy Law requires that a defendant is to enter his defence in the usual manner by making use of the Form TL6A (otherwise Form G) or some other written depositions as in the case of the plaintiff *supra*. Where he intends to rely on written depositions at the trial, Section 34 requires that he may, at the time of filing his defence but not later than five (5) days thereafter, file his witness statements, exhibits and other relevant documents which he intends to tender. All these steps by the defendant are, by implication, to be taken before the matter gets to the trial stage.

In other words, the provision of Section 25 of the regular Recovery Statutes which suggests that the defendant is first to show his innocence or non-liability to the plaintiff's claim is also obtainable under the Lagos Tenancy Law.

The effect of the procedure really is that the defendant has to first enter his defence by 'show(ing) good cause to the contrary' before the plaintiff proceeds to prove his case. So also in Lagos State, the 'trial' in a possession matter begins with the defendant entering his defence by showing good cause why the order for possession should not be made against him by the court. It is when the defendant 'shall not' be able to 'show good cause to the contrary' that proof is then required of the plaintiff of the sundry matters listed[21] in Subsection 4 of Section 27.

This procedure, as pointed out *supra*, is contrary to the rules of procedure and of the law of evidence[22] which is that he who asserts or alleges must prove.

Plaintiff's Case following Default of Defence - Where a defendant fails or neglects to enter any defence as above, then the action proceeds to its 'trial' with the plaintiff discharging the burden of proving the sundry matters listed in subsection 4 of Section 27 of the Tenancy Law. These are that

(a) the defendant is still in possession of the premises,

(b) the annual rental value of the premises,

(c) the nature of the tenancy or the holding,

(d) the expiration or other determination of the tenancy within the time and manner stipulated by law,

(e) his title, if such title accrued after the letting of the premises by the defendant, and,

(f) where the defendant does not appear in court, then the service of the summons or writ on the defendant.[23]

The provision makes a clear distinction between the defendant's appearance in court and his entering of his defence. If he appears in court, then by paragraph (f) of

21. See *infra*.
22. See Sections 131 to 133 of the Evidence Act 2011.
23. Subsection 4 of Section 27.

Section 27 (4), the plaintiff will be relieved of the requirement to prove during the trial that the summons or writ was served on the defendant. It is only when the defendant does not appear in court that the plaintiff will need to prove that the defendant was served with the summons.

The provision dispensing with the requirement to prove service if the defendant appears in court accords with the Court of Appeal decision in *Ido/Osi Local Government v Aluko*[24] to the effect that the rigour of an affidavit of service can be greatly reduced where the defendant who has been served with court processes appears in court and that, in such a situation, there shall be no further need to insist on a proof of service.

Grounds for Possession in Lagos State – Having proved the sundry matters listed *supra*, the court shall then proceed to make orders for possession but only if there has been proof also of the grounds listed in Section 25 of the Tenancy Law and in the circumstances described thereat. These grounds are substantially the same as contained in all other Recovery Statutes nationwide[25] except that the Tenancy Law has classified the grounds into

(a) grounds upon which the court may make the order but subject to the express stipulations of the parties in their tenancy agreement, and

(b) grounds upon which the court may make the order notwithstanding any agreement between the parties.

Subsection 1 of Section 25 of the Tenancy Law provides

24. (2007) All FWLR (Pt. 352) 1807, 1817.
25. See Chapter Three for a full discussion.

that unless the tenancy agreement between the parties expressly stipulates otherwise, the court shall have power to make an order for possession upon proof by the owner/plaintiff of the following grounds

(a) arrears of rent;

(b) breach of any covenant or agreement;

(c) where the premises is required by the landlord for personal use; or

(d) where the premises requires substantial repair.

Subsection 2 thereof on its own part provides that notwithstanding any agreement between the parties, the court shall have power to make an order for possession upon proof of any of the following grounds where

(a) the premises is being used for immoral or illegal purposes;

(b) the premises has been abandoned,[26]

(c) the premises is unsafe and unsound as to constitute a danger to human life or property; or

(d) the tenant or any person residing or lodging with him or being his subtenant constitutes by conduct, an act of intolerable nuisance or induces a breach of a tenancy agreement.

Reconciliation – In the ordinary Nigerian society, court actions, including recovery actions, are regarded as 'war'. It is a kind of war once begun continues, in some situations, for life. Such 'wars' could be passed on from generation to generations of families. To take one member of a family to court is to start a war with everybody in that family who will, in turn, take the war to everybody in the other family. The situation could be worse where the landlord is also

26. Peculiar under the Tenancy Law.

resident with his family in or within the precinct of the suit premises.

Such 'wars' are not good for the peace of society and should be discouraged or reduced to their very barest frequencies. Where discouragement of reduction is not possible their adverse effects on society ought to be ameliorated. It is for these reasons that the establishing statutes of most courts make provisions requiring that the courts should not only promote but also encourage and facilitate reconciliation between the parties.

Section 22 of the Customary Courts Law for Delta and Edo states, for instance, provides in this regard that

> in civil causes or matters a customary court may promote reconciliation among the parties thereto and encourage and facilitate the amicable settlement thereof.

It is to be highly recommended to all courts and, indeed, all counsel practicing in these courts to pay heed to these provisions and give life to them before the actual hearing in the proceedings begins or at the earliest opportunity even after commencement of trial.

Every counsel owes a duty to society to promote good relations among all persons in the interest of peace in the society and must not be blinded by any selfish desires for pecuniary benefits towards encouraging the sustenance of litigation. Indeed it is unprofessional conduct for a legal practitioner to foment strife or instigate litigation.[27]

Reconciliation and Mediation in Lagos – Obviously in recognition of the beauty of moving disputes and their resolution from the tedious and expensive processes of

27. See Rule 25 of the Rules of Professional Conduct in the Legal Profession.

regular courts, the law maker specifically made provisions in the Lagos Tenancy Law for reconciliation, mediation and amicable settlements of recovery disputes. By Section 32 (1) thereof, the Law provides that

> in proceedings under this Law, the court shall promote reconciliation, mediation and amicable settlement between the parties.

Of novel interest is the provision for mediation. This is one of the different informal methods of resolving disputes under what is now generally referred to as Alternative Dispute Resolution. Mediation as a legal term refers to a situation where a neutral third party assists disputants through informal means to negotiate a settlement of their dispute.

Unlike the judge in a formal court, the mediator merely guides the disputants through negotiations with a view to arriving at an amicable settlement in a private, cost effective and confidential process.

Reference to Mediation Discretion of Court - By subsection (2) of Section 32 of the Tenancy Law, a Recovery Court may

> refer tenancy proceedings or any part of it to mediation at a Citizen Mediation Centre or to Lagos Multi-Door Court House[28]

for amicable resolution. Under the provision, consent of the parties to the proceedings shall not be required but it shall be in the absolute discretion of the court to refer any tenancy, which under the Lagos Tenancy Law is the same thing as a recovery proceeding, for mediation.

28. These are specialized Alternative Dispute Resolution fora in Lagos State for achieving speedy out-of-court resolution of disputes.

The mediator, upon completion of his mediation, is required by subsection (3) to submit the result of his mediation i.e. the mediation agreement to the court within three days after the parties have signed it for the purposes of endorsement and enforcement. Endorsement of the mediation agreement by the court renders it a judgement of the court which is then capable of being enforced by way of execution using the machinery of the courts for such purposes.

The Oath – In courts of summary jurisdiction, as most Recovery Courts are, the taking of evidence during trial begins with putting the witness on oath. Section 205 of the Evidence Act 2011expressly provides that every witness giving evidence before the court shall be put on such oath as he declares to be binding on him.

Order X of the Customary Courts Rules also provides for this oath which must be to the effect that the evidence that the witness is about to give is the truth, the whole truth, and nothing but the truth. By Section 206 of the Evidence Act,

> any witness summoned to give oral evidence in any proceedings shall, before giving such evidence, be cautioned by the court, or the Registrar upon the court's direction in the following words:
>
>> You (full name) are hereby cautioned that if you tell a lie in your testimony in this proceeding or willfully mislead this court you are liable to be prosecuted and if found guilty you will be seriously dealt with according to law.

This provision relates only to witnesses who are summoned to give oral evidence and does not affect the parties as witnesses or witnesses called by the parties and who have willingly come to court to testify.

Where the witness objects to the taking of an oath he shall affirm to the like effect that he will tell only the truth in court. The fact of the witness taking an oath or affirming must be recorded by the court.

Child Witness - If the witness is a child and the court is of the opinion that the child does not understand the nature of an oath, the court may receive his evidence albeit that it is not given on oath. The court must however be satisfied that the child understands the duty of speaking the truth.[29]

Generally, the taking of the oath by the witness is not compulsory. A person who has no religion or one whose religious belief does not permit him to make an oath may not be compelled to take an oath before his evidence is received. The court may receive the evidence of such person if the court thinks it is just and expedient to do so.[30]

Clearing the Court - After putting the first witness on oath or, as the case may be, the witness has affirmed or allowed to give his evidence without an oath, the court may 'clear' the courtroom by ordering all witnesses on both sides who are yet to give evidence in the cause to be kept out of court.[31]

The provision is not mandatory and non-compliance does not operate to vitiate the proceedings. Also, the rule does not extend to the parties in the suit or to their respective counsel even though it is intended to call them as

29. Section 209 Evidence Act 2011; Order X Rule 2 of the Customary Courts Rules; Section 9 Oath Act 1963.
30. Section 207 Evidence Act 2011.
31. Section 212 (1) Evidence Act 2011; Order X Rule 11 of the Customary Courts Rules.

witnesses in the proceedings.[32] The order to 'clear' the court may be made by the court upon the application of any of the parties to the proceedings or *suo motun* by the court.

Examination of the Witnesses - Section 215 (1) Evidence Act 2011 provides that every witness shall first be examined (in chief) by the party who calls him as witness and thereafter the other or any other party shall be at liberty to cross examine him. Then he may be re-examined by the party who called him as to matters arising out of the cross examination.[33]

Evidence of Unstamped Documents - A common occurrence at trials before the Recovery Courts is the tendering of documents. Part V of the Evidence Act deals with the subject of documentary evidence but it is intended here to comment briefly on the position of the law where the document sought to be tendered is unstamped and it is generally taken, albeit erroneously, that an unstamped document is incurably inadmissible in evidence.

This follows from the provisions of Section 22 (4) of the Stamp Duties Act (Cap. 411) Laws of the Federation 1990 stipulating that

> … an instrument executed in Nigeria, or relating, wheresoever executed, to any property situate or to any matter or thing done or to be done in Nigeria, shall not, except in criminal proceedings, be given in evidence, or be available for any purpose whatsoever, unless it is duly stamped in accordance with the law in force in Nigeria at the time when the instrument was first executed.

The operative parts in the provision are that

> an instrument executed in Nigeria… shall not… be given

32. *ibid.*

33. See also Order X Rule 3 (1) of the Customary Courts Rules.

> in evidence, or be available for any purpose whatsoever unless it is duly stamped....

There are legal views that the above position is strict and cannot be remedied even by the consent of parties and that such an unstamped instrument will not be admissible in evidence whether directly or for a collateral purpose. Even secondary evidence of such an instrument is neither admissible nor can it be cross examined upon.[34] However, such an unstamped document is admissible to refresh the memory of a witness or to prove fraud or an act of bankruptcy.

For these conclusions, reference and reliance were placed entirely on decisions of foreign courts, mostly English, as authority. With due respect, the conclusions apparently ignored the opening lines of Section 22 (4) of the Stamp Duties Act and the preceding subsections thereto. The said subsection (4) of Section 22 declares that

> except as aforesaid and subject to the provision of section 90 (3) of this Act....

In the preceding subsections, the Act provides for terms upon which instruments not duly stamped may be received in evidence. These are that the court shall take notice of the omission to stamp or the insufficiency of the stamping, and on payment to the court of the amount unpaid as duty together with the penalty payable on stamping the same and of a further sum of two naira, receive the instrument in evidence saving all just exceptions on other grounds.

The reference in Section 22 (4) of the Stamp Duties Act to '*subject to the provisions of Section 90 (3)*' of the

34. M.T. Abdulrazaq (1999) *General Principles of the Law of Stamp Duties in Nigeria* (Tee & Tee, Ilorin).

same Act must be understood as a reference to Section 91 of the Act as there is no subsection (3) to Section 90 of the Act. Section 91 contains a subsection (3) which provides for terms upon which an unstamped receipt (which is inadmissible by reason thereof) may however be admitted upon payment of a penalty of four naira having regard to the illiteracy and ignorance of the party tendering the receipt in evidence.

Also apparently ignored by the learned author was the decision of the Supreme Court in *Okuwobi v Ishola*[36] where, in obvious reliance on the preceding subsections of Section 22 of the Stamp Duties Act, the apex court held that it was wrong to hold a document inadmissible merely on the ground of non-stamping since the requirement of stamping is to ensure that government does not lose revenue thereby and that the court ought to have directed the document to be stamped and thereafter receive same in evidence.

Okuwobi v Ishola must therefore represent the correct position of the law on the point as provided by Section 22 (1) of the Stamp Duties Act. It is therefore correct to say that by the combined effect of subsections (1) and (4) of Section 22 of the Stamp Duties Act together with the decision in the *Okuwobi's* case, an instrument which is not duly stamped in accordance with the law in force at the time when the instrument was first executed is not admissible in evidence,[37] but that it will be wrong to hold the document inadmissible merely on the ground of its non-stamping because the non-stamping can be remedied by a

36. 1973 ANLR 233.
37. Section 22 (4) Stamp Duties Act.

direction of the court that the document be stamped and then be received in evidence.[38] What this means is that the defect of non-stamping in a document is inherently remediable.

Case for the Plaintiff - The plaintiff is usually first to open his case by calling evidence personally and through witnesses. He and each of his witnesses on getting into the witness box is put on such oath as he declares to be binding on him before testifying and during which they may tender documents and other exhibits. This is in accordance with the provisions of the various Rules of court that where a defendant does not admit the plaintiff's claim, he puts the plaintiff to the proof of his claim. This the plaintiff does by adducing evidence in proof thereof.

When the plaintiff is done with his evidence including those of his witness where he calls any, he to closes his case. The defendant is then called upon to enter into his defence. The Rules of evidence require that the defendant be asked by the court if he intends to call evidence since the defendant has a choice not to call evidence in which case he is said to rest his own case on that of the plaintiff. This option is rare in recovery actions.

Defendant Resting Case on Plaintiff's Case - This is a rule of procedure usually provided for in the High Court Rules but the Rules of most Recovery Courts do not make express provisions for this procedure whereby a defendant rests his case on that of the plaintiff. A Recovery Court is however unlikely to deny a defendant who opts for this procedure the right to do so.

38. *ibid.*

A defendant adopts this option where he is certain that from the evidence adduced by the plaintiff, the claim of the plaintiff has not been established and cannot stand. In effect, the defendant argues that the plaintiff has failed to establish a prima facie case against him which should require him, the defendant, to rebut by calling evidence. He therefore elects to be bound by the plaintiff's evidence as correct and as being the truth.

The No Case Submission - Another option open to the defendant is the option to make a 'no-case' submission. The procedure which is more commonly used in criminal proceedings than in civil proceedings may be raised by the court *suo motun.*

By the submission, the defendant avers that even if the evidence led by the plaintiff is conceded as being the truth and correct, the evidence nevertheless cannot sustain the plaintiff's claim in law as to entitle him to judgement.

Under the procedure, whenever a defendant makes a no-case submission, he risks forfeiting his right to call evidence. This will happen where the court puts the defendant to his election whether he intends to call evidence or not before making the submission. Usually, the court will not permit the defendant to make a 'no-case' submission unless he elects upon it alone and to call no evidence.[39]

According to Nwadialo,[40] the difference between resting the defendant's case on that of the plaintiff and a

39. *Fetuga v Western Nigeria Housing Corporation* (1968) NMLR 233.

40. (1990) *Civil Procedure in Nigeria* (MIJ Professional Publishers Ltd Lagos) at 556.

'no-case' submission is that in resting one's case, the defendant decides firmly not to call any evidence and unequivocally so declares to the court by which he can in no circumstance call evidence in the case anymore while by a 'no-case' submission, the defendant's right to call evidence still subsists and could still call evidence if the 'no-case' submission fails and is overruled provided he was not put to his election before making the submission.

The effect of a 'no-case' submission where the defendant had been put to his election before making the submission is that if it is upheld, the claim is dismissed but if overruled, judgment is entered for the plaintiff. Where the defendant was not put to his election and the submission is over-ruled, the case proceeds as usual with the defendant calling his evidence in rebuttal of the plaintiff's case. If the submission is upheld, the suit is dismissed.

Case for the Defendant - Where the defendant desires to call evidence in his defence, he does so, just as the plaintiff did in proof of his claim. He may himself testify and is also free to call other persons as witnesses. To testify, he goes into the witness box where he is put on such oath as he declares to be binding on him. If he has witnesses, he calls each of them into the witness box who are also put on such oath as they declare to be binding on them. They may be allowed to affirm at their option.

As already discussed *supra*, at the commencement of testimonies on each day the case is called, the court is 'cleared' of all persons who are yet to testify and each witness is examined in chief, led by the party who calls him. The witness is thereafter cross examined by the opposing party and then re-examined by the party who called him on matters arising from the cross-examination with a view to clarifying any ambiguities.

A co-defendant is entitled to cross-examine a witness called by any of the defendants. When all the defence witnesses have testified, the defendant closes his case and the proceedings then proceed to the final addresses stage.

Final Addresses – Final addresses have been defined[41] as the procedure whereby parties to a case, at the conclusion of evidence on both sides, address the court on the evidence as adduced during the trial, enumerating the issues canvassed and adverting to the law governing those issues.

The practice has taken such a root in the courts, particularly in the superior courts of record, that it has assumed the nature of a right which, if denied, is not regarded as mere procedural irregularity. Indeed, the place of final addresses in proceedings before the courts has become so entrenched that the 1999 constitution[42] recognizes it as an integral part of court proceedings in providing that

> every court established under this constitution shall deliver its decision in writing not later than ninety days after the conclusion of evidence and final addresses…[43]

Purpose of Final Addresses - Final addresses are designed to assist the court[44] and they form part of the proceedings.[45]

41. Belgore JSC in *Obodo v Olomu* (1987) NSCC 824 at 828.
42. Federal Republic of Nigeria.
43. Section 294 (1).
44. *Niger Construction Ltd v Okugbeni* (1987) 2 NSCC 1258.
45. *Obodo v Olomu* (1987) NSCC 824, 829).

The purpose of final addresses is to let the trial court and the party on the other side know what the party addressing thinks of the whole evidence and the law in relation to the case.

Failure to hear the address of a party to the proceedings who desires to address court vitiates the trial no matter how overwhelming the evidence seems to be on one side. Therefore, whenever the right to address the court exists, a party who is so entitled must not be denied that right as a denial of the right may render the entire proceedings null should a miscarriage of justice be occasioned thereby.

In *Obodo v Olomu*,[46] the trial judge ordered both parties who had led evidence to submit written final addresses and adjourned for judgement. No specific orders were made by the court relating to dates and times when each party was to submit the written addresses. Defence counsel sent his written address to the court without serving the plaintiff who did not send any address. In his judgement, the trial judge dwelt at length on the submissions contained in the defence counsel's written address which the court agreed with. Allowing the appeal of the plaintiff, the Supreme Court held that

> the trial judge was in error in the manner he ordered for the written addresses. He was wrong in deciding the case virtually on the written address of the defendant's counsel which was not served on the plaintiff or his counsel to afford him the opportunity of writing his own address.... The Court of Appeal fell into the same pitfall and erred further by speculating in holding that 'without

46. *Supra.*

> the addresses by both parties the decision arrived at by the learned trial judge would not have been different'.

The apex court then explained that the hearing of a case under the Nigerian legal system is that every party must not only be heard but also must be afforded the opportunity of being heard stressing that

> addresses form part of the case and failure to hear the address of one party, however overwhelming the evidence seems to be on one side, vitiates the trial because in many cases, it is after the addresses that one finds the law on the issues fought not in favour of the evidence adduced.

Final Addresses in Writing - On the issue of written final addresses, the Supreme Court in this same decision expressed the view that since the Rules of court are not clear the point, written final addresses may be allowed for the convenience of the court but that

> perhaps it is better to adhere to (the) tried and tested practice of oral addresses (and that) time would have been saved (in the instant case) if the conventional practice was adhered to whereby oral addresses are made.

This recommendation of the Supreme Court is, with due respects, to be taken seriously as it is very likely that if such written addresses are exchanged between the parties and placed in the court's file only, the constitutional requirement that 'the proceedings of a court … shall be held in public'[47] may be breached as then the contents of the addresses being 'part of the case' shall be unknown to the public who need to see that 'justice is not only done but

47. Section 36 (3) of the 1999 Constitution.

appears to reasonable persons to be done'.[48]

However, final addresses are not an imperative in all cases or situations. Whenever the facts and issues together with the relevant laws are straightforward and mainly not in dispute, a trial court would be free to dispense with the final addresses.[49] This is because cases are decided not on the strength or quality of addresses but on credible evidence. In the absence of credible evidence, no amount of brilliance in a final address can sway a court to arrive at its judgement based on the contents, strength or quality of a final address.

Order of Addresses - The right of parties to address court and the order in which they address court at the close of evidence is provided for by the Rules of court. These are substantially the same in all Rules of courts in Nigeria especially the High Court Rules. For instance, Order 30 Rules 13 - 16 of the High Court of Delta State (Civil Procedure) Rules 2009 provide that

> **13**. When the party beginning has concluded his evidence, the judge shall ask the other party if he intends to call evidence. If the other party does not intend to call evidence, the party beginning shall within 21 days after close of evidence file a written address. Upon being served with the written address, the other party shall within 21 days file his own written address.
>
> **14**. Where the other party calls evidence, he shall within 21 days after the close of evidence file a written address.
>
> **15**. Upon being served with the other party's written address the party beginning shall within 21 days file his own written reply.

48. *Niger Construction Ltd v Okugbeni* (*Supra*).
49. Per Obaseki JSC in *Ariori v Elemo* (1983) ANLR 1, 25.

> **16**. The party who files the first address shall have a right of reply on points of law only. The reply shall be filed within 7 days after service of the other party's address.

The above provisions of the 2009 Delta State High Court Rules are in tandem with the provisions of High Court Rules in all states where 'front loading' has been introduced. These Rules, apart from the introduction of reducing final addresses into writing and allowing the party to address first a right of reply on points of law, remain substantially the same in terms of the order of addresses with the old Rules. For instance, Order 37 Rules 17 and 18 the old Bendel State High Court Rules[50] provided that

> the party beginning shall … produce his evidence and examine his witness. When the party beginning has concluded his evidence, he shall ask the other party if he intends to call evidence (in which term is included evidence taken by affidavit or deposition, or under commission, and documentary evidence not already read or taken as read); and if answered in the negative, he shall be entitled to sum up the evidence already given and comment thereon; but if answered in the affirmative, he shall wait for his general reply.
>
> When the party beginning has concluded his case, the other party shall be at liberty to state his case and to call evidence, and to sum up and comment thereon.[51]

Furthermore, Rules 21 and 22 of the same Order provided that where the party who is opposed to the party beginning calls or reads evidence, the party beginning shall be at

50. Applicable in Delta and Edo states.
51. See also Order 17 Rule 16 of the Lagos Magistrates' Courts Civil Procedure Rules for similar provision.

liberty to reply[52] generally on the whole case or may, by leave of court, call fresh evidence in reply to the evidence given on the other side, on points material to the determination of the issues or any of them but not on collateral matters. Where evidence in reply is tendered and allowed to be given, the party against whom the same has been adduced shall be at liberty to address the court, and the party beginning shall be entitled to the general reply.

Form the above provisions, it is clear that even under the old Rules in Delta State and which Rules are still applicable in some states including Lagos State[53] notwithstanding the introduction of 'front loading' under the Tenancy Law, the order of final addresses is that whenever a defendant calls or reads evidence, he immediately addresses court at the close of his evidence and thereafter the plaintiff addresses the court by way of reply during which he comments generally on the whole case and thereby having the last word.

Final Addresses in Customary Courts - The above discussion on final addresses have been based on the Rules of the Magistrates' Courts and those of the High Courts generally. These are the applicable Rules in recovery actions as has been explained *supra.* But it has also been explained that in some states, the court with exclusive jurisdiction for recovery actions is the customary court which assumes a hybrid character both as a Customary Court and a Magistrates' Court.

In this regard, are the Rules and the practice of final

52. Order 17 Rule 16 (3) of the Lagos Magistrates' Courts Civil Procedure Rules.
53. See *ibid.*

addresses applicable to customary courts when they sit over recovery actions or at all? This question came up indirectly for determination in *Unutame v Bicycle*[54] before the Patani Area Customary Court which held that although the Customary Courts Rules make no provision for final addresses, the practice of final addresses are, notwithstanding, applicable to the court by virtue of the provisions of the 1999 constitution of the federation and binding judicial precedents of superior courts of record. Explaining its persuasive decision regarding the applicability of final addresses in customary courts and the order of addresses, the Delta State Area Customary Court stated thus in part:[55]

> We agree with the learned counsel for the defence that it is a rule of practice for counsel to be allowed to address court. This rule of practice is usually provided for by the rules of the court. See Agbaje JSC in *NIGER CONSTRUCTION LTD v OKUGBENI* (1987) 2 NSCC 1258, 1263.
>
> It is therefore without doubt that the determination of the above stated issue must turn entirely on the construction of the relevant provisions of the Rules of this court i.e. Customary Courts Rules 1978.
>
> Unfortunately, the said Rules contain no provisions whatsoever for final addresses. In the circumstance, it is plausible to hold that the said rule of practice whereby counsel or parties are called upon to deliver final

54. Unreported suit No PACC/6/04 *infra* CORAM Miakpo Emiaso – President, J.D. Ayakoroma and A.W. Titity - Members.
55. For the full report, see Miakpo Emiaso (2010) Law, Practice and Procedure: Area Customary Courts in Nigeria (Peakmans Ltd., Lagos) at 251 *et seq*.

addresses at the end of evidence on both sides do not apply to this court.

This court has no doubts in its mind that the decision of the Supreme Court on final addresses is binding on it. This presupposes that even though the Rules of this court have made no provisions for final addresses, the rule of practice will be applicable to this court via the authorities of superior courts of record which are per force binding on us.

Besides, … there is the constitutional provision which requires that every court established under the constitution *'shall deliver its decision ... after the conclusion of evidence and final addresses…'*. Section 294 Nigerian Constitution 1999.

This constitutional provision is binding on this court and it creates the right for parties to deliver final addresses before judgment and after conclusion of evidence. See *OBODO v OLOMU* (Supra) 831.

However, as earlier stated, the issue for the determination of this court is not whether final addresses are applicable to this court *simplicita* but in what order are the addresses to be taken so as to determine who has the last word. In other words, who addresses first and who addresses last?

Writing under the sub-heading 'Order of addressees' the learned author of CIVIL PROCEDURE IN NIGERIA writes at page 566 in agreement with the learned Supreme Court justices that:

> *'It follows that as a rule, whenever the defendant calls or reads evidence, the plaintiff has the last word, that is, the right of reply'.*

TAKING our guide from the above *ratios decidendi* and learned conclusions, this court holds itself bound that the party who begins to lead evidence has the last word in final address.

We do not hesitate in outrightly disagreeing with the learned counsel that there will be a denial of fair hearing if he is not allowed to reply on points of law.[56] What the rules and authorities permit is for counsel to, having called evidence in defence, have the first shot at addressing the court at the conclusion of his witnesses' testimony summing up his case and commenting thereon.

The rules and the authorities already considered do not say anything concerning a right of reply on points of law. Accordingly, we find ourselves unable to hold that the defendants have any right of reply on points of law. We hold therefore that no such right exists in favour of the defendant.

But all said and done in relation to strict law, this court is struck by the submission of the defence counsel to the effect that this court being a customary court is enjoined to do substantial justice and we take cognizance of the view that

> *'addresses are designed to assist the court. Cases are normally not decided on addresses but on credible evidence. No amount of brilliance in a final speech can make up for the lack of evidence'* - Per Oputa JSC in *Niger Construction Ltd v Okugbeni* (*Supra*).

We are therefore persuaded that notwithstanding the position of the strict law to the contrary, and our conviction that no matter how brilliant the reply sought to be delivered may turn out to be, no miscarriage of

56. But see the later contrary decision of the Court of Appeal (Enugu Division) in *Ugwu v Alaebo* (2006) All FWLR (Pt. 309) 1474 the facts of which are clearly distinguishable.

> justice will be occasioned if the request be granted in furtherance of the doing of substantial justice.

The court's conclusion that the delivery of final addresses as a rule of practice is not applicable to the customary court is supported by the provision of Order IX Rule 6 (1) of its Rules which is to the effect that

> at the conclusion of the evidence on both sides, the court shall consider the whole evidence and give its judgment thereon and the grounds upon which the judgment is based and it shall issue an order …

This provision needs no explanation as it speaks for itself. The judgment of the court is delivered immediately after the close of evidence on both sides and not 'after the conclusion of evidence and final addresses' as contained in Section 294 of the 1999 constitution.

'Final addresses' under the Customary Courts Rules is omitted after the 'conclusion of evidence' before proceeding to judgment. There is no provision in the Rules stipulating final addresses as part of the customary courts procedure.

The position taken by the Patani Area Customary Court allowing a reply on points of law is in accord with the present position of the new Delta State High Court Rules as already discussed *supra.*

Courts Established under the Constitution - It is to be noted in regard to the point under discussion that there is a difference between courts established 'by' the constitution[57] and courts established 'under' the constitution. Courts established by the constitution are specifically named by the constitution[58] while courts

57. See Section 6 (5) (a) to (i) of the 1999 Constitution.
58. *ibid.*

established under the constitution are those courts not specifically named in the constitution but which are established pursuant to powers conferred by the constitution.[59]

All courts with subordinate jurisdiction to a High Court including magistrate and customary courts are courts established not by the constitution but under the constitution. Accordingly, Customary Courts are courts established under the constitution to which Section 294 of the constitution relates and through which it is inferred that the practice of delivering final addresses at the conclusion of evidence in any cause or matter before the court is applicable to the court notwithstanding the provision in Order IX Rule 6 (1) of the Customary Courts Rules which is inferior to the constitution.

The Recovery Judgement - The judgement of the court is the decision of the court arrived at following a consideration of the whole evidence as presented before it by the parties to which the appropriate law has been applied. It is set down in writing and read out in open court by the Judge, Magistrate or President as the case may be. In practice, the judgement is read from handwritten loose sheets and thereafter typed in quadruplicates where there was only one plaintiff and one defendant.

One of the typed copies is placed in the court's file; another copy is pasted in the court's record book where record books are in use otherwise the copy is properly filed in the court's file while the remaining two copies are given to the parties upon request. Where there has been more than one plaintiff and or more than one defendant, as many more

59. See Section 6 (4) (a), (b), (j) and (k) 1999 Constitution.

copies as there were additional parties are typed.

The Judge, Magistrate or President and members must sign every copy of the judgement including the loose sheet from which the judgement is read. The signing is preferably done immediately after the reading of the judgement in open court. This is also applicable to rulings or other orders made by the court.

On judgemet day, the case is called in the usual manner, the Judge, Magistrate or President records the parties and their counsel, if any, in the record book. The fact of the judgement or ruling being read from loose sheets to be typed later and pasted on the record book or placed in the case file (in jurisdictions where record books are not in use) is then recorded. The judgement may be read whether the parties and their counsel are present in court or not and it must be signed by the court upon its delivery.

Enough space is left by visual estimate by the court on the record book for the pasting. Two vertical lines may be drawn over the estimated space left for the pasting and the word 'pasting' written in between the two vertical lines. In the case of the Customary Court, the judgment of the court which must be signed by the President and the members must reflect the opinion of the majority of members sitting at the hearing of the cause or matter.[60] This also is in accord with the provisions of Section 294 (3) of the 1999 constitution to the effect that

> a decision of a court consisting of more than one judge shall be determined by the opinion of the majority of its members.

In the event of members disagreeing, the opinion of the

60. See Section 11 (2) of the Customary Courts Law.

majority shall be deemed and taken to be the decision of the court and where there is an equality of votes the president or other member presiding shall in addition to his original vote have a casting vote.[61]

The judgment is part of the proceedings and must be delivered in public just as the rest of the proceedings must be held in public.[62]

Proceedings in Public - The 1999 constitution of Nigeria makes provisions guaranteeing the right to fair hearing to every person whose civil rights and obligations come up for determination by a court.[63] An integral element of this right is that the proceedings of the court including the announcement of its decision shall be held in public.[64]

By public it is not meant that members of the public must actually be present in court during the proceedings or during the delivery of the judgment. The requirement is satisfied if public access is freely allowed during the proceedings notwithstanding that no member of the public is actually present at the proceedings. The object of the provision is to ensure that trials are conducted in such an environment where members of the public are not excluded and so render the proceedings open and transparent from which the public can see that justice is ultimately fairly

61. See Section 11(2) and (3) of the Customary Courts Law.
62. See Section 36 (3) 1999 Constitution.
63. Section 36 (1) of 1999 Constitution.
64. There are issues in relation to the submission of written final addresses which are not read in open court and especially the provision of the Lagos Tenancy Law that '*any fact required to be proved at the trial of any action evidence shall be by written deposition*' whether this is not in breach of the constitutional provision for trials to be in public.

done. In the words of the Supreme Court in *Oviasu v Oviasu*,[65]

> it is of the essence of justice that … it should be seen to be actually done. Any act of secrecy, however desirable it might seem, detracts from the aura of impartiality, independence, publicity and unqualified respect which enshrouds justice given without fear.

Order 17 Rule 1 of the Lagos Magistrates' Courts Rules provides that trials of civil actions shall be held in open court although the Magistrate may order a hearing to be held in camera where a public hearing would defeat the ends of justice. Also Section 30 (i) of the Customary Courts Law makes provision to the effect that

> the room or place in which a customary court shall sit to hear and determine any cause or matter shall be an open and public court to which the members of the public shall have a right of access while they shall be of good behaviour and to the extent to which the capacity of the court shall allow.

The requirement of open trial is not violated if a court excludes persons, not being parties to the proceedings or being legal practitioners to the parties, from the proceedings in the interest of

(a) defence,
(b) public safety,
(c) public order,
(d) public morality,
(e) the welfare of persons under the age of eighteen,
(f) the protection of the private lives of the parties or
(g) such other special circumstances in which

65. (1973) ANLR 730.

publicity would, in the opinion of the court, be contrary to the interest of justice.[66]

This constitutional provision is substantially provided for in Section 30 (2) of the Customary Courts Law to the effect that the appropriate authority may make Rules of court permitting the exclusion of the public from the proceedings of any Customary Court in cases where:

(a) persons under the age of seventeen years are involved, or

(b) the administration of justice would be rendered impracticable by the presence of the public.

A court may also hold proceedings in private and yet not be in breach of the requirement to hold proceedings in public where a federal minister or state commissioner satisfies the court that it would not be in the public interest for any matter which may come to the knowledge of the public in the course of the proceedings to be so disclosed to the public.[67]

Non Exclusion of the Press - Although the courts may in their discretion exclude members of the public from their proceedings at any stage of the proceedings in circumstances as discussed above where the court considers that the administration of justice so requires, such exercise of discretion shall not extend so as to exclude representatives of the mass media or of the press.

Where however, in the very rare situation where a court makes an order excluding members of the public from its proceedings and such an order includes the press, the order of the court shall specifically state so and

66. Proviso (a) to Section 36 (4) of 1999 Constitution.
67. Proviso (b) to S. 36 (4).

especially the reason for so doing. Such a reason must be very cogent and strong.

Except in the above circumstances or any other situations expressly permitted by law, any proceedings held in camera will be a nullity and liable to be set aside. In *Oviasu v Oviasu*,[68] the hearing took place in the judge's chambers. None of the situations permitted by the constitution under which proceedings could be held in camera was established to be present to necessitate the hearing in camera. The Supreme Court raised the issue *suo motun* and set the judgment aside declaring that

> a judge's chamber is not a court hall to which the public will normally have any right of access. The petition and answer did not contain such matters, which by law, ought to be heard in camera .... It is of the essence of justice that ... it should be seen to be actually done. Any act of secrecy, however desirable it might seem, detracts from the aura of impartiality, independence, publicity and unqualified respect which enshrouds justice given without fear.

Considering the Recovery Judgment – When evidence on both sides of the action has been concluded and the parties have exercised their rights to deliver final addresses, the court shall reflect on the evidence as placed before set the appropriate law against the evidence and come to a judgement. This is what Order 18 Rule 1 of the Lagos Magistrates' Courts Rules states in the following words that

> at the conclusion of the hearing of an action the court shall either at the same or at a subsequent sitting deliver judgement or make a final order in the action ....

68. *Supra*.

Order IX Rule 6 (1) of the Customary Courts Rules also provides for this that

> at the conclusion of the evidence on both sides, the court shall consider the whole evidence and give its judgement thereon and the grounds upon which the judgement is based and it shall issue an order ....

In considering the whole evidence, the court also reflects on the issues as canvassed by the parties. This reflection is done dispassionately. In so doing, the court sets the evidence by both sides against each other with a view to determining which one is of greater probative value not in terms of the number of witnesses or the length or quantum of the evidence but in terms of admissible, relevant and credible evidence.

The 'weighing' of the evidence on both sides is done side by side and almost simultaneously by the court before concluding one way or the other.

The Conclusion - The court must arrive at a conclusion arising from its consideration of the evidence. In other words, the court must make positive pronouncements concerning the result of its consideration of the evidence by stating clearly which of the evidence as adduced by each side it accepts as being more probable and which one it rejects stating the grounds therefor.

Grounds for Conclusion - In giving its 'judgment thereon', the court shall also state the 'grounds upon which its judgment is based'. In *Ojogbue v Nnubia,*[69] the Supreme Court set aside the judgment of the High Court, Onitsha, because the judgment of the High Court did not demonstrate in full a dispassionate consideration of the

69. (1972) ANLR 664.

issues neither did it make any clear findings upon which it had unequivocally upheld the contentions of the defendants against the claims of the plaintiffs.

Therefore a court's judgment must in all cases result from a dispassionate consideration of the evidence and the issues canvassed. It must also contain the court's clear findings arising from the consideration and it must conclude by pronouncing positive orders on the contentious claims of the parties.

Summing up what a standard judgement of a court must contain, the Supreme Court in *Okulate v Awosanya* [70] stated that what a court must watch out for are whether:

(a) the parties have been appropriately stated,

(b) the nature of the claim and cause of action are known and have been considered,

(c) the issues in controversy have been appreciated and dealt with,

(d) the evidence has been properly received, evaluated and given its probative value,

(e) findings supported by evidence have been made and conclusions in fact and in law drawn,

(f) the evidence has been put on the imaginary scale to see which side it tilts favourably and,

(g) verdict or decision has been reached, judgement given and consequential orders made.

The Recovery Order – The heart of all of the above discussion is in the order which the court makes in relation to the action. After considering the evidence and the issues, and after making clear findings and pronouncements as to the result of the exercise of evaluating the evidence before

70. (2000) FWLR (Pt. 25) 1666, 1684.

it including stating the basis for the findings, a court must then make positive orders which must be in the nature of a command or direction[71] in connection with the subject matter of the claim before it.

The possible orders which a Recovery Court can make at the end of a trial are as contained in the Forms J, K, L, and M[72] in the Schedule 1 to the Recovery Statutes. The first three forms contain sundry orders where the judgement is in favour of the plaintiff while the last form is for orders where the judgement is in favour of the defendant. Form J which is entitled *Judgement for Plaintiff in Action for Recovery of Premises* contains orders such as

> it is adjudged that the plaintiff do recover against the defendant possession of the premises mentioned in....

and

> it is further adjudged that the plaintiff do recover against the defendant the sum of ... for rent and *mesne* profits from the ... day of ... 20... up to date hereof and further *mesne* profits at the same time of obtaining possession

while the orders in Form M where the judgement is in favour of the defendant are that[73]

> it is adjudged that the plaintiff is not entitled to recover possession of the ... premises and it is adjudged that judgement be entered for the defendant, and that the

71. See Order 18 Rule 1 Magistrates' Courts Rules, Order XI1 Rule 1 Customary Courts Rules.
72. There is now only one Form numbered TL7 and entitled *Judgement for Claimant in Action for Recovery of Premises* under the Lagos Tenancy Law.
73. See the Forms in Schedule 1 to the Recovery Statutes for other possible orders which the court can make.

The court's order is made in open court and shall be recorded in the record book of the court and must be signed as appropriate.

Orders not Sought

Generally, 'a court has no jurisdiction to grant a relief not asked for'.[74] This is trite. Therefore, the order which the court makes in every recovery action must be in relation to the claim of the parties and as proved before the court.

However, under the Rules, the courts with summary jurisdiction appear to wield great discretionary powers as they may make orders not asked for by the parties if they consider that the justice of the case demands the making of such orders.[75] The Magistrates' Courts Rules provide that

> ... the court may in all causes and matters make any order which the circumstances of the cause or matter justify and which it considers necessary for doing justice, whether such order has been expressly asked for by the person entitled to the benefit of the order or not.[76]

However any such order by the court must be within the court's powers to make. Accordingly, the power of the court to make orders for prayers not sought does not extend to a judgment for a greater sum of money than the amount claimed in the particulars of claim.[77] But the court can award costs for a greater sum than the amount asked for.

Order 18 Rule 3 (2) of the Magistrates' Courts

74. *Bhojson Plc v Daniel-Kalio* (2006) 2 FWLR (Pt 309) 2183; *Ekpenyong v Nyong* (1975) 2 SC 71. But see Kawu JSC's obitre in *First African Trust Bank v Ezegbu* (1993) 7 KLR 1, 18.
75. Order XI1 Rule 1 Customary Courts Rules; Order 18 Rule 5 Magistrates' Courts Rules.
76. Order 18 Rule 5.
77. Proviso to Order X11 Rule 1 of the Customary Courts Rules.

Rules requires that

> every judgement or order requiring any person to do an act act other than the payment of money or costs shall state the time within which the act is to be done

while under the Customary Courts Rules, the court may, in making its order, *suo motun* fix a time frame within which the order must be carried out and, in particular, may direct that any sum of money ordered to be paid may be paid by instalments.[72]

Notice of Court Order - A person affected by an order of court but who did not participate in the proceedings or did not appear in court during the proceedings shall be entitled to a notice of the terms of the order by serving on him a certified true copy of the court's order prior to its execution. This is the provision of Order XI Rule 4 (2) of the Customary Court's old Rules (Delta) which has now been reworded thus:

> when a party affected by an order of a court has appeared in the proceedings it shall not be necessary to bring the terms of the order to his notice before execution.[78]

The rewording has, with due respect, introduced no material change to the procedure under the old Rules except perhaps to emphasize the want of the necessity for bringing the terms of an order of the court to the notice of a party who has appeared in the proceedings.[79]

If it shall be necessary to bring the terms of an order of the court to the notice of a party who has not participated in the proceedings under the Customary Courts Rules, this

77. See also Order 18 Rule 7 Magistrates' Courts Rules.
78. Order XI1 Rule 4 (2).
79. See also Order 18 Rule 3 Magistrates' Courts Rules.

shall be done by the bailiff of the court completing the Formal Order as in Form G in the First Schedule of Forms to the Rules and which the president of the court shall sign. The bailiff then proceeds to serve same and thereafter satisfies the court of the service by way of an affidavit of service in the usual way before commencing the steps that would lead to the execution of the judgement.

Delivery of Judgement within Ninety Days – Every court's judgement in Nigeria must be in writing and delivered in open court within ninety days after the close of final addresses.

Section 294 (1) of the constitution provides that every court established under the constitution shall deliver its decision in writing not later than ninety days after the conclusion of evidence and final addresses. The section also provides that duly authenticated copies of the court's judgement shall be made available to all the parties to the cause or matter within seven days of the delivery of the judgement.

The above provisions of subsection (1) of Section 294 of the 1999 Constitution are however not strict as non-compliance shall not operate to make a court's decision liable to be set aside or to be treated as a nullity by an appeal court except where the appeal court is satisfied that the party complaining has suffered a miscarriage of justice as a result of the non-compliance.[80]

The constitution requires that where it has been determined or observed by the appeal court that there has been non-compliance with the provisions of subsection (1) of Section 294 of the Constitution, the person who presided

80. Section 294 (5) 1999 Constitution.

at the sitting of the appeal court shall send a report on the case to the chairman of the National Judicial Council who shall keep the Council informed of such action as the Council may deem fit.[81]

Attendance at the Proceedings - Every litigant, being a party to a court's proceedings, is expected to attend court every day the cause comes up on the cause list of the court. This is part of diligence which is a duty imposed on all parties to court proceedings including counsel.

Unfortunately, in Recovery Courts, it is a usual occurrence to have defendants deliberately absent themselves from court as a design for delaying the proceedings. Sadly, it is not uncommon that such litigants conduct themselves in this way sometimes on the advice of their lawyers who take turns with their clients for absenting themselves from proceedings with a view to forcing adjournments of their cases upon the court. When it is the turn of counsel to absent himself under the delay tactic, counsel writes letters to court making all sorts of claims including placing a curse on himself with misfortunes such as illness why he is unable to attend court and requesting that the case be adjourned.

Condemning this attitude, the Court of Appeal per Mukhtar JCA in *Muhammed v Kpelai,*[82] declared that

> the business of the court is indeed a serious one and must be seen as such by all and sundry if our judicial system is to be accorded its rightful place in the charter that binds us together as an orderly society. No one is entitled to treat the proceedings of the court ... with disdain or passive indifference

81. Section 294 (6).
82. (2001) FWLR (Pt. 69) 1404, 1415.

by displaying a 'nonchalant and lackadaisical' attitude in the prosecution of his own case. This means that every party to a court proceedings, whether he is the plaintiff or the defendant, must attend court every day the cause comes up on the court's list.

A party who deliberately or for no discernable excuse absents himself from the proceedings does so at his own detriment as equity aids the vigilant and never the indolent. The Rules of court make provisions for the business of the court to go on, in appropriate cases, in the absence of a party and it will not lie in the mouth of such an indifferent and indolent absentee litigant to complain of being denied his constitutional right to fair hearing if the proceedings proceeds in his absence with an unfavourable outcome to himself.

When the cause is called by the clerk or the Registrar of the court, the litigant is expected to answer to his name in clear and audible voice in words such as 'yes sir!' or 'sir!' or 'yes my lord!' or 'present my lord!. He then steps out of the gallery and stands to a side of the court depending as to whether he is plaintiff or defendant behind the bar of the court in the well thereof.

Legal Practitioner as Party - It happens sometimes that a party to a proceedings is also a legal practitioner. The Rules permit such a party, like every other person, to conduct his case himself in person. When he so does, he is not a legal practitioner for the purposes of the particular proceedings but he is only himself as a litigant. He is entitled to speak and conduct his case from the bar and even in his robes (in the High Court) as he continues to be entitled to the privileges of his profession which cannot be denied him merely because he is a plaintiff or defendant in a proceedings.[83]

In recovery actions especially those before Recovery Courts with summary jurisdictions, the incidence of legal practitioners appearing as party is a frequent occurrence. These are legal practitioners who are also landlords, or legal practitioners who have been invested with powers of attorney, or legal practitioners appointed by landlords as agents and all of whom have been invested with authority to eject tenants by action. Such legal practitioners, in practice, usually conduct their cases in court in person themselves. They are entitled to do so.

But such self-representation is not to be encouraged as it makes the proceedings most untidy. This untidiness is usually brought to the fore when the other party is represented by counsel and will have to cross examine his learned friend. Hence it is to be recommended that a legal practitioner who has a personal cause or matter before the court should at all times endeavour to secure the services of a colleague for obvious advantages. As the Supreme Court put it in *Egbe v Adefarasin*,[84]

> ...counsel should endeavour to brief another counsel when cases concern them personally otherwise objectivity and detachment can hardly be maintained *(and that it must always be remembered that)* he who descends into the arena of conflict cannot avoid the dust of the encounter.

However, where counsel decides to ignore the wise counsel of the Supreme Court and opts to conduct his case in

83. *Fawehinmi v NBA (No.1)* (1989) 2 NWLR (Pt. 105) 494
84. (1987) ANLR 1, 19; (1987) 1 NWLR (Pt. 47) 1.

person and to go into the witness box himself to testify, he cannot be denied the right to so do. But he shall step out of the bar when the case is called and he shall stand to a side in the well of the court as is appropriate depending as to whether he is plaintiff or defendant to answer to his name in the usual manner in which every litigant answers to his name in the court.

He shall thereafter be at liberty to seek the leave of the court to resume his privileged position in the bar of the court from where he may then enter appearance 'in person' as plaintiff or defendant but not enter appearance 'for himself' as there is no such thing in law as a barrister representing himself. In the words of the Supreme Court in *Fawehinmi v NBA (No.1)*,[85]

> a party cannot appear both as a person and as counsel for himself[86] (because) the characters should not be mixed (and that although) a barrister litigant has a right to conduct his case in person as any other member of the public or be represented by counsel as any other member of the public, it is not right or correct to say that a barrister represents himself. Such a representation does not exist in law ....[87]

85. *Supra*.
86. *ibid* at 532.
87. *ibid* at 531.

Chapter Seven
Incidental Proceedings at the Recovery Trial

Introduction

In almost every suit in court, developments and situations exist or occur which are incidental or collateral to the main or principal object of the suit requiring that certain steps be taken in the proceedings to address such developments or occurrences before the substantive suit is heard or subsequent to the hearing and even after judgement.

Interlocutory Proceedings – All such incidental steps are generally referred to as interlocutory steps or proceedings. They become necessary where, for instance, the defendant desires to attack the jurisdiction of the court, or where the plaintiff seeks an injunction or any of the parties desires to amend his process etc.

The Magistrates' Courts Rules provide that where under any law or Rule of court any application in the course of an action or matter before or after judgement is expressly or by implication authorized to be made to the court, then such an application may be made by way of an interlocutory application either

(a) in writing on notice to the other party or *ex parte*, or

(b) orally.[1]

Similarly, Order VIII Rule 1 of the Customary Courts Rules defines *'interlocutory application'* as an application made during the pendency of a suit and which is incidental to the principal object of the suit and includes all steps

1. Order 10 Rule 1.

taken for the purpose of assisting the parties in the prosecution of their cases or of protecting the subject matter of the suit or otherwise dealing with the action or of executing the judgment when obtained.

By incidental proceedings therefore, it is meant to refer to those steps which become necessary to be taken by the parties to a recovery suit designed and directed at preparing or generally at packaging the suit for effectual adjudication but only with regard to some collateral issue to the main object of the suit. Such steps include applications for injunctions, amendments, adjournments, consolidation, attacking court's jurisdiction etc.

Injunctions - A very common incidental occurrence to proceedings in the Recovery Court is the application for injunctions. An injunction is an order of the court as court of equity[2] addressed to a particular party to the proceedings which either prohibits the person from doing or continuing to do a certain act or directs him to carry out an act. This means that an injunction could either be prohibitory as in when it prohibits the party from doing an act e.g. where it restrains him from continuing an act of nuisance or mandatory as in when the party is mandated to do a thing e.g. that he should remove or demolish a wall partition he has erected in the premises without the written consent of the landlord.

The injunction is a very useful tool in the administration of justice, for maintaining peace in the society, and for ensuring that the ends of justice are not defeated ultimately.

2. Courts in Nigeria are empowered by the various reception statutes to enforce *'the common law of England and the doctrines of equity …'*.

The concept of injunction has its roots in English equity. It developed from the proceedings of the English courts of Chancery which were the original courts of equity. These courts developed the concept of injunctions to remedy the rigid inadequacies inherent in the English common law. In *Adenuga v Odumeru*[3] the Supreme Court explained that

> an injunction is an equitable order…. A claim for an injunction is a claim in equity.

In recovery proceedings, it is not uncommon therefore to have interlocutory applications for injunctions usually by the defendant praying the court to restrain the plaintiff from such acts as unlawfully ejecting the defendant, harassing or intimidating him, disconnecting facilities such as electricity and water supply.

The application for injunction is not granted by the court on a platter of gold and for the asking. The applicant usually has an uphill task persuading the court to grant it except where the facts are patently clear in relation to the interest of justice. The following discussion is only[4] in outline and intended to show the nature of injunctions and some of the ingredients required for its grant.

Types of Injunctions – Although this chapter is about interlocutory proceedings, it is worthy to note that there are different types of injunctions depending on the purpose which it is intended that the injunction should serve. These include the perpetual injunction which is not interlocutory or temporary in nature but the claim for which is usually a precondition for claiming other types of injunction such as the interim injunction and the interlocutory injunction

3. (2001) FWLR (Pt.37) 1056, 1069.
4. The reader is advised to consult other standard texts on the subject.

which are without regard as to whether the injunction is prohibitory or mandatory.

Interlocutory Injunctions

A plaintiff may sue claiming an injunction which is endorsed on writ of summons and statement of or particulars of claim. Such a claim for an injunction in the writ of summons or plaint is usually in the nature of a permanent nature and is known as perpetual injunction the endorsement of which as above entitles the plaintiff to subsequently apply for an interim or interlocutory injunction. According to the Supreme Court per Karibi-Whyte JSC in *Adenuga v Odumeru*,[5]

> it is settled law ... that any application for relief subsequent to (the filing of) the claim[6] ... shall be within the purview and scope of the claim. This is because a plaintiff is limited by his claim as expressed in his writ of summons and statement of claim. Any departure from the claim so endorsed and to make a new claim gives rise to a new cause of action in respect of which the jurisdiction of the court has not been invoked by the institution of the action. The jurisdiction of the court is determined by the claim of the plaintiff. This is why any ancillary relief must fall within the scope of the claim in the substantive action.

This Supreme Court decision does not necessarily mean that an interim or interlocutory injunction can only be claimed when a perpetual injunction is claimed in the writ but it means that the ancillary relief by way of an application for injunction must be for prayers related to the substantive claim as endorsed on the writ of summons and

5. *Supra.*
6. This is the 'plaint' in courts of summary jurisdiction.

or settled in the statement of claim. This has to be so because the purpose of an ancillary relief is to ensure the maintenance of the claim pending the determination of the substantive action

> hence the (ancillary) relief must be related to the substantive claim which is the subject matter for determination before the court.[7]

Application for Injunction - The application for an interlocutory injunction is made by way of motion to the particular court in which the main suit has been filed and never to another court since the order sought is an interlocutory one and is collateral to the main suit.[8]

Although it is usual to bring every application for interlocutory reliefs by way of formal motion and Rule 3 of Order VIII of the Customary Courts Rules prohibits the court from entertaining a motion unless the applicant files a motion paper in which he states distinctly the terms of the order he seeks and the grounds upon which he relies therefor, the court may however entertain a motion if the applicant makes an oral application for it in open court distinctly stating the terms of the order sought and the grounds upon which the applicant relies for the grant of the order as, in appropriate cases, the court may entertain an application brought otherwise[9] than by way of formal motion.

Affidavit in Support not a Necessity - The provision

7. *ibid* at 1069.
8. *Adebomi v Ilaro DC* (1965) NMLR 242; See Order VIII Rule 2 Customary Courts Rules.
9. See, for instance, Order 10 Rule 1 (b) Magistrates' Courts Rules which permits that an interlocutory application may be made orally in court.

under the Customary Courts Rules does not provide for the filing of a supporting affidavit while Rule 1 (c) (iii) of the Magistrates' Courts Rules provides that

> where an interlocutory application is to be made on notice, no affidavit shall be necessary in the first instance ...[10]

but the Magistrate may direct evidence to be adduced in such manner as he thinks fit.

In practice however and, notwithstanding the above provisions, an affidavit in support of motion whether on notice or *ex-parte,* is almost always a necessity. This is more so in the case of an application for injunctive orders since an application for the grant of an order of injunction is usually never made as a matter of course but entirely at the discretion of the court.

It is therefore almost always an imperative to support a motion containing an application for an order of injunction with an affidavit wherein the facts upon which the applicant relies to persuade the court to exercise its discretion in his favour and which also satisfy the sundry conditions for the grant of an injunction will bc deposed to.[11] In this regard, Order 10 Rule 6 of the Magistrates' Courts Rules provides that

> where any party desires, before the trial, an immediate order
>
> (a) in the nature of an injunction; or

10. Rule 6 of the Customary Court's Order expressly permits the court to receive oral evidence at the hearing of a motion for interlocutory relief.
11. See *Kotoye v CBN* (1989) ANLR 76; *Obeya Memorial Hospital v A.G. Federation* (1987) 3 NWLR (Pt .60) 324.

(b) for the appointment of a receiver; or

(c) for taking any account; or

(d) for making any enquiries;

he may apply to the court on affidavit setting forth the facts rendering the order immediately necessary, and the court may make such order as it thinks fit.

The facts and conditions which the Rules of court and authorities contemplate for the grant of an injunctive relief include that

(a) the applicant has a legal right deserving of protection by the court,

(b) he has a good chance of success at the trial

(c) the balance of convenience is in his favour

(d) damages will not be adequate compensation or that applicant will suffer irreparable damage and

(e) the applicant shows that there is a substantial issue to be tried at the hearing.

Motions on Notice – Safe for where the Rules make provisions allowing a motion to be brought *ex parte*, every motion for an order of interlocutory relief is required to be on notice to the other party or the person likely to be affected by the order. For instance, Rule 4 of Order VIII of the Customary Courts Rules provides that except where the motion is made by oral application in open court in the presence of the person to be affected or where the court considers it desirable and not unjust that a motion should be taken in the absence of any person likely to be affected, a motion shall be taken only after due notice has been served on the persons likely to be affected.

***Ex Parte* Motions** - The Rules of court clearly show that motions *ex-parte* are a part of normal courts procedure.

Explaining the place of the *ex parte* motion in

litigation, the Supreme Court states that

> '*ex parte*' in relation to injunctions is ... used in contradistinction to 'on notice' ... and both expressions ... refer to the manner in which the application is brought and the order procured.[12]

The apex court then went on to explain that an applicant for a non-permanent injunction may bring the application *ex parte*, that is, without notice to the other side as is appropriate. By their very nature, injunctions granted on *ex parte* applications can only be interim in nature.

They are made without notice to the other side so as to keep matters in status *quo* to a named date, usually not more than a few days or until the other side can be put on notice. The rationale for making an *ex parte* order by the court is to avoid an irretrievable or serious mischief which might result from delay by proceeding in the usual and ordinary way of first putting the other side on notice.

Where an order is made by the court *ex-parte,* the order shall be served on the party affected by the order.[13] Such *ex-parte* order shall be liable to be set aside[14] upon application by the person affected if he shall exercise his right to have the order set aside within seven[15] days of the order being served on him.

The Order of Injunction - The court, after listening to argument on both sides if the application is contested as is

12. *Kotoye v CBN* (1989) ANLR 76.
13. Order 10 Rule 8 Magistrates' Courts Rules and Order VIII Rule 5 Customary Courts Rules.
14. Order 10 Rule 10 Magistrates' Courts Rules and Order VIII Rule 5 Customary Courts Rules.
15. Time frame applicable only to the Customary Courts by Order VIII Rule 5 Customary Courts Rules.

usually the case, and upon the applicant satisfying the conditions for the grant of the order of injunction, grants the order. Where the application is for an interim order made upon an *ex-parte* application, it is made to subsist for no more than about seven days[16] or pending the determination of the same application on notice.

All injunctions except a perpetual injunction are temporary in nature and are designed to keep parties in *status quo* for a period of time or pending an event. Another purpose of an injunction is to preserve the *res* of suit. But injunctions are never granted in respect of completed acts.[17]

Upon determination of an application by way of motion on notice, the order of injunction is made to be in place till the determination of the substantive suit.[18] This is known as an interlocutory injunction. It is different from a perpetual injunction which is made usually at the end of the substantive suit and forms part of the final judgment.

Generally, the court will not grant an interlocutory or interim injunction unless the application for same falls within the scope of the claim in the substantive suit.[19] Accordingly, where the claim in the substantive suit does not include a claim for injunction, the court will usually refuse to make an order for an interim or interlocutory injunction as any application for an ancillary relief made to the court subsequent to the claim must be within the purview and scope of the claim. To depart from the claim in

16. *Kotoye v CBN* (*Supra* at 124).
17. *Williams v Dawodu* (1988) 4 NWLR (Pt. 88) 210.
18. *Kotoye v CBN* (*Supra*).
19. *Adenuga v Odumeru* (*Supra*).

a subsequent application for an ancillary relief is to introduce a new cause of action in respect of which the jurisdiction of the court has not been invoked.[20]

An interim injunction which is usually granted *ex-parte* is designed to keep the parties in status *quo* for a period of seven days or thereabout or pending the determination of the same motion on notice while an interlocutory injunction which is entered after hearing both or all sides to the motion is to keep parties in status *quo* pending the determination of the substantive action.

The grant or otherwise of an interlocutory injunction is a discretionary exercise which the court exercises judicially and judiciously being a remedy at equity. In granting an injunction, the court is always careful not to determine the substantive action at this stage of the proceedings.[21]

Ex Parte Injunctions - Although our laws and the Rules of court recognize the granting of *ex parte* injunctions, its grant is made reluctantly and with extra caution on the part of the court. This is because by its nature, an *ex parte* injunction is open to abuse such that the instrument of court which ought always to be used to meet the ends of justice is employed to perpetuate injustice since the court makes the order after hearing only the applicant's side of the story.

The Supreme Court in *Onyesoh v Nnebedum*[22] has therefore cautioned in this regard that

> before granting an order of injunction on an *ex parte* application, the trial court should make sure that there is

20. *ibid* at p. 1068.
21. *Kadiya v Kadiya* (2001) FWLR (Pt.70) 1586, 1597.
22. (1992) 3 NWLR (Pt. 229) 315.

> real urgency shown otherwise the court should direct that the person who would be affected by the order be put on notice.[23]

Undertaking as to Damages - The applicant for an order of injunction must enter into an undertaking as to damages to compensate the other party of any losses or detriments he may suffer as a result of the grant against him of the order of injunction should it turn out at the end of the substantive action that the applicant was not at all entitled to the order granted in his favour. This will happen if at the end of trial the court decides that the legal right, which the applicant relied on for asking for the order of injunction, did not exist in his favour.

But it is not in all cases that the entering into an undertaking is a necessity. A court making an order of injunction ought also to order the applicant to enter into the undertaking for damages but failure to so order does not render the order of injunction invalid or incompetent. As Nnaemeka-Agu JSC pointed out in the *Onyesoh* case,

> an undertaking as to damages is the price which every applicant for an interlocutory injunction has to pay for it and that, save in recognized exceptions, *(an order of interlocutory injunction)* ought not to be granted if no undertaking *(as to damages)* has been given *(but)* it is putting the consequences of the failure to give the undertaking too high to say… that *(it)* renders the order

23. See also National Judicial Council circular No.NJC/CIR/HOC/1/3 of 7th May 2008 which warns all judicial officers to '*desist from granting reckless ex parte injunctions*' and the follow up circular of the Delta State Customary Court of Appeal No. DSCCA/P/2129/35 of 2nd June 2008 which stressed that '*non-compliance will attract dismissal from the service.*'

> made incompetent. The true position is that it renders the order liable to be set aside *(and)* whether it will be set aside in any case will depend upon the facts of the particular case.

Also, where an applicant for an order of injunction has voluntarily deposed to an undertaking to pay damages in his affidavit in support of his application for the order of injunction, it will be unnecessary for the court to extract the undertaking as to damages in its order.

Accelerated Hearing in Lieu of Injunction - In practical terms, a good number of applications for injunction serve no useful purpose. Most times, they only serve to delay the proceedings and consequently the justice of the substantive action. The court is therefore enjoined to, whenever it is possible, accelerate hearing of the substantive case instead of dissipating energies, cost and time in taking interlocutory proceedings before going through, invariably, the same evidence and legal arguments in the substantive trial.[24]

Customary Courts and Injunctions

As already shown, Customary Courts in Delta, Edo, and Osun exercise the jurisdiction for recovery actions and that when they are exercising this jurisdiction, they do so as hybrid courts in that they do not lose their characters as Customary Courts even though they are exercising all the jurisdictions of a regular Magistrate Court sitting as a Rent Tribunal. But does this entitle Customary Courts to also exercise the jurisdiction for orders of injunction? In other words, are injunctions known to customary law? There are views to the effect that customary courts have jurisdiction

24. *Nigeria Civil Service Union v Essien* (1985) 3 NWLR (Pt.12) 185.

only to entertain or apply customary law. [25]

The learned author[26] of *Cases and Texts on Equity Trust and Administration of Estates*[27] is of the view that 'even in traditional law, injunction was not unknown' and that among the *Yorubas* whenever there was a dispute which was generating bad blood capable of endangering peace, the disputants were restrained from taking laws into their hands and an injunction placed on the land forbidding all the disputants from entering the land or dealing with it until the dispute is settled. [28] This clearly means that injunctions are not unknown to customary law and therefore can be granted by Customary Courts not only because they are not unknown to customary law but also because their establishing statutes allow them to entertain

> causes or matters under any law (other than customary law) including bye-laws ....[29]

Clearly, 'any law' and which is not customary law must be a reference to all other forms of law including equity and therefore injunctions which is part of Nigerian law.

Besides, Order XIII Rule 1 of the Customary Courts Rules provides that

> where a court has power to require any person to do or abstain from doing any act or thing other than the payment of money and no other mode is provided by

25. See *Akintayo v Atanda* (1963) ANLR 599; *CCA Edo State v Aguele* (2006) 12 NWLR (Pt.995) 545.
26. Olayide Adigun.
27. (1987) Ayo Sodimu Publishers.
28. See at page 77.
29. Item 6 of Schedule 1 to the Customary Courts Law 1997 (Delta State). For more on this, see Miakpo Emiaso (2010) *Law, Practice and Procedure: Area Customary Courts in Nigeria* (Peakmans Ltd., Lagos) at 21 – 24; 123 *et seq.*

> these Rules for enforcing the requirement, the court may exercise the power by an order and may annex to the order such conditions as the court may see fit, and may suspend or rescind any such order on terms and may make such arrangements for carrying out such order as the court may see expedient.

This provision of Order XIII clearly defines an injunction and indicates that the Customary Court has powers to make and enforce orders of injunction.

Amendments - Another incidental development in proceedings before the Recovery Court is the need to amend processes before the court. A party may be allowed by the court to amend any of his processes under the Rules of court. The Customary Courts Rules, for instance, provide that

> the court may, at any stage before judgment, upon application by any party to the proceedings, amend the particulars of a claim … if the court is satisfied that no injustice will result…[30]

The above provision of the Customary Courts Rules refers only to the possible amendment of the particulars of claim and not necessarily of the claim or of other processes before the court. But it is humbly submitted that the reference to particulars of claim ought also to cover the claim and all other processes before the court. Therefore, it is possible to amend both the claim and the particulars of claim and indeed any other process filed in or before the Customary Court.

The Magistrates' Courts Rules are more detailed in providing that the court may, at any time amend any

30. Order IX Rule 7.

defects and errors in any proceedings whether the defect or error is that of the party applying to amend or not.[31] Rule 3 of this Order provides that any amendment may be made at any stage of the proceedings by the court of its own motion, or on the oral application of any party at the trial, or before the trial on notice.

The court will usually grant the application of a party to the proceedings to amend his claim, particulars of claim, or other process filed in or before the court if the application to amend is designed to or intended to aid the determination of the real questions or questions in controversy between the parties in the suit[32] and where the amendment will not lead to injustice on the part of the respondent. Stating the guiding principles for the grant of an application for amendment of court processes, the Supreme Court of Nigeria in *Ojah v Ogboni*[33] called in aid the *dicta* of Bowen L.J. in *Cropper v Smith*[34] thus –

> … It is a well established principle that the object of courts is to decide the rights of the parties, and not to punish them for mistakes which they made in the conduct of their cases by deciding otherwise than in accordance with their rights …. I know of no kind of error or mistake which, if not fraudulent or intended to overreach, the court ought not to correct, if it can be done without injustice to the other party. Courts do not exist for the sake of discipline, but for the sake of deciding matters in controversy and I do not regard such amendment as matter of favour or grace …. It seems to

31. Order 9 Rule 1.
32. See Rule 1 of Order 9 Magistrates' Courts Rules.
33. See *Ojah v Ogboni* (1976) ANLR 277.
34. (1884) 26 Ch.D 700, 710.

> me that as soon as it appears that the way in which a party has framed his case will not lead to a decision of the real matter in controversy, it is as much a matter of right on his part to have it corrected, if it can be done without injustice, as anything else in the case is a matter of right.

The application will be refused also if it is shown that the application will entail injustice to the respondent, or that the applicant is acting *mala fide* or that the respondent had been exposed to some injury by the blunder of the applicant and which injury cannot be compensated by costs or otherwise.[35]

Necessity for Amendment – In the superior courts of record, particularly the High Courts, the general rule is that parties are bound by their pleadings. By this generally strict rule, a party may not be allowed to adduce evidence in support of a fact he has not pleaded in his pleadings. Any such evidence led inadvertently on the records will go to no issue and the court will be entitled to and usually will discountenance it.

Where such evidence had been led and admitted, the court may subsequently, upon application to it by the party who led such evidence, be bound to amend the pleadings to bring them at tandem with the evidence as led.[36] But in the summary jurisdiction of most Recovery Courts, the strict rules of pleadings are not applicable since pleadings in their technical sense are not used in proceedings thereat.

35. *ibid.*
36. *Ibanga v Asanga* (1982) 5 SC 291; *Oguntimeyin v Gubere* (1964) ANLR 169.

However, sub Rule 2 of Rule 7 to Order IX of the Customary Courts Rules provides that

> if the facts proved at the trial are substantially the same as the particulars of claim ... the court may give judgment and issue an order on the evidence adduced before it without amending the claim ....

This provision seems to suggest that, like pleadings in the High Courts, judgment by the Customary Court may be given only where the evidence led is in agreement or substantially in agreement with the particulars of claim. If this position is correct, then the need for a party who has filed particulars of claim in the Customary Court to when necessary amend same is obvious.

Also, a party may have come or been brought to court in the wrong capacity. Upon the party realizing the mistake, an application for amendment becomes necessary. Mistakes may also have been made with respect to some fundamental element in the processes filed by either party such as in the name of a party or the amount claimed which will require amendment.

A suit by or against a non-juristic person is not a misnomer and cannot be amended. Such a suit must be struck out[37] as there is nothing before the court capable of being amended.

An application to amend the title of a suit is not granted as a matter of course especially where an incorporated company is involved. It must be shown that there were reasonable grounds of excuse for the wrong naming of the party and that the wrong name used could not have led to any reasonable doubt as to the real identity

37. *Agbonmagbe Bank Ltd v GM, G.B. Ollivant* (1961) ANLR 125.

of the person intended to be sued.[38]

Generally, the court will not grant an immaterial amendment or one brought in bad faith. Also, where an amendment will set up a claim which had become statute barred or one which did not exist as at when the summons was issued will not be granted.

Procedure for Amendment – The Rules are silent on the procedure for bringing an application for amendment to the court safe for implied references. For instance, Order 9 Rule 3 of the Magistrates' Courts Rules provides that an amendment may be made by the court *suo motun*, or by oral application of any party to the proceedings at the trial, or, if before trial, on notice.

Similarly, Order IX Rule 7 of the customary Courts Rules provides that the court may at any stage and upon application by any party to the proceedings, amend the particulars of a claim if the court is satisfied that no injustice will result. But unlike the provision in the Magistrate's Courts Rules, the Customary Courts Rules do not expressly empower the court to amend or order an amendment *suo motun.*[39]

An application for amendment may be made orally if the amendment is short, simple, clear and properly couched and formulated. But it is usual that applications for amendment particularly of the claim or particulars of claim be made formally by way of motion on notice to the other party whereby the prayer for amendment is carefully

38. *Njemanze v Shell BP* (1966) ANLR 8.

39. But in appropriate cases, the Customary Court may exercise its inherent powers to so order where no party will suffer prejudice thereby.

couched and properly formulated in simple and clear wordings usually in the following form:

> Take notice etc … for an order granting leave to the plaintiff/applicant to amend his particulars of claim *(or claim or other process as appropriate)* in the manner indicated in the exhibit annexed hereto.

The particular process as was originally filed but now indicating the amendment sought thereon is then annexed to the affidavit in support of the motion as an exhibit. The part sought to be amended is indicated by underlining the new material sought to be introduced into the particulars of claim (or whatever process is being amended) or where it is sought not to introduce new material but to delete or remove material, same is indicated by bold vertical lines on both margins over the part of the process being amended.

The application is then filed and argued in the usual manner except when the other party does not object in which case the motion is moved in terms of the motion paper.

The Order of Amendment - The order of amendment is refused or granted by the court as the court deems proper. When granted, the amendment is usually ordered to be effected by the applicant within a specified time. The amendment must then be effected within the time so specified by the court otherwise the order will lapse. But the party may apply to the court and obtain an extension thereof and except time is extended the order becomes void.

The order of the court allowing amendment must also direct that the amended process be filed and served within the specified time. This is to enable a properly amended process be in the court's file as opposed to a mere exhibit as annexed to the motion paper which may inadvertently be 'missed out' by the court at the time of writing its judgment sometimes many months or even years later.

The amended process which is filed must also be endorsed with fact of the amendment and the date of the order at the bottom of the last page thus:

Amended by order of court made the ... day of ... 20....

Effect of Amendment - The amendment of a court process whether it is the plaint or claim or particulars of claim takes effect not from the date the order of amendment is made by the court but dates back to the original date of the process. This has to be so especially with respect to the writ of summons or other form by which the suit was commenced so as to prevent the action from possibly being caught by the provisions of the statute of limitation.

Conversely, it is not permissible for a party to amend his claim by introducing a new cause of action which had not accrued as at the date of filing the original suit.

Once a court process is amended, the process in its original form before the amendment was ordered becomes immaterial. Hence the proceedings continues after the amendment as if the amended version had been before the court right from the inception of the proceedings[40] while the original process becomes irrelevant as far as the suit is concerned.

Generally, the court allows amendments upon application on terms as to costs. The order of amendment can be made at any time before judgment provided that no

40. *Oguma v IBWA* (1988) I NWLR (Pt.37) 658.

party will be prejudiced thereby and the interest of justice will be better served.

Where under the Rules of court an order of amendment is made *ex-parte*, a notice of the order of the Order of amendment must be served on the other party.[41]

Adjournment – The proceedings may be adjourned by the court either upon the application of any of the parties or *suo motun* at any stage.[42]

The adjournment *suo motun* by the court is one which is made for reasons of the court's convenience. This means that the court takes into consideration its work-load *vis-à-vis* other causes or matters pending before it and all the circumstances of the particular suit in deciding to adjourn a suit on its own motion until such a time as may be convenient for it.

Under the Magistrates' Courts Rules, the court may not only adjourn the hearing of any proceedings at any time but may do so also from time to time. And when such adjournment is ordered in the absence of any of the parties or person interested in the proceedings, notice thereof shall be to them by the Registrar of the court.[43]

Court may Refuse Adjournment – Sub-rule 2 Rule 8 of the Customary Court's Order IX provides that the court shall refuse any request for adjournment by any party to the proceedings 'unless there be good reason for granting it'. This means that refusing an application for adjournment by any party to the proceedings is the rule and not the

41. Proviso to Order IX Rule 7 (1) Customary Courts Rules.
42. Order IX Rule 8 (1) Customary Courts Rules. Section 30 Magistrates' Courts Law and Order 10 Rule 4 of its Rules.
43. Order 10 Rule 4 (2).

exception. Granting such an application is the exception to the rule. This exception is to be observed by the court on one ground only. That is to say only when the court sees 'good reason' to so do.

But 'good reason' could be as vague as it is subjective. Good reason with regard to any proceedings in a court must necessarily be that reason which accords with the attainment of the ends of justice. The grant or refusal by the court of an application for adjournment has implications in the constitutional demand of fair hearing. This constitutional demand is to the effect that

> in the determination of *(a citizen's)* civil rights and obligations, including any question or determination by or against any government or authority a person shall be entitled to a fair hearing within a reasonable time by a court ... established by law and constituted in such manner as to secure its independence and impartiality[44]

Therefore a court will be cautious and circumspect in refusing an application made to it by a party to the proceedings for adjournment lest the court create a situation which may suggest a denial of fair hearing to the applicant.

Adjournment Discretionary - In *Ononuju v Ononuju,*[45] the Court of Appeal held that the question of adjournment is a matter within the discretion of the trial judge but which discretion must be exercised judicially and judiciously.

The primary objective in the grant or refusal of an application for adjournment is the attainment of substantial justice and the cardinal principle is that each party to a dispute has a right to have his dispute determined upon the

44. Section 36 of the 1999 Constitution.
45. (1991) 5 NWLR (Pt. 192) 479.

merits. Therefore the court must do everything to favour the fair hearing of the questions between the parties.[46]

Fair hearing in this regard has been defined to mean a trial conducted according to all the legal rules formulated to ensure that justice is done to the parties to the cause[47] and that the true test of a fair hearing (which is the same thing as fair trial) is the impression of a reasonable person who was present at the trial whether, from his observation, justice has been done in the case.[48]

In *N.B.C.I v M.G.I Co Ltd*,[49] the 'matter came up for the first time for hearing' and the plaintiff was absent in court. His counsel applied for an adjournment on the excuse that his client was 'inevitably absent'. The defendant's counsel however applied to court to dismiss the suit which application was granted.

Allowing the appeal of the plaintiff, the appeal court held that a trial judge being the master of his court has wide discretionary powers in matters of adjournment but that before refusing or granting an adjournment, the court must consider the application carefully and must state the reasons for its decision and it should be 'obvious from the records that (it gave) a deliberate, careful, different and definite consideration' for the grant or refusal.[50]

Accordingly, an application for adjournment to enable the applicant to call additional witness or on ground of medical needs or to enable a party to properly prepare

46. *ibid* per Kolawole JCA at 490.
47. *Ariori v Elemo* (1983) ANLR 1, 25.
48. *Mohammed v Kano Native Authority* (1968) ANLR 411
49. (1992) 2 NWLR (Pt .221) 71.
50. *ibid* at p. 82.

his case will, if granted, be in the interest of justice.[51] In practice, parties and counsel grossly abuse these grounds resulting in delays in justice delivery. Defendants in recovery actions often take to all manner of antics to delay proceedings and thereby 'buy time'. But it has to be stressed that delay cannot amount to a defence.

To discourage the abuses to which applications for adjournments may be subjected by parties and their counsel, the Edo State Customary Courts Rules 1984 by a 2005 amendment imposes a fee of N200.00 for every application for adjournment by a party. The applicant's letter for adjournment is required to be filed at the court's Registry in the usual manner whereat it is assessed at N200.00 which is paid by the applicant for adjournment and an official receipt issued.

The N200 filing fee is without regard to any costs which the court may in its discretion eventually award in favour of the other party in the circumstance of the application for the adjournment.

Fair Hearing Within Reasonable Time – As already shown *supra*, there is a constitutional requirement that in the determination of a citizen's civil rights and obligations, a person shall be entitled to a fair hearing within a reasonable time by a court. 'Reasonable time' has been stated to mean

> the period of time which, in the search for justice, does not wear out the parties and their witnesses and which is required to ensure that justice is not only done but appears to reasonable persons to be done.[52]

---

51. *Ariori v Elemo* (*Supra*) at 25.
52. Per Obaseki JSC (as he then was) in *Ariori v Elemo* (*Supra*).

In effect, it is the attitude of the Nigerian law that recovery actions, like every other action in any court, ought to be disposed of within such period of time which will not wear out parties to an action so that justice will ultimately appear to reasonable persons to have been done where all parties have been afforded fair opportunities to state their respective sides and be heard. Such fair opportunities do not consist in unnecessary delays arising from wanton absence from court.

When an application for adjournment is granted, the court may also make orders on terms as to costs.[53]

Adjournment for Mention – It is said that in a court of summary jurisdiction as most recovery courts are, all adjournments are for hearing and never for mention. This is indeed provided for by the Rules of court where almost all the provisions relating to adjournment speak of 'adjournment for hearing' or 'adjourn the hearing'.

An adjournment for mention, in practice, is that adjournment of the proceedings ordered by the court to enable certain interlocutory steps to be taken in preparation for the hearing of the action while an adjournment for trial or hearing is that ordered by the court to a date for the actual trial of the suit during which evidence will be led by the parties and their witnesses and which evidence shall be recorded. An adjournment for trial or hearing is ordered only when the suit is said or considered by the court to be ripe and ready for the actual hearing.

All court business including adjournments depends on the convenience of the court and it may not always be possible for a court to predict its convenience and be

53. Order IX Rule 8 (3) Customary Courts Rules.

certain that a suit is ready and ripe for hearing so as to give rise for necessarily adjourning same for trial or hearing. Parties may obtain adjournments to take steps such as amending their processes or to wait upon a contingent. In situations as these, it is humbly submitted that even a court of summary jurisdiction may find it compelling, in the interest of justice, to sometimes adjourn for mention. Also, there are instances when parties to the proceedings who are represented by counsel are, together with their counsel, are absent in court and there is no indication as to the reasons for their absence. In such situations, the Rules of court permit that the suit be struck out but the court may keep same on the list for good reasons.

Where the court decides not to strike out the cause but to adjourn it, the court will not be acting with sincerity if it adjourns for hearing as the date to which the suit will be adjourned may not be suitable to any or one of the parties to proceed with a trial. It will accord more with seriousness and sincerity on the part of the court if the adjournment in such cases be for mention and when this is done, on the return date for mention, if the ends of justice including the convenience of the court permit that the matter may be tried or heard notwithstanding that the adjournment was for mention and that, by so doing, no party to the proceedings will be overreached or prejudiced, the court may nonetheless hear the suit.

The converse is also true where the matter was adjourned for hearing and on the return date the ends of justice and the convenience of the court dictate that it be nonetheless adjourned without the trial, then the court shall further adjourn the suit for the hearing or for mention depending on the reason or reasons therefor.

Stand Down – A common occurrence in the courts in recent times is the practice of standing matters down usually for hearing or for argument. It is employed by the court when there is need to attend to some other issues of lesser seriousness or which could be more quickly attended to before settling down to attending to more contentious matters or causes which would require some fairly long time to conclude.

The court may 'stand down' a contentious matter till after it has attended to the 'petty' and non-contentious issues and matters. By so doing, the courtroom is cleared of a crowd and avoids having to waste the time of litigants and especially of the other counsel involved in the less contentious and petty matters.

This practice, unfortunately, is now being misconstrued and abused by some counsel who have fallen into the habit of writing letters to court asking the court to stand down their matters for them because they are otherwise engaged somewhere else. This, it is with due respects submitted, is disrespectful to the court since the real meaning and purport of such a letter is that counsel is asking the court to wait for him while he does other things unconnected with the particular proceedings before the court. The court does not wait for counsel or the litigant. Under the duties of a lawyer to the court, it is required that a lawyer shall maintain a respectful attitude towards the court, not for the sake of the temporary incumbent of the judicial office but for the maintenance of its supreme importance and Rule 1(b) of the Rules of Professional Conduct in the Legal Profession provides that

> a lawyer should be punctual in all court appearances and, whenever possible, should give prompt notice to the court and to all other counsel in the case, of any circumstances requiring his tardiness or absence.

By this rule, counsel shall, by writing to court and to his learned friend on the other side of the case, give prompt notice of circumstances for his tardiness or his absence from court.

Counsel is entitled to write to court asking that his matter be adjourned to another date upon his giving notice of circumstances requiring his absence; but he is not entitled to ask the court to wait for him. Therefore, every such letter in which a lawyer asks a court to wait for him by standing down his case while he does some other thing unconnected with the case he seeks to have the court 'stand down' for him ought to be turned down and refused by the court for being disrespectful

However, it may be necessary sometimes for counsel to make an application for a stand down in open court in the course of proceedings and for reason connected with the particular proceedings. Where the court considers the ground for the application worthy of consideration in the interest of justice, it may grant a stand down. This is especially possible where the application has been made by a senior counsel who may be entitled to the indulgence of the court. Otherwise, an order to stand down a cause or matter in the interest of justice and in consideration of the court's convenience but never for the convenience of counsel or litigant is one which the court only may usually make *suo motun.*

Attacking Court's Jurisdiction - Another incidental occurrence in proceedings before courts is the attack of the court's jurisdiction. The can be done on different grounds such as

(a) that the sum claimed is in excess of the monetary limit of the court's jurisdiction or
(b) that the claim does not disclose any reasonable cause of action or
(c) that the subject matter of the claim has been previously adjudicated upon and thus caught up by the doctrine of *res judicata* or
(d) that the cause of action is statute barred.

Whenever there is an application attacking the court's jurisdiction, the application shall first be considered by the court and a decision given. The decision must be recorded in the court's record book. Where the attack succeeds, the court shall strike out the claim. But if the attack fails, the court shall dismiss it and properly assume jurisdiction therefor and the proceedings shall proceed in the usual way.

Consolidation of Actions - Consolidation of actions is a process whereby two or more otherwise separate and distinct suits pending in the same court are by order of the court joined or combined and tried at the simultaneously.[54] This is another possible incidental occurrence in a court. It is not expressly provided for in the Customary Courts Rules but Order 11 Rule 1 of the Magistrates' Court Rules, expressly provides that

> actions or matters pending in the same court may be consolidated by order of the court of its own motion or on the application of any party on notice. [55]

54. Nwadialo, Fidelis (1990) *Civil Procedure in Nigeria* (MIJ Professional Publishers Ltd, Lagos) at 485A.
55. See also Order 13 Rule 5 of the Magistrates' Court (Civil Procedure) Rules (Cap. 97) Bendel State 1976.

Although the Customary Courts Rules do not provide for the practice of consolidation of actions, but because whenever the Customary Court sits over a recovery action, it does so as hybrid court and makes use of the Magistrates' Courts Civil Procedure Rules, the practice becomes applicable. No one court Rules are in themselves exhaustive and whenever there is a lacuna in the Rules of any court with respect to a particular procedure, recourse may be had to the Rules of some other appropriate court usually as a guide.

Suits that may be Consolidated - The actions or matters which may be consolidated are causes or matters in which it appears to the court that the issues are the same and between substantially the same parties. Order 11 Rule 5 (1) of the Magistrates' Courts Rules for instance provides that

> where several actions by the same plaintiff against several defendants are proceeding in the same court, and the event of the actions depends on the finding of the Magistrate on some question common to all of them, the Magistrate may select one of them for trial, and stay proceedings in all the others until judgement in the selected action is given.[56]

The above described situation in which the same landlord/plaintiff files several actions against several tenants/defendants is a common occurrence in recovery courts but it is hardly ever possible that the event of the actions depends on the finding of the court on some question which is common to all of them. Therefore it is hardly possible that recovery actions be tried in the 'selective' manner as provided in the Magistrates' Courts

56. See also Rule 2 for a converse provision.

Rules. Every recovery action is peculiar in some respect which renders its fact or event different from other actions notwithstanding that they are filed by the same landlord/plaintiff.

In *Balogun v LEDB*,[57] the court declared that 'cases of recovery of action should not in general be consolidated as such question as hardship or reasonableness can only be decided on the facts of each case. Consolidation in such cases serve no useful purpose and can only complicate matters.

Guidelines for Consolidation - In *Nasr v Complete Home Enterprises*,[58] the Supreme Court held that

> the main purpose of consolidation … is to save costs and time *(and that consolidation)* will not usually be ordered unless there is some common question of law or fact bearing sufficient importance in proportion to the rest of the subject matter of the actions to render it desirable that the whole should be disposed of at the same time.

Accordingly, by the relevant Rules and judicial pronouncements, in every situation where

(a) there is some common question of law or fact in each of the actions sought to be consolidated and which can be conveniently disposed of in the same proceedings or

(b) the right to the relief claimed in each of the actions to be consolidated have arisen out of the same transaction or series of transactions or

(c) that for any other reason it is desirable to consolidate two or more actions,

57. (1963) ANLR 520, 521.
58. (1977) ANLR 93.

the court may validly consolidate. Therefore, where two or more actions having any one or more of the above situations are pending in the same court between

(a) the same plaintiff and the same defendant, or
(b) the same plaintiff and different defendants, or
(c) different plaintiffs and the same defendant or
(d) different plaintiffs and different defendants,

such actions may be consolidated by the court either acting *suo motun* or upon the application of any of the parties to any of the actions.

Consolidation avoids a multiplicity of actions with its attendant costs whereas one action would serve to determine all the rights of a number of persons in situations where these persons have the same interests.

But two actions may not be consolidated where the plaintiff in one action is the same person as the defendant in another action except where one of the actions can be ordered to stand as a counterclaim or third party proceedings in another action. Where however the court decides to consolidate, it will be out of a judicial desire on the part of the court to save the suit which is later in time and which clearly must amount to an abuse of court process especially if the plaintiff in the latter suit had been served with the wit of summons in the suit first filed.

The court consolidates the suits by an order in which it is expressly stated which of the parties becomes plaintiff in the consolidated suit and which will be defendant thereat.[59]

Effect of Consolidation - Consolidation of actions in its effect is different from the effects of a joinder of causes of

59. See *Shell BP Ltd v Jammal Eng. Ltd* (1974) ANLR 489, 496.

action. Whereas in a joinder of actions, all the causes of action form a single suit requiring the court to deliver a single judgement in one proceedings, consolidation of actions only requires that two or more distinct and separate actions be tried simultaneously in a single proceedings but nonetheless requiring the court to deliver a judgment in respect of each action.

The two or more cases so consolidated must be considered as a single matter in one proceedings but in which the court cannot determine one or other of the suits and ignoring the other.[60]

Procedure – An application for consolidation of actions can be made orally in open court or by motion on notice[61] supported by affidavit. Actions capable of being consolidated may be easily recognisable from the circumstances of the suits in which case an oral application will do. But, sometimes, the applicant for consolidation may need to justify why it is necessary to consolidate.

In courts where pleadings are filed, the burden on the applicant in justifying the application can be made light by reference to the pleadings. But in courts of summary jurisdiction, the depositions in the affidavit supporting the application to consolidate may have to be profuse as the plaint/claim and particulars of claim[62] as filed may be too laconic to show the common question of law or of fact in

60. *Nasr v Complete Home Enterprises* (*supra*) but compare *Attah v Nnacho* (1964) ANLR 307. Consolidation is also different from joinder of parties – See Nwadialo, Fidelis (*supra*) at page 494.
61. Consider Order 11 Rule 2 (2) Magistrates' Courts Rules.
62. Miakpo Emiaso (2010) *Law, Practice and Procedure: Area Customary Courts in Nigeria* (*Supra*) at Chapter Twelve on Form and Commencement of Actions.

the suits and the fact that the right to relief claimed in each of the actions have arisen from the same transaction etc. It is worse where particulars of claim have not been filed at all.

The Order for Consolidation - Care is usually exercised by the court in wording the order consolidating actions so that there is certainty as to who becomes plaintiff in the consolidated suit and who becomes defendant. Generally, the plaintiffs in the distinct suits, where practicable, remain plaintiffs and the defendants remain defendants. But this is not to be assumed and must be specifically stated in the order of the court.

Counsel filing applications for consolidation can usually be helpful in this regard by ensuring that the prayer for consolidation is properly worded to incorporate indications as to the parties.

Deconsolidation - Actions consolidated may subsequently be taken apart and separated into their original individual suits if the ends of justice would be better met. Orders for consolidation may be made by consent of parties or due to expediency on general principles of equity and justice but if such orders are made by a judge who, subsequently at the trial, becomes satisfied that justice would best be served by taking the cases separately, he has a discretion also to vary or to discharge his previous order.[63] Any court to which the consolidated suit is subsequently assigned or transferred for trial is entitled to the same direction.

Enforcement of Judgments - The enforcement of a court's judgment is an incidental occurrence to the main or principal object of the suit. The principal object of a suit is

63. *Attah v Nnacho* (*supra*).

the judgment of the court in the action and this includes the decree or order or ruling of the court, even where it is a dismissal of any cause or matter as well as any other decision of a court.

Enforcement of judgment is the calling into play the coercive powers of the court in giving effect to its judgment. Accordingly, the need for the enforcement of the court's judgment only arises where there has been a default in complying with the terms of the court's judgment as voluntary compliance renders execution or enforcement unnecessary.[64]

***Locus in Quo* Visit** – Before leaving the subject of incidental matters at proceedings, it is necessary to discuss one other frequent occurrence at trials. This is the subject of the visitation of the court to the venue, place, or site of a material thing, not being a document, the existence or condition of which has been referred to by oral evidence.

Purpose - The purpose of such visitation is for the court to inspect the thing the inspection of which may be material to the proper determination of the questions in dispute.

Generally known as a visit to the *locus in quo*, the practice and procedure therefor is provided for by the Rules of some courts. Most of the Customary Courts Rules do not make provisions for visitation to a *locus in quo* but the 2006 Osun State District and Customary Courts Law provides for it at section 38 thereof in the following words:

> in any cause or matter it shall be lawful for a Customary Court, on the application of either party or of its own motion:
>
> (a) to make an order as the court may think fit for the

64. See Chapter Eight (*infra*) for a fuller discussion.

> inspection by the Customary Court, the parties, or any witness of any immovable or movable property, the inspection of which may be material to the proper determination of the question in dispute….

Also, Section 127 of the Evidence Act 2011 provides that

> (1) if oral evidence refers to the existence or condition of any material thing other than a document, the court may, if it thinks fit,
>
> > (a) require the production of such material thing for its inspection, or
> >
> > (b) inspect any movable or immovable property, the inspection of which may be material to the proper determination of the question in dispute….

Therefore, where, for instance, conflicting oral evidence has been received by the court in relation to the existence or non-existence of a thing, or its condition, the court may, if it thinks fit in the interest of justice and for a clearer understanding of the oral evidence, visit the *locus in quo* i.e. the location in question with a view to inspecting same to enable it better appreciate the evidence already received and further also to enable it arrive at a proper resolution of the conflicting evidence and a proper determination of the issues in question.[65]

According to Belgore JSC (as he then was) in *Umar v Bayero University Kano*,[66]

> there are certain matters of fact that cannot be resolved by the trial court by mere judgement of demeanour of the witness. The *locus in quo* must be seen…. Whether

65. *NNSC v Sabana* (1988) 2 NWLR (Pt 74) 23.
66. (1988) 4 NWLR (Pt 86) 85; (1986) ANLR 361, 367. See also Augie JCA in *Dada v Faleye* (2007) All FWLR (Pt. 349) 1134, 1151.

> the road at a vital scene is straight, level and visible for several miles, or it is curve, undulating with gradients of hills and valleys and thus not permitting visibility over a long stretch is a matter that cannot be resolved with a belief or disbelief of the evidence … rather it is a matter to be resolved by a visit to the *locus in quo*.

For the same reasons, a court may think it fit to visit the locus of an accident in an action for damages resulting from negligent driving or to a land in dispute where it is necessary for the court to better delineate the boundaries or better appreciate the peculiar features relating to the land.

Sometimes the thing referred to in oral evidence may be of such character as in when, for instance, it is immovable or of such large size that it will be impracticable to physically produce it in court. The court may in such situation think it fit to visit the locus to inspect the thing.

Guidelines for a *Locus in Quo* Visit – The following are some guidelines and rules for visits to a locus in quo:

Necessity - From the dicta of Blegore in the *Umar v Bayero University* case, whenever a need for a *locus in quo* visitation presents itself, the court must do so.[67] The court's discretion must be tilted towards making a visit rather than avoiding it since a failure to visit in such situations will, as it happened in this case, lead to a setting aside on appeal of the trial court's judgement and the ordering of a retrial.

Judicial Discretion - However, a trial court's decision to visit a *locus in quo* in civil proceedings is one which is within the discretion of the court [68] but which discretion

67. *Seismograph Services Ltd v Ogbeni* (1976) ANLR 163, 177.
68. *Ezeokeke v Uga* (1962) ANLR 477.

must be judicially and judiciously exercised. If in its exercise of its judicial responsibilities and judgement a court considers a *locus in quo* visitation necessary so as to better appreciate the oral evidence before it, then the court must do so.[69]

Visit not Delegable - The inspection upon a *locus in quo* visitation must be carried out by the court properly constituted with the Judge or the Magistrate or the Customary Court President being in charge as he would in the usual manner if the proceedings were to be held in the courtroom. The inspection at the *locus in quo* must not be delegated to anyone else.

Parties to be Present - All the parties to the suit and their counsel, where they are represented by counsel, must be present at the inspection.[70]

Visit at any Stage - A visit to a *locus in quo* can be made at any stage and at any time during the proceedings before judgement.[71] However, where, upon the visitation and inspection, it becomes necessary for further oral evidence to be called by the parties, especially with a view to clarifying new issues or facts thrown up by the inspection, the court must allow the parties the opportunity to do so.

Visit Part of Proceedings - Proceedings at an inspection forms part of the trial and as such all rules of law, evidence, practice, and procedure must be observed during the inspection. Therefore, any evidence led in chief by any of the parties must be subjected to cross examination in the

69. *Adeponle v Ajalebe* (1969) ANLR 215; *Umar v Bayero University Kano* (*supra*).
70. *Evoyoma v Daregba* (1968) ANLR 191.
71. *Ejidike v Obiora* (1951) 13 WACA 270.

usual manner and to re-examination as the case may be.[72]
Proper Records at Visit - The court must make records of the proceedings at the inspection since the inspection at a *locus* is as much a part of the entire proceedings in any suit and the rules of evidence must apply equally to such inspection as to any other portion of the proceedings and the court does not cease to be a court because it is sitting outside its usual place of sitting.[73]
Evidence at Locus to be on Oath - Witnesses at the *locus in quo* inspection must be put on oath in the usual manner and, if they had been on oath before the movement to the locus in quo, they must be reminded of their subsisting oath.[74]
Personal Observations of Court not Material - The court must be careful not to treat its views at the inspection as evidence since in all cases in which a visit is paid by the court to the *locus in quo* in a civil action, the Judge or the Magistrate, or the President in the case of a Customary Court should be careful to avoid placing himself in the position of a witness and arriving at conclusions based on his personal observations of which there is no evidence upon the records.

Where there is conflicting evidence as to the physical facts, the court may use its own observations to resolve such conflict but it is not open to the court to substitute its own observations for the sworn testimony of witnesses nor to reach conclusions upon something it has

72. *Awoyebe v Ogbeide* (1988) 1 NWLR (Pt 73) 695.
73. *Ogungbemi v Asamu* (1986) 3 NWLR (Pt 27) 161.
74. *Awoyegbe v Ogbeide* (supra); *Nwizuk v Eneyok* (1953) 14 WACA 354

observed in the absence of any testimony on oath to the existence of the facts it has observed.[75]

The court will not only be descending but will also be usurping the position of the witnesses if it does so and, where this materially affects its decision, its judgement will be liable to be set aside and a retrial ordered.

Procedure – The Evidence Act and the Rules of court do not make provisions expressly indicating by whose motion a court may be moved to visit a *locus in quo*. Order 41 Rule 5 of the Lagos State High Court (Civil Procedure) Rules of 1994 simply prescribes that

> it shall be lawful for any judge, by whom any action or matter may be heard or tried, to inspect any property or thing concerning which any question may arise therein.

Clearly, this provision does not state by whom or by whose motion or application the judge may be moved to inspect the property or thing. It can only be inferred therefore that since 'it shall be lawful' for the judge so to do, it is entitled to do so *suo motun* only.

In the same vein, Section 127 of the Evidence Act 2011 simply provides that

> … the court may, if it thinks fit, (a) require the production of such material thing for its inspection, or (b) inspect any movable or immovable property ….

Here again, since 'the court may, if it thinks fit, require … or inspect …', then again, it can only be inferred that this can only be done by the court *suo motun* and not otherwise. Rules 6 and 7 of the same Order 41 of the Lagos High Court Rules each open with

> an application for … may be made to the court or a

75. *Ejidike v Obiora* (*supra* at 274) per Verity Ag. P. (as he then was).

judge in chambers by any party (or by the plaintiff) …. Clearly, because it is intended that parties can make the applications referred to in the Rules 6 and 7, it has been expressly so provided that the 'application … may be made … by any party'. This is against the provisions in Rule 5 and Section 127 of the Evidence Act where this is not expressly so provided and therefore not making the position of the law on the point as clear as should be ideal.

The answer to a question as to whether a party to proceedings can move the court to pay a visit to a *locus in quo* can only be answered therefore in the negative by a strict reference and reliance to the Evidence Act and the Rules of court.

A more liberal reference must therefore be the right attitude so as to avoid a situation of denying justice a vital route to achieving same. In the *Umar v Bayero University* case, the Supreme Court per Belgore JSC (as he then was) declared that

> the statement of defence invited … the trial judge on a visit to the *locus in quo* (but) the learned judge never took advantage of this opportunity.[76]

This supports the view that a liberal attitude which permits a party to proceedings in a proper case may by an appropriate mode move the court to visit a *locus in quo* for the purpose of inspecting same in the interest of justice may permissible.

Proceedings at the *Locus* – Section 127 (2) of the Evidence Act 2011 provides for two modes of taking the proceedings at the locus. The first is for the court to be adjourned and moved to the locus where the subject matter

76. *Supra* at 367.

of the inspection is and there the proceedings shall continue in the usual manner until the needs of the inspection are met and concluded. Subsection 2 to Section 127 of the Evidence Act provides that

> when an inspection of property … is required to be held at a place outside the courtroom, the court shall either (a) be adjourned to the place where the subject matter of the said inspection may be and the proceedings shall continue at that place until the court further adjourns back to its original place of sitting, or to some other place of sitting.

If the area or thing to be inspected and the method of its inspection are such that the business of the inspection cannot be completed in one sitting, the court may adjourn to another day to continue until conclusion.

At the conclusion of the inspection, the proceedings shall then be further adjourned back to the original sitting place of the court. It may also be further adjourned to some other place of sitting as, for instance, where there is another *locus* to be visited.

The second mode of taking proceedings at a *locus in quo* is provided for in paragraph (b) of subsection 2 to Section 127 of the Evidence Act and this is that the court shall attend the *locus*, make an inspection of the subject matter only, move back to its regular place of sitting, and take evidence, if any, of what transpired at the *locus*.

Since the court is to avoid placing itself in the position of a witness and arriving at conclusions based on its own observations of which there is no evidence upon the records, it is to be highly recommended with due respect that the court must take evidence from the parties upon its getting back to its original place of sitting after the visitation and inspection.

In either mode, the guidelines as discussed above must be observed by the court.

Chapter Eight
Enforcement of Recovery Judgements

Even after judgement, unless through legal means by the deputy sheriff with appropriate warrant, a landlord cannot eject a tenant.
– Pan-Asian African Co. Ltd. v Nicon (1982) 9 SC 1

The general rules for enforcement of judgements apply *mutatis mutandi* to enforcement of Recovery judgements. Executing a court's judgment is generally regarded as an interlocutory step in relation to the proceedings. This is because the enforcement of a court's judgment is an incidental occurrence to the main or principal object of the suit.

The principal object of a suit is the judgment[1] itself which has been defined as the reasoned and binding judicial decision of the court [2] while its enforcement when circumstances so dictate is incidental to the judgement. The court's judgement is the decision of the court arrived at following a consideration of the whole evidence as presented before it by all the parties to which the appropriate law has been applied[3] and this includes the court's decree, order[4] or ruling as well as the dismissal of any cause or matter or any other decision of the court.

Enforcement of a court's judgment is the calling into play of the coercive powers of the court with the aim

1. See, for instance, Order VIII Rule 1 of the Delta State Customary Courts Rules 2007.
2. Nwadialo, Fidelis (1990) *Civil Procedure in Nigeria* (MIJ Professional Publishers Ltd., Lagos) at 567.
3. See Miakpo Emiaso (2010) *Law, Practice and Procedure: Area Customary Courts in Nigeria* (Peakmans Ltd., Lagos) at 259.
4. See Section 2 Part I Judgements (Enforcement) Rules.

of giving effect to its judgment. This is only necessary where there has been a default in voluntary compliance with the terms of the court's judgment by the judgement debtor since voluntary compliance will render such use of the court's coercive powers in execution or enforcement of its judgement unnecessary.

The right of a successful litigant to enforce his judgement, and the procedure for the enforcement of the judgment of a court in Nigeria are governed and regulated by the Sheriffs and Civil Process Act[5] and the Judgment (Enforcement) Rules made pursuant to Section 94 of the Act whose preamble is to the effect that it makes provisions for

> ... the enforcement of judgments and orders … of the courts throughout Nigeria.

Most states have their own Sheriffs and Civil Process laws which are substantially *impari materia* with the Federal Act except for arrangement and numbering of sections.

Applicability of the Act in Customary Courts – There are thoughts to the effect that the reference to 'the courts throughout Nigeria' in the above preamble of the Judgment (Enforcement) Rules does not cover customary courts. This is because 'court' with regard to these Rules which have been made pursuant to the Sheriffs and Civil Process Act has been taken to exclude customary courts as, by section 2 of the Act, 'court' is defined simply only as 'include(ing) a High Court and a Magistrate court.'

In this regard, the learned author of *Civil Procedure in Nigeria,*[6] citing the decision of the then Western

5. Cap. 407 LFN 1990.
6. Fidelis Nwadialo.

Region High court in *Ope v Olonje*[7] declares expressly that

> the Judgements (Enforcement) Rules do not apply to proceedings in customary courts[8]

because the Sheriffs and Civil Process Act defines 'court' as including 'only' the High Court and Magistrate courts. But, with due respects, the word 'only' is not part of the definition in Section 2 of the Sheriffs and Civil Process Act. Besides, the usage of the word 'includes' in the definition means that other courts, apart from the High Court and Magistrate courts, are included in what 'court' means.

To buttress this position, a consideration of Section 95 of the Act shows that the same word 'court' is defined as meaning a 'court to which parts III, IV, V and VI apply'. This definition clearly means that any court to which the parts listed do not apply is excluded. It is therefore humbly submitted that the provision of the Sheriffs and Civil Process Act are not inapplicable to customary courts on the basis of the definition attached to 'court' in section 2 of the Act.

A better argument in support of the exclusion of Customary Courts from the application of the Sheriffs and Civil Process Act may be found in construing Item 57 of the Exclusive Legislative List as contained in the Second Schedule to the 1999 constitution which is to the effect that

> service and execution in a state of the civil and criminal processes, judgements, decrees, orders and other decisions of any court of law outside Nigeria or any court of law in Nigeria other than a court of law established by the House of Assemby of that state *(Underlining supplied)*

7. (1962) WNLR 386.
8. *ibid* at 766.

are matters within the Exclusive Legislative powers of the Nigerian Federal Government.

By the said Item 57 of the 1999 constitution therefore, the National Assembly cannot legislate on matters relating to the service and execution of court processes, judgements, decrees, orders and other decisions of any court of law in Nigeria established by a state House of Assembly. The Customary Courts, except the Customary Courts of the Federal Capital Territory,[9] are one such court established by enactments of the state Houses of Assembly where they exist. But so also are the Magistrate Courts throughout Nigeria and the District Courts in the Northern states of the country. Indeed, all courts below the High Courts in Nigeria are courts 'established by the House of Assembly of the states'.

In effect, Item 57 renders the provisions in the Sheriffs and Civil Process Act in relation to Magistrate Courts unconstitutional except where such provisions are only with respect to the service or execution of process in a state other than the state where the process or judgement originates. This is because since these courts are established by states Houses of Assembly, the Federal legislature has no legislative powers to enact those provisions.

Customary Courts Judgements Enforcement Rules – Apparently in reaction to the attitude that the Sheriffs and Civil Process Act does not apply to Customary Courts and

9. These are established by the National Assembly for the Federal Capital Territory pursuant to Section 299 of the 1999 Constitution which empowers the National Assembly to so legislate as if the territory were a state.

notwithstanding the above argument in support of its applicability across board nationwide, most Customary Courts Rules e.g. those of Delta and Edo states[10] make provisions (which may not be exhaustive) for the enforcement of the judgments of the Customary Courts.

The Federal Act contains 112 sections while the Rules made pursuant thereto contain 12 Orders. Yet it has been held that the Act and Rules do not contain exhaustive provisions on the issue of enforcement of judgment and hence, in the case of High Courts, resort may be had to English Rules where there is a lacuna in the local laws and rules.[11]

If therefore, with 112 sections and 12 Orders, the Act and Rules may not be exhaustive, it goes without saying that the provisions in only four orders in the Customary Courts Rules can hardly be anything near being free of inadequacies. Therefore, even if the exclusion views above operate to have effect on customary courts, the need for Customary Court to have resort to the Act and Rules in appropriate cases can never be ignored or avoided.

As stated *supra*, some states including Delta and Edo states have enacted their own Sheriffs and Civil Process laws and Rules which are *impari materia*[12] with the Federal Act and Rules. Lagos State even published the

10. See Orders XIV, XV, XVI and XVII thereof.
11. See *Omolodun v Akinsanya* (1947) 18 NLR 115. See also Nwadialo, Fidelis (1990) *Civil Procedure in Nigeria* (MIJ Professional Publishers Ltd., Lagos) at 766.
12. Except perhaps in the numbering and arrangement of sections. The heading in the index to the 1994 Laws of Lagos State listing these Federal Laws reads: '*List of Some Federal Laws Applicable to Lagos State... and they are Numbered Differently*'

Federal Act and Rules verbatim as a federal law applicable to Lagos State.[13] In this chapter therefore, for reasons of elegance in the discussion, references shall be to the Federal Sheriffs and Civil Process Act (Cap. 407) and the Judgements (Enforcement) Rules made pursuant to Section 94 of the Act except otherwise expressly stated.

Enforceable Judgements - Generally, there are two types of judgments which courts in Nigeria deliver. These are declaratory judgments, which are not amenable to enforcement since such judgments merely declare the rights of parties or interpret statutes or deeds. However, there are judgments which make positive orders directed at persons to do or refrain from doing specified acts or things or for the payment of money.

The second type of judgment can also be divided into two namely judgments for payment of money and other judgments not requiring the payment of money. A judgement for the payment of rent, arrears of rent or *mesne* profits is a money judgement requiring the payment of money by the judgement debtor to the judgement creditor while a judgement in respect of possession is one not requiring the payment of money but the doing of an act i.e. the delivery up of possession of the suit premises by the judgement debtor to the judgement creditor.

Execution of Money Judgment against Property - By Section 20 of the Sheriffs and Civil Process Act (hereinafter throughout this chapter referred to only as 'the Act'),

13. Delta and Edo states published same as Cap. 151 of the 1976 Bendel State Laws which Delta State has republished as Cap. 187 in the Annotated Laws of Delta State 2007.

any sum of money payable under a judgment of a court may be recovered in case of default or failure of payment thereof forthwith or at the time or times and in the manner thereby indicated, by execution against the goods and chattels and the immovable property of the judgment debtor in accordance with the provisions of this Act.[14]

Time Execution Due - Such execution under the provisions of the Act can be carried out immediately following the entry of the court's judgement and upon the failure or default of the judgement debtor to pay up the judgement sum except, by the judgement, there is some other time or some other manner specified for so doing. This is the purport of the above provision to the effect that the sum of money payable under the judgement may be recovered forthwith. The provision appears not to leave the judgement debtor with a breathing space between the entry of the judgement and the execution despite the requirement also that the execution is to take place only 'in the case of default or failure of payment'. There ought to be some period of grace to establish that that there has been such a default or failure.

However, the provision allows for where, by the terms of the judgement, a time or times have been specified for such payment and default or failure of payment has occurred by such specified time or times. Then, upon such default or failure, execution may take place following such default or failure.

Under the Customary Courts Rules for Delta and

14. See also Rule 1of Order 13 of the Lagos State Customary Courts Rules which is a verbatim reproduction of Section 20 of the Act.

Edo states whose provisions are substantially *impari materia* with all other Customary Courts Rules nationwide, an execution of money judegement cannot take place unless three days shall have passed since the judgment was delivered by the court and there has been a default or failure of payment of the judgment sum by the judgment provision of Section 20 of the Act which expressly provides that

> any sum of money payable under a judgment of a court , in case of default or failure of payment thereof at the time or times directed or if no time is directed, within *three days* of the judgement, be recovered by execution against the goods and chattels of the judgement debtor.

There is a three days breathing space allowed the judgement debtor under the above Customary Courts Rules which is absent under the Act.

In practice, this breathing space may be more than three days as the process of raising the necessary papers and putting in place the logistics required for carrying out an execution may take at least an additional day because the court will not issue same unless it has become due so to do. This also applies as with under the Act so that there is some administrative breathing space even though there is none expressly provided statutorily.

Property that may be Seized - The goods and chattels to be attached in execution of the court's judgment must belong to the judgment debtor and should be property within the state where the judgement has been entered. There are special procedures for levying execution on properties outside the state of the court which entered the judgement.

Under the Customary Courts Rules, where the goods are within the state but outside the area of jurisdiction of the court, the warrant or writ of attachment shall be forwarded to the court within whose jurisdiction the writ or warrant is to be enforced or executed.

This process by which the deputy sheriff of the court, upon the application of a judgment creditor, levies execution of the court's judgment in favour of the judgment creditor in satisfaction of the judgment debt upon sale of the seized property is what is generally known as *fieri facias.*[15]

Properties that Cannot be Seized - The writ of *fieri facias* does not permit the deputy sheriff to seize the wearing apparels and beddings of the judgment debtor or of those of members of his family. By Section 25 of the Act, the sheriff, bailiff or any officer of court executing any writ of execution issued from a court against the goods or chattels of any person may, by virtue of the writ, seize

> any of the goods and chattels of that person, except the wearing apparel and bedding of that person or his family and the tools and implements of his trade, to the value of ten Naira,[16] which shall to that extent be protected from seizure.

Also protected from seizure by the sheriff or bailiff by virtue of a writ of execution are such other properties of the judgement debtor such as

---

15. A writ of execution requiring payment of a judgement debt usually shortened as *'fifa'* and addressed to the deputy sheriff directing him to seize the property of the judgement debtor to meet the pecuniary demands of a judgement.
16. The Act was first enacted in 1945 at which date ten Naira would be worth a lot more in value than it is worth today. Order XIV Rule 1 of the more recently amended Delta State Customary Courts Rules provides for '*the value of N1000.00*'.

money, bank notes, bills of exchange, promissory notes, bonds, specialities or securities for money belonging to that person.

All goods or chattels seized shall be deposited in some fit place usually within the court premises by the sheriff or bailiff or in the custody of a fit person approved by the sheriff or president of the court (in the case of a customary court) from which the writ was issued, or be safeguarded in such other manner as the sheriff directs.[17]

Sale of Seized Goods - The object of the seizure of the judgment debtor's goods or chattels is to raise the judgment sum in favour of the creditor by selling the seized goods. Accordingly, all seized goods in execution of the court's judgment shall be sold[18] so as to convert same into money for the purpose of satisfying the judgment debt but no such sale shall take place

until the expiration of a period of at least five[19] days next following the day on which the goods have been so seized unless

(a) the goods are of a perishable nature; or

(b) the person whose goods have been seized so requests in writing.[20]

Such sale shall be by public auction between the hours of seven o'clock in the morning and eight o'clock in the

17. Section 26 of the Act; Rule 8 of Order XIV of the Customary Courts Rules.
18. Section 29 of the Act. Order XIV Rule 10 (i) Customary Courts Rules.
19. Ten days under the Customary Courts Rules. See also Order 13 Rule 9 of the Lagos State Customary Courts Rules.
20. Section 29 (1) the Act. Rule 9 of Order XIV of the Customary Courts Rules.

evening and shall be in the premises of the court where the goods have been attached or in any other place as the court may direct.[21]

Time Sale Due -The sale of seized goods, under the Act, is not to take place before the expiration of five clear days and, under the Customary Courts Rules, ten clear days following after the day of the seizure except where the goods are of perishable nature or the person whose goods have been seized requests in writing an earlier sale .[22]

Seized goods, under the Customary Courts Rules, may be sold on any day except on a Sunday and the judgment debtor must be informed in writing of the date, place and time of the sale prior to the sale[23] while, under the Act,

> notice of the day and hour of sale of any movable property, apparently over forty Naira[24] in value, attached, shall be published four days at least before the day of such sale by being posted upon the door of the court house ….

Whereas the Act provision allows the judgement debtor a four days notice prior to a sale, the Customary Courts Rules simply provides that the judgement debtor shall be informed in writing without specifying a period of notice to which the debtor is entitled. Also, whereas the Act provision requires that the notice of the day and hour of sale be published by posting such notice upon the door of the court, the Customary Courts Rules requires no

---

21. Section 29 (2).
22. Section 29 (1). Rule 9 of Order XIV of the Customary Courts Rules.
23. Rule 10 (2) and (3) of Order XIV of the Customary Courts Rules
24. Unrealistic value. See footnote 16.

publication but only that

> the bailiff shall, prior to the sale, inform the judgement debtor in writing of the date, place and time of the sale.[25]

Payment of Debt Supersedes Execution - Where the judgement debtor pays up the judgment debt or part thereof which the creditor accepts in full settlement thereof before the actual sale of the seized property, then the execution shall be superseded and the sale stopped. By Section 22 (2) of the Act,

> if the judgement debtor, before the actual sale of the property, pays or causes to be paid or tendered to the Registrar of the court from which the writ issued, or to the bailiff holding the writ, the sum of money and costs inserted or endorsed … or such part thereof as the judgement creditor agrees to accept in full satisfaction, together with the fees inserted or endorsed … the execution shall be superseded, and the property of the judgement debtor shall be discharged and set at liberty.[26]

This is that where execution had taken place and the goods and chattels of the judgement debtor taken custody of and before their actual sale the judgement debtor pays up the judgement debt or tenders part of it which the judgement creditor accepts in full settlement thereof, then not only will the goods and chattels so seized liable to be discharged and set at liberty but the payment shall operate in relation to the goods and chattels as if they were not attached in the first place as the 'execution (not the sale) shall be superseded'.

Proceeds of Sale – Under the Customary Courts Rules, [27]

25. Rule 10 (3) Customary Courts Rules.
26. See also Rule 6 of Order XIV Customary Courts Rules and Order IV Rule 18 of the Federal Rules.
27. Rule 16 of Order XIV.

the bailiff, who is the officer of court with statutory responsibility for carrying out the actual execution of the judgment under the direction of the deputy sheriff, is forbidden from paying any moneys realized by him by any process directly to either the judgment creditor or his agent but shall pay to the Registrar all moneys for the time being in his hands at the close of every working day.[28]

By Rule 17, the proceeds of sale of any property sold under writ of execution less the expenses of the sale shall be disbursed by paying:

(a) to the judgment creditor the amount to be levied under the writ together with any costs paid by him subsequent to the issue of the writ and

(b) the balance, if any, to the judgment debtor.

Rule 17 does not state by whom the above disposition of moneys shall be made. But in view of the prohibition in Rule 16 and the payment in Rule 13, it must be presumed that, in practical terms, it is the Registrar of the court who has to make the disposition as provided in Rule 17.

The Act and the Rules thereunder contain similar provisions which are not free of difficulties of interpretation. Order I[29] Rule 15 of the Federal Rules made pursuant to the Act contains the curious provision, similar to the above Customary Courts Rule 16 of Order XIV, which is to the effect that

> no money realized by any process is ever to be paid by the sheriff or a bailiff to the judgement creditor or to his lawyer or agent.

The curiosity in this provision stems from the fact that it

28. Rule 13.
29. This Order deals with the 'duties of the sheriff and bailiffs'.

comes immediately following the provisions of Rules 13 and 14 which require that the deputy sheriff shall render accounts and

> the balance shall be payable to the judgement creditor or other person entitled thereto, who shall give a receipt therefor.

However, Order VII pursuant to the Act which deals with the sale of seized properties, provides that

> where property is sold under a writ of execution the proceeds shall be disposed of as follows –
>
> (a) where the property is sold by the sheriff, he shall follow the procedure prescribed in Rule 13 of Order I; and …
>
> (b) the money so paid into court shall be payable as follows –
>
> (i) any amount then due and unpaid for sheriff's, bailiff's, and appraiser's fees and expenses: to the sheriff, and next, …
>
> (iii) the amount to be levied, together with costs paid by the judgement creditor subsequent to the issue of the writ, if any: to the judgement creditor, directly or through the Registrar of the home court, if any, and next,
>
> (iv) the balance: to the judgement debtor.[30]

The intendment of the law therefore must be that all monies received by the deputy sheriff or the bailiff in the course of all executions of writs of execution must

(a) first be accounted for and thereafter

(b) paid into court before

(c) they are disposed of as provided for in Rule VII of Order 5.

In practice however, because of the reality associated with the difficulty of recovering money paid into government

30. Order VII Rule 5.

treasury, the requirement of the law as in (b) is hardly ever complied with.

Attaching Immovable Property – Generally, the law forbids execution of judgement against the immovable property of a judgement debtor if the debtor has sufficient movable property within jurisdiction to satisfy the judgement debt including the costs awarded and the costs of levying the execution. However if

(a) no movable property of the judgement debtor can with reasonable diligence be found or

(b) if property is found but such property is insufficient to satisfy the judgement and costs and the costs of levying the execution, or

(c) where the proceeds from the sale of goods and chattels seized are insufficient to satisfy the judgment debt and

(d) there are no more movable property belonging to the judgment debtor which with diligence can be found within the jurisdiction, and

(e) the judgement debtor is the owner of any immovable property,

the judgement creditor may apply to the court for a writ of execution against the immovable property of the judgement debtor which the court may issue.[31]

The application, under the Act, shall be in accordance with the provisions of the Act and any rules made thereunder[32] and, under the Customary Courts

31. Section 44 of the Act; Rule 18 of Order XIV.

32. *ibid.* See also Order IV Rules 3, 4, and 5 and Order V Rules 3 and 4 of the Federal Judgement Enforcement Rules.

Rules,[33] must be by way of motion on notice to the debtor for the issue of a fresh writ of attachment and sale of the immovable property of the debtor. The application is to be brought in the court within whose territorial jurisdiction the immovable property of the debtor which is sought to be attached is situated and not necessarily in the court which delivered the judgement.

A house or building which belongs to the owner of the land on which the house or building stands is dealt with by the law as immovable property and may be taken in execution.[34] Also where a house or building is on land not belonging to the owner of the house or building or where the house or building is on land held under the provisions of the Land Use Act, such may nevertheless be attached and sold and the rights, title and interests of the owner of the house or building shall be dealt with as immovable property subject to the provisions of the Land Use Act.[35]

A judgment debtor in occupation of family property allotted to him under customary law cannot alienate the property while it remains an unpartitioned family property. Accordingly, such property cannot be attached by his judgment creditor[36] as immovable property. But where such a judgment debtor is entitled to remove the materials or some of the materials used in construction of the building which is family property, his right, title or interest thereto may be attached or sold but only with leavc of the court to be granted or refused by the court at its discretion with or

33. *ibid.*
34. Section 46 (i) of the Act.
35. ibid.
36. *Majekodunmi v Tijani* (1932) 11 NLR 74.

without conditions attached to it.[37]

Procedure – The procedure for attachment of immovable property under the Act is as contained in Order V Rules 3 and 4 of the Judgements (Enforcements) Rules which require that the attachment

> shall be effected by delivery of the notice of attachment in Form 41… and, unless the court shall otherwise order, by posting in a conspicuous place on the (immovable property) a notice in Form 40 prohibiting all persons from receiving the same by purchase, gift, or otherwise; and the sheriff may also take and retain actual possession of the (immovable property) by putting into possession thereof some fit person approved by the sheriff.

Order IV thereof specifies the procedure for the issuance of execution processes generally and provides that an application for the issue of an execution process shall be made to the Registrar of the court by filling a written request therefor in which the applicant must specify the suit number and title, the date of the judgement, the nature of the process sought, and the name of the party against whom the process is to be executed, and the amount, if any, to be levied[38] and

> upon the application of the judgement creditor, the Registrar shall … issue the proper process for the execution of the judgement.

Under the Customary Courts Rules, the applicant judgement creditor must file an application to court by way of motion on notice to the judgement debtor. If the application for the writ of attachment is filed in a court

37. Section 45 of the Act.

38. Order IV Rule 4 Judgement (Enforcement) Rules.

other than the court which delivered the judgment, the application shall be supported by a certificate from the court which delivered the judgment verifying the judgment and stating:

(a) how much of the judgment debt remains due and unsatisfied

(b) and that movable property of the debtor sufficient to satisfy the judgment debt could not with diligence be found within the state.[39]

The verifying certificate is not necessary where the application is before the court which delivered the judgment but, as is usual, all applications for a writ of attachment must be supported by two affidavits.

The first affidavit in support is deposed to by the bailiff who is in custody of the writ or who has executed, if any, the writ of execution in respect of the movable properties of the judgment debtor. In this affidavit in support of the application for the writ of execution against the debtor's immovable properties, the bailiff must, where he had attempted or carried out an earlier execution against movables, depose to all the steps he had taken in respect of the writ of execution for movables including how much was realized by him from the sale of the goods and chattels.

The bailiff's affidavit is necessary because he is the officer of court with statutory powers to execute all writs and it is him alone who can credibly assure the court on oath of the truth and correctness of the steps taken in respect of the writs.

The second affidavit will be by the applicant judgment creditor whose application activates the court and

39. Order XIV Rule 18 (2) Customary Courts Rules.

its officers in respect of the necessity to enforce the court's judgment. He too will have to depose to the steps taken in respect of the execution and why it has become necessary to apply for the writ of attachment and sale of the debtor's immovable property. Applicant must also depose to the fact and details of the debtor's immovable property within the court's territorial jurisdiction.

Hearing Application for Writ of Execution - The application for the new writ of execution against immovable property is one which may be contested as it is usually on notice to the judgment debtor who may file counter affidavits to the affidavits of the bailiff and the applicant in support.

The application is set down for argument and argued in the usual manner and at the conclusion of which the court, if satisfied that sufficient movable property of the debtor could not with diligence be found, lawfully orders the issue of a fresh writ of attachment and sale of the judgement debtor's immovable property.[37] Where the court is not satisfied as above, the application is refused.

Effecting Attachment – Effecting the attachment on an immovable property under the Act is as contained in Order V Rules 3 and 4 of the Judegemets Enforcement Rules referred to and discussed *supra* while under the Customary Courts Rules, this is accomplished with the bailiff proceeding to attach the lands, buildings or other immovable properties of the debtor as indicated on the writ upon receipt of the court ordered writ of attachment.

This the bailiff does by serving on the debtor the order of the court forbidding the bailiff from alienating the

40. Rule 18 (3) Customary Courts Rules.

immovable property and prohibiting any other person or persons from accepting same. The bailiff then affixes or posts copies of the court's order upon the properties and this completes the attachment.[41]

Sale of Attached Immovable Property – Rule 20 of Order XIV of the Customary Courts Rules provides that the Registrar of the court is to arrange for the sale of an attached immovable property upon the bailiff's report to him that attachment has been completed.

Unlike the provision in Rule 9 of this Order which requires that seized goods be not sold until at least ten days from date of seizure has expired, it appears that sale of attached immovable property under the Rules may be effected by the Registrar immediately upon completion of attachment. This is because the wordings of the Rule 20 is to the effect that

> when the attachment has been completed, the bailiff or messenger executing the writ shall report the same to the Registrar … who shall *thereupon* arrange for the sale of the attached property …

But Order VII Rule 6 (i) of the Judgments (Enforcement) Rules provide that

> no immovable property attached shall be sold ... until the expiration of at least fifteen days….

It is to be humbly submitted therefore that the Registrar, notwithstanding the provision of Order XIV Rule 20 of the Customary Courts Rules, ought to allow himself to be persuaded by the provisions of either Rule 9 or Order VII Rule 6 (i) of the Federal Rules.

The sale, like that for movable property, shall be by

41. Rule 19.

public auction in such manner and under such conditions as the court may direct and the proceeds thereof shall be disposed of in the same manner as for proceeds of movable property under Rule 17 of Order XIV.

The court issues a certificate of purchase to the purchaser upon the sale becoming absolute and the certificate so issued shall be evidence of the valid transfer of such rights, title and interest as the judgment debtor had in the property.

Setting Aside Irregular Sale – There are no statutory provisions for dealing with irregular execution of a writ of attachment or an irregular issue thereof but the Customary Courts Rules provide for the setting aside of an irregular sale of attached immovable property. Order XIV Rule 21of the Rules provide that

> at any time within twenty-one days from the date of sale of any immovable property, application may be made to the court for an order to set aside the sale on the ground of material irregularity in the conduct of the sale ....

The provision is in respect only of an application for the setting aside of a sale following an attachment of immovable property. It does not refer to an application in respect of attachment or execution.

The irregularity upon which the court will set aside the sale must be materially substantial and must be one arising from the conduct of the sale. It must not be an irregularity in relation to the attachment or the execution of the judgement. Accordingly, the setting aside of the judgement under which the execution was levied or the setting aside of the execution itself is not material irregularity to warrant the setting aside of the sale.

The application for setting aside of sale must be made within twenty-one days of the sale otherwise the sale shall become absolute. But where an application has been validly made and the sale is thereupon set aside, the purchaser shall be entitled to a refund of any money already deposited or paid by him.

Notwithstanding the silence of statute with regards to irregular or wrongful execution, our legal system does not permit a wrong to go without a remedy. This is expressed in the maxim *ubi jus ibi remedium.* Accordingly, the Court of Appeal has held that there are consequences for wrongful execution or irregular execution of a writ of attachment.[42] By the decision of the appellate court, not only is such an execution liable to be set aside, a person adversely affected by such execution may be entitled to damages.[43]

As for irregular issue of a writ of attachment, the Court of Appeal stated that there is no such thing as an

> irregular or void issue of a writ of attachment except perhaps_*(one)* based on a judgment ... declared a nullity; or *(one issued but)* which may not be issued without leave of court.[44]

Where there has been a wrongful or an irregular execution, even the court whose judgment has been wrongfully or irregularly executed will be competent to set the execution aside upon an application to it so to do and the application cannot amount to another method of obtaining a stay of

42. *Pavex Int. Co. Ltd v IBWA* (1994) 5 NWLR (Pt.347), 685, 700
43. *ibid.* But see Sections 41 and 42 of the Act for protective provisions for bailiffs and the extent thereof.
44. *ibid* - per Uwaifo JCA (as he then was) but see Tabai JSC in *Akinyemi v Soyanwo* (2006) All FWLR (Pt. 335) 58, 68.

execution which the court had earlier refused. It will only be a situation which calls for the court's intervention to remedy a grievance *ex debito justiciae.* According to the Court of Appeal, an execution is wrongful where:

(a) a writ of *fieri facias* is executed after the judgment debt had been paid or the debt validly tendered. Such an execution would ground an action in trespass.

(b) the execution is neither authorized nor justified by the writ or by the judgment under which it is issued e.g. as in when execution is for more than the judgment permits or

(c) the endorsement on the writ of attachment directs the bailiff to levy execution at a wrong address or on the goods and chattels of a person other than the goods or chattels of the judgment debtor or

(d) after a stay of execution has been ordered by the court or agreed by the parties.

Also, an execution will be irregular where any of the requirements of the Rules of court relating to execution of the judgment of the court has not been complied with. An execution will be irregular where:

(a) it is levied by an unauthorised officer or

(b) the writ does not follow the judgment precisely in terms e.g. of the names of the parties or the terms of the judgment or

(c) several executions are issued on a joint judgment

(d) there is an error in the amount ordered to be recovered or paid.

In any of the above situations of wrongful or irregular execution, the execution will be liable to be set aside.[45]

Execution Against the Person – Another mode of enforcing money judgments is the arrest and imprisonment of the judgment debtor with a view to compelling him to comply with the terms of the court's judgment against him.[46] Section 65 of the Act expressly provides that

> … the court … may commit to prison, for any term not exceeding six weeks, any person who makes default in payment of any debt or instalment of any debt due from him in pursuance of any judgement or order of any court for the payment of any sum.

But the judgement debtor cannot be so arrested and imprisoned unless

(a) he has made default in the payment of the judgment sum and

(b) a judgment summons has been issued and served on him[47] and

(c) an opportunity has been accorded him to show cause why he should not be committed to prison[48] and

(d) the court is satisfied that he has or has had since the date of the judgment the means to satisfy the judgment debt.[49]

The judgement summons is essentially an invitation to the

45. *ibid.*
46. Order XVII Rule 1 of Customary Courts Rules. See also Part IV of the Sheriffs and Civil Process Act.
47. See Section 55 of the Act; Order IX Judgement Enforcement Rules and Order XVII Rule 1 (2) of Customary Courts Rules.
48. Rule 2 of Order XVII Customary Courts Rules.
49. Rule 9 of Order XVII Customary Courts Rules.

judgment debtor to come to the court to explain why he has defaulted in satisfying the judgment debt but it is one which is not open to the debtor to decline honouring. Where he fails to appear in court in obedience to the summons, the court may issue a warrant for his arrest forthwith[50] and he will be brought before the court with all convenient speed.

Upon his being brought to court following his arrest or upon his voluntary appearance in obedience to the summons, he is investigated by the court with respect to:

(a) his ability to pay the debt and

(b) the discovery of any property applicable to such payment and

(c) what other debts he owes and

(d) any other matters the court deems fit in the circumstance.

At the end of the court's investigation, the court makes any one or more of the following orders:

(a) the committal of the judgment debtor to prison for a period not longer than four weeks.

(b) the attachment and sale of the judgment debtor's property and

(c) or the instalmental payment of the debt.

The court may also order the release of the debtor from prison if he had earlier been imprisoned. His imprisonment does not discharge him from eventually paying the judgment debt nor will it preclude the judgment creditor from exercising any of his rights to levy execution against the movable or immovable property of the debtor. He may also be rearrested but not in respect of the same judgment

50. Sections 58 and 66 of the Act. Rule 3 of Order XVII Customary Courts Rules.

debt for which he had earlier been imprisoned and released. Where a judgment debtor is imprisoned at the instance of the creditor, he shall be paid a sustenance allowance of not less than two hundred Naira per day by the creditor who shall pay the allowance in weekly advances to the court.

A judgment debtor who is imprisoned shall be released from prison at any time when he fully pays the debt or at the request of the creditor or where the creditor fails to pay the debtor's daily sustenance allowance.

Interpleader Proceedings: As pointed out in *Pavex Int. Co Ltd v IBWA,*[51] an execution is wrongful if it is levied on the goods of a person other than the goods of the judgment debtor. Such an execution is liable to be set aside and anybody who shall have suffered any damage thereby has a right of action in damages. The person who is the rightful owner of the goods also has a remedy by way of an interpleader action.

Such an action which is generally known as a sheriff's interpleader proceedings is essentially for the purpose of resolving a resulting conflicting claim in respect of property which has been attached in execution of the court's judgment. Neither the Act nor the Rules provide a definition for interpleader proceedings but the provision of Order XV (i) of the Customary Court's Rules provide some direction. Under it, any person who claims that any attached property, movable or immovable, ought not to be sold in execution of a judgment against a judgment debtor, may apply to the court to issue a summons calling upon the judgment creditor to show cause to the court why the

51. *Supra.*

property should not be released from the attachment.[52]

In making the application, the usual reason for the applicant in claiming that the attached property ought not to be sold in execution of the judgement against the judgement debtor is that the attached property does not belong to the judgement debtor.

But it is curious that the Customary Courts Rules require the judgment creditor to discharge the burden of proving that the property attached is not liable to be sold by showing cause why the property should not be released from the attachment. This is clearly in conflict with the provisions of Section 131 of the Evidence Act 2011and the general principle of our adversarial system of administration of justice which requires that he who

> desires any court to give judgement as to any legal right or liability dependent on the existence of facts which he asserts must prove that those facts exist.

Clearly by this provision of the Evidence Act and the stated principle of law, the person who has a burden to prove anything under the provisions of Rule 1 of Order XV of the Customary Court's Rules ought to be the

> person who claims that any property which has been attached ... is not liable to be sold.

This is because it is him who has applied to court for the issue of the interpleader summons under which he asserts that 'property which has been attached … is not liable to be sold' because of an interest to which he claims in the attached property. It should be him who should 'show cause' by proving that the property attached is his property or that, in any event, the property does not belong to the

52. See also Section 34 of the Act and Order VI of the Rules thereto.

judgment debtor. This may have informed the provision in Rule 4 (1) of the same Order that

> every application by a claimant for an interpleader summons shall be supported by a declaration by the claimant, which may be on oath at the discretion of the court, specifying the property claimed and setting out the grounds upon which it is claimed[53]

notwithstanding that Rule 1 has required that the judgement creditor is to show cause why the attached property which is the same as the property claimed should not be released from the attachment.

The position under the Act and the Judgment (Enforcement) Rules is different. Here, the claimant informs the bailiff or the sheriff holding the writ who in turn informs the court's Registrar of the claimant's claim. The Registrar then sends notice of the claimants' claim to the judgment creditor and another notice to the claimant himself requiring him to make appropriate deposits or give security by bond in accordance with Section 33 of the Act.

The sheriff thereafter applies for the interpleader summons if the creditor does not admit the claimant's claim. The summons is served on the creditor and the claimant in accordance with the Rules for serving ordinary summonses. A date not less than fourteen days from date of service is then fixed for the hearing by the Registrar.

Between the service and the return day for hearing, the claimant is required to file particulars of the property he claims and the grounds upon which he makes the claim stating his name, address and occupation.[54] By this Rule,

53. See also Rule 6 (1) of Order VI Judgements Enforcement Rules.
54. *ibid.*

the claimant is called upon to prove his claim and not the other way round as in the Customary Court's Rules.

Also, by Section 34 (3), the Act provides that on the hearing of the summons, 'the court shall adjudicate upon the claim …' which again presumes the adversarial system of adjudication.

Time for Making Interpleader Claim – The Customary Courts Rules, the Act, and the Judgements Enforcement Rules are silent on the time within which a claim may be filed but Rule 3 (1) of Order XV of the Customary Court's Rules requires that 'a claim must be made … at the earliest opportunity'. However where the attached property has been advertised for sale before the claim is made, the sale shall be postponed pending completion of the court's investigation of the claim.

Also, the proceedings shall be dismissed if it appears to the court that there has been a deliberate delay in making the claim or if sale of the property has taken place before the claim was made.

Hearing Interpleader Claim - At the investigation, the court is clothed with the same powers as if the claimant had originally been a party in the suit from which the judgment leading to the execution was generated.

The court under the Customary Courts Rules is required during the hearing to consider the evidence in support of the claim tendered by the claimant by way of a declaration in support of his claim made on oath specifying the property claimed and setting out the grounds upon which it is claimed while under the Act, Section 34 (3) thereof requires that[55]

55. Rule 4 (i) but *cf* Rule 6 of Order VI Enforcement Rules.

on the hearing of the summons the court shall adjudicate upon the claim, and shall also adjudicate between the parties or either of them and the sheriff upon any claim to damages arising or capable of arising out of the execution of the writ by the sheriff, and shall make such order in respect of any such claim and the costs of the proceedings as it thinks fit.

If during the hearing it appears to the court that the value of the property attached exceeds its jurisdiction, the court shall stay the proceedings on the attachment and sale and order the claimant to institute fresh proceedings in any other court with competent jurisdiction.[56]

Order of Court - At the conclusion of the court's investigation, if it appears that the property attached is not liable to be sold in execution of the judgment against the judgment debtor, the court shall make an order releasing the property from the attachment otherwise the court disallows the claim and dismisses the interpleader summons.[57]

Writ of Possession – A writ of possession is the mode of enforcing the court's judgment for possession of land by which the sheriff or bailiff of the court is directed or authorized to enter into or upon the judgment land and take possession thereof for the eventual benefit of the judgment creditor. By it, the bailiff is commanded to enter upon and take possession of land which is the subject of the court's judgment and to give possession thereof to the judgment creditor.[58]

---

56. See Rule 2 (i) of Order XV Customary Courts Rules.
57. Rule 1 (2) and (3) Order XV Customary Courts Rules. See also Rule 15 of Order VI Judgement Enforcement Rules.
58. See Form P in First Schedule of forms to the Law.

Although a writ of possession substantially performs the same function as a warrant[59] of possession, the latter is exclusively used in recovery of premises actions between landlord and tenant while the former is for the enforcement of judgments for the recovery of land or delivery up of possession of land in actions other than actions between landlords and tenants.

For instance, by Order XVI Rule 1 of the Customary Courts Rules, the execution of any judgment relating to land or other immovable property may be carried out by a writ of possession whereby the judgment creditor is placed in possession of the land or immovable property. But if the land so attached is claimed by some other person not being the judgment debtor, such a person may within twenty-eight days of the execution dispossessing him apply to the court by way of an *ex-parte* motion making a claim to the attached land.

The court considers the *ex-parte* application by examining the applicant and if it appears to it that the applicant has good ground for making the application, the court shall make orders converting the application to a writ which shall be served on the judgment creditor as such. Thereafter the court investigates the matter as if it were a claim in a suit filed by the claimant against the judgment creditor.

The decision of the court operates as a judgment arising from an ordinary civil suit as between the parties or any person claiming through them in respect of the property.[60]

59. See *infra* and Form N in Schedule 1 of the Law.
60. Order XVI Rules 2 and 3 Customary Courts Rules.

Warrant of Possession – The Recovery Statutes[61] all provide that where a landlord has been adjudged to be entitled to possession of any premises, the court may issue a warrant of possession of the premises in favour of the landlord against the defendant. This warrant is as in Form N (Form TL9 in Lagos State) of the Schedule of Forms to the Law. The court issues the warrant of possession only when there has been a failure or refusal by the defendant to voluntarily comply with or obey the judgement of the court ordering him to give up possession of the premises.

A warrant of possession[62] performs substantially the same function which a writ of possession performs in land matters. It is a process issued by the court upon the application of the judgement creditor and which is directed at the court's sheriff or bailiff ordering or authorizing him to enter into or upon the premises which is the subject of the judgement and to take possession thereof for the eventual benefit of the judgement creditor. The warrant of possession recites the court's judgement and order in the following manner:

> Whereas at the court holden on the ……. day of ……… 20…. it was adjudged that the plaintiff was entitled to the possession of the premises mentioned in the particulars annexed to the summons … and it was ordered that the defendant should give the plaintiff possession …. etc.

This recitation is then followed by a new order directing the sheriff or bailiff thus:

> And whereas the defendant has not obeyed the said

61. Section 26 of the Law
62. Same as 'Warrant for Possession'.

order:

> These are therefore to authorize and require you forthwith to give possession of the said premises to the plaintiff.[63]

Effective Date of Warrant – There is no statutory provision for when a judgement for possession of premises should take effect. But, like other kinds of judgements, a judgement for possession, takes effect from the date it is pronounced by the court or such other date as the court may name for the delivery up of possession. The language of a court's judgement for possession is such that a specific date is named therein on which the defendant is to give up possession of the suit premises to the plaintiff. This date is usually forthwith i.e. immediately where the defendant had contested the action and the court, taking into consideration all the surrounding circumstances of the case, considers that the justice of the case so demands. A future date may however be named by the court for the giving up of possession.

But no execution may be levied upon it until the date of the day next after the last day named by the court in its judgement for the giving up of possession.[64] A warrant of possession, once issued, takes immediate effect and shall continue in force for three months and shall lapse and become ineffective if not executed within three months of its issue.

Order *in Rem* - Like a writ of attachment, a warrant of possession is an order of court *in rem.* It is aimed at and attaches to the premises - an immovable property. It is not

63. See the Form N (TL9 Lagos).
64. Section 30 of the Law.

necessarily aimed at any named or particular person. Hence it is not an order of court *in personam.* Perhaps this is why the notice of owner's intention to apply to recover possession proclaims that:

> unless peaceable possession of the premises … be given to *(me),* I shall … apply to the *(the court)* for a summons to eject ANY PERSON therefrom. (Emphasis supplied).

Regular Execution of Warrant of Possession - The sheriff or bailiff carries out his authorisation by physically entering onto the premises and thereby taking possession thereof. If upon arrival at the judgement premises at any reasonable time between the hours of 6 a.m. and 6 p.m. on any day of the week not being a public holiday or a Sunday, the bailiff who is to levy a regular execution of a judgement or order for possession of premises finds the entrance unlocked and he is able to gain access thereto, he shall levy execution of the court's judgement by carrying out his authorization whether or not the defendant named in the process is present. This is because the judgement of the court in respect of possession is *in rem* and not *in personam.* It will be lawful execution if the bailiff meets 'any person' who opens the premises to enable him gain access thereto.

Goods or Chattels not to be Removed - However, Section 24 of the Act provides that for the purpose of executing a writ to give possession of any premises, it shall not be necessary to remove any goods or chattels from those premises. This clearly shows that there is a distinction between the writ of execution against goods and chattels and the writ of execution for the recovery of possession. Where however the judgement to be executed is one for both possession and also for rent and or rent arrears and or *mesne* profits, the bailiff shall enter upon the premises for the purpose of recovering same and thereafter demand payment for the rent, rent arrears, and *mesne* profits from the defendant who is personally liable. This part of the judgement is one *in personam* and may be demanded only from the defendant.

If the defendant or any person found in the premises is unable to meet the money demand of the judgement, the bailiff shall seize so much of the defendant's properties as will, in his estimation, be enough to meet the pecuniary value of the judgement and the costs of the execution into his custody to be sold by auction with a view to recovering the judgement sum for the benefit of the judgement creditor.

Execution by 'Force Open' - Where the bailiff is unable to gain access to the suit premises sought to be recovered under the judgement of the court because the premises is locked and the defendant is unavailable to open it, the bailiff shall return to the court with an application for leave of the court permitting the judgement creditor to 'force open' the entrance to the premises for the purpose of carrying out his authorization.

The application to force open is usually made *ex parte* supported by affidavit deposed to by none other but the bailiff detailing the efforts he had made to execute the judgement for possession and why he has been unable to accomplish same.

The bailiff must depose in details to the fact of how many times he has attempted to effect the execution showing dates and time of day in each attempt. These details will enable the court to determine whether the efforts made are sufficient and reasonable to conclude that regular execution is impossible and upon which the court may then grant the prayer to "force open" the door or the entrance to the judgement premises for the purpose of executing the court's judgement.

The above represents the only instance when a court may grant leave to a judgement creditor in a possession matter to 'force open' the judgement premises for purposes of recovering possession. It will be unlawful otherwise e.g. as when the plaintiff files an originating motion *ex parte* praying the court for an order to 'force open' a premises without having first obtained a judgement for possession and relying on affidavit evidence that the defendant had locked up the premises and left for a long period of time during which he had not been seen and nobody knows his whereabouts and his rent had fallen into many months in arrears. Sometimes this kind of situation arises where the plaintiff deposes in the affidavit in support of his motion for an order to 'force open' that the tenant has died and no relation of his has come to remove his things from the premises while rent in respect thereof has remained unpaid for months.

There is no law which supports this kind of practice whereby an applicant is granted leave to 'force open' the premises of the respondent without a valid and subsisting judgement for possession on the merit. The landlord of such an 'absconding' tenant must first serve relevant statutory notices, file an appropriate substantive action for possession, prove his claim as appropriate and obtain judgement in terms of his claim as filed and proved by him before proceeding to a 'force open' process.

In *Iheanacho v Uzochukwu*,[65] a tenant successfully recovered damages for trespass and detinue against a caretaker who, without following the due process of first obtaining a judgement for recovery of possession, proceeded to file an affidavit before a chief magistrate court who endorsed thereon powers to the caretaker to recover possession of a shop from the tenant who was a periodic tenant in respect of the shop.

On the strength of the endorsed powers, the caretaker levied execution on the tenant by breaking into the tenant's shop, taking over possession, and letting same to a third party. This is tantamount to self help which 'does not come within the purview of the law.[66]

The Supreme Court in this case made it clear that even a trespasser in possession can maintain an action in wrongful or forcible ejectment against a defendant since

> a claim for damages for wrongful ejection does not necessarily involve the existence of a tenancy relationship nor does such tenancy relationship constitute an essential precondition to a successful prosecution of the action. A plaintiff in an action for wrongful or forcible ejection needs not therefore be a tenant; and one in lawful possession of land (or premises) may maintain an action in wrongful ejectment notwithstanding the absence of a landlord and tenant relationship between the parties.

In settling the plaint for a suit for recovery of possession in

65. (1997) 2 NWLR (Pt. 487) 257; (1197) 46 LRCN 214.
66. *Eliochin Nig. Ltd v Mbadiwe* (1986) 11 NWLR (Pt. 14) 47. See also *NSC Nig. Ltd v Innis-Palmer* (1992) 1 NWLR (Pt. 218) 422, *Adekunle v Adegboye* (1992) 2 NWLR (Pt. 223) 305, *Ogunsanya v Arab Brothers Ltd* (1952) 14 WACA 107.

which the plaintiff claims that the defendant had locked up the premises and absconded over a long period of time during which he had not been seen and nobody knows his whereabouts and his rent had fallen into many months in arrears, and that therefore he seeks the court's order to force open the premises in execution of the court's judgement, the plaintiff or his counsel may include the prayer for the 'force open' and lead evidence during the trial showing the peculiar circumstance of the case and why it is necessary to make an order for 'force open' as part of the judgement of the court in the suit. This will save cost and time of bringing a separate motion therefor subsequent to the judgement as is the more usual practice.

Of course, the peculiar circumstance of the defendant having absconded also means that service of all processes of the court leading to the judgement including the statutory notices must have been served by substituted means upon leave of the court duly first sought and obtained.

Force Open and Abandoned Premises in Lagos State – In Lagos State, there is now statutory provision for dealing with what its Tenancy Law refers to as 'abandoned premises' in respect of which an 'order to force open' may be obtained from the court as part of the court's judgement for possession.

By Section 15 (1) of the state's Tenancy Law No. 14 of 2011, premises will be deemed to be abandoned where

(i) the tenancy in respect of the premises has expired but

(ii) the tenant has not given up lawful possession

thereof and

(iii) there is evidence that the tenant has not been in occupation[67] of the premises since the tenancy expired.

Whenever there is an abandoned premises as above and the landlord is desirous of recovering possession thereof, he shall, by the provisions of subsection 2 of this section,

(i) issue a seven days notice of his intention to recover possession as prescribed in Form TL4 in the Schedule to the Law and

(ii) serve same on the tenant by pasting the notice on the abandoned premises.

At the expiration of the seven days notice, the landlord shall apply to the court for an order for possession including an order to force open the premises.

Garnishee Proceedings – Part V of the Sheriffs and Civil Process Act and Order VIII of the Rules thereto provide for enforcing the judgement of a court by way of garnishee proceedings. Garnishee proceedings are a method of enforcing payment of money judgment. By it, the judgment creditor attaches the debts owed to his judgment debtor by a third party in execution of the judgment.

Parties to garnishee proceedings – There are usually three parties involved in a garnishee proceedings. The first is the judgment creditor who has obtained a court's judgment in respect of some liquidated sum of money against the

67. This provision is bare and open to abuse. The 'evidence' to prove that the tenant has not been in occupation should include a minimum duration during which the premises has been without occupation by the tenant before it can be held to have been abandoned.

second party who is the judgment debtor.

The third party is usually not a party to the suit from which has arisen the judgment but is a third party who is indebted to the second party. Such third parties are usually banks with whom the second party i.e. the judgment debtor maintains an account having a credit balance. The third party could also be any other person or organisation who is indebted to the second party.

Under the proceedings, the judgment creditor i.e. the first party is known as the garnishor while the third party is known as the garnishee. Therefore, the garnishor is the person who applies to court for an order of the court empowering him to attach or garnishee an amount of money belonging to the judgment debtor but which amount of money is in the custody or under the control of the garnishee.

Such an amount of money could be a debt owed the judgment debtor in the ordinary course of business or otherwise but it must be due or accruing to the judgment debtor as at the date of the commencement of the garnishee proceedings. In other words, the debt owed to the judgment debtor must be a present and existing debt but never one which is to accrue in the future.

Procedure – The garnishor commences the proceedings by way of a motion *ex-parte* to which is annexed a statutory affidavit as in Form 25 contained in the First Schedule to the Act.

Upon hearing the *ex-parte* application the court, if satisfied that the applicant is entitled to attach the debt, makes a garnishee order *nisi* which is then served upon the garnishee and the judgment debtor.

The service of the garnishee order *nisi* on the garnishee attaches the amount of money which the garnishee owes to the judgment debtor and any dealings with the money thereafter by the garnishee will be null and void and could attract unpleasant consequences to the garnishee.

The garnishee order *nisi* commands the garnishee to appear in the court making the order so as to show cause why an order should not be made on him for the payment to the garnishor of the amount of the debts due and owing or accruing from the garnishee to the judgment debtor or so much thereof as will satisfy the debt due under the judgment and the costs.[68]

The Rules require that between the service of the garnishee order *nisi* on the garnishee and the return date, there shall be no less than fourteen days but the garnishee may within eight days of the service pay into court the amount claimed due from him to the judgment debtor. This puts an end to the proceedings.

But the garnishee may protest the debt and contest the making of an order absolute. In such a situation, the court conducts a trial with a view to determining the garnishee's liability or otherwise.[69] The court thereafter makes an order either directing the garnishee *nisi* to become absolute leaving the garnishee open to the levying of execution on him or an order discharging the garnishee order *nisi* particularly where the court is in doubt whether the attached debt is in fact due from the garnishee to the judgment debtor.

Sequestration – This is another method of enforcing the

68. Form 26.
69. Section 87 of the Act.

court's judgment not provided for by the Rules but provided for in the Act and Enforcement Rules.[70] But by Rule 13 of Order IV of the Enforcement Rules, only a High Court has powers to issue a writ of sequestration. Therefore, where the court is confronted with a proper situation for an order for the issue of sequestration, the court shall transfer same to the appropriate High Court.

An order for sequestration may be made where:

(a) an order or warrant for commitment or imprisonment had been made against a judgment debtor who cannot be found thereby making the execution of the order impossible or

(b) a judgment debtor has been arrested and detained in custody for not obeying the court's judgment but notwithstanding his arrest and detention he persists in his disobedience.

In either situation, the court may make an order, upon application, directing that the movable and immovable property of the judgment debtor be attached but not to be sold. The property so attached are only held and detained from the debtor until he purges himself of his disobedience to the court's order which is in the nature of contempt of court.

70. Section 82.

Chapter Nine
Appeals Against Recovery Judgements

Either party to a recovery action shall with leave of the High Court, appeal from the decision of the court
– S.35 Recovery Statute (Delta/Edo).

Appeals

An appeal against the decision of a court is a right conferred on an aggrieved party to an action to call upon a higher court to judicially re-examine the decision of an inferior court upon grounds that the decision of the inferior court is wrong and with a view to moving the higher court to correct the wrong.

This the higher court, as an appellate court, does by 'rehearing' the case, not by listening to the witnesses all over afresh, but by reconsidering all the evidence as presented before the inferior court from a record of the proceedings as transmitted from the inferior court.[1] Describing what appeal courts do when they 'rehear' cases, Oputa JSC (as he then was) had this to say in *Egbe v Adefarasin*[2]

> now (the Supreme Court) as well as the Court of Appeal are appellate courts. They do not try issues. Rather they examine the way issues had been tried by trial courts in order to ensure that the case was properly tried.[3]

Appeals in recovery of possession actions are an uncommon occurrence in Nigeria. In relation to the volume of such cases at the level of courts of first instance, it will be correct to state that less than five per cent of recovery of

1. *University of Lagos v Olaniyan* (1985) 1 SC 285.
2. (1987) ANLR 1.
3. *ibid* at 16

possession actions nationwide ever proceed to appeal. When they do, they usually involve mostly corporate organisations and fairly well-to-do individuals as parties.

Be that as it may, the Recovery Statutes make provisions for appeals in respect of recovery actions. These provisions are not *sui generis* but are substantially the same in all the states of the federation and the Federal Capital Territory of Abuja and as applicable to all other types of appeals.

It is intended to briefly examine these provisions in this chapter using the Lagos State provisions as standard guide and reference and which reference must be understood as the same in all other states as appellate rules and principles are substantially the same throughout Nigeria.

The filing and prosecution of appeals can be very technical and the discussion herein cannot replace the primary sources of the sundry statutory provisions and judicial pronouncements on the subject.

Generally, recovery actions commence in the Magistrate Courts, the Rent Tribunals in states where they exist, and in Customary Courts in states where the jurisdiction is conferred on them. These courts of first instance are courts of co-ordinate jurisdiction and appeals from them usually lie to the High Courts and further from there to the Court of Appeal and thence to the Supreme Court. In this chapter, the discussion is restricted to appeals from these courts of first instance to the High Courts only.

Courts with Appellate Jurisdiction - No court exercises

4. *Ikeakwu v Nwankpa* (1967) NMLR 224, *Nafiu Rabiu v State* (1980) 2 N.C.R 117.

an appellate jurisdiction unless it is statutorily invested[4] with such jurisdiction and the jurisdiction is usually conferred by the statute which establishes the court hence Section 35 of the Recovery Statutes, for instance, makes provision allowing

> either party to any proceedings in relation to any provision of the (Law), shall with leave of the High Court, appeal from the decision of the (court) to the High Court of the state.[4]

By this provision, no decision of the court in respect of a possession action may be appealed against without the leave of the High Court first obtained. The provision is curious as the general rule is that, with respect to final decisions of courts, there is a right of appeal and no leave of court is required before an aggrieved party can appeal.[5] This right of appeal with respect to appeals from High Courts is a constitutional right.[6] The jurisdiction of the High Court to hear and determine appeals from the Magistrate Courts is usually conferred by the High Court Law.[7]

In *Mabinuori v Ogunloye*[8] the court held that where a court is conferred with appellate jurisdiction simply that an appeal lies without stating whether it is as of right or otherwise, then it shall be taken that the appeal is as of right. According to the Supreme Court per Lewis JSC,

4. Other Recovery Statutes contain similar provisions but without the requirement of the leave of the High Court.
5. See Obaseki JSC in *Eveson v Sanusi* (1984) 4 SC 115.
6. See Section 241 (1) (a) of the 1999 Constitution.
7. See, for instance, Section 28 of the 1994 Lagos State High Court Law.
8. (1970) ANLR 17.

> we do not consider it necessary … for the legislation to state specifically that the appeal shall be as of right, because a provision enabling an appeal to be brought should be read as being 'as of right' unless the contrary is stated, as the granting of the right of appeal where it would not otherwise exist implies of itself in our view that it shall be exercised without further fetter unless the legislation states to the contrary.[9]

Also, where, in respect of the decision of a court, there is no statutory provision stating that an appeal may lie therefrom, then such decision of the court shall be taken as a final decision and from which there is an appeal as of right.[10]

Under the Lagos State Tenancy Law No. 14 of 2011, it is provided that a party to any proceedings may appeal to the High Court in accordance with the provisions of the Magistrate Courts Law while a party to any proceedings in the High Court may appeal in accordance with the provisions of the 1999 Constitution of Nigeria.[11]

Similarly, subsection 2 of Section 49 of the Customary Courts Law for Delta and Edo states which have exclusive jurisdiction for recovery actions under the Rent Control and Recovery of Residential Premises Law makes provision in respect of civil causes or matters in the customary courts that

> any party who is aggrieved by the decision of a customary court in a civil cause or matter may within 30 days of the date of such decision or order appeal to
>
> (a) the Customary Court of Appeal on issues

---

9. *ibid* at 19.
10. *Mekwunye v Director of Audit* (1967) ANLR 238.
11. See Section 45 of the Tenancy Law.

involving questions of customary law; and

(b) the appropriate High Court on issues not involving questions of customary law.[12]

A recovery action under the Recovery Statutes is an issue not involving questions of customary law and as such an appeal thereon must lie to the appropriate High Court.

Procedure on Appeal – As already stated *supra*, under the Lagos State Tenancy Law, for instance, a party to any proceedings may appeal to the High Court in accordance with the provisions of the Magistrate Courts Law. Section 60 of the Lagos State Magistrates Courts Law of 1994 provides that

> the procedure, practice and manner of appeals in civil proceedings shall be in accordance with Rules of court made under the High Court Law ...[13]

Similarly, Section 50 of the Customary Courts Law provides that appeals from the Customary Court are to be regulated and made subject to the conditions and in accordance with the provisions of any law or Rules of court regulating practice and procedure of the court to which the appeal lies.

This is the general position under the various High Court Rules which also make provisions to the effect that every appeal from a decision of a lower court may be commenced by the filing of a notice of appeal by the appellant within 30 days of the delivery of the judgement appealed against. The filing must be done at the Registry of the court which delivered the judgement and must, also within the same period of thirty days, be served on all the

12. Other states Customary Courts Laws have similar provisions.
13. See also Section 32 of the 1994 Lagos State High Court Law.

parties directly affected by the appeal.

There are forms in the Appendix to the Rules which may be used with substantial compliance in filing the notice of appeal. The notice of appeal should specify the

(a) suit name as on the records in the lower court,
(b) suit number,
(c) names of the parties,
(d) date the judgement appealed against was given,
(e) substance of the decision, judgement or order appealed against,
(f) grounds of appeal,
(g) part of the decision appealed against especially where the complaint is not against the whole decision, judgement, or order,
(h) name and address of appellant's legal practitioner (if any), and
(i) addresses of the parties where processes can be served on them.[14]

Order XIX of the Customary Courts Rules makes similar provisions in relation to the procedure for filing of appeals against judgements of Customary Courts and states that an appeal shall be commenced by an aggrieved party desirous of appealing against the judgement of the court by either giving oral notice of his desire in open court or by filing a notice of appeal.

Where oral notice has been given, the appellant shall nevertheless file his notice of appeal within the time prescribed by the court and not otherwise. Therefore, an oral notice of a desire to appeal given in open court may not ultimately be sufficient as an appeal duly filed.

14. See Order 3 Rule 2 of the 1994 Lagos State High Court Appeal Rules.

Time to Appeal and Enlargement Thereof - Although the Rules allow the appellant thirty days from the date of the decision appealed against within which to file his notice of appeal, he may be granted leave to appeal out of time[15] upon his showing reasonable cause. Such leave is usually upon terms as the court shall consider just.

Order 3 Rule 8 (2) of the Lagos State High Court Appeal Rules of 1994 provides for the enlargement of time within which an appellant may appeal. The Rule provides that every application for enlargement of time within which to appeal shall be by motion on notice to the respondent supported by an affidavit which shall set out the facts upon which the applicant relies.

Such facts shall disclose good and substantial reasons for the failure to appeal within the prescribed period[16] since the grant of an order enlarging time within which to appeal is not made as a matter of course but entirely at the discretion of the court. When granted, the court may impose such terms as it deems fit in the circumstance of the application.[17]

For this purpose, the mistake, negligence or inadvertence of the applicant's counsel will be taken as the 'sins' of counsel which generally will not be visited on the litigant. In such situations, the application for enlargement

15. See Section 48 of the 1994 Lagos State High Court Law and Order 3 Rule 8 High Court Appeal Rules Lagos.
16. See also Order 3 Rule 8 (2) of the 1994 Lagos State High Court Appeal Rules.
17. Rule 8 (3).

of time will nevertheless be granted.[18]

The application for enlargement of time must also set forth the grounds of appeal. Such grounds of appeal must, *prima facie*, disclose good cause why the appeal should be heard. A copy of the judgement or ruling appealed against must be annexed to the application for extension of time. Where the judgement or ruling is not so annexed, the Rules require that sufficient reasons explaining the non-availability shall be provided.[19]

The only court with the statutory powers to enlarge time within which to appeal is the appellate court.[20] This is because Order 3 Rule 8 (1) is to the effect that

> the Registrar of the court below shall not accept a notice of appeal for filing ... after the period fixed by Rule 1 of this Order has elapsed, unless an order enlarging time has first been obtained in the appeal court by the party who wished to appeal.

Grounds of Appeal – Every notice of appeal must contain grounds upon which the appeal is brought. The grounds of appeal constitute the most important part an appeal since they represent the complaints of the appellant and indicate the issues which the appellate court is called upon to determine. In *Egbe v Adefarasin*,[21] the Supreme Court held that

> a ground of appeal is one which touches an issue of fact

18. *Jozebson Industries Co. v R. Lauwers Import-Export* (1988) ANLR 310; *Bowaji v Adediwura* (1976) 6 SC. 143 and *Doherty v Doherty* (1976) 1 ANLR 279.
19. See generally Order 7 Rule 5 (2) Customary Court of Appeal Rules 2001.
20. High Court Appeal Rules (Lagos).
21. (1987) ANLR 1, 23.

or law or of procedure in a case and which, if upheld, will lead to the appeal being allowed.

Accordingly, a notice of appeal which contains no ground of appeal is like a person without a heart. It is dead on arrival and the court will unhesitatingly dismiss[22] it if such a notice of appeal gets past the Registrar to the court.

The purpose of grounds of appeal is to give notice of the appellant's case to the other side i.e. the respondent so that he will know what he has to contend with and to the court so that the court will know what it is being called upon to determine.[23] Grounds of appeal operate like pleadings in the High Courts so that parties are bound[24] by their grounds of appeal the way they are bound in the High Courts by their pleadings and the rules relating to grounds of appeal are as technical as those relating to pleadings.[25]

As stated *supra*, by Rule 2 of Order 3 of the High Court of Lagos Appeal Rules, every notice of appeal shall, among other details, set out the grounds of appeal upon which the appeal has been brought. Rule 3 of the same Order provides that each ground of appeal shall be stated clearly, succinctly, separately, and that where a ground of appeal alleges an error in law, the nature of such error shall be stated.

A ground of appeal may contain sundry complaints such as allegations that the court

22. *Akeredolu v Akinremi* (1986) 2 NWLR (PT. 25) 710.
23. *National Investment & Property Co. Ltd v Thompson Organisation Ltd.* (1987) ANLR 134.
24. See Rule 13 of the High Court Civil Procedure Rules 1994.
25. See Lewis JSC in *National Investment & Property Co. Ltd v Thompson Organisation Ltd.* at 138.

(a) erred in law or that
(b) it erred in law and in fact,
(c) misdirected itself in law or that
(d) it misdirected itself in law and in fact.

Order 2 Rule 9 of the Lagos High Court Appeal Rules makes provision for the kind of complaints which a ground of appeal may contain in respect of a notice of appeal filed by an accused and these include that

(a) the court had no jurisdiction to entertain the case,
(b) the court exceeded its jurisdiction,
(c) the court was personally interested in the case,
(d) the court acted corruptly or maliciously in the case,
(e) the court's decision was obtained by fraud,
(f) the decision is unreasonable or cannot be supported having regard to the evidence,
(g) the decision is erroneous in point of law.

These grounds are in respect of criminal appeals but, it is humbly submitted that, they also form possible grounds upon which civil appeals may be founded.

Particulars – Sub Rule 2 of the same Rule 9 provides that an appellant shall set forth in his grounds of appeal the particular matter on which he relies or of which he complains. By this is meant that a ground of appeal must be accompanied by the particulars of the error or the particulars of the misdirection in the case which the appellant relies on for bringing the ground of appeal.

In litigation generally, *particulars* serve the purpose of providing further details concerning the allegations which inform or give rise to the ground of appeal which is usually expressed in very concise form with a tendency for being vague. Particulars therefore give some insight into the grounds such that the issues required to be determined by the appeal court become delimited and narrowed.

A ground of appeal without particulars is bad in law and is liable to be struck out.[26] The Rules usually require that the particulars to the grounds of appeal shall be set out separately under the ground to which they relate.

However, in *Jozebson Industries Co. Ltd v Lauwers Import-Export*[27] the Supreme Court has held that the particulars need not necessarily always come under a separate heading as

> where a ground of appeal in itself has furnished the particulars needed, there will not be a further need for a separate paragraph stating the particulars of the errors alleged.[28]

Also as stated *supra*, under the Lagos State Tenancy Law, a party to any proceedings in the High Court may appeal in accordance with the provisions of the 1999 Constitution of Nigeria. This has the effect of qualifying certain grounds of appeal as grounds which may require the leave of court before they can be valid filed. The constitutional provisions[29] relating to rights of appeal are with respect only to proceedings in the High Court and do not extend to or include proceedings in the Magistrate Courts or the Rent Tribunals or the Customary Courts.

Accordingly, in all appeals to the High Courts, there

26. *Akwiwu Motors v Songonuga* (1984) ANLR 309.
27. *Supra.*
28. *ibid* at 321.
29. See Sections 241 and 242 of the 1999 Constitution.

is a right of appeal irrespective as to the rules in the constitution relating to rights of appeal with respect to appeals from the High Court to the Court of Appeal. There is therefore no need for leave of court before any grounds of appeal in an appeal to the High Court except under Section 35 of the Rent Control and Recovery of Residential Premises for Delta and Edo States which require that a party to any proceedings in relation to any provision of the law shall with leave of the High Court appeal from a decision of the court to the High Court.

However, with respect to all other Recovery Statutes, the view that no leave is required before filing an appeal to the High Court irrespective of the nature of the ground of appeal is supported by the wordings of the various sections of the statutes conferring the appellate jurisdiction on the High Court[30] and the tenor of the Supreme Court's decision in *Mabinuori v Ogunloye.*[31]

Outside the above exception with regards to the rules relating to the filing and arguing of grounds of appeal, most of the other rules will affect and bind the grounds of appeal in appeals to the High Court. These include that

(a) every ground ground of appeal shall be stated clearly, succinctly, separately, and that where a ground of appeal alleges an error in law, the nature of such error shall be stated.

(b) cvcry ground of appeal must disclose a complaint against the judgement of the court i.e. against the *ratio decidendi* of the case and not

30. See *supra*. See also Section 45 of the Lagos Tenancy Law, Section 49 (2) of the Customary Courts Law.

31. *Supra*.

against a mere *obitre*[32]

(c) parties are bound by their grounds of appeal and therefore cannot argue any ground of appeal not filed before the court without first obtaining leave of the court to do so by way of amendment of his grounds or to file additional grounds[33]

(d) the court is also bound by the grounds of appeal as filed and must restrict itself to pronouncing in its judgement only upon the grounds as validly filed.[34]

(e) the appeal court must consider and pronounce on all grounds of appeal as validly filed and argued by the parties[35]

(f) a ground of appeal filed but not argued is deemed abandoned and therefore must be struck out[36]

(g) every appellant is entitled to include in its grounds of appeal and argue the omnibus ground that the judgement of the court is against the weight of evidence

Conditions of Appeal – Upon the filing of the notice of appeal, it is usual for the court to impose certain conditions to be performed by the appellant aimed at ensuring that the cost of processing the record of proceedings and for taking certain other incidental steps necessary for timeously getting the appeal listed before the appeal court are

32. *Egbe v Adefarasin* (*Supra*).
33. *Awote v Owodunni No. 1* (1986) 5 NWLR (Pt. 46) 941.
34. *Olusanya v Olusanya* (1983) 3 SC 4, *Western Steel Works Ltd v Iron and Steel Workers Union* (1987) 1 NWLR (Pt. 49) 284.
35. *Balogun v Labiran* (1988) 3 NWLR (Pt. 80) 66.
36. *Are v Ipaye* (1986) 3 NWLR (Pt.29) 416.

diligently met. In this regard, Order 2 Rule 4 of the Lagos State High Court Appeal Rules provides that a person wishing to appeal

> shall apply to the Registrar of the court below for certified typewritten copies of the proceedings and shall deposit such amount as is deemed sufficient by the Magistrate to cover the cost of the number of copies bespoken

and thereafter,

> it shall be the duty of the Registrar of the court below to have the necessary copies of the proceedings prepared with utmost dispatch[37]....

In the very unusual but interesting case of *Engineering Enterprise of Niger Contractor Co. of Nig. v Attorney-General of Kaduna State*,[38] the plaintiff's case before the Kaduna State High Court was dismissed whereupon she appealed to the Court of Appeal but the judgement of the High Court could not be produced at the Court of Appeal in proof thereof because it was missing through the

> inadvertence, carelessness or negligence of the High Court[39] of Kaduna State.

Setting aside the decision of the Court of Appeal striking out the appellant's appeal for failure to prove the High Court's judgement before it, the Supreme Court held that

> our law is quite clear that once an appellant has deposited the money for making up and forwarding the record (of proceedings), he has performed his duty. The record shows that the plaintiff deposited with the

37. *Engineering Enterprise of Niger Contractor Co. of Nig. v Attorney-General of Kaduna State* (1987) ANLR 396.
38. *Supra*.
39. *ibid* at 404.

> Registrar of the High Court of Kaduna State the sum of N47.40 for filing, hearing service and records. He had done his duty. It was the Registrar of the High Court who failed to discharge his duty of transmitting the judgement to the Registrar of the Court of Appeal because it was missing.[40]

Similarly, Rule 2 of Order XIX of the Customary Courts Rules which are more explicit and specific in this respect stipulates that the Registrar of the court shall file the appeal in the usual manner and issue a receipt therefor upon the delivery to him of the notice of appeal. This is a typewritten notice of appeal in duplicate and, of course, not an oral notice made in open court.

Thereafter, the Registrar presents same to the President of the Customary Court who approves an imposition of conditions of the appeal which will usually include

(i) a deposit by the appellant into court of a sum of money not exceeding one thousand Naira to cover the cost of compiling and transmitting the record of appeal.

(ii) An order on the appellant to deposit a further sum of money or to enter into a recognizance with or without sureties for the sum of money to cover the costs awarded in the Area Customary Court or which may be awarded in the appeal court.

Service of Notice of Appeal - It is the duty of the Registrar of the court below to cause service of the notice and the grounds of appeal on the respondent within ten[41] days of his

40. *ibid.*
41. Order XIX Rule 4 of the Customary Courts Rules. But compare Rule 5 of Order 3 of the High Court Appeal Rules (Lagos).

receipt of_the notice and grounds. Order 3 Rule 5 of the High Court Appeal Rules is silent on the length of time within which the service of the notice of appeal on the respondent has to be done but simply provides that

> the Registrar of the court below shall cause a copy of the notice of appeal to be served on the respondent or respondents.

The Registrar shall also, within three months[42] of his receipt of the notice of appeal and the grounds of appeal, compile and forward the record of appeal to the appeal court. The High Court Appeal Rules do not specify the length of time within which the Registrar of the court below is to forward 'copies of proceedings required for an appeal' to the appeal court but Order 3 Rule 7 thereof provides that he shall

> have copies of proceedings required for an appeal prepared with the utmost dispatch

and that as soon as the required number of copies of proceedings have been prepared, the Registrar shall

> forward them duly certified by him, together with a copy of the notice of appeal and other documents concerning the appeal to the Registrar of the appeal court

and then the appeal shall be deemed to have been entered in the appeal court.

In doing so, the Registrar shall ensure that the appellant shall have complied with the conditions of appeal especially with regards to the charges for the cost of the compilation and forwarding of same which, under the Customary Courts Rules is one thousand Naira[43] at the most while under the High Court Appeal Rules it is such

42. Rule 5 of Order XIX of the Customary Courts Rules.

43. Rule 3 (a) of Order XIX of the Customary Courts Rules.

amount as is deemed sufficient by the Magistrate to cover the number of copies bespoken.[44] While under the High Court Rules the Registrar is to certify the copies of the proceedings required for the appeal, it is the President of the Customary Court or any of the members authorised by him to do so who certifies the record of appeal before they are forwarded under the Customary Courts Rules. The Registrar, under the Customary Courts Rules is further required to certify the exhibits typed and incorporated in the record book of appeal as correct before they are forwarded to the appeal court.

Appeal Entered - Upon receipt of copies of proceedings required for an appeal or the record of appeal (as the case may be) by the appeal court, the appeal shall be deemed to have been entered[45] in the appeal court. Thereafter the Registrar shall notify the parties directly affected by the appeal of the date fixed for the hearing of the appeal and the place and date of the hearing by causing a notice thereof to be served on them.[46]

The notice, under the High Court Rules, is to be served 'in due course' by the Registrar of the appeal court after the appeal has been entered and shall be served in the manner prescribed for the service of writs of summons issued by the High Court. Notice served by registered post to the address for service given by the party to whom the

44. Rule 4 Order 2 and Rule 6 Order 3 Lagos High Court Appeal Rules.
45. Rule 7 (2) of Order 3 High Court Appeal Rules (Lagos).
46. Rule 10 of Order 3 High Court Appeal Rules (Lagos); Rule 6 Customary Courts Rules which provides for the appeal court to fix the date and notify the parties.

notice is addressed shall also be sufficient and good service.[47]

Stay of Execution Pending Appeal - A judgement of court takes effect from the moment it is delivered. Therefore, subject to the provisions of the Sheriffs and Civil Process Act limiting time within which execution of the judgement may be levied, a party in whose favour judgement has been entered may, without further requirement, proceed to enforce the judgement if not voluntarily complied with.[48]

However, where an appeal has been filed against the judgement, it becomes usually necessary that the execution be stayed in order to protect the *res* and so as not to render the decision of the court of appeal nugatory in the event that the appeal succeeds.

General Position of the Law - Generally, the position of the law is that the bare fact of filing an appeal does not operate as a stay of execution. Section 63 of the Lagos State Magistrates Court expressly provides that

> an appeal shall not operate as a stay of execution but a Magistrate or the High Court may order a stay of execution either unconditionally or upon the performance of such conditions as may be imposed in accordance with the Rules of court.

Where the judgement debtor, having filed an appeal against the judgement desires that the judgement be stayed pending the outcome of the appeal, he must also file a formal application by way of motion[49] on notice in the lower court in the first instance where the appeal has been filed but not

47. *ibid.*
48. See Enforcement of Recovery Judgements *supra* at Chapter Eight.
49. Rule 9 (2) of Order 3 High Court Appeal Rules (Lagos).

entered for an order staying execution of the judgement pending the result of the appeal.[50] Where the appeal has been entered before the application for stay is brought, it shall be filed in the appeal court.

The motion, whether at the court below or at the appeal court, shall be supported by an affidavit setting out the facts upon which the applicants relies for bringing the application. The respondent is also entitled to file a counter affidavit in opposition.

An application for stay of execution can be made at any time but only validly after the filing of an appeal.[51] It is filed at the appeal court if the appeal has been entered by the appeal but must be filed in the court below if filed before the appeal is entered.

The basis for the filing and the grant of an application for stay of execution of a judgement pending the determination of an appeal against the judgement is the appeal itself. Therefore the existence of an appeal must be established before the court. This the applicant can do by annexing to his affidavit in support of the application

(i) a copy of the notice of appeal as already filed showing the grounds of appeal and

(ii) the official receipt for filing the notice of appeal as further proof of the filing of the notice of appeal since it is the filing of the notice of appeal that brings an appeal into existence.

A notice of appeal in draft but which is not filed is not an

50. Rule 9 (1) of Order 3 High Court Appeal Rules (Lagos).

51. See the first proviso to Rule 9 (1) of Order 3 High Court Appeal Rules (Lagos). See also *Martins v Nicannor* (1988) 2 NWLR (Pt. 74) 75; *Mobil Oil Ltd v Agadaigo* (1988) 2 NWLR (Pt.77) 383.

appeal. A sure proof of the filing is the official treasury receipt issued from the court's Registry showing that appropriate filing fees thereof has been paid.

In order to avoid complications arising from a wrongful execution of the judgement despite an appeal, extreme diligence is required of the appellant. He must make sure that the notice of appeal together with the application for stay of execution should also not only served on the deputy sheriff but should be timeously served on him and the respondent.

Conditions for Grant of Stay - A stay of execution is not granted by the court as a matter of course. It is an order of the court made entirely at its discretion and which discretion is exercised judicially and judiciously under well-defined legal principles.

To succeed, the applicant must show substantial reasons to justify the grant thereof. This is because the court will not make a habit of depriving a successful litigant the fruits of his success unless under special circumstances.

Such special circumstances will involve a consideration of some collateral issues and in some cases inherent matters which may, unless the order is granted, destroy the subject matter of the proceedings or foist upon the court, especially the court of appeal, a situation of complete helplessness or render nugatory any order or orders of the court of appeal or paralyse, in one way or the other, the exercise by the litigant of his constitutional right of appeal or generally provide a situation in which whatever happens to the case, and in particular even if the appellant succeeds in the court of appeal, there will be no return to *status quo*.[52]

In granting the application for stay of execution of judgement pending appeal, the court will usually impose one or more of the following conditions that the appellant

(a) deposits a sum of money fixed by the court not exceeding the amount of the money or the value of the property affected by the decision, judgement or order appealed from or give security to the court's satisfaction for the said sum,

(b) deposits a sum equal to the amount of the costs allowed against him or give security to the court's satisfaction for the said sum,

(c) give security to the court's satisfaction for the performance of or compliance with the decision, judgement or order of the court in the event that the appeal fails, where the decision, judgement or order appealed from relates to possession of lands or houses, and

(d) pending the making of a deposit or the giving of security therefor, the appellant's property shall be seized and attached, including a deposit or security for the expenses incidental to the seizure and attachment.[53]

Once the appeal has been validly filed, the appeal court becomes *dominus litis* and every subsequent step including every application must thenceforth be brought before the appeal court.

52. *Vaswani Trading Co. v Savalakh & Co* (1972) ANLR 922.
53. See Order 3 Rule 9 (3) of the Lagos State High court Appeals Rules 1994.

The notice of appeal and grounds of appeal may be amended with leave of the appeal court at any time before judgement and upon such terms as the court may deem fit.

Special Position of the Customary Court of Appeal - As shown above a recovery action under the Recovery Statutes and the judgement thereof is not an issue of customary law and therefore appeals therefrom lie to the High Cout. Also, the Rules of court of the appeal court are the appropriate Rules which govern appeals.[54]

But it is also correct that the appeal court Rules do not regulate appeals to the absolute exclusion of the law and Rules of the lower court. Hence whereas the above discussion represents the general position of the law applicable to all courts in Nigeria, there are special provisions in relation to the Customary Courts especially in Delta, Edo and Osun states which are variance with the above general position of the law.

Of special interest in this regard are the provisions of paragraph 2 of Rule 3 of Order XIX of the Customary Courts Rules which is to the effect that

> the court *(i.e. the Customary Court)*, having made an order under Rule 2[55] in respect of a civil cause or matter and being satisfied by the appellant that the order has been complied with, shall order a stay of execution upon such terms as it thinks fit.

The provision does not provide for the filing by the appellant of an application for a stay of execution and by implication suggests that the court is to order the stay of execution on its own motion once it is satisfied that the

54. See *supra* and Section 32 of the 1994 Lagos State High Court Law.
55. This Rule deals with conditions of appeal as discussed above.

appellant has complied with the conditions of appeal as ordered by it pursuant to Order XIX Rule 2 of its Rules.

In other words, the Customary Court shall, as a matter of course and without the need for the appellant showing any 'special circumstances' justifying an order for stay of execution of its judgement, 'order a stay of execution' once the appellant complies with the conditions of appeal.

In effect, the Customary Court may be permitted by its Rules to be 'guilty' of making

> a practice of depriving … successful litigants of the fruits of (their) success.

This is possible as the appellant who files a vexatious or frivolous appeal containing no arguable points of law may promptly go to sleep on the prosecution of his appeal having picked up an order of stay of execution without even asking for it and as a matter of course. This he does with a view to frustrating the judgement creditor from reaping the fruit of his judgement and thereby ridiculing our justice system.

APPENDIX A

WRIT OR PLAINT AGAINST TENANT OR PERSON REUSING TO DELIVER UP POSSESSION (FORM F)

(APPROPRIATE GENERAL TITLE – as in Appendix C)

The plaintiff is entitled to the possession of........... premises (*describe shortly*) situate at .... which were let by the plaintiff to the defendant for .... which said tenancy expired (or was determined by operation of law or notice to quit given by the plaintiff.............. as the case may be) on the ...... day of......... 20...... and on the...... day of.............. 20... the plaintiff did serve on the defendant................ a notice in writing of his intention to apply to recover possession of the said premises (*a duplicate of which notice is hereto annexed*) by ....(*describe the mode in which the service was effected*); and that notwithstanding the said notice the said defendant refuses (or neglects) to deliver up possession of the said premises and still detains the same.

The plaintiff claims possession and N....................k for arrears of rent and N.........................k for *mesne* profits.

(OR)

The plaintiff claims possession and N................k for arrears of rent and *mesne* profits at the rate of N.................. per .... being the rate of the said premises from the......day of....................... 20...... until possession is given up.

(OR)

The plaintiff claims possession and N...................k for arrears of rent and *mesne* profits from the .... day of .... 20...... until possession is given up.

Grounds for Possession: (a) Reasonableness (b) Arrears of rent (c) Personal use (d) Nuisance (e) Substantial repairs (f) Etc etc

Signed:....................
(Plaintiff)

APPENDIX B

SUMMONS FOR RECOVERY OF POSSESSION OF TENEMENTS

(APPROPRIATE GENERAL TITLE as in Appendix C))

You are hereby summoned to appear before the ..... Court at .... on the .... day of .... 20... at the hour of .... in the forenoon to answer the plaintiff's claim to recover possession of .... situate at .... within the jurisdiction of this court on the ground(s) stated in the particulars of claim hereto annexed, and also to recover the sum of N.............k mentioned in the said particulars.

If you dispute the claim or have a counter claim you should, within.................... days after the service of this summons on you, inclusive of the day of service, send to the Registrar a defence or counterclaim for which the form below may be used.

If you dispute part only of the money claimed you may pay into the district office of the Rent Tribunal *(or the court)* the amount admitted ...

If you admit the whole or part of the claim and desire time for payment or giving up possession you should within the said ...... days send to the Registrar an admission for which the form below may be used.

	N	k
Claim Fee for plaint/ Legal Practitioner's fees		
Total amount of claim and cost		

Sending the form to the Registrar does not relieve you from appearing at the Tribunal *(the court)* on the day named, but delay in sending a defence or admission or in giving possession or in paying into the Tribunal *(the court)*, may add to the costs.

To the Defendant ....

Dated this .... day of .... 20.........

....

Officer Issuing Summons

Take notice that if you hold the above mentioned premises as the tenant of any person other than the plaintiff, you must give notice of this summons to that person or to his agent immediately it comes to your knowledge. If you fail to do so you will be liable to forfeit three years' rent of the premises to him.

I dispute the plaintiff's claim because............................ (state facts relied on in support of defence)

OR

I admit the plaintiff's title and his right to immediate possession and offer to give up possession on the .... day of........................... 20................

OR

I admit the claim for N ......or (I admit N .... part thereof) and I ask leave to pay the same with the costs on that amount on the ...... day of ....20... or by instalments of N.........because ....

OR

I have a counter-claim against the plaintiff for N ....
N..

....

Defendant

Defendant's address to which
notices can be sent...........
....

APPENDIX C

TENANCY AGREEMENT

(A Precedent)

THIS TENANCY AGREEMENT made this … day of …20……

BETWEEN

……………………………….of……………………………..

(hereinafter called 'the landlord' which expression shall where the context so admits include his heirs executors administrators and assigns) of the one part

AND

……………………………….of……………………………..

(hereinafter called 'the tenant') of the other part

1. WHEREAS

(a) The landlord is the owner of the property being lying and situate at and known as ……………………………………

(b) The landlord has agreed to let and the tenant agrees to take a two bedroom flat in the said property under a monthly tenancy.

2. NOW IT IS HEREBY AGREED that in pursuance of the said agreement and the tenant paying the rent reserved the landlord lets and the tenant takes the two bedroom flat at ……..under a monthly tenancy from the … day of … 20… the tenant having paid before the execution of this agreement the sum of N…k being rent for the period of … months from the … day of … 20….

3. THE TENANT COVENANTS with the landlord

(a) to pay rent annually in advance on or before the anniversary of this tenancy

(b) to contribute proportionately with other tenants or occupants in the property to the payment of all rates and outgoings levied now or in the future on the said premises by an appropriate authority

(c) to maintain the interior of the premises in good repair and condition (fair wear and tear excepted) and to vacate same at the end of the tenancy in tenantable condition

(d) to be responsible for the clearing and cleaning of lavatory and soak-away pits serving the let premises provided that any maintenance or cleaning arising through faulty construction or structural wear and tear

shall be the responsibility of the landlord
(e) not to do anything within the flat or in the common corridors, passages and stairways which will constitute a nuisance, annoyance, noise or other form of disturbance to other tenants or occupants of the property
(f) to settle all electricity and water bills promptly otherwise to have these services disconnected if such bills are not settled after reasonable notice of their due date
(g) not to assign sublet transfer or part with possession of the premises
(h) not to keep any form of livestock in the premises
(i) not to make any structural alterations to the premises without first obtaining the written consent of the landlord therefor
(j) not to pound yam or any such like activity in any part of the premises
(k) not to accommodate any visitor within the premises for more than two days without informing the landlord of the presence and particulars of such visitor.

4. THE LANDLORD HEREBY COVENANTS with the tenant that the tenant paying the rent hereby reserved any increase thereof from time to time and observing and performing the agreements herein on his part contained shall peaceably hold and enjoy the let premises during the said term without any interruption by the landlord or any person rightfully claiming under or in trust for him.
PROVIDED ALWAYS and it is expressly hereby agreed that if the tenant shall at any time fail or neglect to perform and observe any covenant on his part to be performed and observed and fails to remedy such default or breach within a reasonable time after written notices served on him by the landlord to remedy same then in such case the landlord may at any time thereafter re-enter the let premises or any part thereof in the name of the whole and thenceforth hold and enjoy the same as if this tenancy had not been granted but without prejudice to any right of action or remedy of the landlord for any antecedent breach of covenant by the tenant.

SIGNED SEALED AND DELIVERED
By the within named landlord ....

IN THE PRESENCE OF

……………………………………………

of………………………………………

Occupaton…………………………….   ………………..

SIGNED SEALED AND DELIVERED
By the within named tenant   ……………….

IN THE PRESENCE OF

……………………………………………

of………………………………………

Occupaton……………………………   ………………

APPENDIX D

APPLICATION TO LET PREMISES

(To be completed in full by prospective tenant)

TO THE LANDLORD/AGENT OF ....
(Address of premises to be let)

1. SURNAME..
2. OTHER NAMES..
3. MARRITAL STATUS ....SEX..
4. AGE .... DATE OF BIRTH ....
6. STATE OF ORIGIN............... LOCAL GOVT...................................
7. HOME TOWN ADDRESS...
(Not Postal Address)
8. TRIBE/NATIVE LANGUAGE..
9. NATIONALITY .... RELIGION......................................
10. OCCUPATION/PLACE OF WORK...
11. ANNUAL INCOME ....
12. NUMBER OF (a) WIVES......... (b) CHILDREN.............................
13. PRESENT RESIDENTIAL ADDRESS...
14. NAME/ADDRESS OF PRESENT LANDLORD........... ....
15. HOW LONG HAVE YOU LIVED HERE.......................................
16. WHY ARE YOU LEAVING PRESENT ADDRESS......... ....
....

IMPORTANT: This is not a tenancy agreement. We are not bound hereby to provide accommodation.

Please Give Names of Two Guarantors:

(1) Names.. Sign ....
Occupation..
Addresses: (a) Office...
(b) Residence ....

(2) Names.. Sign ....
Occupation..
Addresses: (a) Office...
(b) Residence ....

....
Tenant's Signature/Date

....

FOR OFFICE USE ONLY

1. Rent paid ....2. Period ....
3. Agreement fee .... 4. Agency ....

APPENDIX E

POWER OF ATTORNEY

(A Precedent)

BY THIS POWER OF ATTORNEY given this … day of … 20 ……,
I Mr. ………………………… of ………………………………………
do hereby appoint ………….. of ………………………………………
my true and lawful attorney for me in my name and on my behalf to do all or any of the following things or acts, that is to say
(a) manage my property situate being and known as …………………...
(b) demand receive and collect rents or other revenue from tenants in the said property
(c) let lease the said property or parts thereof to tenants and to warn off and prohibit all trespassers from the said property and, if necessary, to commence prosecute defend answer or oppose all actions and other legal proceedings including the recovery of possession from any tenant thereat
(d) issue and serve necessary and appropriate statutory notices on any or all of the tenants in the said property
(e) charge usual fees for doing all or any of the above things or acts including a first charge of …% on all rents or other revenue received or collected
(f) AND GENERALLY to act as my attorney in relation to the said property and on my behalf to execute and do all things and acts as fully and effcctually in all respects as I can do.
AND I HEREBY AGREE AND DECLARE that the power of attorney hereby given shall be irrevocable except by a … months notice in writing from the date of service of such notice on the done.
IN WITNESS WHEREOF I, ……………………….. for myself and on my behalf herein have hereunto set my hand and seal the day and year first above written.

SIGNED SEALED AND DELIVERED
by the within named donor …………………

IN THE PRESENCE OF
………………………………………………

APPENDIX F

LAGOS STATE TENANCY LAW NO. 14 OF 2011

ARRANGEMENT OF SECTIONS

SECTION

33. Claims against persons in unlawful occupation
34. Defence supported by written deposition
35. Service on persons in unlawful occupation
36. Defendant not defending claim
37. Unreasonable increase of rent
38. Application to set aside or vary judgement of court
39. Warrant for possession may be issued at any time
40. Form and purpose of warrant for possession
41. Duration of warrant
42. Warrant for possession justifies entry on premises
43. Enforcement of order of court
44. Offences and penalties
45. Appeals
46. Regulations and procedure
47. Interpretation
48. Repeal
49. Citation and commencement

LAW NO. 14 2011

Lagos State of Nigeria

LAW TO REGULATE RIGHTS AND OBLIGATIONS UNDER TENANCY AGREEMENTS AND THE RELATIONSHIP BETWEEN THE LANDLORD AND THE TENANT INCLUDING THE PROCEDURE FOR THE RECOVERY OF PREMISES AND FOR CONNECTED PURPOSES

Commencement: 24th August 2011

THE LAGOS STATE HOUSE OF ASSEMBLY enacts as follows:

1. APPLICATION OF THE LAW

(1) This Law shall apply to all premises within Lagos State, including business and residential premises unless otherwise specified.

(2) The Law shall not apply to –

(a) residential premises owned or operated by an educational institution for its staff and students;

(b) residential premises provided for emergency shelter;

(c) residential premises –

(i) in a care or hospice facility

(ii) in a public or private hospital or a mental health facility; and

(d) that is made available in the course of providing rehabilitative or therapeutic treatment.

3. The following areas:

(i) Apapa

(ii) Ikeja GRA

(iii) Ikoyi; and

(iv) Victoria Island

are exempted from the application of this Law, however, the Governor may from time to time by Order published in the state official gazette exempt the application of this Law to any other area or premises in thie state.

2. JURISDICTION OF THE COURTS

(1) A court shall have jurisdiction to determine matters in respect of the tenancy of any premises let before or after the commencement of this Law.

(2) The jurisdiction of a court shall not be ousted by the defendant or respondent setting up the title of any other party.

(3) The parties' agreement to resort to court connected Alternative Dispute Resolution (ADR) or other facilities such as the Lagos Multi-Door Court House or to the Citizens Mediation Centre for amicable dispute resolution shall not however be construed as an ouster of court's jurisdiction.

4. Proceedings shall be brought under this Law at the High Court where the rental value of the premises exceeds the jurisdiction of the Magistrate Court as provided by the Magistrates' Courts Law.

(5) Subject to the provisions of the Law, a court shall be bound by the practice and procedure in civil matters in the Magistrates' Court or the High Court of Lagos State.

3. TENANCY AGREEMENT

A tenancy agreement shall for the purposes of this Law, be deemed to exist where premises are granted by the landlord to a person for value whether or not it is –

(a) express or implied;

(b) oral or written or partly oral or partly written; or

(c) for a fixed period

4. ADVANCE RENT

(1) It shall be unlawful for a landlord or his agent to demand or receive from a sitting tenant rent in excess of six (6) months from a monthly tenant and one (1) year from a yearly tenant in respect of any premises without prejudice to the nature of tenancy held at the commencement of the tenancy.

(2) It shall be unlawful for a sitting tenant to offer or pay rent in excess of one (1) year for a yearly tenant and six (6) months for a monthly tenant in respect of any premises.

(3) It shall be unlawful for a landlord or his agent to demand or receive from a new or would be tenant rent in excess of one (1) year in respect of any premises.

(4) It shall be unlawful for a new or would be tenant to offer or pay rent in excess of one (1) year in respect of any premises.

(5) Any person who receives or pays rent in excess of what is prescribed in this section shall be guilty of an offence and shall be liable on conviction to a fine of one hundred thousand Naira (N100,000.00) or to three (3) months imprisonment.

5. RENT PAYMENT RECEIPT

(1) As from the commencement of this Law, all landlords shall upon payment of rent by the tenants, be obliged to issue a rent payment receipt to their tenants in respect of such payments.

(2) The receipt shall state the –

(a) date on which rent was received;

(b) names and addresses of the landlord and the tenant;

(c) description and location of premises in respect of which the rent is paid;

(d) amount of rent paid; and

(e) period to which the payment relates.

(3) Any landlord who fails to issue a rent payment receipt to his tenant as prescribed under this section, shall be liable on conviction to a fine of one hundred thousand Naira (N100,000.00).

6. RIGHTS OF A TENANT

(1) The tenant's entitlement to quiet and peaceable enjoyment of the premises includes the right to –

(a) privacy;

(b) freedom from unreasonable disturbance;

(c) exclusive possession of the premises, subject to the landlord's restricted right of inspection; and

(d) the use of common areas for reasonable and lawful purposes.

(2) Where a tenant with the previous consent in writing of the landlord, effects improvements on the premises and the landlord determines the tenancy, such a tenant shall be entitled to claim compensation for the effected improvements on quitting the premises.

7. OBLIGATIONS OF THE TENANT

Subject to any provision to the contrary in the tenancy agreement the tenant shall:

(1) pay the rents at the times and in the manner stated;

(2) pay all existing and future rates and charges not payable by the landlord by law;

(3) keep the premises in good and tenantable repair, reasonable wear and tear excepted;

(4) permit the landlord and his agent during the tenancy at all reasonable hours in the daytime after previous written notice,

to view the condition of the premises and to effect repairs in necessary parts of the building;

(5) not make any alterations or additions to the premises without the consent of the landlord;

(6) not assign or sublet any part of the premises without the written consent of the landlord; and

(7) notify the landlord where structural or substantial damage has occurred to any part of the premises as soon as practicable.

8. OBLIGATIONS OF THE LANDLORD

Subject to any provision to the contrary in a tenancy agreement, the landlord shall:

(i) not disturb the tenant's quiet and peaceable enjoyment of the Premises.

(ii) pay all rates and charges as stipulated by law.

(iii) keep the premises insured against loss or damage.

(iv) not terminate or restrict the use of a common facility or service for the use of the premises.

(v) not seize any item or property of the tenaqnt or interfere with the tenant's access to his personal property.

(vi) effect repairs and maintain the external and common parts of the premises.

9. OBLIGATIONS OF THE LANDLORD REGARDING BUSINESS PREMISES

A tenancy agreement in respect of business premises shall be deemed to provide that where the landlord –

(a) inhibits the access of the tenant to the premises in any substantial manner;

(b) takes any action that may substantially alter or inhibit the flow of the customers, clients or other persons using the tenant's business premises;

(c) causes or fails to make reasonable efforts to prevent or remove any disruption to trading or use within the business premises which results in loss of profits to the tenant;

(d) fails to rectify as soon as practicable, any breakdown of plant or equipment under his care and maintenance which results in loss of profits to the tenant; or

(e) fails to maintain or repaint the exterior or the common parts of the building or buildings of which the premises is comprised, and after being given notice in writing by the tenant requiring him to rectify the matter, does not do so within such time as is reasonably practicable,

the landlord is liable to pay to the tenant such reasonable compensation as shall be determined by the court, where the tenant effects the repairs or maintenance.

10. SERVICE CHARGE, FACILITY AND SECURITY DEPOSITS

In any case where the landlord or his agent in addition to rent requires the tenant or licensee to pay –

(a) a security deposit to cover damage repairs to the premises;

(b) for services and facilities for the premises; or

(c) service charges in flats or units that retain common parts of the premises,

The landlord or his agent shall issue a separate receipt to the tenant for payments received and such tenant shall be entitled to a written account at least every sic (6) months from the landlord of how monies paid were disbursed.

11. PAYMENT OF PROFESSIONAL FEES

From the commencement of a tenancy, it shall be the duty of the party who engages the services of a professional in respect of the tenancy agreement to pay the fees for such professional fees.

12. PROVISION FOR RE-ENTRY

Where there is a breach or non-observance of any of the conditions or covenants in respect of the premises, the landlord shall subject to –

(a) any provision to the country in the agreement between the parties; and

(b) the service of process in accordance with the relevant provisions of the Law,

Have the right to institute proceedings for an order to re-enter and determine the tenancy.

13. LENGTH OF NOTICE

(1) Where there is no stipulation as to the notice to be given by either party to determine the tenancy, the following shall apply –

(a) a week's notice for a tenant at will

(b) one (1) month's notice foe a monthly tenant;

(c) three (3) month's notice for a quarterly tenant;

(d) three (3) month's notice for a half-yearly tenant; and

(e) six (6) month's notice for a yearly tenant.

(2) In the case of a monthly tenancy, where the tenant is in arrears of rent for six (6) months, the tenancy shall lapse and the court shall make an order for possession and arrears of rent upon proof of the arrears by the landlord.

(3) In the case of a quarterly or half-yearly tenancy, where the tenant is in arrears of one (1) year rent, the tenancy shall lapse and the court shall make an order for possession and arrears of rent upon proof of the arrears by the landlord.

(4) Notice for tenants under subsection 1 (c), (d), and (e) of this section need not terminate on the anniversary of the tenancy but may terminate on or after the date of expiration of the tenancy.

(5) In the case of a tenancy for a fixed term, no notice to quit shall be required once the tenancy has been determined by effluxion of time and where the landlord intends to proceed to court to recover possession, he shall serve a seven (7) days written notice of his intention to apply to recover possession as in Form TL5 in the Schedule to this Law.

(6) The nature of a tenancy shall, in the absence of any evidence to the contrary, be determined by reference to the time when the rent is paid or demanded.

14. NOTICE TO LICENSEE

Where a person is a licensee and upon the expiration or withdrawal of his licence, he refuses or neglects to give up possession, he shall be entitled to service of a seven (7) days notice of the owner's intention to apply to recover possession as in Form TL4 in the Schedule to the Law.

15. NOTICE REQUIRED FOR ABANDONED PREMISES

(1) A premises will be deemed to be abandoned where the –

(a) tenancy has expired; and

(b) tenant has not occupied the premises since the tenancy expired and has not given up lawful possession of the premises.

(2) Following subsection (1) above, the landlord shall –

(a) issue a seven (7) days notice of the landlord's intention to recover possession as prescribed in Form TL4, which shall be served by pasting the notice on the abandoned premises; and

(b) apply to the court for an order for possession and an order to force open the premises.

16. TENANT REFUSING OR NEGLECTING TO GIVE UP POSSESSION

As soon as the term or interest on any premises has been determined by a written notice to quit as in Form TL2 or TL3, in the Schedule to this Law and the tenant neglects or refuses to quit and deliver up possession of the premises or any part of it, the landlord or his agent may cause the tenant to be served with a written notice as in Form TL4, signed by the landlord or his agent, of the landlord's intention to proceed to recover possession, stating the grounds and particulars of the claim, on a date not less than seven (7) days from the date of the notice.

17. SERVICE OF NOTICES

(1) Notices referred to under Sections 13 – 16 of this Law shall be by proper service as prescribed under Sections 18 and 19.

(2) Proper service shall be service in such a manner that it can be established to the satisfaction of the court that the person to be served will have knowledge of any of the notices.

18. SERVICE OF NOTICES FOR RESIDENTIAL PREMISES

Proper service on a tenant of residential premises shall be personal service, for residential premises which includes but not limited to the following:

(a) service on the tenant in person;

(b) delivery to any adult residing at the premises to be recovered;

(c) by courier where the tenant cannot be found, by delivering same at the premises sought to be recovered and the courier shall provide proof of delivery; or

(d) affixing the notice on a prominent part of the premises to be recovered and providing corroborative proof of service.

19. SERVICE OF NOTICES FOR BUSINESS PREMISES

Proper service on a tenant of a business premises shall be by –

(a) delivery to a person at the business premises sought to be recovered; or

(b) affixing the notice on a prominent part of the premises to be recovered and providing corroborative proof of service.

20. DUTY TO NOTIFY OTHER PERSONS IN OCCUPATION

Where the tenant is a person other than an individual (including corporate entity), the landlord shall ensure proper service of all notices required under this Law on the tenant:

Provided that the failure of the tenant to notify any other person in occupation shall not affect the proceedings to recover possession.

21. PERSONS IN UNLAWFUL OCCUPATION

Where a person claims possession of premises which he alleges is occupied solely by a person in unlawful occupation, the proceedings for recovery of the premises shall be by the summary procedure contained in the Civil Procedure Rules of the relevant court without prejudice to the necessary need to serve upon the unlawful occupant Form TL4.

22. SERVICE OF PROCESSS

Service of any summons, warrant or other process shall be effected in accordance with the provisions of the law for the time being in force relating to the service of the civil process of Magistrates' Court or the High Court of Lagos State.

23. USE OF FORMS

Subject to the provisions of this Law, the forms contained in the Schedule to this Law, may be used in the cases to which they apply and when so used, shall be sufficient in Law with such adaptation and modification as may be necessary.

24. INSTITUTION OF PROCEEEDINGS TO RECOVER POSSESSION

Upon the expiration of the time stated in the notice as in Form TL4, if the tenant neglects or refuses to quit and deliver up possession, the landlord may file a claim by way of summons as in Form TL6A and B for recovery of possession, either against the tenant or against such person so neglecting or refusing, in the Magisterial District or High Court Division where the premises is situated.

25. GROUNDS FOR POSSESSION

(1) Unless the agreement expressly stipulates otherwise, the court shall have power to make an order for possession upon proof of any of the following grounds –

(a) arrears of rent;

(b) breach of any covenant or agreement;

(c) where the premises is required by the landlord for personal use; or

(d) where the premises requires substantial repair.

(2) Notwithstanding any agreement between the parties, the court shall have power to make an order for possession upon proof of any of the following grounds where –

(a) the premises is being used for immoral or illegal purposes;
(b) the premises has been abandoned;
(c) the premises is unsafe and unsound as to constitute a danger to human life or property; or
(d) the tenant or any person residing or lodging with him or being his subtenant constitutes by conduct, an act of intolerable nuisance or induces a breach of a tenancy agreement.

26. RECOVERY OF PREMISES FOR A FIXED TERM CERTAIN

The landlord shall be entitled to recovery of the premises where –

(a) a tenancy is proved to be for a fixed term certain;
(b) the period of the tenancy has expired by effluxion of time; and
(c) Form TL5 has been served in accordance with Section 13 (5) of this Law.

27. TRIAL

(1) In any matter under this Law, relating to any fact required to proved at the trial of any action, evidence shall be by written deposition or oral examination of witnesses in open court or a combination of both.

(2) All agreed documents or other exhibits shall be tendered from the bar or by the party where he is not represented by a legal practitioner.

(3) The oral examination of a witness during his evidence-in-chief shall be limited to confirming his written deposition and tendering in evidence all disputed documents or other exhibits.

(4) Where the tenant does not enter any defence and the landlord can prove –

(a) that the defendant is still neglecting or refusing to deliver up the premises;
(b) the annual rental value of the premises;
(c) the nature of the tenancy or holding;
(d) the expiration or other determination of the tenancy within the time and manner stipulated by law;
(e) his title, if such has accrued since the letting of the premises;
(f) the service of the summons or writ if the defendant does not appear,

the court may make an order as in Form TL7 for possession of the premises mentioned either immediately or on or before such date within six (6) months from the date of the order as the court may direct.
(5) Subject to the provisions of Section 13 (2) and (3), the court shall, in making an order for possession of premises, have regard to all circumstances of the case including where appropriate, the question as to whether other premises are available for the landlord or the tenant.
(6) If the claimant named in the summons or writ fails to obtain an order under subsection (1) of this section, the defendant may be awarded such costs as the court may direct.

28. PAYMENT OF ARREARS

(1) Where there is any matter for determination before a court under this Law, and the tenant admits the arrears of rent or a portion of the rent, the court may order the tenant to pay such arrears of rent while the court proceeds with the matter.
(2) Where arrears of rent are claimed for the use and occupation of the premises, the claim shall show the rate at which such sum is claimed, and where it is proved, judgement shall be entered for the amount so proved.

29. COURT AS RECEIVER OF REFUSED RENT

(1) In any proceedings under this Law, where a landlord refuses to accept the current rent from a tenant, the tenant may, upon application to the court, pay such rent to the court's Registry.
(2) The landlord in such case shall be entitled to collect the rent from the court, less ten percent (10%) to be retained by the court.

30. ARBITRATION

(1) A valid agreement to arbitrate shall be upheld and be enforceable in the court while an arbitration clause or agreement in a tenancy or lease agreement shall not be construed as an ouster of the court's jurisdiction.
(2) In the absence of any agreement to the contrary or where the parties cannot agree on the appointment of an arbitrator or tribunal, the court on receipt of a written application by any of the parties, shall act as the appointing authority, upon payment of the prescribed fees.
(3) An arbitration award shall be enforceable as a judgement or order of the court upon registration.
(4) Applications to enforce awards shall be made to the court.
(5) An arbitration award in any matter covered by this Law must be registered within three (3) months of the date of the award.

31. LANDLORD MAY CLAIM MESNE PROFITS OR FOR USE AND OCCUPATION OF PREMISES

Where mesne profits or a sum for the use and occupation of the premises are claimed, the claim shall show the rate at which such sum is claimed, and where it is proved, judgement shall be entered for the amount so proved.

32. MEDIATION

(1) In proceedings under this Law, the court shall promote reconciliation, mediation and amicable settlement between the parties.

(2) A court may refer tenancy proceedings or any part of it to mediation at a Citizen Mediation Centre or to Lagos Multi-Door Court House.

(3) Referrals to mediation under the provisions of subsection (2) of the section shall not require the consent of the parties to the proceedings.

(4) The mediator shall submit the Mediation Agreement to the court for endorsement and enforcement within three (3) days after execution by the parties.

33. CLAIMS AGAINST PERSONS IN UNLAWFUL OCCUPATION

Where, in a possession claim against persons in unlawful occupation, the claimant does not know the name of a person in occupation of the premises, the claim shall be brought against 'persons unknown' in addition to any other description available.

34. DEFENCE SUPPORTED BY WRITTEN DEPOSITION

Where in accordance with Section 27 of this Law, the defendant intends to rely on a written deposition, he may at the time of filing the defence but not later than five (5) days thereafter, file witness statements, exhibits and other relevant documents to be tendered.

35. SERVICE ON PERSONS IN UNLAWFUL OCCUPATION

Where in a possession claim against trespassers, the claim has been issued against 'persons unknown', the claim, particulars of claim, any witness statements, exhibits and any other relevant document shall be deemed served on those persons by –

(a) attaching copies of the claim form, particulars of claim and any other relevant document to the main door or some other part of the premises so that they are clearly visible;

(b) if practicable, inserting copies of those documents in a sealed transparent envelope addressed to 'the occupiers' through the door or gate of the premises or letter box if there is one; or

(c) placing stakes in the land in places where they are clearly visible and attaching to each stake copies of the claim form, particulars of claim and any other relevant document in a sealed transparent envelope addressed to 'the occupiers'.

36. DEFENDANT NOT DEFENDING CLAIM

Where the claim is based on documentary evidence and the defendant does not file a defence or appear at the trial and does not defend the claim, the Magistrate shall be entitled to adjudicate upon the clam in Chambers but shall give judgement in open court.

37. UNREASONABLE INCREASE OF RENT

(1) Subject to any agreement to the contrary, an existing tenant may apply as in Form TL11 to the court for an order declaring that the increase in rent payable under a tenancy agreement is unreasonable.

(2) In determining whether an increase in the rent is unreasonable, the court shall issue hearing notice as in Form TL12 to the landlord and shall consider the application on the following grounds –

(a) the general level of rents in the locality or a similar locality for comparative analysis;

(b) evidence of witnesses of the parties; and

(c) any special circumstances relating to the premises in question or any other relevant matter.

(3) If satisfied that the increase in the rent is unreasonable, the court may order as in Form TL13 that the increase in the rent be changed to a specific amount.

(4) Notwithstanding the provisions of any law, it shall be unlawful for a landlord to eject a tenant from any premises pending the determination of the action.

38. APPLICATION TO SET ASIDE OR VARY JUDGEMENT OF COURT

Any judgement by default under this Law shall be final and remain valid and may only be set aside upon application to the Magistrate on grounds of fraud, non-service, lack of jurisdiction or upon such terms as the court may deem fit.

39. WARRANT FOR POSSESSION MAY BE ISSUED AT ANY TIME

Where a landlord is entitled to possession of any premises, the court may issue a warrant for possession, notwithstanding that the counterclaim is undetermined or unsatisfied.

40. FORM AND PURPOSE OF WARRANT FOR POSSESSION

A warrant for possession shall entitle the landlord to be put in possession of the premises to which the warrant relates and the certificate of warrant execution shall be as in Form TL10.

41. DURATION OF WARRANT

Notwithstanding any provision in any other law, every warrant for possession shall bear the date after the day mentioned in the order for possession of the premises in question and shall be in force for three (3) months from such date:

Provided that a warrant may be renewed every three (3) months but shall not exceed three (3) renewals.

42. WARRANT FOR POSSESSION JUSTIFIES ENTRY ON PREMISES

Any warrant to give possession of the premises to the person named in the warrant or to whom it may be directed, shall justify entry to him with such assistance as he deems necessary and be given possession of the premises:

Provided that no entry upon such warrant shall be made on a Sunday or public holiday.

43. ENFORCEMENT OF ORDER OF COURT

At the expiration of the time ordered by the court, if an order of possession of the court is not obeyed, the court at the instance of the landlord shall, where such order can be proved to have been served on the tenant, issue a warrant for possession, and if the order is that possession of the premises be given up by the tenant to the landlord, the court shall immediately at the instance and at the cost of the landlord, issue a warrant for possession to the landlord.

44. OFFENCES AND PENALTIES

(1) Subject to the provisions of any law, -

(a) any person who demolishes, alters, or modifies a building to which this Law applies with a view to ejecting a tenant and without the approval of the court; or

(b) any person who in respect of any premises –

(i) attempts to forcibly eject or forcibly ejects a tenant;

(ii) threatens or molests a tenant by action or words, with a view to ejecting such tenant; or

(iii) willfully damages any premises

shall be guilty of an offence and is liable to a fine not exceeding two hundred and fifty thousand Naira (N250,000.00) or a maximum of six (6) months imprisonment and any other non-custodial disposition.

(2) A court shall have power to punish for contempt in the face of the court but may in other cases order the arrest and bring before it any person suspected of having committed contempt of court and such a person shall as soon as practicable be brought to trial before a court of law.

(3) Following subsection (2) of this section, any person who-

(a) resists, molests, assaults, or in any way obstructs any officer of the court or any other person from carrying out an order of the court to serve any process or execute a warrant for possession; or

(b) has been put out of possession, by virtue of a warrant for possession, and unlawfully retakes possession of the premises after possession has been given to the landlord

Shall be charged with contempt and is liable on conviction to a fine not exceeding two hundred and fifty thousand Naira (250,000.00) or a maximum of six (6) months imprisonment and any other non-custodial disposition.

(4) (a) Any landlord who obtains an order for possession of any premises under this Law by intentionally providing false information shall be guilty of an offence and liable under the Criminal Code.

(b) Any tenant who deprives the landlord of any premises under this Law by intentionally providing false information shall be guilty of an offence and liable under the Criminal Code.

(c) Without prejudice to any criminal proceedings, where -

(i) any landlord has obtained an order of possession of premises under this Law and upon an application made by summons by the tenant, the court is satisfied that such order was obtained by intentionally providing false information; the court shall order the landlord to pay reasonable compensation to such tenant; and

(ii) the tenant has deprived the landlord of possession of premises under this Law and upon application made by summons by the landlord, the court is satisfied that the landlord was so deprived by the tenant intentionally providing false information; the court shall order the tenant to pay reasonable compensation to such landlord.

45. **APPEALS**

(1) A party to any proceedings in the Magistrates' Court may appeal from the decisions of the Magistrates' Court to the High Court in accordance with the provisions of the Magistrates' Court Law.

(2) A party to any proceedings in the High Court may appeal in accordance with the provisions of the constitution.

46. REGULATIONS AND PROCEDURE

The Chief Judge may, as required, make regulations for the procedure through which matters relating to the conduct of proceedings shall be carried out.

47. INTERPRETATION

In this Law, unless the context otherwise requires -

'Agent' means any person usually employed by the landlord in the letting or leasing of the premises or in the collecting of the rents, or a person specially authorized to act in a particular manner by writing under the hand of the landlord;

'Business Premises' except where it is expressly stated otherwise by this Law, includes premises used wholly or in part for non-residential purposes, such as, places let out for business, shops, offices, shopping malls, sporting facilities, events centres, lodgings, gaming houses, clubs and club houses, religious worship, institutions and voluntary services structures amongst others;

'Commissioner' means Commissioner for Justice, Lagos State;

'Common Area' means any part of the premises the use of which is jointly shared by tenants or by a landlord and onc or more tenants;

'Court' means the High Court and Magistrates' Court of Lagos State but specifically excludes the Customary Court;

'Current Rent' means the subsisting rent;

'Functions' includes powers and duties;

'Governor' means the Governor of Lagos State;

'Interested Person' includes any person claiming through the landlord or the tenant or who has an interest in the proceedings;

'Landlord' in relation to any premises means the person entitled to the immediate reversion of the premises or ift he property is held in joint tenancy or tenancy in common, any of the persons entitled to the immediate reversion and includes –

(a) the attorney, solicitor, agent or caretaker of any such landlord;

(b) any person receiving (whether in his own right or as an attorney or agent) any rent from any person for the occupation of any premises in respect of which he claims a right to receive the same; or

(c) a former landlord where the context so requires;

'Licensee' means a person who comes into occupation by mere permission, without the creation of a landlord and tenant relationship and has no estate or legal interest in the premises;

'Mesne Profits' means the rent and profits which a tenant WHO holds over OR A TRESPASSER HAS OR MIGHT HAVE RECEIVED during his occupation of the premises and which he is liable to pay as compensation to the person entitled to possession;

'Persons in Unlawful Occupation' means any person or corporate body who –

(a) enters into occupation through the tenant or remains in ay residential or business premises without the consent of the landlord; or

(b) enters into or remains in occupation of the premises after an order for possession against a tenant without the consent of the landlord;

'Premises' except where it is expressly stated otherwise by this Law, includes premises used for business, residential and non-residential purposes;

'Prescribed' means prescribed by this Law or Schedule or rules or regulations or orders;

'Proceedings' includes any proceedings instituted in court in respect of this Law;

'Rents' includes any consideration or money paid or agreed to be paid or value or a right given or agreed to be given or part of any crop rendered or any equivalent given in kind or in labour, in consideration of which a landlord has permitted any person to use and occupy any land, premises, or other corporeal hereditaments, the use of common areas but does not include any charge for services or facilities provided in addition for the occupation of the premises;

'Rules' means the rules for the time being in force relating to the practice and procedure of the courts in the exercise of their respective civil jurisdiction made under the law by which such courts were established or any law amending same;

'Services or Facilities' includes any of the following that are provided or agreed to be provided by the landlord to the tenant of premises: appliances and furnishings, cleaning and maintenance services, parking spaces, cable, television and dish services, laundry services, storage facilities, elevator services, common recreational facilities, intercom systems and security surveillance, housekeeping facilities, security services and waste removal services;

'Sitting Tenant' means a tenant in lawful occupation after the expiration of the first tenancy term according to the provisions of this Law and includes a tenant renewing an existing tenancy following an expired term of years;

'State' means Lagos State;

'Substantial Repair' means any work required to remedy anything which threatens the structure or renders the premises inhabitable, creates an intolerable nuisance or could be construed as a breach of the landlord's covenant in the head-lease;

'Sub-tenant' means a person who occupies a premises or a portion of the premises previously occupied by a tenant which has been sublet to the sub-tenant by virtue of the written consent of the landlord;

'Tenant' includes a sub-tenant or any person occupying any premises whether by payment of rent howsoever or by operation of law and not persons unlawfully occupying any premises under a bona fide claim to be the owner;

'Tenancy' means holding of interest in land or property by a tenant under a tenancy agreement;

'Tenancy Agreement' means an agreement whether written or oral, express or implied between a landlord and a tenant regarding possession of premises and use of common areas and includes leases and sub-leases.

48. REPEAL

The Rent Tribunals (Abolition and Transfer of Functions) Law 2007 is repealed.

49. CITATION AND COMMENCEMENT

This Law may be cited as the Tenancy Law and shall come into force on the 24th day of August 2011

SCHEDULE

There is only one schedule of 14 Forms numbered TL1 to TL14 thus:

TL1 - General Form of Title of Proceedings
TL2 - Notice to Quit Signed by the Landlord in Person
TL3 - Notice to Quit Given by an Agent or Legal Practitioner of the Landlord
TL4 - Notice to Tenant of Owner's Intention to Apply to Recover Possession
TL5 - Notice to Tenant of Owner's Intention to Apply to Recover Possession for Effluxion of Time
TL6A - Summons for Recovery of Possession of Premises
TL6B - (Annexed Claim Against Tenant or Person Refusing to Deliver up Possession
TL7 - Judgement for Claimant in Action for Recovery of Premises
TL8 - Judgement for Defendant in Action for Recovery of Premises
TL9 - Warrant for Possession of Premises
TL10 - Certificate of Executing of Warrant of Possession
TL11 - Application for Order Against Unreasonable Increase of Rent
TL12 - Notice of Hearing
TL13 - Order
TL14 - Record of Unreasonable Increase in Rent

APPENDIX G

RENT CONTROL AND RECOVERY OF RESIDENTIAL PREMISES LAW

LAWS OF DELTA STATE OF NIGERIA 2007(CHAPTER 180)

1. SHORT TITLE

The Law may be cited as the Rent Control and Recovery of Residential Premises Law.

2. INTERPRETATION

In this Law, unless the context otherwise requires –

'Accommodation' includes any building or premises used as residence whether or not approved by the building approving authorities in the state and regardless of user;

'Agent' means any person usually employed by the landlord in the letting of a premises or in the collection of the rents thereof or specially authorized to act in a particular manner by writing under the hand of the landlord in relation to a premises;

'Court' includes District Customary Courts, Area Customary Courts, and the Customary Court of Appeal of the state;

'Functions' includes powers and duties;

'Landlord' in relation to any premises means the person entitled to the immediate reversion of the premises or if the property therein is held in joint tenancy or tenancy in common, any of the persons entitled to the immediate reversion and includes –

(a) the attorney or agent of any such landlord; or

(b) any person receiving (whether in his own right or as an attorney or agent) any rent from any person for the occupation of any accommodation in respect of which he claims a right to receive same;

'Mesne Profits' means the rents or profits, as the case may be, which a tenant who holds over or a trespasser has or might have received during his occupation of the premises and which he is liable to pay as compensation to the person entitled to possession;

'Governor' means the Governor of Delta State of Nigeria;

'Premises' includes a house or building or any part thereof together with its gardens or other appurtenancies;

'Prescribed' means prescribed by this Law or regulations and orders made thereunder;

'Rent' includes any money or money's worth whether in the form of crops, labour or otherwise paid or given as the case may be, in consideration of which a landlord has let a premises to a tenant;
'The Rules' means the rules for the time being in force relating to the practice and procedure of a court in exercise of its civil jurisdiction, made under the law by which such court is established or any law amending the same;
'Standard Rent' means in relation to any accommodation any rent fixed by order under Section 6 of this Law;
'State' means Delta State of Nigeria;
'Tenant' includes a sub-tenant or any person occupying any premises whether on payment of rent or otherwise but does not include a person occupying a premises occupying a premises under a bona fide claim of right as the owner of the premises;

3. APPLICATION

(1) This Law shall apply to all residential accommodation throughout the state.
(2) The Governor may from time to time by order classify the types and categories of residential accommodation, zone the areas of the state and fix the standard and maximum rents for such accommodation for the purpose of this Law.
(3) The Governor may from time to time by order exempt the application of this Law to any particular accommodation or areas.
(4) Any order made under sub-section (2) of this section may be made to have effect from any date (not however being a date earlier than the date of commencement of this Law whether before or after the date of the making thereof, according as the Governor may deem necessary or expedient.

4. RENT TRIBUNALS

(1) There shall be established courts to be called District and Area Customary Courts and the Customary Court of Appeal (hereinafter in this Law referred to as 'the courts') as provided in the Customary Courts Law and the Customary Court of Appeal Law of the state.
(2) No proceedings of the court shall be rendered invalid by reason of any defect in the appointment of the chairman or any member.
(3) The court may, on the application of any person who in the opinion of the tribunal has an interest in the matter, or of its own motion, sit

with one or more assessors in any case where the tribunal is satisfied that it is necessary for the determination of any issue before it.

5. AGREEMENT

(1) As from the commencement of this Law, it shall be unlawful for a landlord to accept an agreed rent in respect of any accommodation to which this Law applies which is in excess of the standard rent prescribed for the type of accommodation.

(2) Where the agreed rent is higher than the standard rent prescribed for the type of accommodation under this Law, the tenant shall pay, as from the commencement of this Law, the standard rent.

(3) Where the agreed rent is lower than the standard rent prescribed for the type of accommodation under this Law, the tenant shall continue to pay, as from the commencement of this Law, the agreed rent save that after the expiration of six months of the commencement of this Law, the landlord may make an application to the court for an order to vary the agreed rent.

6. STANDARD RENT

(1) The court shall have jurisdiction, on application made to it by a landlord, or a tenant or any interested person to determine in respect of any accommodation let before, on or after the commencement of this Law the standard rent payable in respect of such accommodation within the limit of the rent prescribed in the order made under Section 3 of the Law.

(2) Every order of the court fixing the standard rent of any accommodation shall be signed by the chairman and be issued under the seal of such tribunal.

(3) The standard rent fixed by the court shall supersede the agreed rent as between the landlord and the tenant and any order made by the tribunal shall bind all persons including the landlord, tenant or mortgagee of the building in which the accommodation is situated.

(4) As from the commencement of this Law, it shall be unlawful for anyone in consideration of the grant, continuance, surrender or giving up of a tenancy of any accommodation to require or receive the payment of any loan or premium in respect of the same, and any such payment made in respect of any accommodation to a landlord by a tenant shall be recoverable by the tenant, and may, without prejudice to any other method of recovery, be deducted from any rent payable by him to the landlord, at any time.

(5) For the avoidance of doubt, the provisions of this Law shall not render unlawful or invalid any agreement whereby any bona fide contractor invests in the development of any property to which this Law applies, and in consideration of such investment, takes a lease of the property for any period of time at a rent lower than the standard rent.

(6) It shall be unlawful for the agreed or standard or maximum rent of any accommodation to which this Law to be demanded or received in excess of three months for individual tenants and twelve months for commercial or institutional tenants.

(7) Where before the commencement of this Law an agreed rent has been paid to a landlord in advance and in excess of that provided in sub-section (6) above, such rent shall not be recoverable by a tenant.

7. GENERAL JURISDICTION

(1) Proceedings under this Law may be brought before the court established under the Customary Court Law.

(2) The jurisdiction of the court shall not be ousted by the defendant or respondent bona fide setting up the title of a third person.

(3) Subject to the provisions of this Law, the court shall be bound by the practice and procedure in civil matters in the Magistrates' Courts

(4) Where a tenant has defaulted in paying –

(a) his rent before the coming into force of this Law; or

(b) the agreed rent as at the commencement of this Law, and there is an application for the determination of the standard rent before the court, the court may order the tenant to pay such arrears of rent before the determination of the application.

8. TRANSFER OF LIABILITY: EFFECT ON RENT

(1) Any transfer to a tenant of any burden or liability previously borne by the landlord shall, for the purposes of this Law, be treated as an alteration of rent and where, as a result of such transfer the terms on which any premises are held are on the whole less favourable to the tenant than the previous terms, the rent shall be deemed to be increased whether or not the sum periodically payable by way of rent is increased.

(2) Any increase of rent in respect of any transfer to a landlord of any burden or liability previously held by the tenant where, as a result of such transfer, the terms on which any premises are held are on the

whole not less favourable to the tenant than the previous terms, shall be deemed not be an increase of rent for the purposes of this Law.

9. DISTRESS FOR RENT

(1) A landlord shall not exercise the power of distress for rent except in execution of the judgement of a court and in accordance with the Sheriffs and Civil Process Law, but the court, on being satisfied that a tenant has defaulted in paying –

(a) the standard rent fixed by the tribunal; or

(b) an agreed rent which is lower than the standard rent,

may order that the tenant's property be distrained until such payment is made.

(2) Sections 18, 19, 20, 21 and 26 of the Sheriffs and Civil Process Law shall apply in relation to distress made under this section as they do in relation to attachment in execution under process of a court.

10. PROCEEDINGS TO BE IN PUBLIC, ETC.

(1) The proceedings of the court shall be held in public unless on any occasion the tribunal considers it to be in the interests of justice for the same to be held in private, and accordingly to exclude any person therefrom.

(2) Proceedings of the court shall be deemed to be judicial proceedings and the members to be judicial officers.

(3) A tribunal shall, in the course of its proceedings, have power to examine witnesses on oath, and to summon any person to give evidence or to produce any document which the tribunal may consider relevant including any document of title.

11. PROTECTION OF MEMBERS OF TRIBUNAL

(1) No member or officer of the court shall be liable to be prosecuted or sued in any court for any act done or ordered to be done by him in good faith in the discharge of his functions under this Law.

(2) No person duly authorized to carry out the orders of the court shall be liable to be prosecuted or sued in any court for so doing.

12. REPRESENTATION OF PARTIES

In respect of any matter before the court any landlord, tenant, class of landlords or tenants or any other person who in the opinion of the tribunal has any interest in such matter may be represented either by himself or by a legal practitioner, an in respect of any such matter the Governor may be represented by a law officer or by any other person authorized in that behalf by or on behalf of the Attorney-General.

13. SUB-TENANTS DEEMED TO BE TENANTS OF LANDLORDS

Where a landlord at any time lets any premises and his tenant not being expressly prohibited in writing from sub-letting sub-lets such premises or any part thereof, the sub-tenants of such premises or any part thereof shall be deemed for the purposes of this Law to be tenants of the landlord.

14. RESTRICTION ON CONTRACTING OUT

Any agreement relating to the tenancy of any accommodation to which this Law applies shall be void in so far as it purports to preclude the tenant from making any application or otherwise exercising any rights conferred upon him under or by virtue of this Law or provides for the termination or the surrender of the tenancy of the accommodation in the event of his making such application or exercising such a right or for the imposition of any penalty or disability on the tenant in that event.

15. COURTS TO CONFORM TO PROVISIONS OF LAW

Every court established by the laws of the state whether of civil or criminal jurisdiction shall, so far as is necessary, and subject to sub-section (1) of Section 7 of this Law, conform to the provisions of this Law and shall not recognize or enforce any measures, transactions or other arrangements which in its opinion are tended for, or calculated to result in, the evasion or default of any of the provisions or purposes of this Law, in all or any proceedings, actions, suits or cases between landlords and tenants or between any of them and other persons and in all applications, suits, actions, cases and matters in which the rights, remedies, duties, or titles of any of these afore-mentioned are in question.

16. SECURITY OF TENANCY

(1) Where an application has been made to the court by a tenant in respect of accommodation to which this Law applies, any notice issued by the landlord and served on the tenant to quit the accommodation thereafter shall be of no effect and no similar notice to quit shall be given by the landlord before the decision of the court is given.

(2) Notwithstanding the provisions of any law or enactment, the court may declare as invalid and of no effect a notice to quit served on a tenant if it is satisfied that such a notice was not issued in good faith, and the tribunal's endorsement to that effect on the purported notice to

quit shall be sufficient evidence of such decision before any court of law.

17. TENANT REFUSING, NEGLECTING TO GIVE UP POSSESSIOM

When and so soon as the term or interest of the tenant of any premises, held by him at will or for any term either with or without being liable to the payment of any rent, shall have ended or shall have been duly determined by a written notice to quit as in form B, C, OR D, whichever is applicable to the case, or otherwise duly determined and such tenant, or, if such tenant does not actually occupy the premises or only occupies a part thereof, any person by whom the same or any part thereof shall then be actually occupied, shall neglect or refuse to quit and deliver up possession of the premises or of such part thereof respectively, the landlord of the said premises or his agent may cause the person so neglecting or refusing to quit and deliver up possession to be served, in the manner hereinafter mentioned, with a written notice as in Form E signed by the landlord or his agent, of the landlord's intention to proceed to recover possession on a date not less than seven days from the date of service of the notice.

18. LENGTH OF NOTICE

Where the is no express stipulation as to the notice to be given by either party to determine the tenancy, the following periods of time shall be given –

(a) in the case of a tenancy at will or a weekly tenancy, a week's notice;

(b) in the case of a monthly tenancy, a month's notice;

(c) in the case of a quarterly tenancy, a quarter's notice; and

(d) in the case of a yearly tenancy, half a year's notice.

Provided that in the case of a monthly tenancy, where a tenant is in arrears of rent for three months after the commencement of this Law, the tenancy shall determine and the court shall on the application of the landlord make an order for possession and arrears of rent.

19. GIVING OF NOTICE AND EXPIRY THEREOF

Notices referred to in Section 18 may be given at any time prior to the date of termination of current terms of tenancy, but they shall not be effective if the time between the giving of the notice and the time when the tenancy is to be determined is less than the respective periods set out in Section 18, provided that where rents are payable in advance in the case of monthly and quarterly tenancies, it shall not be lawful for a landlord to give notice to quit or recover possession during the first six months of the tenancy except on the order of the tribunal or with the consent of the tenant.

20. INSTITUTION OF PROCEEDINGS

(1) Upon the expiration of the time stated in any such notice of the landlord's intention to recover possession, if such tenant or any person holding or claiming by, through or under him, neglects or refuses to quit and deliver up possession accordingly, the landlord may apply to the court for the issue of a writ or enter a plaint as in Form F, at his option either against such tenant or against such person so neglecting or refusing, for the recovery of the same and thereupon a summons as in Form G shall issue to such tenant or person so neglecting.

(2) If mesne profits are claimed and the writ or plaint shows that the rate at which such mense profits are claimed is the same as the standard rent of the premises, judgement shall be entered for the ascertained amount as a liquidated claim and if mesne profits are at the rate of the said rent up to the time of obtaining possession the judgement shall be extended to include such claim and shall be as in the second alternative in Form J.

(3) Where a claim for recovery of possession is joined with a claim for arrears of rent and the defendant admits liability for arrears of rent, the court shall upon such admission enter judgement for the arrears of rent and may subsequently proceed with the claim for recovery of premises.

21. SUB-TENANT SERVED WITH SUMMONS TO RECOVER POSSESSION MUST GIVE NOTICE TO HIS IMMEDIATE LANDLORD

Where any summons for the recovery of any premises as is herein before specified shall be served on or come to the knowledge of any sub-tenant of the plaintiff's immediate tenant, such sub-tenant being an occupier of the whole or of a part of the premises sought to be recovered, he shall forthwith give notice thereof to his immediate landlord, failure to give such notice rendering him liable to forfeit such sum as the tribunal may consider just but not exceeding three year's rent of the premises held by such sub-tenant to such landlord by action in the court from which such summons shall have issued, and such landlord, on the receipt of such notice, if not originally a defendant, may be added or substituted as a defendant to defend possession of the premises in question.

22. LANDLORD MAY CLAIM FOR MESNE PROFITS

The landlord may, either together with his writ or plaint for the recovery of the premises or in answer to any claim or counter-claim made in respect of any unexhausted improvements as hereinafter provided, claim to recover, or to set-off, rent or mesne profits, or both accruing in respect of such premises from the determination of the tenancy to the day appointed for the hearing, or to any preceeding day named in the writ or plaint.

23. CLAIMS FOR ARREARS OF RENT AND MESNE PROFITS

The amount claimed under any writ or plaint for arrears of rent and mesne profits shall be treated as one claim.

24. IMPROVEMENT OF ACCOMMODATION BY TENANTS

Where a tenant with the previous consent in writing of the landlord executed on his accommodation any improvements he shall be entitled, at the termination of the tenancy, on quitting his accommodation to receive compensation from his landlord in respect of any such improvement.

25. HEARING OF SUMMONS

(1) If the defendant shall not at the time named in the summons or any adjournment thereof, show good cause to the contrary, then on proof –

(a) of the defendant still neglecting or refusing to deliver up the premises;

(b) of the yearly rent of the premises;

(c) of the holding;

(d) of the expiration or other determination of the tenancy within the time and manner thereof;

(e) of the service of the summons, if the defendant does not appear thereto,

The court may order as in Form J, K, or L, whichever is applicable to the case, that possession of the premises mentioned in the plaint be given by the defendant to the plaintiff either forthwith or on or before such day as the tribunal shall think fit to specify.

(2) If the plaintiff at the time named in the summons or at any adjournment thereof shall fail to obtain an order under sub-section (1) above, the defendant shall be entitled to judgement and may be awarded costs, such judgement and award being as in Form M.

26. WARRANT OF POSSESSION MAY ISSUE AT ANY TIME

Where a landlord is entitled to possession of any premises, the court may issue a warrant of possession –

Provided that every counterclaim connected with or arising from the writ or plaint shall have been determined or satisfied.

27. LIMITATIONS OF ORDERS AND JUDGEMENTS

(1) No order or judgement for the recovery of possession of any premises to which this Law applies or for the ejectment of a tenant therefrom shall be made or given unless the court considers it reasonable to make such order or give such a judgement, and unless either –

(a) the court has power so to do under the provisions set out in the Second Schedule to this Law; or

(b) the court is satisfied that suitable alternative accommodation is available for the tenant.

(2) Accommodation shall be deemed to be suitable if it is in the opinion of the tribunal, reasonably suitable to the needs of the tenant and his family as regards proximity to place of work, to the means of the tenant and to the needs of the tenant and his family as to extent and character.

28. ENFORCEMENT OF ORDER OF COURT

If the order of the tribunal given under Section 26 be not obeyed, the tribunal, whether such order can be proved to have been served on the defendant or not, shall, at the instance of the plaintiff, issue a warrant of possession, and if such order is to the effect that possession of the premises be given forthwith by the defendant to the plaintiff, the court shall at the instance and cost of the plaintiff issue a warrant of possession forthwith.

29. FORM AND PURPOSE OF WARRANT OF POSSESSION

A warrant of possession shall entitle the plaintiff to be put in possession of the premises to which the warrant relates and shall be as in Form N and the certificate of execution thereof shall be as in Form O.

30. WARRANT OF POSSESSION TO BE IN FORCE FOR THREE MONTHS

Every warrant of possession shall on whatever day it may be issued bear the date of the day next after the last day named by the court in the order for the delivery of possession of the premises in question and shall continue in force for three months from such date, and no longer, but any order for delivery of possession made subsequent thereto need not be served.

31. WARRANT OF POSSESSION JUSTIFIES ENTRY ON POSSESSION

A warrant of possession shall entitle the person named therein or to whom it is directed to enter upon the premises with such assistants as may be reasonably necessary, and to take possession accordingly:

Provided that no entry upon such premises shall be made on a Sunday or public holiday or at any time except between the hours of six o'clock in the morning and six o'clock in the evening.

32. SERVICE OF PROCESS INCLUDING SUBSTITUTED SERVICE

Service of any notice under the provisions of this Law or any summons, warrant or other process shall be effected in accordance with the provisions of the law for the time being in force relating to the service of civil process of Magistrates' Courts and if the defendant cannot be found, and his place of dwelling shall either not be known, or admission thereto cannot be obtained for serving any such process, a copy of the process shall be pasted on some conspicuous part of the premises sought to be recovered, and such pasting shall be deemed good service on the defendant.

33. RENT BOOKS

(1) As from the commencement of this Law, all landlords of premises in the areas to which this Law applies shall issue prescribed Rent Books in addition to receipts to their tenants.

(2) The Rent Book shall be in the custody of the tenant and necessary entries shall be made by the landlord therein when rents are paid by the tenant.

(3) Any landlord who fails to issue the prescribed Rent Book to his tenant or who fails to make necessary entries in a Rent Book in accordance with sub-section (2) of this section shall be guilty of an offence and shall be liable on summary conviction to a fine of fifty Naira or to imprisonment for one month or to both such fine and imprisonment.

34. USE OF FORMS

(1) Subject to the express provisions, if any, of the rules, the forms contained in the First Schedule may, in accordance with any instructions contained in the said forms, and with such variation as the

circumstances of the particular case may require, be used in the cases to which they apply, and when so used, shall be good and sufficient in Law.

(2) The forms may be added to, repealed, replaced or varied by rules made as aforesaid in all respects as if the forms had originally been so made under this Law.

35. APPEALS

Either party to any proceedings in relation to any provision of this Law shall with the leave of the appropriate appellate court appeal from the decision of the court to the appropriate appellate court of the state.

36. CESSER OF JURISDICTION OF HIGH COURT AND MAGISTRATE COURT

(1) In so far as jurisdiction is conferred on the courts in respect of the causes or matters mentioned in the foregoing provisions of this Law, the High Court or Magistrate Courts of the state shall, to the extent that jurisdiction is so conferred on the courts, cease to have jurisdiction in relation to such causes or matters:

Provided that the High Court shall have appellate jurisdiction.

(2) Nothing in the foregoing provisions shall affect the jurisdiction and all other powers of the court to continue to hear and determine causes and matters which are part-heard before any other court at the date when jurisdiction is conferred on the courts, and any proceedings in any such causes and matters, which are part-heard at the expiration of the period of three months beginning with the date when jurisdiction is conferred on the courts, shall abate on the expiration of that period.

37. SAVINGS. LAW NO. 14 OF 1970

Any court or appointment of a member of a court or assessors, set up or made, and any application, proceedings or other thing whatsoever made, commenced or done in pursuance of any provision of the Rent Control Law, 1970 shall, on the commencement of this Law be deemed to have been duly set up, made, commenced or done under the provisions of this Law, subject to such modifications and adaptations as may be required to bring the same in conformity with this Law.

38. OFFENCES AND PENALTIES

(1) Subject to the provisions of any Law in force, any person who demolishes, alters or modifies a building to which this Law applies with a view to ejecting a tenant and without the approval of the appropriate court is guilty of an offence and is liable on summary

conviction, to a fine of two hundred Naira or imprisonment for three months or both.

(2) (i) Any person who in respect of any accommodation to which this Law applies –

(a) attempts to eject or forcibly ejects a tenant; or

(b) harasses or molests a tenant by action or words with a view to ejecting such tenant; or

(ii) Any person who in respect of any accommodation to which this Law applies –

(a) harasses or molests a landlord in respect of accommodation let by him by action or words; or

(b) does any act or thing whatsoever calculated to stultify the provisions of this Law, or fails to comply with the requirements of any order made by a court,

shall be guilty of an offence and is liable on summary conviction, to a fine of two hundred Naira or imprisonment for three months or both.

(3) The court shall have power to punish for contempt in the face of the tribunal but it may in other cases, order the arrest of and bring before it any person suspected of having committed contempt of the tribunal and such a person shall as soon as practicable be brought to trial before a court.

(4) Any person charged with contempt of a tribunal shall be liable on conviction to a fine of one hundred Naira or to imprisonment for three months or both.

(5) Any person who, in respect of any type of accommodation to which this Law applies, receives a loan or premium from the tenant which, in the opinion of the tribunal, contravenes the provisions of this Law especially in relation to advance payment of rent shall be guilty of an offence and shall be liable on summary conviction to a fine equal to twice the amounts received as such loan or premium.

(6) Any landlord who demands or receives from a tenant rent in excess of the standard rent or receives or demands rent in advance in excess of -

(a) in the case of an individual tenant, three months; or

(b) in the case of commercial or institutional tenants, twelvemonths,

shall be guilty of an offence and liable on conviction to a fine of one hundred Naira and shall in addition refund to the tenant the amount of the excess of the rent received.

(7) Any person who resists, molests, assaults or in any way obstructs any officer (or any other person) engaged in the service of any process or in execution of a warrant of possession, in carrying out an order of a tribunal shall be guilty of an offence against this Law and shall be liable on summary conviction to a fine of two hundred Naira or to imprisonment for twelve months or to both such fine and imprisonment.

(8) Any person who has been put out of possession under a warrant of possession, and unlawfully retakes possession of the premises after possession has been given to the landlord shall be guilty of an offence against this Law and shall be liable on summary conviction to a fine of two hundred Naira or to imprisonment for twelve months or to both such fine and imprisonment.

(9) It shall be unlawful for any landlord to obtain order for possession of any accommodation under this Law by fraud, misrepresentation or concealment of any material fact.

(10) Where any landlord has obtained an order for possession of any accommodation under this Law and the court is satisfied upon an application made by summons by such tenant that such order was obtained by fraud, misrepresentation or the concealment of any material fact, the court shall order the landlord to pay reasonable compensation to such tenant.

(11) Any person who contravenes any provision of this Law shall be guilty of an offence and shall on summary conviction, where no punishment is specifically provided, be liable to a fine of fifty Naira or to imprisonment for one month.

39. APPLICATION TO LEASES

This Law shall apply to leases.

40. COMPULSORY ACQUISITION OF PREMISES

(1) Where the court has found that any landlord has violated any of the provisions of this Law or any regulations or order made thereunder on two occasions, the Governor may on the recommendation of the court, acquire the interest of the landlord in the premises in relation to which the offences have been committed.

(2) Where premises are compulsorily acquired pursuant to sub-section

(1) of this section, there shall be paid such compensation as may be determined under the provisions of the Public Lands Acquisition Law.

41. REPEALS NO. 14 OF 1970

(1) The Rent Control Law, 1970 is hereby repealed.

(2) The Recovery of Premises Law is hereby repealed to the extent that it relates to accommodation in residential premises.

(3) The provisions of the Magistrates Court Law to the extent that it relates to all actions between landlord and tenant in respect of residential accommodation are hereby repealed.

42. REGULATIONS

The Governor may make regulations providing for any matter for which provision appears to him to be necessary for the purpose of giving effect to the provisions of this Law and in particular, without prejudice to the generality of the foregoing, for all or any of the following matters –

(i) the procedure on applications to and hearing by, the court and the fixing of fees for the filing, service and hearing of application;

(ii) the manner in which rents may be paid to a landlord who refuses to accept any rent tendered to him;

(iii) the forms to be used for the process and procedure of a tribunal;

(iv) the amount of increase or reduction to be allowed by court in relation to repairs to premises according as the liability to make them is established before the appropriate tribunal;

(v) the type and nature of repairs or fixtures in premises where the accommodation is and the amount to be allowed in computing a standard rent where the court is satisfied that the repairs of fixtures, as the case may be, are necessary to make the premises reasonably fit for human habitation;

(vi) the forms and records to be used or kept by a tribunal or as record of payment under any tenancy agreement;

(vii) the imposition of penalties (other than for non-compliance with any order fixing standard rent); and

(viii) such other matters coming before a tribunal as the Governor may deem fit.

SCHEDULES

There are two main Schedules I and II. Schedule I has 15 Forms numbered A to O while Schedule II has the rules pursuant to Section of the Law as to when the court may make orders for recovery of possession without proof of alternative accommodation.

SCHEDULE I
Schedule I contains the following forms –
A - General Form of Title of Proceedings
B - Notice to Quit Signed by the Landlord Himself
C - Notice to Quit Given by an Agent or Legal Practitioner of the Landlord
D - Notice by Landlord to Quit Lodgings
E - Notice to Tenant of Owner's Intention to Apply to Recover Possession
F - Writ or Plaint Against Tenant or Person Refusing to Deliver up Possession
G - Summons for Recovery of Possession of Tenements
H - Appointment of Appraisers
I - Report of Appraisers
J - Judgement for Plaintiff in Action for Recovery of Premises
K - Judgement in an Action for Recovery of Premises for Plaintiff Where Title has Expired Before the Return Day
L - Judgement for Plaintiff in Action for Recovery of Premises for Non-Payment of Rent
M - Judgement for Defendant in Action for Recovery of Premises
N - Warrant for Possession of Premises
O - Certificate of Execution of Warrant of Possession

SCHEDULE II
Possession or Ejectment Without Proof of Alternative Accommodation (See primary source).

RENT CONTROL AND RECOVERY OF RESIDENTIAL PREMISES REGULATIONS
These are regulations made by the Governor of the state pursuant to powers conferred on him by Section 42 of the Law.
(See primary source).

APPENDIX H
THE LAWS OF THE FEDERATION OF NIGERIA (ABUJA) 1990

RECOVERY OF PREMISES ACT

CHAPTER 544

ARRANGEMENT OF SECTIONS

PART I - PRELIMINARY
Short title and interpretation

PART III - EJECTMENT

21. Enforcement of order of court
22. Form and purpose of warrant of possession
23. Warrants of possession to be in force for three months
24. Warrants of possession justifies entry on premises
25. Protection of officers of the court
26. Penalty for resisting or assaulting officers
27. Penalty on person unlawfully retaking possession

PART IV - MISCELLANEOUS

Service

28. Service of process

Landlord's liability to special damages

29. Landlord's liability to special damages

Appeal

30. Appeal from order of possession in all cases

Forms

31. Use of forms

SCHEDULE

THE LAWS OF THE FEDERATION OF NIGERIA (ABUJA) 1990

RECOVERY OF PREMISES ACT/LAW[1]

CHAPTER 544

An Act/Law to make provision for the recovery of possession of premises

F. & L. 1958 Cap. 176; L.N. 112 of 1964; W.R. 1959 Cap. 110; 1976 No. 3

PART I - PRELIMINARY

Short title

SHORT TITLE AND APPLICATION

1. (1) This Act/Law may be cited as the Recovery of Premises Act/Law.

(2) The Minister[2] may, from time to time by order, declare that the provisions of this Act/Law shall not apply to an area specified in the order and the order coming into force the provisions of this Act/Law shall cease to apply to such areas as may be specified in the order.

(3) A proceeding instituted prior to and which is pending at the date of the coming into force of the order and which is in respect of any premises in an area referred to in the order may be continued and carried through to completion, notwithstanding the order, in all respects as if this Act still applied to the area in which are situate the premises in question.

(4) Where the provisions of this Act are withdrawn from the area by order as from aforesaid the withdrawal shall remain operative only so long as there is in force an order effecting the withdrawal.

2. INTERPRETATION

In this Act/Law, unless the context otherwise requires,

'agent' means any person usually employed by the landlord in the letting of the premises or in the collection of the rents thereof or specially authorized to act in a particular manner by writing under the hand of the landlord;

1. The wordings and section numberings of this Act is the same in the states which have retained this enactment. Wherever the word Act occurs, the word Law fits in respect of state enactments.
2. Executive Council in some states.

'court' includes the High Court and Magistrates' Courts but does not include a customary court;

'landlord' in relation to any premises means the person entitled to the immediate reversion of the premises or if the property therein is held in joint tenancy or tenancy in common, any of the persons entitled to the immediate reversion, and includes the attorney or agent of the landlord, and also any person appointed to act on behalf of the state in dealing with any land, building, premises or corporeal or incorporeal hereditament vested in the state;

'mesne profits' means the rent and profits which a tenant who holds over or a trespasser has or might have received during his occupation of the premises and which he is liable to pay as compensation to the person entitled to possession.

'minister' means the minister charged with the responsibility for the administration of the Federal Capital Territory, Abuja;

'premises' includes

(a) a house or building or any part thereof together with its grounds or other appurtenancies, and

(b) the land without any building thereon;

'rent' includes any part of any crop rendered, or any equivalent given in kind or in labour, in consideration of which a landlord has permitted any person to use and occupy any land, house, premises, or other corporeal hereditament;

'rules' means the rules for the time being in force relating to the practice and procedure of the courts in exercise of their respective civil jurisdiction made under law by which the court were established or any law amending those laws;

'tenant' includes any person occupying premises whether on payment of rent or otherwise but does not include a person occupying premises under a bona fide claim to be the owner of the premises.

(2) A reference to a Form means a reference to that Form as set out in the Schedule to this Act/Law.

Jurisdiction

3. GENERAL JURISDICTION

Proceedings under this Act/Law may be brought in any court of competent jurisdiction.

4. COSTS IN THE HIGH COURT

Where proceedings under this Act/Law are brought in the High Court and the amount recovered or the value of the rent as ascertained does not exceed any amount which could have been recovered without any set-off or with an admitted set-off in a Magistrates' Court the plaintiff shall not be allowed costs in excess of those which he could have recovered had he brought the action in a Magistrates' court provided that –

(a) the proceedings were in respect of a bona fide claim of right set up by the defendant under Section 5 of this Act/Law; or

(b) the court certifies that there was a question of law involved which rendered it advisable for a decision thereon to be made by the High Court.

5. JURISDICTION OF MAGISTRATE IN CASES OF TITLE OF THIRD PERSON

The jurisdiction of a Magistrate shall not be ousted by the defendant bona fide setting up the title of a third person, unless he holds under, or claims through, that third person.

6. JURISDICTION IN RESPECT OF RENT OTHER THAN IN MONEY

(1) Where the rent includes a part of a crop or a value given in kind or labour or any amount which is not specified as of a precise monetary value proceedings under this Act/Law may be brought in a Magistrates' Court.

(2) If during the hearing it appears that the amount of the claim is a sum exceeding the rate of four hundred Naira a year, the plaintiff may abandon the excess and proceed and thereupon the Magistrates' Court shall have jurisdiction to hear and determine the action, so howsoever that –

(a) subject to the provisions of any law limiting the jurisdiction of the Magistrate hearing the action, the plaintiff shall not recover in the action a sum greater than hundred Naira;[3] and

(b) the judgement of the court shall be in full discharge of all demands in respect of the particular cause of action.

3. In some state laws e.g. Delta and Edo states, this reads: '... *a sum greater than the limit of the civil jurisdiction of the presiding Magistrate...*'.

PART II – PROCEEDINGS LEADING UP TO JUDGEMENT

Notices to Quit and if Intention to Recover Possession

7. NOTICES TO QUIT: FORM B, C OR D

When and so soon as the term or interest of the tenant of any premises, held by him at will or for any term either with or without being liable to the payment of any rent, ends or is duly determined by a written notice to quit as in Form B, C or D, whichever is applicable to the case, or is otherwise duly determined, and the tenant, or if the tenant does not actually occupy the premises or only occupies a part thereof, a person by whom the premises or any part thereof is actually occupied, neglects or refuses to quit and deliver up possession of the premises or of such part thereof respectively, the landlord of the premises or his agent may cause the person so neglecting or refusing to quit and deliver up possession to be served, in the manner hereinafter mentioned, with a written notice as in Form E signed by the landlord or his agent, of the landlord's intention to proceed to recover possession on a date not less than seven days from the date of service of the notice.

8. LENGTH OF NOTICE TO DETERMINE CERTAIN TERMS

(1) Where there is no express stipulation as to the notice to be given by either party to determine the tenancy, the following periods of time shall be given –

(a) in the case of a tenancy at will or a weekly tenancy, a week's notice;

(b) in the case of a monthly tenancy, a month's notice;

(c) in the case of a quarterly tenancy, a quarter's notice;

(d) subject to subsection (2) of this section, in the case of a yearly tenancy, half a year's notice.

(2) In the case of a yearly tenancy, the tenancy shall not expire before the time when any crops growing on the land, the subject of the tenancy, would in the ordinary course be taken, gathered, or reaped if such crops were crops which are normally reaped within one year of planting and such planting was done by the tenant prior to the giving of the notice.

(3) The nature of the tenancy shall, in the absence of any evidence to the contrary, be determined by reference to the time when the rent is paid or determined.

9. GIVING OF NOTICE AND EXPIRY THEREOF

Notices referred to in Section 8 of this Act/Law may be given at any time prior to the date of determination of the current terms of tenancies, but they shall not be effective if the time between the giving of the notice and the time when the tenancy is to be determined is less than the respective periods set out in Section 8 of this Act/Law.

10. INSTITUTION OF PROCEEDINGS

(1) On the expiration of the time stated in any such notice of the landlord's intention to recover possession, if the tenant or any person holding or claiming by, through or under him, neglects or refuses to quit and deliver up possession accordingly, the landlord may apply, according to whether he is taking action in the High Court or the Magistrates' Court, for the issue of a writ or enter a plaint, as in Form F, at his option either against the tenant or against the person so neglecting or refusing, in the court of the division or district, as the case may be, in which the premises are situate for the recovery of the premises and thereupon a summons as in Form G shall issue to such tenant or person so neglecting.

(2) If mesne profits are claimed and the writ or plaint shows that the rate at which the mesne profits are claimed is the same as the rent of the premises, judgement shall be entered for the ascertained amount as a liquidated claim and if mesne profits are claimed at the rate of the rent up to the time of obtaining possession the judgement shall be extended to include that claim and shall be as in the second alternative in Form J.

11. OBLIGATION OF SUBTENANT TO GIVE NOTICE TO HIS IMMEDIATE LANDLORD

(1) Where any summons for the recovery of any premises as is hereinbefore specified is served on or come to the knowledge of any subtenant of the plaintiff's immediate tenant, the subtenant being an occupier of the whole or of a part of the premises sought to be recovered, he shall forthwith give notice thereof to his immediate landlord.

(2) Failure to give notice shall render the subtenant liable to forfeit such sum as the court may consider just but not exceeding three year's rent of the premises held by the subtenant to such landlord.

(3) The sum to be recoverable, whatever the amount thereof, by the landlord shall be by action in the court from which the summons shall have been issued, and the landlord, on the receipt of such notice, if not

originally a defendant, may be added or substituted as a defendant to defend possession of the premises in question.

12. LANDLORD MAY CLAIM FOR MESNE PROFITS

The landlord may, either together with his writ or plaint for the recovery of the premises or in answer to a claim or counterclaim made in respect of any unexhausted improvements as hereafter provided, claim to recover or to set-off, rent or mesne profits, or both, accruing in respect of the premises since the ending or determination of the tenancy down to the day appointed for the hearing, or to a preceding day named in the plaint.

13. CLAIMS FOR ARREARS OF RENT AND MESNE PROFITS

The amount claimed under any writ or plaint for arrears of rent and mesne profits shall be treated as one claim.

14. TENANT'S TITLE TO COMPENSATION

Where a tenant executes on his holding any improvements he shall be entitled, subject to the provisions of Section 15 of this Act/Law, at the termination of the tenancy or quitting his holding, to receive compensation from his landlord in respect of any such improvement which continues unexhausted.

15. CONSENT OF LANDLORD

A tenant shall not be entitled to compensation in respect of any improvement, unless he has executed it with the previous consent in writing of the landlord.

16. COURT MAY HEAR COUNTERCLAIM WITH CLAIM TO RECOVER THE LAND

A tenant may at any time make any claim or counterclaim before a court against the landlord in respect of any unexhausted improvement, and the court may, if it thinks it expedient, hear and determine any counterclaim together with any claim to recover possession of the holding in respect of which the counterclaim is made:

Provided that –

(a) in the case of a counterclaim, notice in writing of the particulars of the counterclaim shall be given to the landlord three clear days before the day fixed for the hearing of the claim to recover possession, and

(b) the court at the hearing shall have power to enlarge the time for the delivery of the notice or for the hearing of the counterclaim.

Appraisers

17. COURT MAY APPOINT PERSON TO VALUE IMPROVEMENTS

(1) A court may

(a) from time to time, and at any time, appoint by writing as in Form H one or more persons to estimate the value of any unexhausted improvements in respect of which a claim or counterclaim is made, and to report in writing as in Form I to the court thereon, and

(b) make such order as it thinks fit in respect of the expenses and remuneration of those persons.

(2) The provisions of the Stamp Duties Act shall not apply to persons appointed by the court under this section.

18. REPORT OF APPRAISERS TO BE EVIDENCE

A report in writing, purporting to be signed by the person, or persons, appointed by the court under Section 17 of this Act/Law, shall be received in evidence in all courts until it is shown that the report was not so signed.

Hearing and Judgement

19. HEARING OF SUMMONS

(1) If the defendant is not at the time named in the summons or an adjournment thereof, show good cause to the contrary, then on proof –

(a) of the defendant still neglecting or refusing to deliver up the premises;

(b) of the yearly rent of the premises;

(c) of the holding;

(d) of the expiration or other determination of the tenancy with the time and manner thereof;

(e) of the title of the landlord, if the title has accrued since the letting of the premises; and

(f) of the service of the summons, if the defendant does not appear thereto,

the court may order as in Form J, K or L, whichever is applicable to the case, that possession of the premises mentioned in the plaint be given by the defendant to the plaintiff either forthwith or on or before the day as the court shall think fit to specify.

(2) If the plaintiff at the time named in the summons or at any adjournment thereof fails to obtain an order under subsection (1) of this section, the defendant shall be entitled to judgement and may be awarded costs, the judgement and the award being as in Form M.

20. ISSUE OF WARRANT OF POSSESSION

Where a landlord is entitled to possession of any premises, the court may issue a warrant of possession, notwithstanding that the counterclaim is undetermined or unsatisfied.

PART III - EJECTMENT

21. ENFORCEMENT OF ORDER OF COURT

If the order of the court given under Section 19 of this Act/Law –

(a) is not obeyed, the court, whether the order can be proved to have been served on the defendant or not, at the instance of the plaintiff, issue a warrant of possession; and

(b) is that possession of the premises be given forthwith by the defendant to the plaintiff, the court shall, at the instance and cost of the plaintiff, issue a warrant of possession forthwith.

22. FORM AND PURPOSE OF WARRANT OF POSSESSION

A warrant of possession shall entitle the plaintiff to be put in possession of the premises to which the warrant relates and be as in Form N and the certificate of execution thereof shall be as in Form O.

23. WARRANTS OF POSSESSION TO BE IN FORCE FOR THREE MONTHS

Every warrant of possession shall, on whatever day it may be issued, bear the date of the day next after the last day named by the court in the order for the delivery of possession of the premises in question, and continue in force for three months from the date and no longer, but no order for delivery of possession need be drawn up or served.

24. WARRANT OF POSSESSION JUSTIFIES ENTRY ON PREMISES

Any warrant to give possession of premises shall justify the person named thereon or to whom it is directed in entering upon the premises named therein, with such assistants as he shall deem necessary, and in giving possession accordingly:

Provided that no entry upon such warrant shall be made on a Sunday or a public holiday or at any time except between the hours of six o'clock in the morning and six o'clock in the afternoon.

25. PROTECTION OF OFFICERS OF THE COURT

No action and no prosecution may be brought against the judge, Magistrate or other officer of the court by whom a warrant of possession was issued, or against any sheriff or other person by whom the warrant may be executed, or document affixed, for issuing the warrant or executing the warrant respectively, or affixing such document, by reason that the person by whom the same shall be issued out had no lawful right to the possession of the premises.

26. PENALTY FOR RESISTING OR ASSAULTING OFFICERS

Any person who resists, molests, assaults or in any way obstructs any officer when engaged in the execution of such warrant as aforesaid, or any person appointed under Section 17 of this Act/Law and engaged in carrying out an order of a court is guilty of an offence under this Act/Law and liable, on summary conviction, to a fine of one hundred Naira or to imprisonment for six months or to both fine and imprisonment.

PART IV - MISCELLANEOUS

Service

28. SERVICE OF PROCESS

Service of any notice of determination of a tenancy or of a notice to quit or any summons, warrant or other process shall be effected in accordance with the provisions of the law for the time being in force relating to the service of the civil process of Magistrates' Courts and if the defendant cannot be found, and his place of dwelling is either not be known, or admission thereto cannot be obtained for serving any such process, a copy of the process shall posted on some conspicuous part of the premises sought to be recovered, and such posting shall be deemed good service on the defendant.

Landlords liability to special damages

29. LANDLORD'S LIABILITY TO SPECIAL DAMAGES

(1) Where the landlord at the time of applying for a warrant of possession of the premises as aforesaid had lawful right to the possession of the premises, or of the part thereof so held over as aforesaid, neither the said landlord or his agent, nor any other person

acting on his behalf, shall be deemed to be a trespasser by reason merely of any irregularity or informality in the mode of proceeding for obtaining possession under the authority of this Act/Law, but the party aggrieved may, if he think fit, bring an action for such irregularity or informality, in which the damage alleged to be sustained thereby shall be specially claimed, and may recover full satisfaction for such special damage with costs of suit.

(2) If the special damage claimed is not proved, the defendant shall be entitled to a judgement, and if proved, but assessed by the court at any sum not exceeding fifty kobo, the plaintiff shall recover no more costs than damages, unless the court before which the trial shall have been (or was) brought) shall certify on the record that full costs ought to be allowed.

Appeal

30. APPEAL FROM ORDER OF POSSESSION IN ALL CASES

Either party to a proceeding to recover possession of any premises under this Act/Law may appeal from the decision of the court to the appropriate court of appeal whatever may be the value of the subject matter in dispute.

Forms

31. USE OF FORMS

(1) Subject to the express provisions, if any, of the Rules, the forms contained in the Schedule to this Act/Law may, in accordance with any instruction contained in the forms, and with such variation as the circumstances of the particular case may require, be used in the cases to which they apply, and, when so used, shall be good and sufficient in law.

(2) The forms may be added to, repealed, replaced or varied by Rules made as aforesaid in all respects as if the forms had originally been so made.

SCHEDULE

There is only one schedule containing 14 Forms as in the Appendix G

Table of Cases

Index

Made in United States
North Haven, CT
05 November 2026

21861531R00275